Psychology A Level
Year 1 and AS

The Revision and Exam Companion

Psychopathology

Biopsychology

Social Influence

Memory

Research methods

Attachment

Mike Cardwell • Rob McIlveen

Rachel Moody • Joseph -Sparks

OXFORD
UNIVERSITY PRESS

OXFORD
UNIVERSITY PRESS

Great Clarendon Street, Oxford, OX2 6DP, United Kingdom

Oxford University Press is a department of the University of Oxford. It furthers the University's objective of excellence in research, scholarship, and education by publishing worldwide. Oxford is a registered trade mark of Oxford University Press in the UK and in certain other countries

British Library Cataloguing in Publication Data
Data available

978 019 837640 8

10 9 8 7 6 5 4 3 2 1

Paper used in the production of this book is a natural, recyclable product made from wood grown in sustainable forests. The manufacturing process conforms to the environmental regulations of the country of origin.

Printed in Great Britain by Bell and Bain Ltd, Glasgow

Acknowledgements

The publishers would like to thank the following for permissions to use their photographs:

p49: Alamy; p55: Clive-Wearing02.jpg ©Jiri Rezac Photography; p61: Bettmann/Corbis; p65: gpointstudio/iStock; p75: AlexanderSm/iStock; p85: Oxford University; p105: Universal History Archive/UIG/Science Photo Library; p109: Alamy; p171: Mauro Fermariello/Science Photo Library.

Cover images by: Eric Isselee/Shutterstock

All other photographs by Shutterstock

Although we have made every effort to trace and contact all copyright holders before publication this has not been possible in all cases. If notified, the publisher will rectify any errors or omissions at the earliest opportunity.

Acknowledgements

Our thanks and appreciation go to Sarah Flynn and Alison Schrecker at OUP for driving through the original proposal for the book and to Fiona MacColl for her design inspiration. Alison in particular has project managed the book with quiet efficiency and a sharp eye for detail. A special thanks too should go to Mark Billingham for his input. We are also grateful to Gill Ries, Sally Morris, Jackie Stanbury and Jane Williams for their assistance in checking the answers to the activities. Finally we are indebted to Veronica Wastell for making the whole thing look good on the page and for working above and beyond her remit in order to turn this into something of which we can all be justifiably proud.

Rob McIlveen would like to thank Clare Compton for her invaluable assistance with this project. Joseph Robinson-Sparks would like to thank Kate Tapper for her pedagogical inspiration and Joseph Vu for his continued support.

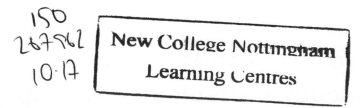

Contents

This book is part of our 'Companion' series, and shares the same aim of providing a companion to help turn your understanding of psychology into even better exam performance.

There are many features in this book that we think make it distinctive:

1. INTRODUCTION and skill practice

In the introductory section of this book we have provided activities to help you develop the skills you need in order to to perform well. You might believe that 'doing well' just means knowing the psychology, but that is only really half of the formula for success. You also have to be able to express your knowledge appropriately – i.e. know and follow the 'rules of the game'. 'Doing well', therefore, is not just knowing the content, but knowing how to use it.

2. Must know and should know

The content in this book focuses on preparing answers to the extended writing questions worth 12 marks (16 marks for Year 1 A level). If you fully understand the material AND can answer these questions, then you should be able to cope with all other kinds of questions that are asked.

We have divided this material into:

MUST. For some students this will be sufficient. If you can produce this material in an exam you are likely to get a Grade C.

Once you have mastered the 'must' content, then move on to **SHOULD**. Knowing this extra material should lift your answer to a Grade A.

For students who are in the first year of an A level course, the **A LEVEL ONLY ZONE** provides extra evaluation points, necessary for 16 mark extended writing questions.

3. Activities

On the right-hand side of each spread there is a range of exam-focused activities to help consolidate your knowledge. These activities aim to help you construct better exam answers. Other activities will help you process your knowledge and enhance your understanding and memory of the material on that spread.

Answers to most activities are given at the end of this book.

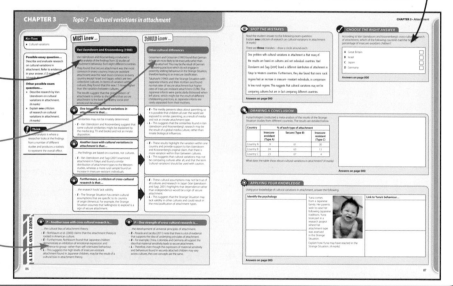

For each topic we provide a sample extended writing (i.e. essay) question. We have alternated these so they are sometimes 12 marks (for AS students) and sometimes 16 marks (for Year 1 A level students).

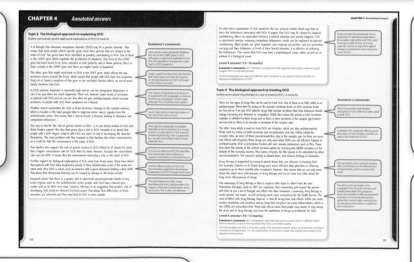

Examiner comments are given as a form of running commentary on the answers. These indicate the strengths of the answer and offer suggestions how it might be improved.

We have added a final assessment, indicating the mark range for this answer and giving the reasons why this particular level would be appropriate.

As well as providing sample questions, we have also given you sample student answers to give you an idea of what a student response to this question would look like. These are not designed to be 'model' answers to the questions, but are typically of Grade A or B standard.

On pages 18 and 19 we have included a sample mock examination, with suggested answers at the back of the book.

The AS examination

Paper 1 (7181/1) Introductory topics in psychology

You will have one-and-a-half hours to answer all the questions.

This paper is divided into three sections, each worth 24 marks.

Section A Social Influence

Section B Memory

Section C Attachment

Paper 2 (7181/2) Psychology in context

You will have one-and-a-half hours to answer all the questions.

This paper is divided into three sections, each worth 24 marks.

Section A Approaches in psychology

Section B Psychopathology

Section C Research methods

The A level examination

Paper 1 (7182/1) Introductory topics in psychology

You will have two hours to answer all the questions.

This paper is divided into four sections, each worth 24 marks.

Section A Social Influence

Section B Memory

Section C Attachment

Section D Psychopathology

Paper 2 (7182/2) Psychology in context

You will have two hours to answer all the questions.

This paper is divided into three sections. Sections A and B are each worth 24 marks, Section C is worth 48 marks.

Section A Approaches in psychology

Section B Biopsychology

Section C Research methods

Paper 3 (7182/3) Issues and options in psychology

The content and exam information for Paper 3 will be covered in the Year 2 book.

Assessment objectives

The examinations assesses three separate skills, known as **assessment objectives**. These are as follows:

AO1 (description of knowledge)
AO2 (application of knowledge)
AO3 (evaluation of knowledge)

We look further at these three assessment objectives, how you can master them and how they are examined on the next few spreads. In practice, the differences between these three skills can be quite subtle, as it is a case of what you *do* with material that makes it AO1, AO2 or AO3 rather than any inherent properties of the material itself. Let's look at a (completely fictional) example from a galaxy far, far away.

'Snoke (2016) found that uniforms lead to greater obedience than do ordinary clothes. He found that galactic police were more likely to be obeyed when they were wearing their police uniforms than when they were wearing civilian clothes. When orders were given by uniformed officers, civilians obeyed more quickly and with less protest than when orders were given by non-uniformed officers.'

Now let's look at how this material can be used as a way of responding to three very different types of question. Note that the underlying material is more or less the same in all three cases, but it has been 'tweaked' so that it is being used in either a descriptive (AO1), application (AO2) or evaluative (AO3) way.

An AO1 question

Outline the findings of one psychological study of the relationship between obedience and uniforms. *(3 marks)*

Snoke (2016) found that uniforms lead to greater obedience than do ordinary clothes. He found that galactic police were more likely to be obeyed when they were wearing their police uniforms than when they were wearing civilian clothes. When orders were given by uniformed officers, civilians obeyed more quickly and with less protest than when orders were given by non-uniformed officers.

An AO2 question

Kylo Ren is fed up of wearing his mask and cloak when conquering planets but finds his stormtroopers don't take him seriously when he wears t-shirt, jeans and sandals. Using your knowledge of the relationship between obedience and uniforms, explain why this happens. *(3 marks)*

Snoke (2016) found that galactic police were more likely to be obeyed when they were wearing their police uniforms than when they were wearing civilian clothes. As Kylo Ren's mask and cloak is his uniform, this would explain why his stormtroopers are less likely to obey his orders when he is dressed more casually. Uniforms such as those worn by galactic police and by Kylo Ren cause people to take authority more seriously and so are more likely to obey the orders they give.

An AO3 question

Explain one critical point concerning the relationship between obedience and uniforms. *(3 marks)*

The claim there is a relationship between obedience and uniforms is supported by research by Snoke (2016), who found that galactic police were more likely to be obeyed when they were wearing their police uniforms than when they were wearing civilian clothes. This supports the claim that uniforms cause people to take authority more seriously and so are more likely to obey the orders they give.

Types of exam questions

There isn't a comprehensive list of the questions that might be asked in your exams. If questions are too predictable then students tend to focus on memorising answers rather than gaining a good understanding of the specification content.

Therefore the unpredictable nature of the questions should encourage you to focus on the specification rather than being concerned with what questions can be asked.

As long as you have covered the specification you should be able to answer the exam questions.

Having said that the exam questions are unpredictable, it is possible to identify certain question types that are predictable. We have, therefore, attempted to produce a breakdown of the types of questions that you are likely to encounter. Please note that this is not a definitive list!

Knowing these question types should help you to be better prepared for the exam and focus on how to turn your knowledge of psychology into exam success.

On each spread of this book we have indicated likely questions that might be set to assess the topic of the spread.

Question type	Example	Advice
Simple selection/ recognition	Which **one** of the following is a dispositional factor affecting obedience? **A** Location **B** Personality **C** Proximity **D** Uniform *(2 marks)* Which of the following types of memory is being used in each of the examples below? Choose one type of memory that matches each example and write A, B or C in the box next to it. Use each letter once only. • Justin remembers how to brush his teeth without consciously thinking about it. ☐ • Justine remembers how awful she felt when she went to the dentist surgery yesterday. ☐ **A** Episodic memory **B** Procedural memory **C** Semantic memory *(2 marks)*	*Questions such as these should be straightforward enough, so the trick is making sure you have selected the right answer to gain maximum marks. If you aren't sure which answer is the right one, try crossing through those that are obviously wrong, thus narrowing down your options.* *It is well worth reading each question very carefully (and then reading it again) to make sure you follow the exact instructions in the question. For example, you might, contrary to instructions, be tempted to use the same answer in both boxes.*
Description questions (E.g. Describe, Outline, Identify, Name)	Give **two** features of the concept of the critical period. *(2 marks)* Identify and outline **two** techniques that might be used in a cognitive interview. *(4 marks)* Outline the fight or flight response. *(6 marks)*	*These AO1 description questions can come in lots of different forms, but will never be worth more than 6 marks for any one part of a question.* *To judge how much to write in response to a question, simply look at the number of marks available and allow about 25 words per mark.* *However, where the sole command word is 'Name' or 'Identify', there is no need to develop a 25 word per mark response, simply identifying or naming (as required by the question) is enough.* *Sometimes the phrasing of a question (such as the second question) is a prod to get students to go beyond just naming or identifying something and to offer additional detail to flesh it out.*
Differences/Distinguish between	Distinguish between proactive and retroactive interference as explanations of forgetting. *(2 marks)* Identify **two** differences between insecure-resistant and insecure-avoidant attachment. *(2 marks)*	*Students often ignore the instruction to 'distinguish between' or 'identify differences' and simply outline the two terms or concepts named in the question. This is not what is required, and would not gain credit.* *The word 'whereas' is a good linking word to illustrate a difference between two things. However, the difference must be related to the same thing, e.g. it would not be appropriate to point out that an insecure-resistant infant displays high levels of stranger anxiety whereas an insecure-avoidant infant avoids contact with the caregiver at reunion. This is because the two types are not being compared on the same thing (e.g. stranger anxiety).*
Applying knowledge	Nadia is passionate about a charity that supports children living in developing countries. However, most of her classmates want to raise money for an animal charity. The class are due to vote for the class charity at the end of the week. Using your knowledge of minority social influence, explain **two** ways in which Nadia could try to persuade her classmates to vote for her charity. *(6 marks)* Kelly was chatting to her friend about her new son, Henry, who was now 3 months old. She told her friend how amazing it was that when she smiled at Henry, he smiled back, and when she poked her tongue out, so did he. 'It's as if he's trying to copy everything I do', Kelly said to her friend. With reference to Kelly's conversation with her friend, outline two features of caregiver-infant interaction. *(4 marks)*	*In these AO2 questions, you will be provided with a scenario (the question 'stem') and asked to use your psychological knowledge to provide an informed answer.* *You must make sure that your answer contains not only appropriate psychological **content**, but that this is set explicitly within the **context** outlined in the question stem.* *In the first example on the left, some students would ignore the question stem and simply provide a description of minority influence research for changing attitudes. Other students might ignore the underlying psychology completely and simply engage with the material in the stem in some other way. Neither approach is appropriate, and would result in a disappointingly low mark.* *The same warning applies to the second example. There is a temptation to either ignore Kelly's conversation with her friend completely or just mention it in passing. Examiners will be looking for total engagement with the question stem, so ignore it at your peril!* *We have included a number of 'Apply your knowledge' features throughout the book so you can practise your skills in this area as well as going a little deeper with some of the issues of the page. The scenarios in these features tend to be lengthier than in actual exam questions, but the skill in answering them is the same.*

Question type	Example	Advice
Research methods questions	You will be given a description of a study and then a number of short questions such as: (i) Write a suitable hypothesis for this study. *(3 marks)* (ii) Identify the experimental design used in this study and outline one advantage of this experimental design. *(3 marks)* (iii) Name a measure of dispersion the researcher could use. *(1 mark)* (iii) At the end of the study the researcher debriefed each participant. Write a debriefing that the researcher could read out to the participants. *(6 marks)*	*Most research methods questions are set within the context of a hypothetical research study. This means that your answers must also be set within the context of that study. If you don't set your answers within the specific context of the study, you cannot receive full marks.* *Most research methods questions have a fairly low tariff (i.e. 1, 2 or 3 marks), although, as with the last question, they can be worth as much as 6 marks.* *We have included a large number of sample research methods questions throughout the book. The more you practice these, the better you will become at them, and with mastery comes increased confidence.*
Maths questions	Time taken (secs) for six different participants to complete a task over consecutive attempts: 24, 22, 19, 16, 15, 12. Calculate the mean time for participants to complete the task. Show your calculations. *(2 marks)* **Table 1** Median accuracy scores for anxious and non-anxious participants. |	Anxious	Non-anxious
Median	18	28 | Sketch an appropriate graphical display to show the median accuracy scores in Table 1. *(6 marks)*	*'Maths' questions can appear anywhere on the paper, and can assess your ability to carry out simple calculations, construct graphs and interpret data. For example, in the first question, a correct answer and appropriate working are necessary for maximum marks.* *Six marks may seem a lot for the second question, but 1 mark is given for each of six aspects of the requested graph, e.g. displaying the data as a bar chart, correct plotting of the bars, labeling axes correctly, having an informative title etc.*
Evaluation questions	Briefly evaluate Bowlby's theory of maternal deprivation. *(4 marks)* Explain **one** strength and **one** limitation of the biological approach in psychology. *(6 marks)* Discuss **two** limitations of the cognitive approach in psychology. *(6 marks)*	*Evaluation can be 'general' as in the first question on the left, or specific as in the second. For the latter question, marks will only be given for that specific content. Miss part of it out and you miss out on marks, put more than one strength or limitation and it won't be creditworthy.* *It is important that you elaborate your evaluative points for maximum marks. We have shown you how to achieve this in some of the 'Upgrade' features throughout this book.*
Mixed description and evaluation questions	Briefly outline and evaluate the cognitive interview as a technique for improving the accuracy of eyewitness testimony. *(4 marks)* Briefly outline and evaluate **one** explanation for the working memory model. *(6 marks)*	*Not all questions are straightforward 'description only' or 'evaluation only', but may be mixed.* *The command words (e.g. outline, evaluate) will tell you that description and evaluation are required.* *As a rule of thumb, in questions like these you should divide your AO1 and AO3 content equally.*
Extended writing questions	Outline and evaluate research into the effects of anxiety on the accuracy of eyewitness testimony. *(8 marks)* Describe and evaluate **two** studies of social influence. *(12 marks)* Describe and evaluate the multistore model of memory. *(16 marks)*	*Although the distinction between this and the previous category is somewhat arbitrary, questions worth more than 6 marks are usually referred to as extending writing questions.* *As a rough guide, you should write 25 words per mark so for a 8-mark answer 200 words would be appropriate and 300 words for a 12-mark answer. Three well-developed AO3 points are usually sufficient for a 12-mark question, and that is the approach we have taken throughout this book.* *If you are doing the A level course, you may face a 16-mark question. The only difference between this and a 12-mark question is the requirement for further evaluation, taking your word count to around 400 words. We have included this further evaluation on spreads where appropriate.*
Extended writing questions with specific instructions	Describe and evaluate the two-process model as an explanation of phobias. Refer to evidence in your answer. *(12 marks)* Read the item and then answer the question that follows. Thomas has a phobia of clowns. He relates this to a scary experience he had as a child. He was at the circus when a clown jumped up from the row behind Thomas and startled him so much that his parents had to leave before the show ended. Thomas was so disturbed that he has not even been able to look at a picture of a clown since, let alone go anywhere near one. Describe and evaluate the two-process model as an explanation of phobias. Refer to the example of Thomas as part of your answer. *(12 marks)*	*Some extended writing questions have an extra specific instruction, as in the two examples on the left. Both require a discussion of the two-process model (i.e. AO1 and AO3), but each has a slightly different additional requirement.* *The first simply asks you to include evidence (i.e. research evidence as AO3) in your answer. You might well have been going to do this anyway, but now it is required. It doesn't mean that all your AO3 has to be 'evidence', but perhaps a couple of research studies that either support or challenge the two-process model would suffice.* *The second question requires you to discuss not only the model but to do this in the context of the stimulus material provided. Although the model is the key requirement of the question, don't make the mistake of assuming the applied aspect of the question is less important.* *Questions such as this, where you are asked to incorporate discussion of a person or persons' experience, have an AO2 component. This is reflected in the allocation of marks for that question. For example, in the case of Thomas and his clown phobia, there would be 6 marks allocated for AO1 (description), 4 for AO3 (evaluation) and 2 for AO2 (Application). For an 16 marks A level question with an AO2 component the allocations are AO1 (6 marks), AO3 (6 marks) and AO2 (4 marks). Remember that these skills are not assessed independently, but knowing the relative weighting of each allows you to plan your answer accordingly.*

You'll probably recognise these four animals, but how would you describe them? Each has its own distinctive characteristics, the qualities that make that animal what it is rather than something else. For example, if you correctly identified the top left animal as an elephant (well done), you are showing **knowledge**. If you then think about what makes it an elephant (rather than a lion or a rhino) – i.e. its size (big), its trunk (long), what it eats (it's a herbivore), the texture of its skin (rough) and so on, you are adding **detail**. If you used the term 'elephant' rather than 'a big grey thing with flappy ears' then you are using **specialist terminology**. These are the skills of **description**.

Assessment Objective 1 (AO1) assesses your knowledge and understanding of the different topics covered in this book.

Being able to do this effectively and efficiently takes practice, so throughout this book you will be given opportunities to practice your AO1 skills.

What skills are needed for AO1?

Giving psychological information

First and foremost in an AO1 question you are required to present your psychological knowledge. However, many students make the mistake of thinking that's all there is to it – learn a chunk of psychology and then 'dump' it into an exam question. Unfortunately, this is neither effective nor efficient as we shall see.

Showing your understanding

You are marked on your understanding as well as your knowledge. Consider the question 'Briefly explain the deviation from social norms definition of abnormality' (2 marks).

The deviation from norms definition sees abnormality in terms of people not conforming to the norms in society.

This doesn't really explain this definition (it simply rewords the terms) so doesn't demonstrate understanding. A better answer might be:

The deviation from social norms definition classifies people as abnormal if they constantly deviate from social standards of acceptable behaviour such as politeness, sexual behaviour etc.

This answer does show understanding because the examples demonstrate that the student is aware of the underlying behaviour that would lead to a classification of abnormality.

Including detail

What does 'detail' mean? It is **SPECIFIC** information – not just more information but being precise. It is about giving a fuller and more informative description of something. Consider the question 'Explain what is meant by conformity' (2 marks). A typical answer to this might be:

Conformity is when we behave the same way as the majority.

This is not particularly informative as it lacks detail. We could extend it with an example, e.g.

Conformity is when we behave the same way as the majority. For example when we change the way we dress to be the same as our peers.

Alternatively we could extend our answer by making it more precise.

Conformity is when we change our behaviour as a result of exposure to the majority position.

Selecting appropriate material

Students often write much more than they need to in an exam answer and often include material that is not really relevant. It is difficult to decide what should be put in and what should be left out. Knowing what to include and what not to include in your answer is an indication of your understanding of a topic, and is an important AO1 skill.

Clear and coherent presentation

You are only assessed on your ability to use English and organise information clearly in the extended writing question worth 12 marks (or 16 marks if you are first year A level). However, this ability matters throughout the exam because the examiner has to understand what you are trying to say. Learning to express yourself clearly is a skill.

AO1 mark scheme

The mark scheme below shows you how the skills on the left contribute to your AO1 mark on a **6 mark question**.

Description questions (AO1: 6 mark questions)			
Marks	Knowledge	Organisation	Specialist terminology
5–6	Generally accurate and well detailed	Clear and coherent	Used effectively
3–4	Evident with some inaccuracies	Mostly clear and organised	Some appropriate use
1–2	Limited and lacks detail	Lacks clarity and organisation	Absent or used inappropriately
0	No relevant content		

For AO1 questions worth 4 or 5 marks a similar mark scheme to the one above is used.

For AO1 questions worth 2 or 3 marks:

- 1 mark for a very brief explanation.
- Further marks for increasing detail/explanation (which can include an example).

We suggest that 150 words would be adequate for a question worth 6 marks. For questions worth fewer than 4 marks the length is usually less important. One sentence per mark is a useful guideline.

On the right-hand side of most spreads in this book there are activities for you to do.

In order to practise the skill of AO1 we need some content, so we have used content from Chapter 1.

How many marks?

Below are two answers to the question 'Describe how the authoritarian personality explains obedience to authority'. *(6 marks)*

How many AO1 marks would you give them? In order to help you in this task:

- Underline key words or phrases.
- Consider how much detail has been included.
- Watch out for material that is repeated.

Alice's answer

The authoritarian personality explanation argues that obedience is caused by personality characteristics that are a consequence of a particular parenting style. Parents of someone with an authoritarian personality place great importance on obedience and tend to use physical punishment with their children when they disobey.

As a result of this type of parenting, children tend to develop very definite views of right and wrong and demand strict adherence to social rules. They value obedience above all else and so are more likely to obey themselves.

83 words

Suggested mark for Alice's essay _____ marks

Tom's answer

The authoritarian personality is measured by a questionnaire called the California F scale. This measures the degree to which a person agrees with statements such as 'Respect for authority is the most important virtue a child can learn'. People who score high on the F scale are more likely to have an authoritarian personality.

Altemeyer claimed that there are different aspects of the authoritarian personality such as conventionalism, authoritarian aggression and submission to authority. He referred to this as right-wing authoritarianism.

Although there is evidence to support the relationship between the authoritarian personality and obedience, Milgram claimed that situational factors, such as the legitimacy of authority or uniform, were more important in determining obedience.

114 words

Suggested mark for Tom's essay _____ marks

Answers on page 269

Selecting material

Tom included a lot of unnecessary material. So even though his answer was longer, it wasn't as good as Alice's. You can improve his answer by:

1 Crossing out the irrelevant material.
2 Add in a few more details such as how obedience and the authoritarian personality are related.
3 Can you think of any other details that could be added?

Detail and understanding

How would you define the term 'obedience to authority'?

_____
_____
_____

Now add a sentence that extends this definition into an explanation of the term.

_____
_____
_____

Now add an example.

_____
_____
_____

Getting the details

Choose a theory in the specification, such as the working memory model or learning theory of attachment.

Look at your textbook or this book.

Identify 6 key words for this theory.

Theory

1 _____
2 _____
3 _____
4 _____
5 _____
6 _____

Now try to write one or two sentences for each key word.

This is your 6 mark answer.

Getting the details

Choose a research study in the specification (For example, Milgram's study of obedience (p26) or Asch's study of conformity (p22)).

From your textbook or this book identify 4 key words related to procedures (how the study was done).

1 _____
2 _____
3 _____
4 _____

From your textbook or this book identify 4 key words related to findings and conclusions (what the study showed).

1 _____
2 _____
3 _____
4 _____

Now try to write one sentence for each key word.

Clear and coherent

Try to rewrite the student answer below so it is clearer and more detailed.

Question: Outline **one** feature of the working memory model. *(3 marks).*

One feature is the central executive. It has little storage. It transfers things.

Do you really understand your psychology?

One way to assess this is to give you a pretend situation and see if you can apply your psychological knowledge to it.

For example:

> **The stem**
>
> *Rob's dad has just come back from a business meeting in Scotland. He flew there and back and is complaining about how he was treated during the security screening at his local airport. He describes the staff as 'rude' and 'power crazed' and wonders if they only employ rude and aggressive people.*

Question ➤ **Using your knowledge of research into conformity to social roles, explain why the security staff might be behaving in the way described by Rob's dad.** *(4 marks)*

> **The stem**
>
> *Marian enjoys singing along to music while completing a still-life drawing for her art homework. However, she finds the same songs distracting when trying to listen to her friend explain events in a chapter of a novel they are studying in English class.*

Question ➤ **Use your understanding of the working memory model to explain Marian finds the songs distracting.** *(4 marks)*

> **The stem**
>
> *Shortly after eating breakfast with coffee, while listening to music on his headphones, a traveller is sea-sick during a ferry crossing. Following this, the smell and taste of coffee makes him feel nauseous but the music does not.*

Question ➤ **Using your knowledge of classical conditioning, explain why the smell and taste of coffee makes the traveller feel nauseous.** *(4 marks)*

> **The stem**
>
> *Mrs Watkins is a secondary school teacher. She notices that some of the children in her class constantly call out answers without raising their hands, which ruins the learning for other students.*

Question ➤ **Using your knowledge of social learning theory, how Mrs Watkins might use vicarious reinforcement to change the behaviour of these children? Explain your answer with reference to both positive reinforcement and punishment** *(4 marks)*.

> **The stem**
>
> *Tamsin loves rollercoasters. She explains she enjoys the adrenaline rush they give her, the feeling of her heart racing and breathlessness. Once she has ridden the rollercoaster she finds she quickly returns to a 'normal' state and so queues up to ride again and again.*

Question ➤ **Using your knowledge of the autonomic nervous system, explain Tasmin's experience of riding the rollercoaster.** *(3 marks)*

Answering AO2 Application questions

You must make sure that your answer to 'application of knowledge' questions contains two parts:

1   Reference to the material in the stem.
2   Psychological knowledge.

Look at the examples on the left. Each one begins with a 'stem' – a description of how people have behaved in certain situations.

At the end is the question for you to answer. This question generally contains two parts:

1   Reference to the material in the stem.
2   A phrase that asks you to use your psychological knowledge.

Let's look at the example of Tamsin and her love of rollercoasters.

Students might explain why Tamsin finds rollercoasters so exciting but forget to refer to the autonomic nervous system.

OR

Students might describe the autonomic nervous system but say nothing about Tamsin's experience of riding rollercoasters.

Neither approach would get better than half marks.

YOU MUST DO BOTH.

NB In the Tamsin example, it is not enough just to insert the word 'Tamsin' occasionally.

* You must engage with the stem included in the question.
* Your answer must demonstrate psychological knowledge.

Chloe was shopping in her local branch of Kwiksave when she heard a loud argument coming from the till. When she glanced over, a man was shouting at the woman behind the counter, arguing that he had already paid for the bottle of whisky on the counter. Suddenly he punched her and, grabbing the bottle, he ran out of the shop. When the police arrived they questioned Chloe, using a cognitive interview. They asked her to report everything she could remember about the incident even if it seemed unimportant.

Apart from 'report everything', explain two other techniques from the cognitive interview that the police might have used to investigate what Chloe remembered about the assault on the shop assistant.

In your answer you must refer to the details of the passage above.
(4 marks)

In the above exam question outline:

1   The psychology that is needed:

2   How this is linked specifically to the context in the stem?

An effective way of revising is to work in small work groups, helping each other to understand material and to answer exam type questions. If you practise making up your own application questions (most are worth 4 marks although this is not a hard and fast rule), then other members of the group can have a go at answering them and then you can mark them as a group. This will work, and you will find yourself rapidly becoming competent at handling this sort of question. Even if you work by yourself you can still make up application questions, answer them and then practice marking them using the mark scheme below.

Application questions (AO2: 4 mark questions)				
Marks	Knowledge	Application	Organisation	Specialist terminology
3–4	Clear, detailed and mostly accurate	Appropriate and effective	Generally coherent	Effective use of terminology
1–2	Lacking accuracy and detail	Not always effective	Lacks clarity	Either absent or inappropriate
0	No relevant content			

Sample stem:

Sample question:

Below are four answers to the application question about Chloe above. What mark would you give each of these?

Amalia's answer

A cognitive interview is an interview based on trying to find out as much information as possible. The interviewee must take down every single thing that happens in an interview even though the details may appear unuseful. Also the interviewee will try to change the order of information to see if that provides a different answer. The interviewee must ask for the participant to take on other people's perspective and views on what happened. Also Chloe could be asked to tell the story from one of the men in the argument and could be asked to say what events happened from the end to the start.   106 words

Mark = _____ out of 4 marks

Melissa's answer

As well as asking Chloe to remember everything they would have to ask her to tell her story from a different perspective. They could ask 'If you were standing on the other side of the road what would you have seen?' They may also ask Chloe to tell the story in a different order, asking 'What happened last?' or 'What started the argument?' The police officers may repeat the story back to her to see that it's correct.   79 words

Mark = _____ out of 4 marks

Write your own answer

Combine the best elements from all of these answers to produce your own 4 mark answer.

Pedro's answer

After reporting everything the police could ask Chloe to alter her mental context and imagine what the victim would have seen. This helps reliability if witnesses are lying because then they have several versions of the report. They could then change the order of the incident to try and gain further information which would help them work out who did what. Finally they could ask her to put the incident in perspective with what other witnesses may have seen.   79 words

Mark = _____ out of 4 marks

Roy's answer

After report everything, the police can ask her to mentally context everything which happened. Also changing the order/ perspective will help Chloe remember everything. Schemas are also used when memory may be inaccurate. It helps people remember things from previous experiences and expectations of events.   44 words

Mark = _____ out of 4 marks

Answers on page 269

What skills are needed for AO3?

Understand what evaluation is

'Evaluation' simply means 'What is the value of this thing?' Think about our elephant. How can we think about its value?

One strength of an elephant is that it never forgets.

One limitation of an elephant is that it tends to make a lot of mess.

One application of an elephant is that we could use it to carry heavy loads.

You probably wouldn't think of these if you were asked to 'evaluate' an elephant. Asking for 'evaluation' is just a way of asking 'What are the problems (or advantages)' with something?

State the AO3 Point (P)

So, when we start evaluating, the first thing we must do is to state the criticism. For example:

One strength of Bowlby's theory is the idea that attachments are adaptive.

One limitation of minority influence is that it isn't always effective.

Elaborate the AO3 point (E)

The second thing that is required is elaboration. 'Elaboration' means 'to develop thoroughly'. In particular you need to provide **EVIDENCE** or **EXAMPLES** to support your claim. For example:

(P) One strength of Bowlby's theory is the idea that attachments are adaptive. (E) According to Bowlby, infants become attached during the critical period of three to six months, at the same time human infants start to crawl.

(P) A limitation of the cognitive interview is the time taken and training required by police. (E) For example, police often use deliberate strategies to limit an interview to save time and many police forces have not provided the necessary training to conduct a cognitive interview.

(P) One limitation of conducting research on eyewitness testimony in a lab is that it's artificial. (E) It is artificial because the participants didn't feel emotionally involved; (E) for example, they would in a real accident.

AO3 mark scheme

The mark scheme below shows you how the skills on the left contribute to your AO3 mark on a **6 mark question**.

Evaluation questions (AO3: 6 mark questions)			
Marks	Evaluation	Organisation	Specialist terminology
5–6	Clear and effective	Coherent and well-organised	Used effectively
3–4	Mostly effective	Mostly clear and organised	Used appropriately
1–2	Lacks detail and/or explanation	Poorly organised	Absent or used inappropriately
0	No relevant content		

'Broad range' = 5 critical points

'Range' = 4 critical points

'Restricted range' = 3+ critical points but no elaboration.

Boosting your marks – making AO3 effective

The mark scheme on the right indicates that for an AO3 mark in the top band (5–6 or 3 if a 3 mark question) the evaluation must be 'clear and effective'. But what would you have to do to push your evaluation into this band as opposed to the band below?

Grade C answers tend to provide more superficial evaluation.

Grade A answers tend to provide clear and effective evaluation.

Superficial elaboration = state the point (P) + a bit of elaboration (E). You could write 10 critical points but if they are all superficial you would get no more than 3 out of 6 AO3 marks.

This is the four-point rule = P E E L.

Clear and effective evaluation = state the point (P) + a bit of elaboration (E) + further elaboration (E) + further elaboration OR a link back (L). **E can be evidence, examples, explanation. An example of a link back: 'This shows that …' where you explain what the critical point demonstrates.**

The activities on the facing page will help you practise these elaboration skills and link back.

Issues or evidence

What kinds of things count as AO3?

Appropriate forms of AO3 include:

- The research methods used, for example a strength of a study might be that it was well-controlled or a limitation might be that it caused psychological harm to participants.
- Arguments for or against an explanation, such as suggesting an explanation is too simple.
- Individual differences or gender differences – not everyone responds the same way but many psychological explanations assume that they do.
- Real-world applications, which provide support for any explanation because they show that the explanation is useful.
- Research studies that support or challenge an explanation/ theory.
- The strengths or limitations of alternative explanations – a comparison needs to be made between the current explanation and an alternative one focusing on why one is stronger than the other (but for AO3 make sure you don't just *describe* any alternative explanation).

Using research evidence as AO3

If you *describe* a research study, then you are doing AO1.

If you use a research study as an evaluation it becomes AO3 but only if you say that's what you are doing. Use a **LEAD-IN SENTENCE**. For example:

One study that supports this theory is …

For any AO3 point, effectiveness is determined by:

1 The lead-in sentence (see examples on facing page).

2 The amount of elaboration to make your point clear.

We will start with the **three-point rule**: P E E

Fill in the table with your answer to the questions given:

Outline **one** strength of the multi-store model. *(3 marks)*

State	
Evidence	
Example	

Outline **one** limitation of the multi-store model. *(3 marks)*

State	
Evidence	
Example	

Practise this with other AO3 questions on strengths and limitations.

For each criticism in the box above now write the **link back**.

Outline **one** strength of the multi-store model. *(3 marks)*

Link back	This suggests that …

Outline **one** limitation of the multi-store model. *(3 marks)*

Link back	This suggests that …

Sometimes the link back may work better to say 'This shows that …' or 'Therefore we can conclude that …'

Strengths and limitations are not the only way to 'do AO3'. On the facing page we give you some other ideas.

Write down two other possible ways to make an AO3 point:

1 ....

2 ....

One strength of this study is …	This explanations is supported by …
One limitation of this study is …	This explanations is challenged by …
A real-world application is …	An alternative explanation could be …
However …	There may be cultural variations …
On the other hand …	This would imply …
Not everyone reacts the same way, for example …	A consequence would be …

You should start start an AO3 point by saying, for example 'One strength is …' or 'One limitation is …'. The lead-in phrases above can all be used as a way to start an AO3 point.

Select one of the phrases above and write your own critical point related to the multi-store model.

....

....

....

....

Evaluation in the extended writing question

In a 12 mark extended writing question at AS level, there are 6 marks for evaluation (AO3). In a 16 mark question at A level, there are 10 marks allocated for evaluation.

You are aiming to:

1 **Give the right amount** – about 180 words of AO3 (AS level) and 300 words (A level).

2 **Provide elaboration** – all points should have some elaboration, aiming for about 60 words for each evaluative point.

3 **Make AO3 effective** – each AO3 point should begin with a lead-in phrase and form a distinct AO3 paragraph.

How many AO3 points?

You need 3 elaborated AO3 points at AS level.

You need 5 elaborated AO3 points at A level.

You could have fewer points with more elaboration, but we feel 3 (AS) and 5 (A level) are an appropriate mix of breadth and depth in your answer.

Use paragraphs to show structure

Examiners have to mark thousands of answers in only a few weeks. The clearer your answer is, the better.

For an extended writing answer on a theory:

• Do all your AO1 and then all your AO3.

• Divide the AO1 content into paragraphs.

• Write each AO3 criticism as a separate paragraph.

Content checklists

The following content checklists are based on what is required by the specifications. You can use them to record your progress as you move from a basic understanding of a topic (column 1) to complete mastery of it (column 3).

1. In each 'describe, apply and evaluate' cell tick when you have produced brief notes.

2. Once you feel you have a good grasp of the topic add a second tick to the cell.

3. When you feel you have complete mastery of the topic and would be able to answer an exam question without the aid of notes highlight the cell.

Chapter 1 Social influence

I am able to...	Describe	Apply	Evaluate
Types of conformity and explanations for conformity			
Variables affecting conformity			
Conformity to social roles			
Situational variables affecting obedience			
Explanations for obedience			
A dispositional explanation: the authoritarian personality			
Resistance to social influence			
Minority influence			
Social influence processes in social change			

Chapter 2 Memory

I am able to...	Describe	Apply	Evaluate
Multi-store model			
Features of STM (coding, capacity, duration)			
Features of LTM (coding, capacity, duration)			
Types of LTM – Episodic			
Types of LTM – Semantic			
Types of LTM – Procedural			
Working memory model (including coding and capacity)			
Explanations for forgetting – Proactive interference			
Explanations for forgetting – Retroactive interference			
Explanations for forgetting – Retrieval failure			
Accuracy of EWT – misleading information: leading questions			
Accuracy of EWT – misleading information: post-event discussion			
Accuracy of EWT – Anxiety			

Chapter 3 Attachment

I am able to...	Describe	Apply	Evaluate
Caregiver–infant interactions: reciprocity and interactional synchrony			
Stages of attachment identified by Schaffer			
Multiple attachments and the role of the father			
Animal studies of attachment: Lorenz			
Animal studies of attachment: Harlow			
Explanations of attachment: Learning theory			
Explanations of attachment: Bowlby's monotropic theory			
Concepts of a critical period and an internal working model			
Ainsworth's Strange Situation			
Types of attachment: secure, insecure-avoidant, insecure-resistant			
Cultural variations in attachment including van Ijzendoorn			
Bowlby's theory of maternal deprivation			
Romanian orphan studies: the effects of institutionalisation			

Chapter 4 Psychopathology

I am able to...	Describe	Apply	Evaluate
Deviation from social norms and statistical infrequency			
Failure to function adequately			
Deviation from ideal mental health			
Clinical characterisitics of phobia, depression and OCD			
The behavioural two-process model of phobia, including classical and operant conditioning			
Systematic desensitisation of phobia, including relaxation and the use of hierarchy as a behavioural treatment for phobia			
Flooding as a behavioural treatment for phobia			
Cognitive explanation of depression: Beck's (1967) negative triad			
Cognitive explanation of depression: Ellis' (1962) ABC model			
Cognitive treatment for depression: Cognitive Behaviour Therapy (CBT)			
Cognitive treatment for depression: Challenging irrational thoughts			
Biological explanations of OCD: genetic			
Biological explanations of OCD: neurological			
Biological treatment of OCD: drug therapy			

Chapter 5 Approaches

I am able to...	Describe	Apply	Evaluate
AS and A Level			
Origins of psychology: Wundt, introspection and the emergence of psychology as a science			
Learning approaches: the behaviourist approach, including classical conditioning and Pavlov's research, operant conditioning, types of reinforcement and Skinner's research			
Learning approaches: social learning theory including imitation, identification, modelling, vicarious reinforcement, the role of meditational processes and Bandura's research			
The biological approach: the influence of genes, biological structures and neurochemistry on behaviour. Genotype and phenotype, genetic basis of behaviour, evolution and behaviour			
The cognitive approach: the study of internal mental processes, the role of schema, the use of theoretical and computer models to explain and make inferences about mental processes. The emergence of cognitive neuroscience.			
A Level only			
The psychodynamic approach: the role of the unconscious, the structure of personality, id, ego and superego, defence mechanisms including repression, denial and displacement, psychosexual stages			
Humanistic psychology: free will, self-actualisation and Maslow's hierarchy of needs, focus on the self, congruence, the role of conditions of worth. The influence on counselling psychology.			
Comparison of approaches			

Chapter 6 Biopsychology

I am able to...	Describe	Apply	Evaluate
AS and A Level			
The divisions of the nervous system: central and peripheral (somatic and autonomic)			
The structure and function of sensory, relay and motor neurons			
The process of synaptic transmission including reference to neurotransmitters, excitation and inhibition			
The function of the endocrine system; glands and hormones			
The fight-or-flight response including the role of adrenaline			
A Level only			
Localisation of function in the brain: motor, somatosensory, visual, auditory, language centres; Broca's area and Wernicke's area			
Hemispheric lateralisation and split-brain research			
Plasticity and functional recovery after trauma			
Ways of studying the brain: scanning techniques including fMRI, EEGs, ERPs; post-mortem examinations			
Biological rhythms: circadian, infradian and ultradian and the difference between these rhythms			
The effect of endogenous pacemakers and exogenous zeitgebers			

Chapter 7 Research methods

Content checklist

Column 1: tick when you have produced brief notes.

Column 2: tick when you have a good grasp of this topic.

Column 3: tick during the final revision when you feel you have complete mastery of the topic.

Methods	1	2	3
Experimental method: laboratory and field experiments; natural and quasi experiments			
Observational techniques: naturalistic and controlled observation; covert and overt observation; participant and non-participant observation			
Self-report technique: questionnaires; interviews, structured and unstructured			
Correlations. analysis of the relationship between co-variables			
The difference between correlations and experiments			
Scientific processes			
Aims: stating aims, the difference between aims and hypotheses			
Hypotheses: directional and non-directional			
Sampling: the difference between population and sample; random, systematic, stratified, opportunity and volunteer sampling; bias and generalisation			
Pilot studies and the aims of piloting			
Experimental designs: repeated measures, independent groups, matched pairs			
Observational design: behavioural categories; event sampling; time sampling			
Questionnaire construction, open and closed questions; design of interviews			
Variables: manipulation and control of variables, including independent, dependent, extraneous, confounding; operationalisation of variables			
Control: random allocation and counterbalancing, randomisation and standardisation			
Demand characteristics and investigator effects			
Ethics, including the role of the British Psychological Society's code of ethics; ethical issues in the design and conduct of psychological studies; dealing with ethical issues in research			
The role of peer review in the scientific process			
The implications of psychological research for the economy			
Data handling and analysis			
Quantitative and qualitative data; the distinction between qualitative and quantitative data collection techniques			
Primary and secondary data, including meta-analysis			
Descriptive statistics: measures of central tendency – mean, median, mode; calculation of mean, median and mode; measures of dispersion; range and standard deviation; calculation of range; calculation of percentages; positive, negative and zero correlations			
Presentation and display of quantitative data: graphs, tables, scattergrams, bar charts			
Distributions: normal and skewed distributions; characteristics of normal and skewed distributions			
Statistical testing: the sign test			

Answers are given, along with examiner comments, on pages 256 to 262.

Section A Social influence

Answer all questions.

1 Which **two** of the following are factors affecting conformity investigated by Asch? *(2 marks)*

A agentic state   C task difficulty

B locus of control   D unanimity

2 Read the item below and answer the question that follows.

> When David started university he believed that the UK should have nuclear weapons. However, nearly all of the new friends he made were against this idea. David felt under pressure to conform so would say that he was also against nuclear weapons. By the time David graduated three years later, he strongly believed that the country should disarm and would even organise protests against nuclear weapons.

Referring to the above item, explain the difference between compliance and internalisation. *(6 marks)*

3 **(a)** Outline **one** of Milgram's findings from his research into obedience. *(2 marks)*

  (b) Briefly explain **one** limitation of this finding. *(2 marks)*

4 Describe and evaluate **one** dispositional explanation of obedience. *(12 marks)*

Section B Memory

5 Which of the following types of memory is being used in each of the examples below? Choose one type of memory that matches each example and write A, B or C in the box next to it.

Use each letter once only. *(2 marks)*

A Episodic memory

B Procedural memory

C Semantic memory

- Daniel remembers how to mow the lawn without consciously thinking about it. ☐

- Danielle remembers how upsetting it was when she once destroyed a flower bed when mowing the lawn. ☐

6 Name **two** components of the working memory model. *(2 marks)*

7 Read the item below and then answer the questions that follow.

> A psychologist investigated whether it was easier to recognise faces when in their normal configuration than when the faces' features were scrambled. Participants had to identify ten faces they had been shown before from a set of 30 faces. Some participants chose from scrambled faces while others chose from normal faces. The psychologist recorded how many they correctly identified, and the results are shown in **Table 1**.
>
> **Table 1** The number of faces correctly identified (out of 10) for scrambled faces and normal faces.

Condition 1 (Scrambled faces)	5 7 3 3 4 1 0 5
Condition 2 (Normal faces)	6 0 7 8 9 8 7 8

(a) Calculate the median for Condition 1. Show your workings. *(2 marks)*

(b) Explain why the median is a better of measure of central tendency compared to the mean in this study. *(2 marks)*

8 Outline **one** strength and **one** weakness of the cognitive interview as a technique for improving the accuracy of eye witness testimonies. *(4 marks)*

9 Briefly evaluate retrieval failure as an explanation of forgetting. *(4 marks)*

10 Describe the multi-store model of memory. *(8 marks)*

Section C Attachment

11 Name two of the countries studied by van Ijzendoorn in his research into cultural variations in attachment. *(2 marks)*

12 Outline **two** limitations of Ainsworth's research into the 'Strange Situation'. *(4 marks)*

13 Read the item below and answer the questions that follow.

> A psychologist compared two groups of adolescent participants who either had secure or insecure attachments as infants. He used a questionnaire to identify their attachment type but also to rate the quality of their friendships. The higher the rating, the more positive the friendships were for the participant. The results of the study are shown in **Table 2**.
>
> **Table 2** The median rating for quality of friendships for participants with secure attachments in infancy and those with insecure attachments.

	Secure	Insecure
Median rating for quality of friendship	12.1	10.3

(a) Explain why this study is an example of a quasi experiment. *(2 marks)*

(b) Outline one limitation of using a questionnaire to collect the data in this study. *(2 marks)*

(c) Sketch a bar graph to show the median ratings for quality of friendships in **Table 2**. *(4 marks)*

14 Explain how reciprocity and interactional synchrony are involved in caregiver-infant interactions. *(4 marks)*

15 Briefly discuss one of Harlow's animal studies on attachment. *(6 marks)*

Mock exam: AS Paper 2 Psychology in context

Section A Approaches in psychology

1 Which **one** of the following divisions of the nervous system is made up of the brain and spinal cord? *(1 mark)*

A Autonomic nervous system C Peripheral nervous system
B Central nervous system D Somatic nervous system

2 Name the type of neuron that forms synapses with muscles. *(1 mark)*

3 Read the item below and then answer the question that follows.

> Jasmine is a girl who has inherited a disorder that will potentially affect her verbal ability in the future. However, her parents have worked hard to stimulate her development and psychologists are amazed with the progress she is making.

Distinguish between the concepts of genotype and phenotype. Refer to Jasmine's case in your answer. *(4 marks)*

4 Read the following item and then answer the question that follows.

> Rory looks up to his older sister Rosie, and tries to copy many things he sees her doing. Rory is particularly keen to be as sporty as her as he sees their parents give her lots of praise and attention for this. Rosie is also aware that Rory pays attention to what she does so she is always careful to play fair when she knows that he is watching.

With reference to social learning theory, explain Rory's sporty behaviour. *(6 marks)*

5 Describe and evaluate the cognitive approach in psychology. *(12 marks)*

Section B Psychopathology

6 Identify **one** behavioural characteristic of;

(a) depression **(b)** obsessive-compulsive disorder **(c)** phobias
(3 marks)

7 Read the item below and then answer the question that follows.

> Ewan was diagnosed with depression having felt overrun with despair for the last twelve weeks. His doctor suggested that the cause of this was the fact that Ewan's long-term partner walked out on him three months ago. After this happened, Ewan was convinced he would never find another boyfriend.

Using Ellis' ABC model, explain why Ewan is suffering from depression. *(6 marks)*

8 Describe **one** research study that supports the behavioural approach to explaining phobias. *(4 marks)*

9 Read the item below and answer the questions that follow.

> A psychologist tested the effectiveness of drug therapy in treating the symptoms of obsessive-compulsive disorder by comparing drugs with a placebo (a fake drug). To do this, she used a matched pairs design.

(a) Identify the independent variable in this study. *(1 mark)*
(b) Outline **one** advantage of using a matched pairs design in this study. *(2 marks)*

10 Outline and briefly discuss **two** definitions of abnormality. *(8 marks)*

Section C Research Methods

Read the item and then answer the questions that follow.

> A psychologist investigated the relationship between children's diet and how well they behaved in school. He used a sample of 30 children aged from 5 to 11 years. Participants were randomly selected from children where both the parents and the child's school had agreed to taking part. The psychologist measured diet by asking parents to complete a questionnaire which gave a score for how healthy the child's diet was. The higher the score, the more healthy the diet. He measured behaviour by doing an overt observation of each child, for one hour, in their normal classroom. Using a series of behavioural categories, he counted how many times a child displayed a certain behaviour. The categories were all examples of poor behaviour, so the higher the total score, the worse the classroom behaviour was.

11 Write a suitable directional hypothesis for this study. *(3 marks)*

12 Outline **one** advantage and **one** disadvantage of using a random sample in this study. *(4 marks)*

13 Five of the children in the study were from Year 1. What fraction of children in the sample were from Year 1? Show your workings. *(2 marks)*

14 Explain why the psychologist needed the parents to agree to the study taking place. *(2 marks)*

15 The psychologist used closed questions in his questionnaire. Give **one** strength and **one** limitation of using closed questions. *(2 marks)*

16 Give one example of a behavioural category which could have been used in the observation. *(1 mark)*

17 (a) Briefly explain **one** limitation of using an the observational method in this study. *(2 marks)*

(b) Briefly outline how this limitation could have been addressed. *(2 marks)*

The results of the study are shown in the scattergram on the right.

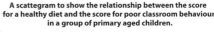

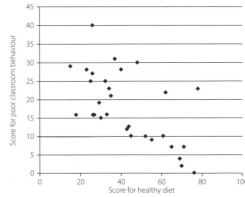

A scattergram to show the relationship between the score for a healthy diet and the score for poor classroom behaviour in a group of primary aged children.

18 Describe what the scattergram shows. What would the psychologist conclude from this data? *(3 marks)*

19 What is the range of the data taking from the observations of poor classroom behaviour? Show your workings. *(2 marks)*

20 Give **one** limitation of using a correlation to investigate diet and behaviour. *(1 mark)*

KEY TERMS

- Compliance
- Conformity
- Identification
- Internalisation
- Informational social influence
- Normative social influence

Possible essay question …

Discuss normative social influence **and** informational social influence as explanations for conformity. *(12 marks AS, 16 marks A)*

Other possible exam questions …

+ Outline what is meant by the terms 'compliance', 'internalisation', and 'identification'. *(2 + 2 + 2 marks)*
+ Explain what is meant by the terms 'normative social influence' and 'informational social influence'. *(2 + 2 marks)*
+ Outline **one** explanation for conformity and explain **one** criticism of this explanation. *(3 + 3 marks)*

MUST know …

Types of conformity

Compliance is going along with a group without accepting their point of view.

Internalisation is going along with a group because we accept that their perceptions and beliefs are accurate.

Identification is when we adopt an attitude or behaviour because we want to be associated with a group.

Explanations for conformity

Normative social influence is when we conform in order to gain approval or avoid disapproval. It explains why compliance occurs.

Informational social influence is when we conform because we believe the majority to be right. It explains why internalisation occurs.

The power of normative social influence is supported by…

…research on adolescent smoking.

- **E** – This showed a relationship between people's normative beliefs and the likelihood of them starting smoking.

Informational social influence helps explain…

…why social stereotypes develop.

- **E** – Research has shown that exposure to others' beliefs has an important influence on the way we stereotype others.

Informational social influence also explains how…

…political opinions are shaped.

- **E** – Research shows that people's judgements about politicians can be influenced by their knowledge of others' reactions.

SHOULD know …

Types of conformity

There is no change in our underlying attitudes, only in our public behaviour.

As well as our public behaviour changing, our underlying attitudes also change.

Identification includes both internalisation (accepting a group's attitudes or behaviour) and compliance (acceptance is for the purpose of becoming part of a group).

Explanations for conformity

An important condition for normative social influence is that we must believe we are under surveillance by the group.

The human desire to be right means that informational social influence is more likely if it is not clear to us how we *should* behave.

- **E** – Linkenbach and Perkins (2003) found that adolescents who were told that most of their peers didn't smoke were less likely to start smoking themselves.
- **L** – This supports the claim that people shape their behaviour to fit in with their peer group.

- **E** – Wittenbrink and Henley (1996) found people exposed to a negative, but supposedly majority, view about African Americans later reported more negative views about a black individual.
- **L** – This suggests that we are influenced by others when we believe they know more about an issue than we do.

- **E** – Fein *et al.* (2007) found judgements about presidential candidates in a debate were influenced by how others were supposedly reacting towards them.
- **L** – This suggests that we are influenced by others when we believe they have more information than we do.

A LEVEL ONLY ZONE

Normative social influence research has real world applications…

…such as making people behave more responsibly.

- **E** – Nolan *et al.* (2008) investigated whether people detected the influence of social norms on their energy conservation behaviour.
- **E** – They found that people believed the behaviour of their neighbours had the least impact, but results showed it had the strongest impact.
- **L** – This suggests people underestimate/under-detect the impact of normative social influence and instead rely on beliefs about what should motivate their behaviour.

Informational social influence's impact depends on…

…the judgements we are making.

- **E** – How much we're influenced depends on whether we're making judgements about social reality (e.g. how 'fun' a city is) or physical reality (e.g. its population size).
- **E** – Laughlin (1999) found people are more likely to be influenced when judgements have to be made about social reality.
- **L** – This supports the idea that informational social influence is more likely to occur when judgements are made on the basis of social consensus.

CHOOSE THE RIGHT ANSWER

Which **two** of the following are explanations for conformity? Tick **two** boxes only.

A Agentic state ☐

B Compliance ☐

C Normative social influence ☐

D Internalisation ☐

E Informational social influence ☐

Answers on page 269

 MATCH THEM UP

Match up the following concepts with their appropriate definitions.

1	Compliance is…	A	…conforming because we believe the majority to be right.
2	Internalisation is…	B	…going along with a group without accepting their point of view.
3	Identification is…	C	…adopting an attitude or behaviour because we want to be associated with a group.
4	Normative social influence is…	D	…conforming in order to gain approval or avoid disapproval.
5	Informational social influence is…	E	…going along with a group because we accept that their perceptions and beliefs are accurate.

Answers on page 269

 WRITE YOUR OWN EVALUATION POINT

"Informational social influence helps to explain the development of social stereotypes." Using this evaluation point, write it out in your own words below.

Point	
Evidence	
Explain	
Link	

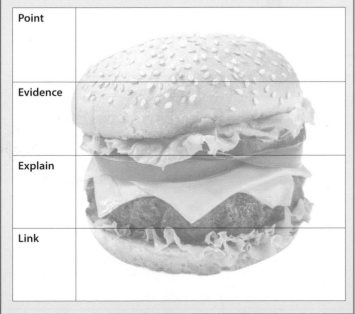

 SPOT THE MISTAKES

Read this answer to the following exam question:

Explain what is meant by compliance and identification. Give an example of each type of conformity.

There are **three** mistakes – draw a circle around each.

Compliance is a form of conformity in which we go along with the group's view and accept what we are being told. Our underlying attitude therefore changes. An example of compliance would be if we were pressured by our friends into stealing something from a shop, but we didn't want to do that. Internalisation is when we go along with the group's view and accept what we are being told. In internalisation, our underlying attitude also changes. An example of internalisation would be agreeing to go to a party when we didn't really want to.

Answers on page 269

APPLYING YOUR KNOWLEDGE

Using your knowledge of types of conformity and explanations for conformity, answer the following.

Dave and his friends were walking home from school. One of his friends picked up a stone and threw it at the window of an abandoned building. Dave's other friends did exactly the same, and then all looked at Dave. He didn't want to throw a stone, but he thought that if he didn't his friends wouldn't let him walk home with them anymore.

(a) Explain Dave's behaviour in terms of normative social influence. *(2 marks)*

Pete was going to Wembley to watch England play football for the first time. When he got to London he didn't know which tube train to get on. He saw a group of people dressed in England shirts and draped in flags all shouting 'En-ger-land'. They headed off to King's Cross. Pete followed them, confident that he would get to Wembley in time for the kick-off.

(b) Explain Pete's behaviour in terms of informational social influence. *(2 marks)*

Answers on page 269

KEY TERMS

- Confederate
- McCarthyism
- Self-efficacy

Possible essay question ...

Outline and evaluate research into group size, unanimity, and task difficulty as variables affecting conformity. *(12 marks AS, 16 marks A)*

Other possible exam questions ...

+ Explain the role of group size as a variable affecting conformity. *(4 marks)*
+ Describe how unanimity affects conformity. *(4 marks)*
+ Outline **one** study which investigated the effects of task difficulty on conformity and describe the results that were found. *(2 + 2 marks)*

MUST know ...

Asch (1956) studied conformity using a 'visual discrimination' task in which a group of participants had to say out loud which of three comparison lines matched a standard line.

Asch found that conformity was lower when group size was smaller and increased as group size increased.

Asch also found that conformity decreased when the group's unanimity was disturbed, and one of them gave the correct rather than incorrect answer.

Asch made the task much more *difficult* by making the comparison and standard lines very similar, so that the correct answer was much less obvious. Conformity increased the more difficult the task was.

Not all participants in Asch's experiments conformed...

...when the majority unanimously gave wrong answers.

- *E* – In two-thirds of trials, participants kept their original answer, despite a large majority expressing a completely different view.

Asch's findings may not be true today

...as the research took place at a time when conformity was high.

- *E* – The USA was affected by McCarthyism at the time, so people were scared to go against the majority.

One weakness of research in conformity is that...

...studies have only used a limited range of majority sizes.

- *E* – Asch believed that a majority of three was a sufficient number for maximum influence.

SHOULD know ...

All but one of the participants were actually 'confederates' who were initially instructed to give a unanimously incorrect answer on two-thirds of the eighteen trials.

There was very little conformity with one or two confederates, but three increased conformity to 33%. However, further increases in group size did not lead to more conformity.

When the confederates were unanimous, conformity occurred 33% of the time. When one confederate dissented, conformity dropped to 6%.

When the task is easy, normative social influence operates and participants show compliance. When the task is more difficult, conformity probably occurs because of informational social influence.

- *E* – Asch argued this indicated a tendency for participants to show independent behaviour rather than simply conform.
- *L* – This suggests that majority influence is not as strong as it might seem as a higher proportion of trials produced an independent response rather than conforming to the majority position.

- *E* – Perrin and Spencer (1980) replicated Asch's study in the 1980s and only had one conforming response in 386 trials.
- *L* – This suggests that conformity levels change over time and that Asch's research could be regarded as a 'child of its time' rather than a universal phenomenon.

- *E* – Bond (2005) says that only Asch used a majority greater than nine, and most studies have used a majority of between two and four.
- *L* – This suggests that we know very little about the effect of a larger majority on conformity rates given that most research has studied only the influence of relatively small majorities.

 A LEVEL ONLY ZONE

Asch's confederates may have been unconvincing...

...and so participants may not have believed their incorrect answers.

- *E* – If confederates were not convincing, the validity of the study would be low.
- *E* – Mori and Arai (2010) overcame this by giving each participant glasses which altered what they saw, removing the need for confederates.
- *L* – Conformity levels were similar to Asch's findings, suggesting his confederates did act convincingly and that his findings are valid.

There are important cultural differences...

...in conformity rates.

- *E* – Therefore we should expect different results in different cultures.
- *E* – Smith *et al.* (2006) found that the average conformity rate in individualist cultures was 25%, while the average conformity rate in collectivist cultures was 37%.
- *L* – This suggests that culture has an impact on conformity rate in that cultures that value interdependence more (collectivist cultures) are more likely to show higher levels of conformity than those that value independence (individualist cultures).

CHOOSE THE RIGHT ANSWER

Which **two** of the following statements about variables affecting conformity are correct? Tick **two** boxes only.

A	Conformity increases when the size of the group increases. ☐
B	Conformity decreases when the group's unanimity is disturbed. ☐
C	Conformity decreases when the size of the group increases. ☐
D	Conformity increases when the task is easy. ☐
E	Conformity increases when the size of the group increases, but only up to a point. ☐

Answers on page 269

 DRAWING CONCLUSIONS

 In an experiment into conformity, a researcher varied both the number of confederates and the difficulty of the task. The bar chart below shows the findings.

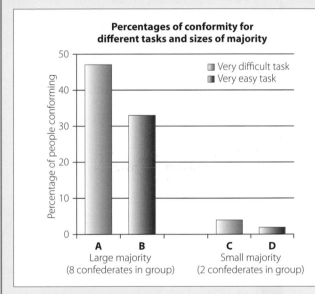

Percentages of conformity for different tasks and sizes of majority

■ Very difficult task
■ Very easy task

Percentage of people conforming (y-axis: 0–50)

A B — Large majority (8 confederates in group)
C D — Small majority (2 confederates in group)

Identify **three** things the bar chart shows about conformity. *(3 marks)*

Answers on page 269

 RESEARCH ISSUES

When Asch studied conformity, he used confederate participants who had been instructed to behave in certain ways during a visual discrimination task. Asch was interested in how people would behave when they found themselves in a group situation but believed that the other participants were genuine rather than confederates.

Identify **two** ethical issues that arise in this study. Suggest how **one** of these ethical issues could be dealt with. *(4 marks)*

Answers on page 269

 KEY WORDS

(1) Exam question:

Identify **three** variables that have been shown to affect conformity. Describe how conformity is affected by these three variables. *(6 marks)*

The three variables and their effect on conformity are shown on the opposite page. For each one, select **two** key words or phrases. The first one has been done for you:

Variable	Key word 1	Key word 2
Unanimity	Dissent	Decreased

(2) Now try to write an answer to the exam question using your key words. Your answer should make reference to the nature of the variable and the way in which conformity is affected.

Answers on page 269

 APPLYING YOUR KNOWLEDGE

Using your knowledge of variables affecting conformity, answer the following.

Mark went to his local pub's quiz night. The first question was: "What is the capital of Outer Mongolia?" Mark knew that the answer was Ulan Bator, but he kept quiet while his friends made suggestions. One of the quiz team was sure the answer was Kathmandu. His six team mates all agreed. Mark was asked was he thought the answer was. "Kathmandu," he replied.

(a) Explain Mark's behaviour in terms of one of the variables that affects conformity. *(3 marks)*

Just as the team captain was about to write down the answer, a team member who had only just arrived said: "Kathmandu? Are you mad, it's Ulan Bator!" The rest of the team said they'd never heard of Ulan Bator. Mark said: "He's right you know. You need to write down Ulan Bator."

(b) Explain the change in Mark's behaviour in terms of one of the variables that affects conformity. *(3 marks)*

Answers on page 269

KEY TERMS

- Demand characteristics
- Social roles

Possible essay question ...

Discuss conformity to social roles as investigated by Zimbardo. *(12 marks AS, 16 marks A)*

Other possible exam questions ...

+ Outline how Zimbardo studied conformity to social roles. *(4 marks)*

+ Describe the findings of any **one** study which has investigated conformity to social roles. *(4 marks)*

MUST know ...

Zimbardo and his colleagues' Stanford Prison Experiment (SPE) investigated how participants behave when given the role of either 'prisoner' or 'guard' in the *absence* of an obvious authority figure.

Guards wore uniforms and reflective sunglasses, which prevented eye contact with the prisoners. Prisoners wore a smock with an identification number on it.

The guards quickly became tyrannical and abusive towards the prisoners. The prisoners became increasingly passive and accepting of their plight. Both guards and prisoners conformed to their social role.

The SPE was supposed to last for two weeks, but was ended after only six days.

SHOULD know ...

The 24 participants had all been judged to be psychologically stable before the study began. They were randomly assigned to be a 'prisoner' or a 'guard'.

Guards referred to prisoners by their number rather than their name. The guards carried truncheons, but were told beforehand that they could not use them.

Some of the guards were so enthusiastic about their role that they volunteered to do unpaid overtime.

Five prisoners had to be 'released' early because of their extreme reactions to the situation they found themselves in. These reactions had begun after only two days of the SPE.

 EVALUATION — *Not all the guards behaved sadistically...*

...so such behaviour might not be due to an automatic embracing of the role.

- **E** – For example, some guards were aware that what they were doing was wrong.

- **E** – Haslam and Reicher (2012) argue this shows participants did not automatically conform to their roles, but chose how they behaved.
- **L** – This suggests that Zimbardo was wrong to claim the guards' behaviour was an automatic consequence of them conforming to their role.

EVALUATION — *The SPE was a controversial study...*

...but it was conducted ethically.

- **E** – The study was approved by the ethics committee at the university where it was conducted. Participants were not deceived because they were told beforehand that many of their usual rights would be temporarily suspended.

- **E** – However, Zimbardo acknowledges that the SPE could have been stopped earlier, given the emotional distress the 'prisoners' experienced. He did, however, debrief participants.
- **L** – Even though Zimbardo claims there were no lasting negative effects, the SPE highlights the importance of ethical considerations in psychological research.

 EVALUATION — *Demand characteristics may have affected the SPE...*

...weakening its internal validity.

- **E** – Participants' behaviour may have been the result of powerful demand characteristics created by the situation they found themselves in.

- **E** – Banuazizi and Movahedi (1975) found that students unfamiliar with the SPE correctly guessed its purpose and could accurately predict the behaviour of the prisoners and guards.
- **L** – This suggests that the internal validity of the SPE might have been seriously threatened by the presence of demand characteristics.

A LEVEL ONLY ZONE

EVALUATION — **Conformity to social roles has real world applications...**

...such as Abu Ghraib.

- **E** – Zimbardo believes that the same conformity to social roles in the SPE occurred at Abu Ghraib, a military prison in Iraq in which Iraqi prisoners were tortured and abused by American soldiers in 2003 and 2004.
- **E** – This, along with no accountability to higher authority, made the abuse more likely.
- **L** – This suggests that certain situational factors, combined with an opportunity to misuse the power associated with certain roles, can lead to people behaving in tyrannical and abusive ways.

EVALUATION — **It may not be mindless conformity...**

...that leads to people behaving in a tyrannical way.

- **E** – The guards' brutality may not be a natural consequence of the role and its associated power.
- **E** – Reicher and Haslam (2006) found the way members of strong groups behave depends on their social identity and its norms and values, not the role they take on.
- **L** – This means group behaviour is not necessarily mindless, but that people's behaviour depends on the norms and values of their social identity.

CHOOSE THE RIGHT ANSWER

Which **two** of the following statements about Zimbardo's prison study are correct? Tick **two** boxes only.

A	Both guards and prisoners conformed to their social role.	☐
B	Only the guards conformed to their social role.	☐
C	The prisoners were unaffected by their experiences.	☐
D	The guards became tyrannical and abusive towards the prisoners.	☐
E	Increasing the number of guards had a negative effect on morale.	☐

Answers on page 269

 MATCH THEM UP

Match the researchers to the appropriate evaluation of the SPE.

1	Banuazizi and Movahedi	**A**	Participants' behaviour in the SPE was a result of powerful demand characteristics created by the situation they found themselves in.
2	Haslam and Reicher	**B**	The same conformity to social roles in the SPE occurred at Abu Ghraib.
3	Reicher and Haslam	**C**	'Prisoners' and 'guards' did not conform automatically to their assigned roles.
4	Zimbardo	**D**	The SPE guards' brutality was not a natural consequence of that role and asserting the power associated with it.

Answers on page 269

 WRITE YOUR OWN EVALUATION POINT

Select one evaluation point from the page opposite and write it out in your own words below.

Point	
Evidence	
Explain	
Link	

 SPOT THE MISTAKES

Read this answer to the following exam question:

Evaluate research into conformity to social roles. *(6 marks)*

There are **three** mistakes - draw a circle around each.

> Zimbardo's study is important because conformity to social roles can also be seen in the real-world. At Abu Ghraib, the guards were abusive towards the prisoners even though the guards were accountable for their behaviour. However, Zimbardo's study raises important ethical issues. One of these is deception, because the prisoners did not know what the study was about. Another criticism of Zimbardo's study is demand characteristics. A study has shown that when given details about the procedure, students who were unfamiliar with the study were able to correctly predict how the prisoners and guards would behave. However, one strength of Zimbardo's study is that it has been replicated by Haslam and Reicher in a simulated prison setting in Britain.

Answers on page 269

 APPLYING YOUR KNOWLEDGE

Using your knowledge of conformity to social roles, answer the following.

Mike successfully applied for a job as a steward at Liverpool's Anfield football stadium. He was told that his job was to ensure that people were safe during the game. On his first day at work, Mike was told he would be stewarding the supporters in the Kop end of the ground. He was given a bright yellow high-visibility jacket. Because it was a hot sunny day, Mike wore his 'Aviator' sunglasses. Five minutes into the game, a young boy stood up and cheered his favourite player. Mike stormed into the crowd and gave the boy a serious telling off. Even if the boy shuffled in his seat, Mike told him off. After half an hour of continually being told off, the boy burst into tears. He told Mike he wanted to leave at half-time, but Mike said he wouldn't allow him to leave. The boy spent the second half of the game staring at the ground, avoiding eye contact with Mike.

Explain Mike's behaviour and the boy's behaviour in terms of conformity to social roles. *(6 marks)*

Answers on page 270

KEY TERMS

- Deception
- Ecological validity
- Historical validity
- Informed consent
- Obedience to authority
- Protection from harm

Possible essay question …

Discuss **two or more** situational variables that affect obedience (e.g. proximity, location, uniform). *(12 marks AS, 16 marks A)*

Other possible exam questions …

+ Outline **one** study which has investigated obedience to authority. *(4 marks)*
+ Explain how proximity influences obedience to authority. *(3 marks)*
+ Explain how location influences obedience to authority. *(3 marks)*
+ Explain how uniforms influence obedience to authority. *(3 marks)*

MUST know …

Milgram (1963) studied obedience by seeing if participants would give a series of increasingly severe electric shocks to a person in a different room if an experimenter told them to.

Although they protested, 26/40 (65%) participants administered the maximum 450V when the experimenter told them to do so.

When the experimenter's proximity to the participant changed, obedience decreased dramatically.

Changing the location of the study did not have a major effect on how obedient participants were.

Obedience also decreased dramatically when the experimenter did not wear his laboratory 'uniform' (his lab-coat).

SHOULD know …

The person did not actually receive any electric shocks. Both he and the experimenter were confederates of Milgram.

None of the participants disobeyed before the 300V shock, and only five refused to continue with the procedure at 300V.

Obedience fell from 65% to 21% when the experimenter issued his instructions from another room via a telephone.

Obedience fell from 65% in the university laboratory to 48% when the study was conducted in a privately-rented office.

When the experimenter wore his lab-coat, 65% of participants gave the maximum 450V shock. When he did not wear the lab-coat, very few participants obeyed him.

 EVALUATION

Many of Milgram's participants didn't believe…

…the shocks were real.

- **E** – Despite the fact the learner cried in pain, the experimenter in Milgram's studies remained cool and distant.

- **E** – This might have led to the participants not believing any real harm would come to the learner.
- **L** – This means that the research may lack internal validity because if the deception hadn't worked then any conclusions drawn about why participants obeyed would be invalid.

 EVALUATION

Milgram's research has many ethical issues…

…including deception and no real right to withdraw.

- **E** – Participants were deceived about the true nature of the study, believing it to be a study about the effect of punishment on learning.

- **E** – While Milgram claimed they had the right to withdraw, the prods from the experimenter made it more difficult for them to leave.
- **L** – This study highlights the importance of ethics when conducting psychological research and the need to safeguard the well-being of participants above the aims of any research study.

EVALUATION

Gender differences may have been overestimated…

…in Milgram's study of obedience.

- **E** – We might expect to find gender differences in obedience, with women behaving more obediently than men.

- **E** – However, neither Milgram nor Blass (1999) (in a meta-analysis of obedience studies) found any difference in obedience rates between men and women.
- **L** – This shows that gender differences did not have an impact on obedience levels.

A LEVEL ONLY ZONE

 EVALUATION

Milgram's research is not relevant…

…to real-life atrocities.

- **E** – Mandel (1998) claims that the situational factors Milgram's research says influence obedience do not occur in the real world.
- **E** – Despite the presence of factors which would, according to Milgram, increase defiance, very few people refused to take part in a mass killing of Jews in Poland.
- **L** – This suggests that situational factors are not the only explanation for obedience.

EVALUATION

Milgram's research is over 50 years old…

…so may lack historical validity.

- **E** – It has been argued that people today would not behave in the same way as Milgram's participants.
- **E** – However, Burger (2009) found levels of obedience almost identical to those found by Milgram. Similarly, a statistical analysis by Blass (1999) found no more or less obedience in studies conducted after Milgram's.
- **L** – This suggests Milgram's research findings do still apply today, rather than being relevant only to one particular point in time.

CHOOSE THE RIGHT ANSWER

Which of the following statements A–E best matches the terms below? Choose **one** statement that matches **each** term and write one of A–E in the box next to it.

1	Proximity	☐
2	Location	☐
3	Uniform	☐

A Increases obedience when instructions are issued by telephone.

B Results in no obedience when the study is carried out in the real world.

C Does not differ much from that seen in the laboratory.

D Increases how obedient participants are.

E Decreases how obedient participants are when instructions are issued by telephone.

F Increases how obedient participants are when the participant and the person receiving electric shocks are in the same room.

Answers on page 270

 DRAWING CONCLUSIONS

 The bar chart below shows how much obedience Milgram found when he made variations to his original study.

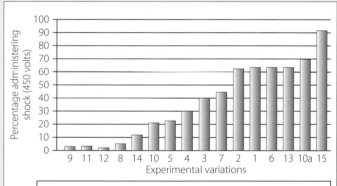

1. Remote victim
2. Voice feedback
3. Proximity
4. Touch proximity
5. Remote authority
6. Women as participants
7. Institutional context
8. Participants free to choose shock level
9. Learner demands to be shocked
10. An ordinary man gives orders
10a. The participant as bystander
11. Authority as victim—an ordinary man commanding
12. Two authorities—contradictory commands
13. Two authorities—one as victim
14. Two peers rebel
15. A peer administers shock

Milgram found 65% obedience in his original study (variation 2). In variation 3, Milgram varied the proximity of the teacher and learner, by having the learner in the same room as the teacher. In variation 7, Milgram varied the location of the study, and conducted it in a run-down office rather than the psychological laboratory at Yale. He called this 'institutional context'. In variation 10, Milgram varied the uniform the experimenter wore. In this variation, he did not wear his laboratory coat. Milgram called this 'an ordinary man gives orders'.

Approximately what percentage of obedience did Milgram find when he varied proximity, location, and uniform? *(3 marks)*

Answers on page 270

 SPOT THE MISTAKES

Read this student answer to the following exam question:

Explain how uniforms and location influence obedience to authority. *(6 marks)*

There are **three** mistakes – draw a circle around each.

> Research has shown that uniforms can have a powerful impact on how obedient people are. In one study, Bushman found that people obeyed more when they were told to do something by a person dressed as a business executive compared with when they were dressed in a police-style uniform. Mllgram found that people were more obedient when the experimenter wore a laboratory coat compared with when he was dressed as an ordinary man. Milgram found that compared with his laboratory study, people hardly obeyed at all when the experiment was conducted in a privately-rented office. However, when Milgram conducted his study in a police station he found that nearly everyone obeyed the experimenter.

Answers on page 270

 RESEARCH ISSUES

Identify **four** examples of deception in the passage below, and identify and explain **one** other ethical issue that is evident in the passage. *(6 marks)*

Milgram obtained participants for his study by placing an advertisement in a local paper asking for volunteers for a study on the effects of punishment on learning. When participants arrived at the laboratory, they were told that one of them would be the 'teacher' and the other the 'learner'. They drew lots to decide which they would be, but the draw was arranged so that one of them was always given the role of 'teacher'. The 'teacher' was told that he would be required to give a series of increasingly severe electric shocks to the 'learner'. However, in reality, no electric shocks were actually administered, and the person who was the 'learner' was actually an actor hired by Milgram to play that role.

Answers on page 270

APPLYING YOUR KNOWLEDGE

Using your knowledge of situational variables affecting obedience, answer the following.

For Mike's second time being a steward at Liverpool's ground, it was another hot sunny day. This time, all of the Liverpool fans followed his instructions to remain seated during the game. At half-time, Mike removed his bright yellow high-visibility jacket because it was so hot. During the second half, Liverpool scored a goal and the supporters started jumping up and down. Mike told them to sit down, but most of them ignored him and remained standing up for the rest of the game.

In terms of research into situational variables affecting obedience, explain the Liverpool fans' behaviour. *(3 marks)*

Answers on page 270

KEY TERMS

- Agentic shift
- Agentic state
- Autonomous state
- Legitimate authority

Possible essay question …

Discuss how the agentic state **and** the legitimacy of authority can explain why people behave obediently. *(12 marks AS, 16 marks A)*

Other possible exam questions …

+ Explain what is meant by the term 'agentic state'. *(3 marks)*
+ Outline **one** psychological study which has investigated the legitimacy of authority as an explanation for obedience. *(4 marks)*

MUST know …

Milgram (1974) defined the agentic state as being when we see ourselves "as an agent for carrying out another person's wishes".

When we move from seeing ourselves as being responsible for our behaviour to seeing someone else as being responsible for it, 'agentic shift' has occurred.

A legitimate authority figure is someone who is perceived to be in a position of social control in a situation.

For authority to be perceived as legitimate, it must occur within some sort of institutional structure, such as the military.

Legitimate authority can be used to justify…

…harming others.

- **E** – When directed by a legitimate authority figure to engage in immoral actions, people are willing to do so.

People are not always in the agentic state…

…and can revert back to an autonomous state.

- **E** – When participants considered the experimenter a legitimate authority, they underwent an agentic shift, but reverted to an autonomous state afterwards.

'Plain cruelty' might explain obedience…

…better than agentic shift.

- **E** – Milgram's participants may have used the situation to express their sadistic tendencies.

SHOULD know …

The agentic state is contrasted with the autonomous state, in which we see ourselves as being responsible for our behaviour.

Agentic shift may occur as a way of maintaining a positive self-image. Because behaviour is no longer our responsibility, our self-image is unaffected.

For a shift to the agentic state to occur, we must perceive the person telling us how to behave as a legitimate authority.

In Milgram's studies, it was the *category* of the institution (the 'scientific' laboratory) rather than the university itself which was the institutional structure.

- **E** – This unquestioning obedience to authority occurs no matter how destructive the actions that these orders called for. This is especially true in the military.
- **L** – This implies that when people authorise another person to make judgements for them about appropriate conduct, they no longer feel that their own moral values are relevant to their conduct.

- **E** – However, Lifton (1986) found that doctors at Auschwitz showed a gradual and irreversible transition from caring professionals to individuals who carried out evil acts.
- **L** – Therefore, carrying out evil actions over time may change people's behaviour more than a sudden and reversible agentic shift.

- **E** – The SPE results support this (see page 24). Guards inflicted rapidly escalating cruelty to prisoners, even though there was no authority figure telling them to do this.
- **L** – This shows it may not be agentic control which causes obedience. Instead it may be certain aspects of human nature.

Agentic shift can explain other behaviours…

…such as bystander behaviour.

- **E** – When we feel less in control of our actions, we tend to show an increased acceptance of external sources of control to compensate for this.
- **E** – Fennis and Aarts (2012) showed reducing personal control resulted in bystander apathy and greater obedience to authority.
- **L** – This suggests agentic shift is caused by a reduction in our feelings of personal control.

It can be very dangerous…

…accepting another person's authority as legitimate.

- **E** – Tarnow (2000) looked at aircraft accidents in the USA where flight crew actions were known to be a contributing factor.
- **E** – There was excessive dependence on the captain's authority in over half of the accidents. One officer claimed he didn't question the captain's behaviour because he assumed the captain knew what he was doing.
- **L** – These findings show that even when confronted with dangerous situations, we might not question authority.

CHOOSE THE RIGHT ANSWER

Which **two** of the following are characteristics of the agentic state? Tick **two** boxes only.

A Obeying because we want to be liked by other group members. ☐

B Obeying because we see ourselves as no longer responsible for our actions. ☐

C Obeying because we understand that we are responsible for our actions. ☐

D Obeying because we are uncertain how to behave. ☐

E Obeying because we see others as being responsible for our actions. ☐

Answers on page 270

MATCH THEM UP

Match the researchers to the statement which best describes their research.

1	Tarnow	**A**	Agentic shift can also explain bystander behaviour.
2	Lifton	**B**	Carrying out evil acts over a long period of time, rather than agentic shift, changes how people think and behave.
3	Milgram	**C**	Excessive dependence on an authority figure can be dangerous.
4	Fennis and Aarts	**D**	People shift back and forth between the agentic and autonomous states.

Answers on page 270

WRITE YOUR OWN EVALUATION POINT

Select one evaluation point from the page opposite and write it out in your own words below.

Point	
Evidence	
Explain	
Link	

APPLYING YOUR KNOWLEDGE (1)

Using your knowledge of the legitimacy of authority, answer the following.

Phil was walking around town when he saw a man fall, clutching his chest. The man was obviously in pain, and very quickly a crowd gathered around him. Nobody appeared to be helping. Then, Phil heard a voice shout: "Let me through, I'm a doctor." The crowd immediately made way and watched whilst the man was treated. Phil wondered if the same thing would have happened if he had shouted, "Let me through, I know first aid."

Explain whether the crowd would have been more likely to make way for a trained doctor or someone who 'knew first aid'. *(3 marks)*

Answers on page 270

APPLYING YOUR KNOWLEDGE (2)

Using your knowledge of agentic state and legitimacy of authority, answer the following.

Susan, the head of sixth form, received a telephone call from the head teacher. She told Susan to announce to the sixth form that they will have to wear uniform starting next term. Susan made the announcement at the next assembly. The students booed and hissed when Susan gave them the news. "Don't blame me, I'm only the messenger," she said, as she left the assembly hall.

Explain Susan's reaction in terms of Milgram's agency theory. *(4 marks)*

Answers on page 270

KEY TERMS

- Authoritarian aggression
- Authoritarian personality
- Authoritarian submission
- Conventionalism
- Dispositional explanation
- F Scale
- Right-wing authoritarianism

Possible essay question …

Outline and evaluate the Authoritarian Personality as a dispositional explanation for obedience. *(12 marks AS, 16 marks A)*

Other possible exam questions …

+ Explain what is meant by the term Authoritarian Personality. *(2 marks)*
+ Describe how the Authoritarian Personality explains obedience to authority. *(4 marks)*
+ Outline and evaluate **one** research study relating to the Authoritarian Personality explanation of obedience to authority. *(6 marks)*

MUST know …

Dispositional explanations propose that obedience is caused by personality characteristics rather than situational factors. A specific personality type that has been proposed to explain obedience to authority is the Authoritarian Personality (AP).

The California F Scale questionnaire measures the different components of the AP. An AP is indicated by strongly agreeing with statements such as, "Obedience and respect for authority are the most important virtues children should learn."

Adorno *et al.* (1950) proposed that the AP was a result of an authoritarian parenting style. They found that the parents of high F Scale scorers tended to emphasise obedience and physically punished their children.

 There is a relationship between…

…authoritarianism and obedience.

- **E** – For example, Elms and Milgram (1966) found higher authoritarianism levels in twenty obedient participants in Milgram's research compared with twenty disobedient participants.

 The social context may be more important than…

…personality factors.

- **E** – Milgram's research showed variations in social context, such as location, caused differences in obedience levels. He argued that they were a better predictor of obedience than personality factors.

Research has shown that…

…authoritarian personalities are more obedient.

- **E** – Participants are often suspicious about whether the shocks are real or fake.

SHOULD know …

People with an AP tend to see the world in 'black and white', enforce strict adherence to social rules, and are rigid thinkers who obey authority.

Altemeyer (1981) refined the concept of the AP. His right-wing authoritarianism personality (RWA) has three important characteristics that predispose people to obedience. These are conventionalism, authoritarian aggression, and authoritarian submission.

Adorno *et al.* argued that children who grow up in an authoritarian family see this system as the norm and acquire the same authoritarian attitudes through learning and imitation. This makes them more likely to behave obediently.

- **E** – A further finding was that obedient participants reported being less close to their fathers in childhood compared with disobedient participants.
- **L** – But many obedient participants also reported having good parental relationships, so this may not be the best explanation for obedience.

- **E** – It was the specific social situation participants found themselves in that caused them to obey, not their personalities.
- **L** – Therefore, according to Milgram, a person's authoritarian personality may not be the best explanation for obedience.

- **E** – Dambrun and Vatiné (2010) found participants' RWA scores were correlated with the maximum shock given, even when they were told the shocks were not real.
- **L** – Participants with a higher RWA score were the most obedient, showing that authoritarianism is a good explanation for obedience.

A LEVEL ONLY ZONE

 Education level may determine obedience…

…and authoritarianism.

- **E** – Some research, such as that by Middendorp and Meloen (1990), has shown less-educated people are consistently more authoritarian than well-educated people.
- **E** – However, other research has shown that when education level is controlled for, the more obedient participants still showed higher levels of authoritarianism.
- **L** – This suggests education level may have some influence, but authoritarianism is a better explanation for obedience.

 People with right-wing views are more likely to obey…

…according to Altemeyer.

- **E** – If people on the political right are more likely to obey, then people on the political left might be less likely to obey.
- **E** – Bègue *et al.* (2014) found participants who defined themselves as being left-wing gave lower intensity (fake) shocks to another participant.
- **L** – This suggests that the situational context does not exclude the possibility of individual differences as a determining influence on obedience.

CHOOSE THE RIGHT ANSWER

Which of the following statements (A–E) best matches the terms below? Choose **one** statement that matches each term and write one of A–E in the box next to it.

1 The California F scale	☐
2 Dispositional explanation	☐
3 Authoritarian personality	☐

A The view that obedience is caused by personality characteristics rather than situational factors.

B A tendency to see the world in 'black and white' and enforce strict adherence to social roles.

C The view that obedience is a product of both personality characteristics and situational factors.

D The view that situational factors are responsible for obedience.

E A way of measuring the authoritarian personality.

Answers on page 270

 DRAWING CONCLUSIONS

A student asked 24 members of her class to complete two questionnaires. One of these was the California F Scale. The higher the score, the more authoritarian the person is. The other was a measure asking people how obediently they would behave in various situations. The higher the score, the more obedient the person is. The scores on the questionnaires were plotted in a scattergram, which is shown below:

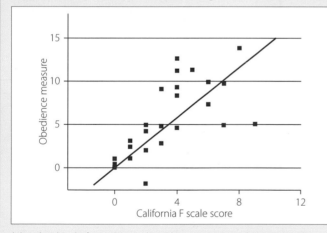

(a) What kind of correlation does the scattergram show? *(1 mark)*

(b) What conclusion would be drawn about the relationship shown in the scattergram? *(2 marks)*

(c) In terms of the two variables measured, what is the main limitation of correlational analysis? *(2 marks)*

(d) Why was it important for the order of presentation of the two questionnaires to be counterbalanced? *(1 mark)*

Answers on page 270

 SPOT THE MISTAKES

Read this student answer to the following exam question:

Describe how the authoritarian personality explains obedience to authority. *(6 marks)*.

There are **four** mistakes – draw a circle around each.

> Adorno says that it is a person's personality and the situation they find themselves in that causes them to be obedient to authority figures. To measure the Authoritarian Personality, Adorno devised the California AP-scale. Authoritarian people are flexible thinkers who see the world in black-and-white terms. They also believe that respect for authority is an important virtue that children should learn. However, authoritarian personalities believe that social rules are there to be broken. There is a correlation between scores on Adorno's measure of authoritarianism and how likely it is that people will behave obediently.

Answers on page 270

 MATCH THEM UP

Match the researchers to the statement which best describes their research findings.

1	Altemeyer	**A**	Less-educated people are consistently more authoritarian than the well-educated.
2	Elms and Milgram	**B**	Participants high in RWA were more willing to give themselves increasing levels of electric shock whenever they made a mistake if the experimenter told them to do so.
3	Middendorp and Meloen	**C**	There were higher levels of authoritarianism in 20 people who had given the maximum 450V shock than in 20 who had behaved disobediently.

Answers on page 270

 APPLYING YOUR KNOWLEDGE

Using your knowledge of the authoritarian personality, answer the following.

Tony and Guy are very different characters. One night they watched a film. It was about the trial of a Police Officer who had been physically abusive to prisoners supposedly in his care? As the judge was about to give the verdict, Tony said: "The prosecution have a good case against him. I think he's guilty." Guy replied: "How can he be guilty? He was just doing what he'd been told to do."

How might the fact that Tony and Guy are 'very different characters' explain their differences of opinion? *(3 marks)*

Answers on page 270

KEY TERMS

- Externality
- Internality
- Locus of control
- Meta-analysis
- Social support

Possible essay question …

Discuss how social support **and** locus of control can explain resistance to social influence.
(12 marks AS, 16 marks A)

Other possible exam questions …

+ Using psychological research, describe how social support explains resistance to social influence. *(6 marks)*

+ Describe how locus of control explains resistance to social influence. *(6 marks)*

MUST know …

Social support is the perception that a person has assistance available from other people, and that they are part of a supportive network. Social support enables us to resist pressures from a majority to conform or obey.

Locus of control (LOC) is a person's perception of personal control of their own behaviour. People with a strong *internal* LOC believe that what happens to them is largely a result of their own ability and effort. People with a strong *external* LOC believe that what happens to them is determined by external factors, such as the influence of others or luck.

 LOC helps us resist pressure to conform…

…but not always.

- **E** – According to Spector (1983), there is a correlation between LOC and a predisposition to normative social influence. However, there is no correlation between LOC and a predisposition to informational social influence.

 Social support does not have to be valid…

…to be effective.

- **E** – Even if our social support isn't particularly convincing, we can still use it to help us resist pressure to conform.

There is a historical trend…

…in LOC research.

- **E** – Twenge *et al.*'s (2004) meta-analysis found young Americans increasingly believed luck influenced their fate more than their own actions.

SHOULD know …

In conformity, an important aspect of social support is that it breaks the unanimity of the majority. In obedience, disobedient peers act as role models on which a person can base their own behaviour. Defiant peers enable us to remove ourselves from situations where we are expected to obey.

Most people are neither strongly internal nor external. 'Internals' rely less on others' opinions, which enables them to resist social influence. 'Externals' take less personal responsibility for their actions and are less likely to display independent behaviour and more likely to accept others' influences.

- **E** – Externals were more likely than internals to conform because of normative social influence, but LOC was not a significant factor when conformity was the result of informational social influence.
- **L** – This suggests a high degree of internality is only helpful when conformity occurs to gain approval.

- **E** – In Allen and Levine's (1971) study, a dissenting confederate wore glasses with thick lenses during a visual task. Although this support was not valid, given the nature of the task, conformity was reduced.
- **L** – This suggests any form of social support is effective, but it is more effective when it is perceived as valid.

- **E** – They found that LOC scores have become substantially more external over time.
- **L** – This externalisation may be due to the increasing levels of alienation experienced by young people and a tendency to explain misfortunes in terms of outside forces in the latter years of the twentieth century.

 Using social support to resist pressures to obey…

…can be seen in the real world.

- **E** – For example, in the Rossenstrasse protest during the Second World War, German women challenged Gestapo agents threatening to open fire if they did not disperse.
- **E** – The women demanded their husbands and sons be released. The support they gave each other eventually resulted in this happening.
- **L** – This illustrates Milgram's finding that a disobedient confederate gives a person the confidence and courage to resist obeying.

 Internals have various characteristics…

…that help them to resist obedience.

- **E** – Internals are more achievement orientated and actively seek out information, as compared with externals.
- **E** – Hutchins and Estey (1978) found that high internals are also better able to resist coercion from others.
- **L** – These findings indicate that having an internal locus of control is a powerful factor in resisting social influence.

CHOOSE THE RIGHT ANSWER

Which **two** of the following statements about resistance to social influence are correct? Tick **two** boxes only.

A Social support has to be valid in order to be effective.	☐
B Locus of control always helps us to resist pressures to conform.	☐
C People with an internal locus of control are generally better able to resist pressures to conform.	☐
D Social support from defiant peers enables us to remove ourselves from situations where we are expected to obey.	☐
E The effects of social support are limited to laboratory studies of obedience.	☐

Answers on page 271

 DRAWING CONCLUSIONS

A researcher was interested in seeing if Locus Of Control (LOC) was an important variable in resistance to social influence. She measured LOC in a large sample of students, and then classified them according to whether they were 'strong internals' or 'strong externals'. She then asked the school's caretaker to act as a confederate. He was asked to inform the students that they couldn't park their cars, even though the car park was obviously empty, without giving them a reason. Other students were told they couldn't use the car park because it was going to be resurfaced. The caretaker recorded which students asked him why they couldn't park their cars and which did not. The results are shown in the table below:

	Percentage of internals questioning caretaker	Percentage of externals questioning caretaker
No reason given	89	14
Reason given	15	14

Outline **two** findings and **two** conclusions that you might draw from this table. *(4 marks)*

Finding 1:

Conclusion1: This shows that ...

Finding 2:

Conclusion 2: This shows that ...

Answers on page 271

 MATCH THEM UP

Complete the statements on the left below with the correct part on the right.

1	Locus of control is	**A**	the perception that a person has assistance available from other people
2	Social support is	**B**	believe that what happens to them is determined by things such as luck
3	People with a strong internal locus of control	**C**	that it breaks the unanimity of the majority
4	People with a strong external locus of control	**D**	a person's perception of personal control of their own behaviour
5	Defiant peers	**E**	believe that what happens to them is a result of their own ability
6	In conformity, an important aspect of social support is	**F**	enable us to remove ourselves from situations where we are expected to obey

Answers on page 271

 APPLYING YOUR KNOWLEDGE

Using your knowledge to resistance to social influence, answer the following.

Javed and Steve were discussing their test results. Steve said that although he'd revised it was only because he'd taken his lucky pixie charm to the test that he'd passed. Javed said that he'd worked really hard for the test and that he deserved to pass it given how much effort he'd put in.

(a) Which type of locus of control does Javed have? *(1 mark)*

(b) Which type of locus of control does Steve have? *(1 mark)*

(c) Which of the two students is least likely to resist pressures to conform? Use your knowledge of psychology to explain your answer. *(3 marks)*

Answers on page 271

KEY TERMS

- Commitment
- Consistency
- Dissent
- Dogmatic
- Flexibility
- Minority influence

Possible essay question ...

Outline and evaluate the role played by consistency, commitment and flexibility in minority influence. *(12 marks AS, 16 marks A)*

Other possible exam questions ...

+ Define the term 'minority influence'. *(2 marks)*
+ Explain how consistency, commitment, or flexibility affect minority influence. *(4 marks)*
+ Outline **one** research study that has investigated minority influence. *(4 marks)*

MUST know ...

The issue of whether a numerical minority can influence a numerical majority was first investigated by Moscovici *et al.* (1969) in their 'blue or green slides' study.

Moscovici *et al.* found that when the minority consistently claimed that the blue slides were green, the majority were influenced about 8% of the time.

Moscovici *et al.*'s findings demonstrate that although conformity levels are nowhere near as high as those seen in studies where a numerical majority attempts to influence a numerical minority, a consistent numerical minority can exert at least some influence over a numerical majority.

 Minority influence is not always effective...

...because we do not process a minority's message as deeply.

- *E* – If the majority express a different view to ours, we might consider their view carefully to understand it.

 Better quality decisions can be made by numerical minorities...

...for example in work groups.

- *E* – Van Dyne and Saavedra (1996) studied *dissent* as a form of minority influence. They found that better decisions were made when a dissenting minority was present.

 Flexibility is important in minority influence...

...and there is research to support this.

- *E* – In a simulated jury trial, Nemeth and Brilmayer (1987) found confederates holding a minority view who *compromised* with the majority were more influential.

SHOULD know ...

In a group of six, a minority of two confederates consistently said that an obviously blue slide was green. The aim of the study was to see if the other four participants would be influenced by the minority's incorrect view.

When the minority behaved inconsistently, and only sometimes called the blue slides green, the majority were influenced about 1% of the time.

Moscovici *et al.* claimed that conversion to a minority position tends to be deep and long-lasting. As well as consistency, commitment to a position and a flexible rather than dogmatic negotiating style are also important in minority influence.

- *E* – However, Mackie (1987) claimed we do not spend as much time processing why a minority's message is different to that of the majority.
- *L* – Therefore, the minority's message tends to be less, rather than more, influential than the position advocated by the majority.

- *E* – Nemeth (2010) claims dissent 'opens' the mind, making us search for more information and consider more options.
- *L* – This shows dissenters liberate people to say what they believe, and stimulate thought even when they are wrong.

- *E* – As minorities are relatively powerless, they must negotiate rather than enforce their position.
- *L* – However, being too flexible too early on in negotiations weakens the minority's position as this suggests they have caved in to the majority.

A LEVEL ONLY ZONE

 There is a tipping point for commitment...

...in minority influence.

- *E* – This is where the number of people holding a minority position is sufficient to change majority opinion.
- *E* – Xie *et al.* (2011) found just 10% of committed opinion holders was necessary to 'tip' a majority into accepting the minority position.
- *L* – The minority were only successful in influencing the majority if they were also *consistent* in their expression of their alternative viewpoint.

Convincing people dissenting minorities are valuable...

...remains difficult.

- *E* – We superficially accept dissent to appear tolerant and democratic. However, dissent is seen as disrupting group harmony.
- *E* – Nemeth argues majority viewpoints persist because a minority viewpoint is often belittled, and dissenters are marginalised or threatened by repercussions.
- *L* – This means opportunities for innovative thinking, which minority influence brings, is often lost.

CHOOSE THE RIGHT ANSWER

Which **two** of the following statements about minority influence are correct? Tick **two** boxes only.

A Minorities are more influential the more dogmatic they are. ☐

B Minorities are more influential if they demonstrate commitment to their position. ☐

C A minority that expresses a viewpoint inconsistently is more effective than one that expresses a viewpoint consistently. ☐

D A minority that is flexible in its viewpoint can never be influential. ☐

E Less conformity is seen when a numerical minority influences a numerical majority than when a numerical majority influences a numerical minority. ☐

Answers on page 271

 RESEARCH ISSUES

Moscovici *et al.* (1969) found that when a numerical minority behaved consistently they were able to influence a numerical majority around 8% of the time. However, when the numerical minority behaved inconsistently, the majority were influenced only about 1% of the time. Moscovici *et al.* also included a control condition in their study.

Explain why a control condition was necessary, and how the numerical minority behaved in it. *(4 marks)*

Answers on page 271

 SPOT THE MISTAKES

Read this student answer to the following exam question:

Explain how consistency, commitment **or** flexibility affect minority influence. *(4 marks)*

There are **five** mistakes - draw a circle around each. There is also one exam technique mistake. Can you spot what it is?

Moscovici studied minority influence in his slides experiment. A group of six participants were used, but one of these was a confederate who was told to always say blue even though all the slides were clearly green. Moscovici found that the minority influenced the majority about 8% of the time. In another condition, the confederates were told to sometimes call the blue slides green. Conformity decreased to about 1%. Moscovici says that minorities are more influential if they are consistent and that it is important because it suggests to the minority that there must be a reason for holding a view if the majority maintain it all the time. Flexibility is the willingness to be flexible and to compromise when expressing a position.

Answers on page 271

 APPLYING YOUR KNOWLEDGE (1)

Using your knowledge of minority influence, answer the following.

Estefan knows the views he holds are very much in the minority. He has approached you for advice on how he should present his views when he is interviewed by the media. Use your knowledge of findings from minority influence research to try to help Estefan alter the attitudes of the majority. One finding and one piece of advice are already in the table.

Finding from minority influence research	Advice to Estefan
Consistency	
	Estefan needs to be willing to compromise when he expresses his position. He must be prepared to negotiate with the majority rather than enforce his position.

Answers on page 271

 APPLYING YOUR KNOWLEDGE (2)

Using your knowledge of minority influence, answer the following.

Sylvia told her friends that she ate nothing but sushi, which her friends thought was a little bit strange. Every day Sylvia told them of the benefits of eating raw fish, which she said increased her intelligence and made her feel super-fit. Sylvia seemed so convinced of the benefits of sushi that her friends decided to buy some and try it. On their way to the supermarket they passed the burger restaurant. There was Sylvia eating a super deluxe beef burger. Later, Sylvia asked her friends if they were going to become sushi-eaters. "NO!" they all replied.

Using your knowledge of research into minority influence, explain why Sylvia was unsuccessful in changing her friends' eating behaviour. *(3 marks)*

Answers on page 271

KEY TERMS

- Augmentation principle
- Boomerang effect
- Snowball effect
- Social change
- Social norms interventions

Possible essay question ...

Discuss the role of social influence processes in social change. *(12 marks AS, 16 marks A)*

Other possible exam questions ...

+ Outline research into the role of social influence processes in social change. *(6 marks)*

+ Using psychological research, explain how social change can be brought about by social influence processes. *(6 marks)*

+ Outline a study of social influence that can be used to explain why social change occurs. *(4 marks)*

MUST know ...

People exposed to a persuasive argument may, under certain conditions, change their views to match those of the minority:

Drawing attention to an issue: Minorities can bring about social change by drawing attention to an issue.

Creating a conflict: Minorities create a conflict in the minds of the majority between what they currently believe and what the minority believe.

Consistent with each other and over time: Social change is more likely when the minority is consistent in their position.

The augmentation principle: If a minority appears willing to suffer for their views, they are taken more seriously.

The snowball effect: Minority influence initially has a small effect, but this spreads more widely until it eventually leads to large scale social change.

 Social change happens gradually…

…if it is done through minority influence.

- *E* – History challenges the claim that minority influence, such as the suffragettes, brings about social change quickly.

 Minority groups are considered deviant…

…which limits their influence.

- *E* – The influence of minorities is often decreased by the majority believing them to be deviant.

 Social change does not always happen…

…after social norms interventions.

- *E* – Research has shown that when people were given normative information correcting their misperception of drinking norms, there was no positive change in behaviour.

SHOULD know ...

The suffragette movement is an excellent example of how a minority can bring about social change.

The suffragettes used educational, political and military tactics to **draw attention** to the fact that women could not vote.

They **created a conflict** between the existing status quo (only men being allowed to vote) and their own position.

The suffragettes were **consistent** in their views regardless of other people' attitudes. Protests and political lobbying continued for years.

Because the suffragettes were willing to risk imprisonment or even death, their influence was **augmented** and became more powerful.

Several years after the suffragettes' actions, women were finally permitted to vote. At this point, the idea had finally spread to the majority, and the **snowball effect** occurred.

- *E* – People have a strong tendency to conform to the majority and maintain the status quo, so groups are less likely to engage in social change.
- *L* – This explains why social change happens so slowly. Some minorities influence the *potential* for social change rather than direct social change.

- *E* – The majority may avoid agreeing with minorities to avoid being seen as deviant themselves.
- *L* – The message of the minority would then have very little impact because the focus of the majority's attention would be the *source* of the message (i.e. the deviant minority) rather than the message itself.

- *E* – DeJong *et al.* (2009) found students did not lower their alcohol consumption or change their perceptions about student drinking levels.
- *L* – This suggests that social norms interventions alone are not sufficient for social change to occur.

A LEVEL ONLY ZONE

 Social change occurs through majority influence…

…as well as minority influence.

- *E* – If people perceive something to be the norm, their behaviour typically changes to fit that norm. Behaviour is based more on what we *think* others do rather than what they *really* do.
- *E* – When a social norms intervention campaign informed people the actual social norm was not drink-driving, such behaviour fell by 13.7%.
- *L* – This finding shows that when peoples' misperceptions about others' behaviour is corrected, positive changes in behaviour can occur.

 The opposite effect to that intended can sometimes occur…

…after social norms interventions.

- *E* – People already behaving constructively may begin behaving destructively.
- *E* – Schultz *et al.* (2007) found that a campaign was effective in lowering heavy electricity users' consumption, but increased consumption in those originally using less.
- *L* – Therefore, social norms interventions can produce a 'boomerang effect', increasing undesirable behaviour in people previously behaving desirably.

CHOOSE THE RIGHT ANSWER

Which **two** of the following are involved when social change occurs through minority influence? Tick **two** boxes only.

A Cognitive interview ☐

B The boomerang effect ☐

C The augmentation principle ☐

D Cognitive conflict ☐

E Consistency conflict ☐

Answers on page 271

DRAWING CONCLUSIONS

The table below is a summary of the percentage of violent and non-violent minorities that were successful in overthrowing regimes and bringing about social change between 1940 and 2006.

Years	1940-1949	1950-1959	1960-1969	1970-1979	1980-1989	1990-1999	2000-2006
Violent minorities	41	35	20	39	38	25	11
Non-violent minorities	39	31	40	56	51	50	67

State **two** findings and for each one draw a conclusion (state what the finding shows). *(4 marks)*

Finding 1:

Conclusion 1: This shows that ...

Finding 2:

Conclusion 2: This shows that ...

Answers on page 271

MATCH THEM UP

Match the different aspects of minority influence with examples of suffragette actions.

1	Drawing attention to an issue	**A**	Continued to protest and lobby politicians for many years until social change was achieved.
2	Creating a conflict	**B**	After several years the acceptance of women being able to vote had spread to the majority of people.
3	Consistency with each other and over time	**C**	Used educational, political and moral tactics, such as chaining themselves to railings.
4	The augmentation principle	**D**	Made members of the majority re-examine what they had previously held to be true after learning about the views of the minority.
5	The snowball effect	**E**	Showed willingness to risk imprisonment or even death to express their views.

Answers on page 271

APPLYING YOUR KNOWLEDGE

Using your knowledge of social influence processes in social change, answer the following.

At the end of every football match, Mike the steward had to pick up litter the supporters had thrown away. It was a job he hated. Mike knew that most of the supporters put their litter in bins, but when he asked some supporters why they didn't put *their* litter in bins, they said: 'Nobody else does, so why should we?'

(a) Identify an approach Mike could use to try to change their behaviour. What would you advise Mike to do to change the behaviour of those supporters who don't put their litter in bins? *(4 marks)*

Mike told Paul about the advice you gave him. Paul said: "It might work, but you need to beware of the boomerang effect." Mike said: "That won't be a problem, boomerangs are banned at football grounds."

(b) Explain what Paul meant by 'the boomerang effect'. What would you tell Mike might happen if Paul was correct about the boomerang effect? *(4 marks)*

Answers on page 271

Agentic shift	People may move from being in a state where they take personal responsibility for their actions (an autonomous state) to a state where they believe they are acting on behalf of an authority figure (an agentic state).
Agentic state	A state where people believe they are acting on behalf of an authority figure.
Augmentation principle	If a minority appears willing to suffer for their views, they are seen as more committed and taken more seriously by others.
Authoritarian aggression	Aggressive feelings toward people who violate conventional norms.
Authoritarian personality	A personality type characterised by strict adherence to conventional values and a belief in absolute obedience or submission to authority.
Authoritarian submission	An uncritical submission to legitimate authorities.
Autonomous state	A state where people take responsibility for their actions.
Boomerang effect	An unintended consequence of social norms interventions where people adopt the opposing position to that intended.
Commitment	The degree to which members of a minority are dedicated to a particular cause or activity. The greater the perceived commitment, the greater the influence.
Compliance	Going along with others to gain their approval or avoid their disapproval. There is no change in the person's underlying attitude, only their public behaviour.
Confederate	An individual in a study who is not a real participant and has been instructed how to behave by the investigator.
Conformity	A form of social influence that results from exposure to the majority position and leads to compliance with that position. It is the tendency for people to adopt the behaviour, attitudes and values of other members of the group.
Consistency	Minority influence is effective provided there is consistency in the expressed position over time and agreement among different members of the minority.
Conventionalism	An adherence to conventional norms and values.
Deception	This occurs when a participant is not told the true aims of a study (e.g. what participation will involve). Thus, the participants cannot give truly informed consent.
Demand characteristics	Cues that makes participants aware of what the researcher expects to find or how participants are expected to behave.
Dispositional explanation	An explanation of behaviour that emphasises the individual's own personal characteristics rather than situational influences within the environment.
Dissent	Holding an opposing view to that of the majority.
Dogmatic	Refusing to consider that other opinions might also be justified.
Ecological validity	A form of external validity. The ability to generalise a research effect beyond the particular setting in which it is demonstrated to other settings.
Externality	Individuals who tend to believe that their behaviour and experience is caused by events outside their control.
F Scale	Also known as the 'California F scale' or the 'Fascism scale', the F scale was developed in California in 1947 as a measure of authoritarian traits or tendencies.
Flexibility	A willingness to compromise when expressing a position.
Historical validity	The extent to which a research finding can be generalised over time.
Identification	A form of influence where an individual adopts an attitude or behaviour because they want to be associated with a particular person or group.
Informational social influence	The result of wanting to be right, i.e. looking to others for the right answer, and conforming to their opinion.
Informed consent	In terms of ethics, participants must be given comprehensive information concerning the nature and purpose of a study and their role in it. This is necessary in order that they can make an informed decision about whether to participate.
Internalisation	Going along with others because we accept their point of view. This is a result of examining the group's position, which may lead to *validation* of our own views, or acceptance of the group's view, both in public and in private.
Internality	Individuals who tend to believe that they are responsible for their behaviour and experience rather than external forces.
Legitimate authority	A person or organisation who has been given command through legislation or general agreement.
Locus of control	An aspect of our personality. People differ in their beliefs about whether the outcomes of their actions are dependent on what they do (internality) or events outside their personal control (externality).

McCarthyism	The practice of making accusations of disobedience and treason without proper regard for evidence, based on the activities of American Senator McCarthy in the 1950s.
Meta-analysis	A researcher looks at the findings from a number of different studies in order to reach a general conclusion about a particular hypothesis.
Minority influence	A form of social influence where members of the majority group change their beliefs or behaviour due to the actions of one or a few people (a minority group).
Normative social influence	The result of wanting to be liked and be accepted as part of a group by following its norms.
Obedience to authority	A type of social influence whereby somebody acts in response to a direct order. There is also the implication that the person receiving the order is made to respond in a way they would not have done without the order.
Protection from harm	During a research study, participants should not experience negative physical effects, such as physical injury, nor psychological effects, such as lowered self-esteem or embarrassment.
Right-wing authoritarianism	A cluster of personality variables (conventionalism, authoritarian submission and authoritarian aggression) that are associated with a 'right-wing' attitude to life.
Self-efficacy	A person's belief that they can perform competently in a given situation.
Snowball effect	Minority influence initially has a relatively small effect but this then spreads more widely as more and more people consider the issues being promoted.
Social change	Occurs when a society as a whole adopts a new belief or behaviour, which then becomes accepted as the norm.
Social norms interventions	An attempt to correct misperceptions of the normative behaviour of peers in an attempt to change the undesirable behaviour of a target population.
Social roles	The behaviours expected of an individual who occupies a given social position or status.
Social support	Care and assistance from other people.

Topic 1 Types of conformity and explanations for conformity

Discuss normative social influence and informational social influence as explanations for conformity. *(12 marks AS)*

Normative social influence is where you go along with the majority, even though you don't really accept their point of view. For example, we may laugh at a joke someone tells, even though we do not find it funny. This is likely to be because we want to be accepted by the group and not feel rejected by them. For normative social influence to happen, we have to believe that the group is watching us to see if we conform or not.

Informational social influence is where you go along with the majority because you think they have more information about a situation than you do. We want to feel confident that our perceptions and beliefs are correct, so we use the majority's opinion to check. This is more likely to happen if the situation is ambiguous or if others are experts. For example, if we are unsure about which piece of cutlery to use at a formal dinner, we might look to others for advice on which fork to use for each course.

There is a lot of research support for normative social influence. For example, Schultz *et al.* found that we can use normative social influence to make people behave more responsibly, as with energy conservation. They found that hotel guests who were exposed to a message about how 75% of guests reused their towels reduced towel use by 25%. These findings support the idea that people go along with the majority because they want to fit in.

Some studies have shown how exposure to the beliefs of others can affect our judgement. Fein *et al.* found that knowledge of other people's reactions can influence how people judge candidate performance in US election debates. When participants saw what they thought was the reaction of their fellow participants on a screen, there were large shifts in participants' judgements of the candidate's performance. This shows that people are affected by informational social influence.

The power of normative social influence can be seen in research on adolescent smoking. This research, done by Linkenbach and Perkins, found a relationship between the likelihood of people starting smoking and people's normative beliefs. When teenagers were told most of their peers didn't smoke, they were less likely to start smoking themselves. This shows that people do shape their behaviour to fit in.

Examiner's comments

Always a good idea, as here, to get straight into answering the question rather than long rambling introductions that don't really contribute much. A good start.

This is another accurate and detailed description, this time of informational social influence. An appropriate example adds the right sort of detail.

The careful construction of this answer is obvious. Clearly dividing your answer into descriptive and evaluative paragraphs is an effective way of controlling what you write. This is a good example of the PEEL technique that we advocate throughout this book.

Another clear and effective paragraph, this time dealing with informational social influence. It states the point, provides evidence *and* elaboration then links back to the material being evaluated.

This answer keeps the effective development of AO3 points going right through to the end.

Level 4 answer (10–12 marks)

Examiner's comments: There is no wasted content in this essay; everything is accurate and detailed, and above all, highly organised. There are two AO1 paragraphs and three AO3 paragraphs, which seems about right for an AS essay.

AO1 description of the two explanations of conformity is accurate and detailed with effective use of specialist terminology.

AO3 evaluation was well balanced across the two explanations, clearly organised and effective.

Topic 2 Variables affecting conformity

Outline and evaluate research into group size, unanimity, and task difficulty as variables affecting conformity. *(16 marks A level)*

Examiner's comments

Asch's research shows that there are many variables that affect conformity, including group size, unanimity and the difficulty of the task. He conducted several different experiments to see which variables had the most significant effects on conformity.

In questions such as this, it is better to stick to *findings* of research, but this context setting paragraph is appropriately brief.

Examiner's comments

Asch found that there was very little conformity when the majority consisted of one or two confederates, but when there were three confederates, the conforming responses rose to 30%. Having more than four confederates didn't change the conformity rate any more, showing that the size of the majority is important, but only up to a point. He also found that when he made the tasks more difficult, the conformity level increased. Lucas *et al.* found that the influence of task difficulty depends on the self-efficacy of the individual and that those who have higher levels of self-efficacy are less likely to conform than those who have lower levels of self-efficacy. This shows that both the situation and the individual participants themselves are important in conformity behaviour.

> This second paragraph contains a mix of AO1 description on group size and task difficulty, although the Lucas *et al.* study could count as AO3 evaluation.

When the majority are unanimous in their wrong decision, conformity was the highest. But when the real participant was given support from someone else, the level of conformity dropped from 33% to 6%. This shows that breaking the unanimity of the group's position was a major factor in reducing conformity.

> Although this paragraph contains appropriate and accurate content on the importance of unanimity, it lacks detail.

One of the major criticisms of Asch's research is that it may be a 'child of its time'. The research took place when America was highly conformist. People were scared to go against the majority and so were more likely to conform. When Perrin and Spencer repeated this research in 1980, they did not see as much conformity as the original studies, suggesting that we have become less conformist over time. This may be because the perceived costs of not conforming were higher in the 1950s than they are today.

> This AO3 evaluation is mostly effective, but it could be more effective if it had justified why the costs of not conforming were higher in the 1950s, and how Perrin and Spencer justified this claim.

Another limitation of conformity research is that it only looks at conformity behaviour when there are a limited number of confederates. No studies, other than Asch's, have used a majority of more than nine and most have typically only used between two and four confederates. According to Bond, this suggests that we do not know very much about the effect of larger majority sizes on conformity levels.

> This is an effective AO3 paragraph that follows the PEEL route and so makes the most of the point.

Not all participants in Asch's experiments conformed when the majority unanimously gave wrong answers. In two thirds of trials, participants kept their original answer, despite majority influence. Asch argued this showed a tendency for participants to show independent behaviour. This suggests that majority influence is weaker than it might seem.

> There is a little confusion over whether it was a low number of *people* or a low number of *trials* that led to this conclusion.

Asch's research took place in America, so it might be that there are cultural variations in conformity rates. This means that we should expect different results if we were to do this research in different cultures. Smith *et al.* did a meta-analysis and found that there was a difference between individualistic cultures and collectivist cultures, with the individualistic cultures having an average conformity rate of 25% and the collectivist cultures having an average conformity rate of 37%. This shows that collectivist cultures are more conformist, suggesting that culture does have an impact on conformity rates.

> Both of these final two paragraphs are well developed and used effectively.

It is possible that participants may not have believed the confederates' incorrect answers because the confederates themselves were unconvincing. If this is true, then the study would have low validity. Mori and Arai modified Asch's study and gave each participant a pair of glasses with different filters in them, altering what they saw. This meant that confederates were not needed. They found that conformity rates were similar to what Asch found, which suggests that the confederates were acting convincingly and the original findings are valid.

Level 3 answer (10–12)

Examiner's comments: AO1 Description is mostly accurate although it could have been more detailed in places.

AO3 Lots of points made. These were mostly effective, although some of the points could have been clearer. Effective use of specialist terminology. Evaluation was well balanced across the two explanations, clearly organised and effective.

Topic 3 Conformity to social roles

Discuss conformity to social roles as investigated by Zimbardo. *(12 marks AS)*

Zimbardo *et al.*'s prison simulation study investigated conformity to social roles, with participants being randomly assigned the role of a guard or a prisoner. They wanted to see how both groups would behave in their role when there was no authority figure telling them what to do.

The guards wore reflective sunglasses, which stopped the prisoners being able to see their eyes and prisoners wore a smock with an ID number on it. The prisoners were referred to by their ID number, not their name, and only allowed certain rights, such as toilet breaks and two visits per week. The guards quickly conformed to their role, becoming tyrannical and abusive, while the prisoners became passive and accepted their more lowly position. This showed that both groups conformed to their social role. Even though it was due to last for two weeks, Zimbardo was forced to stop the experiment after six days as it had become too abusive to allow it to continue.

Zimbardo believed that the guards' change in behaviour was an automatic result of them conforming to their social role. However, not all of the guards behaved in this way. Some of the guards did not degrade or abuse the prisoners, showing that the guards chose their behaviour and so conforming to social roles is not as automatic as Zimbardo claimed it is.

Zimbardo's experiment was conducted ethically, as participants were given fully informed consent, and it was approved by an ethics committee. But it is still controversial because of the extreme distress the participants experienced. Zimbardo did stop the study early, but he could have stopped it even earlier. Afterwartds, he debriefed his participants time and found no long lasting effects of the study. This shows the importance of ethics in research.

It has been argued that demand characteristics may have affected the Stanford Prison Experiment, weakening its internal validity. This means that the behaviour of the participants was not due to the prison environment, but instead it was a response to powerful demand characteristics from the experiment itself. Banuazizi and Movahedi found that students unfamiliar with the experiment could accurately predict the behaviour of the prisoner and guards. This suggests that demand characteristics affected the study's internal validity.

Examiner's comments

This is sufficient contextual information to explain what the study was attempting to do.

As a general rule, 'findings' work better in response to questions such as this rather than procedural details.

This is an effective point of evaluation, of an appropriate length and linking the critical point back to Zimbardo's claim.

Another clear AO3 point, well developed and used effectively. The conclusion was a little vague, but the point would still work if this sentence was ignored.

A little repetition between the opening identification of the critical point and the conclusion drawn. The latter might have been a bit more insightful, perhaps suggesting why this is such a problem for our interpretation of the findings.

Level 4 answer (10–12 marks)

Examiner's comments: AO1 Description is accurate, well-detailed and concentrating (mostly) on the findings from Zimbardo's research.

AO3 Three relevant critical points, each is elaborated appropriately although at times the conclusions drawn do not add that much to the critical nature of the point. The answer would just about make it to Level 4 of the mark scheme.

Topic 4 Situational variables affecting obedience

Discuss **two or more** situational variables that affect obedience (e.g. proximity, location, uniform). *(12 marks AS)*

Examiner's comments

Milgram's research required people to give electric shocks to another person. He told his participants that this was a test of learning on memory and that they were the 'teacher' and the other person was a learner, although he was actually a confederate of Milgram's. Every time the learner got a question wrong, they were told to give him an electric shock by the experimenter. These shocks increased by 15V each time, going up to 450V. This research found that 65% of the participants went to 450V and all went to at least 300V.

This opening paragraph is too general. It doesn't really identify which of the situational variables is being discussed. Many students would make the same mistake, i.e. launching into their standard 'Milgram answer' without looking at the specific demands of the question.

Milgram believed that it was the situation that people find themselves in which determines if they obey or not. When Milgram moved his experiment from Yale University to a run-down office block, the obedience rate dropped from 65% to 48%.

Whether the experimenter wore a uniform had a much larger impact on the level of obedience shown. Bushman's research had a female researcher dressed either as a beggar, a business executive or in a police-style uniform asking people to give a confederate some money for a parking meter. When she was in uniform, 72% of people obeyed, compared to 48% when she was dressed as a business executive.

The main criticism of Milgram's research is it has many ethical issues, including deception and no real right to withdraw. Participants were deceived about the true nature of the study, believing it to be an experiment about learning. Also, while the participants were given the right to withdraw, the prods from the experimenter, telling them to continue, made it much more difficult for them to exercise this right.

Level 2 answer (5–8) marks

AO1 Description is a bit too general at times. Although two appropriate situational variables are covered, too much time has been wasted simply giving an overview of Milgram's findings.

AO3 Again, not really focused on the explicit requirements of the question, which detracts from the overall effectiveness of the evaluation.

Topic 5 Agentic state and legitimacy of authority

Discuss how the agentic state and the legitimacy of authority can explain why people behave obediently. *(12 marks AS)*

The agentic state is defined as being when we see ourselves as an agent for carrying out another person's wishes. When we see ourselves as being in control of our actions, we are considered to be in an autonomous state, but when we see others as being responsible for our actions, we are in an agentic state. When we stop seeing ourselves as being responsible for our own actions and move to seeing someone else as being responsible for them, an agentic shift has occurred. This can be seen when people say that they were 'just following orders' after an atrocity, such as the one at My Lai during the Vietnam War.

A legitimate authority figure is someone who is considered to be in a position of social control in a given situation. It is this power, not any personal characteristics they have, which gives them the legitimate authority. For an authority to be perceived as legitimate, it must occur within some sort of institutional structure, such as a university or the military. This is especially true if an authority figure's commands are potentially harmful or destructive.

It has been suggested that 'plain cruelty' might explain obedience better than agentic shift can. Milgram might have detected signs of cruelty in his participants, who may have used the situation to express their sadistic tendencies. This suggestion was supported by Zimbardo's Stanford Prison Experiment. Guards inflicted rapidly escalating cruelty to prisoners, even though there was no authority figure. This shows it may not be agentic control which causes obedience. Instead it may be certain aspects of human nature.

The process of agentic shift is not confined to obedience but can also explain other forms of social influence. The reason for agentic shift is a reduction in someone's experience of personal control. We accept more external sources of control when we feel less in control. Fennis and Aarts showed that reducing personal control resulted in bystander apathy as well as a greater obedience to authority. This suggests agentic shift is caused by a reduction in our feelings of personal control.

Legitimate authority can be used to justify harming others. In the military, obedience to legitimate authority is vital and this extreme obedience occurs no matter how destructive the instructions are. This implies that when people allow others to make moral decisions for them, they no longer feel personally morally responsible.

Examiner's comments

"Location' is identified as a situational variable, and an appropriate finding used to illustrate how obedience rates change. Why and how this changes could have been made clearer.

The same treatment is given to a second situational variable - uniform. This time it is a little more detailed, and so is more effective.

This first AO3 paragraph makes a general critical point about Milgram's research. It might have pointed out, for example, that our understanding of situational influences on obedience has been acquired at the expense of the abuse of participants.

Examiner's comments

A good clear, accurate and well-developed descriptive paragraph. The use of an example (My Lai) adds important detail to the answer.

Another impressive AO1 paragraph, showing good understanding of the material and offering appropriate detail and development.

Nicely developed AO3 paragraph. Good identification of the critical point with appropriate and clear elaboration followed by a good link back to show why this is an important point that limits the 'agentic state' argument.

Another well-developed AO3 point, supported by research evidence and used effectively as evaluation of the agentic state explanation.

Not quite of the same high standard as the previous two paragraphs, this one tails away a little at the end. However, it makes an appropriate critical point, i.e. that there are moral consequences of obeying a legitimate authority, but this could have been better developed.

the instructions are. This implies that when people allow others to make moral decisions for them, they no longer feel personally morally responsible.

Level 4 answer (10–12 marks)

AO1 Description is clear, accurate and well-detailed and clearly located in the top level criteria within the mark scheme.

AO3 Again, the three AO3 paragraphs approach works well. It is worth remembering that had this been a 16 mark A level question then two more AO3 paragraphs would have been in order.

Topic 6 The authoritarian personality

Outline and evaluate the authoritarian personality as a dispositional explanation for obedience. *(16 marks A)*

Examiner's comments

The authoritarian personality is a dispositional explanation of obedience, which says it is an individual's personal characteristics that make them obedient, not the situation they are in. Adorno used the F Scale to measure the different personality traits which make up the authoritarian personality. Agreeing with statements such as 'rules are there for people to follow and not change' indicates an authoritarian personality. People with an authoritarian personality have rigid thinking patterns and see things in black and white. They also think that social rules should be followed at all times. Adorno thought that people had learned these attitudes from their authoritarian parents, who placed a lot of importance on obedience.

> Good opening paragraph explains the relationship between early upbringing, the development of an authoritarian personality and obedience.

Robert Altemeyer developed the idea of the authoritarian personality and identified three of the personality traits which would lead to right-wing authoritarianism. The first was conventionalism where someone feels it is vital to follow conventional norms and values. The second was authoritarian aggression, where someone has aggressive feelings towards people who do not follow these norms. The third was a blind submission to legitimate authorities, which Altemeyer called authoritarian submission. These characteristics predispose someone to obedience.

> Accurate description of Altemeyer's development of right-wing authoritarianism which explains how this predisposes someone to obedience. Good use of specialist terminology.

This dispositional explanation for obedience is supported by several studies, including one by Elms and Milgram, who selected 20 obedient and 20 dissenting participants from Milgram's original experiment. They were asked to complete a personality questionnaire and the F Scale questionnaire to measure their level of authoritarianism. The obedient participants were found to have higher levels of authoritarianism, suggesting that having an authoritarian personality does predispose you to obedience.

> Good 'PEEL' paragraph identifies, provides evidence and elaboration and draws an appropriate conclusion.

Elms and Milgram's research did, however, show that many of the fully obedient participants reported a happy childhood and not a strict one. It is also unlikely that the vast number of people who were obedient in Milgram's original obedience study all came from strict family upbringings with an authoritarian parenting style, suggesting that obedience may be caused by something other than a strict upbringing.

> Another good critical paragraph that follows the same effective format as the previous paragraph. Although it is not necessary to use these distinct AO3 paragraphs, it is an effective way of planning an answer.

The authoritarian explanation is dispositional and so it ignores situational factors. Milgram's study showed that the social context is more important than someone's personality as the obedience level changed depending on the location or the presence of other dissenting peers. Explaining obedience though authoritarianism cannot account for these variations in obedience levels as they have nothing to do with the participants' personality.

> Nice closing sentence in this paragraph that explains why situational variations in obedience pose a problem for the authoritarian personality explanation.

Education level may determine obedience and authoritarianism. Middleton and Meloen found that less-educated people are consistently more authoritarian than well-educated people. This suggests that it is a lack of education which is responsible for both authoritarian and obedience. However, when Elms and Milgram controlled for education, the more obedient participants still showed higher levels of authoritarianism. This shows that education level may have some influence, but authoritarianism is a better explanation for obedience.

People with right wing views are more likely to obey according to Altemeyer. Therefore, it seems sensible to expect that people who define themselves as left-wing may be less obedient. Bègue et al. found that when participants were asked to give electric shocks to another participant as part of a game show, the participants who defined themselves as being left-wing gave lower intensity shocks. This suggests that the situational context does include individual differences as a determining influence on obedience.

> These final two paragraphs offer the extra evaluation that is necessary for a 16 mark A level answer. Both these paragraphs have the necessary elaboration to make them effective AO3 and guarantee very high marks.

Level 4 answer (13–16 marks)

AO1 Well-detailed and accurate with good use of specialist terminology.

AO3 Five very effective AO3 paragraphs make up an excellent answer to the question.

Topic 7 Resistance to social influence

Discuss how social support and locus of control can explain resistance to social influence. *(12 marks AS)*

Examiner's comments

A lot of research has found that people conform to the majority, but not everyone does. This may be because they have support from other people. This means that if another person also resists the majority, we find it easier to do the same. Asch found that when one confederate gave the right answer, the participant was more likely to do the same, with conformity dropping from 33% to 6%. The main reason for this is that it breaks the unanimity of the majority and so they show that there are other legitimate ways to respond.

> Good opening paragraph that explains how and why social support helps people to resist conformity. Effective use of research findings to add detail.

Locus of control is another explanation for resistance to social influence. This is a person's perception of personal control over their own behaviour. If someone has an internal locus of control then they believe that they are in control of their own actions, while someone with an external locus of control believes that what happens to them is controlled by an external factor, such as luck or the actions of others. People with an internal locus of control are better at resisting social influence.

> Although accurate and appropriate, this material might have been more explicitly linked to *resistance* to social influence.

Social support does not have to be valid to be effective. Even if our social support isn't valid, we can still resist pressure to conform. In Allen and Levine's study, a dissenting confederate wore glasses with thick lenses during a visual task. Although this support was not valid, given the nature of the task, conformity was reduced. This suggests any form of social support is effective, so long as it is perceived to be effective

> Appropriate as AO3, although the conclusion could have been clearer as it isn't clear that the social support referred to here *was* perceived as being effective.

One problem with explaining resistance to social influence using locus of control is that characteristics other than locus of control also help when resisting obedience. Those with an internal locus of control are more achievement orientated and actively seek out information, compared to those with an external locus of control. Hutchins and Estey found that people with an internal locus of control resisted an interrogator better than those with an external locus of control. This suggests that while locus of control is an important factor in resisting social influence, it is not the only one.

> Another paragraph that isn't quite as clear as it might be. The link between the different aspects of this point need to be made more explicit.

Locus of control does not always help us resist pressure to conform. Spector found a significant correlation between locus of control and a hpredisposition to normative social influence, where people with an external locus of control were more likely to conform than those with an internal locus of control. However, there was no relationship between locus of control and a predisposition to informational social influence. This shows that an internal locus of control is only helpful when conformity occurs to gain approval.

> This is a much clearer and more effective AO3 paragraph where everything is tied together for maximum effect.

Level 3 answer (7–9 marks)

AO1 Mixed. Very good first paragraph, accurate and detailed. Second paragraph could have been more explicitly related to *resistance*.

AO3 Not always effective although appropriate material with some elaboration. Reasonably effective first two points and very effective final point.

Topic 8 Minority influence

Outline and evaluate the role played by consistency, commitment, and flexibility in minority influence. *(16 marks A)*

Examiner's comments

Minority influence is where members of the majority group change their beliefs and behaviours as a result of their exposure to a persuasive minority. In order for this to be effective, the minority needs to be committed to their message and consistent in their approach. At first, the majority often assume the minority is wrong, but if they are consistent, then others will reassess their point of view and consider the issue more carefully. If the minority stays consistent, then there must be a reason for it.

If the minority are committed to their message, then it is more likely to be listened to because it is difficult to ignore a group of people who are committed to their position. It suggests that they are confident in their belief and the minority demonstrate courage as they go against the norm, sometimes encountering hostility from the majority. The degree of commitment shown by minority group members is greater because of the cost involved in being in the minority and this commitment may persuade majority group members to change their position to that of the minority.

> Three very effective AO1 paragraphs that cycle through the required topics of consistency, commitment and flexibility. Each is covered in appropriate (and accurate) detail and having three distinct paragraphs makes it easy (for the examiner and the student) to check that the different requirements of the question are being met.

Minorities are relatively powerless so they need to be flexible in their approach, too. They need to negotiate their position with the majority, rather than try to enforce it. A rigid minority who doesn't compromise may be seen as narrow minded and unwilling to consider alternative points of view, which will not help them to change the opinions of the majority.

Minority influence is not always effective because we tend to believe we share majority beliefs. If the majority express a different view to ours, we might consider their view carefully to understand why they think what they do. However, we do not process a minority's message in the same detail as we may consider it a waste of time. Therefore, the minority's message tends to be less, rather than more, influential.

> Good AO3 paragraph, following the PEEL route. Whilst this is not the only way to elaborate evaluative material, it does work well here.

However, better quality decisions can be made by numerical minorities, for example in groups at work. Van Dyne and Saavedra found that better decisions were made when a dissenting minority was present. Nemeth argues that exposure to dissenting opinions makes us search for more information and think about more options. This shows that, even if dissenters are wrong, they liberate people to think more about an issue.

> Both these AO3 paragraphs begin by identifying the critical point, showing evidence to support it and then offer further elaboration to make the point effective. It is not required to draw a conclusion (as in the first of these two paragraphs) but if it says something new (as here), then it is an excellent way of rounding off a critical point.

Flexibility is important in minority influence. This is supported by Nemeth and Brilmayer who found that confederates holding a minority view who compromised were more influential. However, they also found that being too flexible too early on weakens the minority's position because it looks like they have simply conformed to the majority view, rather than being seen as being flexible.

One problem with minority influence is that convincing people dissenting minorities are valuable remains difficult. We may superficially accept dissent to appear tolerant. However, persistent dissent is seen as disrupting group harmony. Nemeth argues majority viewpoints persist because a minority viewpoint is often belittled, and dissenters are marginalised. This means opportunities for innovative thinking, which minority influence brings, is often lost.

There is a tipping point for commitment where the number of people holding a minority position is sufficient to change majority opinion. Xie et al. found 10% of committed opinion holders was necessary to 'tip' a majority into accepting the minority position. The minority were only successful if they were also consistent in their viewpoint, showing that commitment and consistency are both needed if minority influence is to be effective.

> These last two paragraphs extend the overall quantity of AO3 evaluation to justify the 10 marks nominally assigned to AO3 in this question. In an A level extended writing question worth 16 marks, there should be proportionately more AO3 than AO1, which is what has happened here.

Level 4 answer (13–16 marks)

AO1 Lots of detail, accurate and well-organised places this clearly in the top level of the mark scheme.

AO3 Appropriate proportion of AO3 to AO1. Each of the five paragraphs is clear and effective and, like the AO1, puts it well into the top level of the mark scheme.

Topic 9 Social influence processes in social change

Discuss the role of social influence processes in social change. *(12 marks AS)*

Examiner's comments

If an individual is exposed to a persuasive argument, they may change their position to match that of the minority. If the minority draws attention to the issue, and the majority holds a different view, then there is a conflict, which the majority are motivated to reduce. This cognitive conflict doesn't always result in the majority changing their position, but it does mean that they think more deeply about an issue. It's been found that if the minority is consistent in their message, then they are more influential and so it is important for the message to be consistent over time. Initially, the minority's influence has a relatively small effect, but over time, it spreads more widely as more people consider the issues being considered. When it reaches a tipping point, there is a wide-scale social change, such as the vote being given to all adults in the UK due to the minority influence of the Suffragettes.

> Good clear description of of how minority influence works, but apart from a brief mention of the Suffragettes, this isn't explicitly linked to social change. It would have been more effective to choose a couple of aspects (e.g. cognitive conflict and consistency) and show how these related to the actions of the Suffragettes and the ensuing social change).

However, the majority can affect social change, too. Behavioural choices are often related to group norms and so if people believe something to be the norm, then they are more likely to alter their behaviour to fit that norm. Behaviour is, therefore, based more on what people think others believe or do, rather than what they actually believe or do. Social norms interventions typically start by identifying a risky behaviour in a target population. Perception correction strategies can then be used to help change people's behaviour. The aim of these strategies is to tell the target population the actual norms, rather than the perceived ones.

> This is marginally better as the link to social change (through social norms interventions) is made more explicit.

History has shown us that social change happens gradually if it is done through minority influence. People have a strong tendency to conform to the majority, so groups are less likely to engage in social change. The influence of the minority is frequently more latent than direct, so minorities influence the *potential* for social change rather than direct social change.

> Good clear AO3 point, that highlights that minority influence may only have the *potential* for social change.

Another problem with minority groups influencing social change is that minority groups are often considered deviant by the majority, which limits their influence. The majority may avoid agreeing with minorities to avoid being seen as deviant themselves. The message of the minority might, therefore, be less influential because the majority are focusing on the source of the message rather than the message itself.

> Another limitation of minority influence is the problem of deviance. This is explained well and appropriate argument used to support the claim being made.

Social change does not always happen after social norms interventions. For example, some students were given normative information that corrected their misperception of how much students drink. DeJong et al. found that students' perceptions didn't change and they did not change their drinking habits. This suggests that social norms interventions alone are not sufficient for social change to occur.

> A final limitation is identified (social norms interventions don't always work) with evidence to support it and an appropriate conclusion drawn at the end.

Level 4 answer (10–12 marks)

AO1 First paragraph could have been more explicitly linked to social change but rest of the material was clear and well-detailed.

AO3 Three very good AO3 paragraphs, well developed and clearly effective.

KEY TERMS

- Capacity
- Coding
- Duration
- Long-term memory (LTM)
- Short-term memory (STM)

Possible essay questions …

Describe and evaluate research that has investigated capacity in STM. *(10 marks)*

Describe and evaluate research that has investigated duration in STM and/or LTM. *(10 marks)*

Describe and evaluate research that has investigated coding in memory. *(10 marks)*

Other possible exam questions …

+ Explain what is meant by the terms duration, capacity and coding in relation to memory. *(2 marks + 2 marks + 2 marks)*

+ Explain how the findings of one or more studies demonstrate that STM and LTM are different. *(4 marks)*

+ Outline **one** difference between the capacity in STM and LTM. *(2 marks)*

MUST know …

Short- and long-term memory. Capacity, duration and coding (part 1)

Your memory for events in the present or immediate past is referred to as short-term memory (STM). Your memory for events that happened in the more distant past is referred to as long-term memory (LTM). STM and LTM have their own capacity, duration and coding.

- **Capacity** is the measure of how much can be held in memory.
- **Duration** is the measure of how long a memory lasts before it is no longer available.
- **Coding** is the way in which information is changed so that it can be stored in memory.

 One criticism of the research investigating STM is that…

…the capacity may be even more limited than 7+/-2.

- **E** – Cowan (2001) reviewed a variety of studies on the capacity of STM and found that the STM is likely to be limited to about four chunks of information, rather than 7+/-2.

 Another criticism of research investigating STM is that…

…the testing methods are artificial.

- **E** – Trying to memorise strings of digits or consonant syllables does not reflect memory in everyday life.

 A final criticism of research investigating STM is that…

…memory improves with age.

- **E** – Jacobs (1887) found that recall (digit span) increased steadily with age; eight-year-olds could remember an average of 6.6 digits, whereas 19-year-olds could remember an average of 8.6 digits.

SHOULD know …

Short- and long-term memory. Capacity, duration and coding (part 2)

The capacity of STM can be assessed using a digit span test and is said to be 7+/-2 'chunks' of information (Miller, 1956). The duration of STM is less than 18 seconds (Peterson and Peterson, 1959) and information is coded in an acoustic format (Baddeley, 1966a and 1966b).

The capacity of LTM is supposedly unlimited and the duration is up to a lifetime. Bahrick *et al.* (1975) found that participants could remember the names of former classmates with 90% accuracy within 15 years of graduation, but this figure declined to 70% after 48 years. Finally, information in LTM is coded semantically (Baddeley, 1966a and 1966b).

- **E** – These results contradict the original findings of Miller (1956) who suggested that humans can hold 7+/-2 'chunks' of information.
- **L** – This matters because the original findings have not been replicated by subsequent studies and suggest that STM is more limited than originally thought.

- **E** – Although it must be noted that we do occasionally try to remember fairly meaningless things, such as phone numbers or postcodes.
- **L** – This matters because the studies may lack ecological validity, although the research may be useful for understanding memory for certain types of information (e.g. phone numbers).

- **E** – This increase with age might be due to a gradual increase in brain capacity or it may be that people develop strategies to improve their memory as they get older.
- **L** – This suggests that the capacity of STM is not fixed at 7+/-2 and that individual differences may play a role in the differences found.

 P – Another criticism of research investigating STM is that…

…STM may not be exclusively acoustic.

- **E** – Brandimote *et al.* (1992) found that participants used visual coding in STM when they were given a visual task (pictures) and prevented from verbally rehearsing.
- **E** – Usually, we 'translate' visual images into verbal codes in STM, but, as these participants were prevented from using verbal rehearsal, participants used visual codes.
- **L** – This suggests that there might be multiple types of coding in STM and that STM is not exclusively acoustic.

 P – A criticism of research investigating LTM is that…

…LTM may not be exclusively semantic.

- **E** – Frost (1972) showed that long-term recall was related to visual as well as semantic categories.
- **E** – Furthermore, Rothbart (1972) found evidence for acoustic coding in LTM.
- **L** – This suggests that LTM might be encoded using acoustic, visual and semantic information, depending on the type of information being remembered.

CHOOSE THE RIGHT ANSWER (1)

The following concepts relate to memory:

A Coding

B Capacity

C Duration

In the table below, write which **one** of the concepts listed above (**A**, **B** or **C**) matches each definition.

Definition	Concept
The length of time a memory lasts before it is no longer available.	
The quantity of information that can be held in memory.	
The way in which information is changed so that it can be stored.	

Answers on page 272

 SPOT THE MISTAKE

Read this student answer to the following exam question:

Explain how the findings of one or more studies demonstrate the STM and LTM are different. *(4 marks)*

There are **three** mistakes – draw a circle around each.

According to Peterson and Peterson (1959) the capacity of short-term memory is approximately 18 seconds, whereas according to Bahrick *et al.* (1975) long-term memory has a 70% accuracy after 34 years. Furthermore, Miller (1956) suggests that the capacity of short-term memory is between 5–9 'chunks' of information, whereas long-term memory is supposedly limited.

Answers on page 272

 CHOOSE THE RIGHT ANSWER (2)

The concepts below relate to short- and long-term memory. Write the appropriate letter in the box below to complete the table.

A Unlimited

B Approximately 18 seconds, according to Peterson and Peterson (1959)

C Semantic

	Short-term memory	Long-term memory
Encoding	Acoustic	
Capacity	7 ± 2	
Duration		Lifetime

Answers on page 272

 APPLYING YOUR KNOWLEDGE

Short-term memory		Long-term memory

Yasmin is 18 years old. She can vividly remember a holiday she took to Disneyland when she was 5 years old, however she can't remember her new mobile phone number which is 11 digits long. Using your knowledge of short- and long-term memory, explain why Yasmin can remember her holiday to Disneyland but not her new mobile number. *(4 marks)*

Answers on page 272

KEY TERMS

- Multi-store model
- Sensory register
- Short-term memory
- Long-term memory
- Attention
- Rehearsal
- Retrieval

Possible essay question ...

Discuss the multi-store model of memory. Refer to research evidence in your answer.
(12 marks AS, 16 marks A)

Other possible exam questions ...

+ Outline the multi-store model of memory. *(6 marks)*
+ Explain one criticism of the multi-store model of memory. *(4 marks)*

MUST know ...

Sensory register, short-term memory and long-term memory

The multi-store model (MSM) (Atkinson and Shiffrin, 1968) consists of three memory stores, the sensory register, short-term memory (STM) and long-term memory (LTM).

The **sensory register** is where information is held at each of the five senses. The capacity of these registers is very large, however, as most of the information is lost as it receives no attention. The duration is very limited (milliseconds).

Information is held in **STM** for immediate tasks. STM has a limited duration, of approximately 18 seconds and a capacity of 7+/-2.

Finally, **LTM** is potentially unlimited in duration and capacity.

 One strength of the multi-store model comes from…

…supporting laboratory evidence.

- *E* – Controlled lab studies on capacity, duration and coding support the existence of separate short- and long-term stores.

 Another strength of the multi-store model comes from…

…supporting case studies.

- *E* – Scoville and Milner (1985) reported the case of patient HM. His brain damage was caused by an operation to remove the hippocampus from both sides of his brain, to reduce his severe epilepsy.

 However, the multi-store model has been criticised for…

…being overly simplistic.

- *E* – The MSM suggests that both STM and LTM are single 'unitary' stores. However, research does not support this idea.

SHOULD know ...

Attention, maintenance rehearsal and retrieval

The three memory stores are linked to each other by different processes that enable the transfer of information from one store to the next.

If a person's **attention** is focused on one of the sensory stores, then the information is transferred to STM.

Rehearsal (repetition) keeps information in STM, but eventually rehearsal will create a LTM. According to Atkinson and Shiffrin, the more information is rehearsed, the better it is remembered.

Finally, information that is stored in LTM can be returned to the STM by the process of **retrieval**.

- *E* – For example, Miller (1956) found that the duration of STM is 7+/-2tt and Bahrick *et al.* (1975) found that the duration of LTM is approximately 48 years.
- *L* – This supports the idea of separate short- and long-term memory stores, which is the basis of the multi-store model.

- *E* – HM's personality and intellect remained intact but he could not form new LTMs, although he could remember things from before the surgery.
- *L* – This provides support for the MSM as HM was unable to transfer information from his STM to LTM, but was able to retrieve information from before his surgery, supporting the different processes involved in the MSM.

- *E* – The working memory model suggests that STM is divided into a number of different stores. Furthermore, research has also found different types of LTM, for example episodic, procedural and semantic memory.
- *L* – This suggests that the MSM provides a simplistic model of memory and does not take into account the different types of STM and LTM.

 P – Another criticism of the multi-store model is that…

…long-term memory involves more than just maintenance rehearsal.

- *E* – Craik and Lockhart (1972) suggest that long-term memories are created by the level of processing and not rehearsal.
- *E* – Information that is processed more deeply is memorable because of the way it is processed. Therefore, doing more complicated things with information will make the memories more enduring.
- *L* – This suggests that the process of rehearsal does not fully explain the process of remembering information in LTM.

 P – A final criticism of the multi-store model is that…

…STM and LTM are not separate stores.

- *E* – Logie (1999) suggested that STM actually relies on LTM and therefore cannot come 'first' as suggested in the MSM.
- *E* – Furthermore, Ruchkin *et al.* (2003) found that when participants process a list of real words, other areas of the brain were activated, in comparison to when participants processed a list of pseudo-words (fake words).
- *L* – This suggests that STM relies on LTM and may just be another part of LTM and not a separate store.

✓ CHOOSE THE RIGHT ANSWER

Tick **two** of the boxes below to indicate which of the following are true in relation to the sensory register.

A The capacity of the sensory register is very large. ☐

B The duration of the sensory register is very limited (milliseconds). ☐

C Attention is required to transfer information from the sensory register to LTM. ☐

D The capacity of the sensory register is limited. ☐

Answers on page 272

✏ COMPLETE THE DIAGRAM

Match the key terms with the diagram by writing the appropriate number from the diagram next to the related key term.

- Sensory register ☐
- Long-term memory ☐
- Maintenance rehearsal ☐
- Transfer ☐
- Retrieval ☐

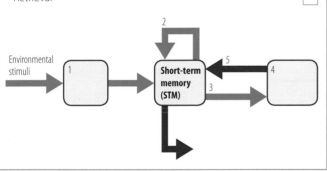

Answers on page 272

✏ FILL IN THE BOXES

In each box below write one sentence describing an aspect of the multi-store model in about 20 words.

In each box below expand the content on the left, writing about another 20 words.

Sensory register is…	Another aspect of sensory register is…
Short-term memory is…	Another aspect of short-term memory is…
Long-term memory is…	Another aspect of long-term memory is…
OPTIONAL: Elaborative rehearsal is…	Another aspect of elaborative rehearsal is…

✓ A MARKING EXERCISE

Read this student answer to the following exam question:
Describe the multistore model of memory. *(6 marks)*

The multistore model consists of three stores which are the sensory memory, the short term memory and the long term memory. First of all information leaves the senses (sight, hearing and so on) and is stored in sensory memory. Then that information is passed to the short-term memory. If any information is not important then it decays or disappears. Once in the short term memory informed can be rehearsed and passed into long term memory. If the information is interrupted during rehearsal it may be forgotten.

Task 1 What mark do you think this would get?

YOUR MARK
AO1

Hint
To help you decide:
How many critical points have been covered?
How much detail is there?
See marking scheme on page 8

Task 2 Write some additional sentences to improve the answer here…

Answers on page 272

51

KEY TERMS

- Central executive
- Episodic buffer
- Phonological loop
- Visuo-spatial sketchpad
- Working memory model

Possible essay question …

Discuss the working memory model. Include strengths and limitations in your answer.
(12 marks AS, 16 marks A)

Other possible exam questions …

+ Outline the working memory model. *(6 marks)*
+ Describe **one** research study that supports the working memory model. *(4 marks)*
+ Explain **one** criticism of the working memory model. *(4 marks)*

MUST know …

The working memory model

Baddeley and Hitch (1974) proposed the working memory model (WMM) because they felt that the STM was not just one store, but multiple stores.

The WMM consists of separate stores for processing acoustic and visual information, which are controlled by a **central executive (CE)**.

The function of the CE is to direct the brain's resources to one of the three slave systems.

The **phonological loop (PL)** deals with auditory information and the order of information. The **visuo-spatial sketchpad (VSS)** is used for the planning of spatial tasks and the temporary storage of visual and/or spatial information.

 ### One strength of the WMM comes from…

…dual task studies.

- **E** – Hitch and Baddeley (1976) found that participants were slower in a dual task study that involved both the central executive and the articulatory loop, in comparison to a task which required just the articulatory loop.

 ### Another strength of the WMM comes from…

…supporting case studies.

- **E** – Shallice and Warrington (1970) studied a man called KF whose short-term forgetting of auditory information was much greater than his forgetting of visual information.

 ### However, one criticism of the WMM is…

…the central executive.

- **E** – Eslinger and Damasio (1985) studied EVR, who had a cerebral tumour removed. Although he performed well on some tests requiring reasoning, he had poor decision-making skills and would spend hours making simple decisions.

SHOULD know …

Episodic buffer

Baddeley (2000) later added the **episodic buffer** as a general store for both visual and acoustic information. The episodic buffer integrates information from the CE, PL and VSS. It also sends information to LTM.

The PL and VSS are also broken into various subcomponents.

The PL contains the phonological store which holds the words you hear and the articulatory process which allows for maintenance rehearsal of acoustic information.

The VSS contains the visual cache which stores information about visual items and the inner scribe which deals with spatial relationships whilst storing the arrangements of objects in the visual field.

- **E** – This demonstrates the dual task performance effect and shows that the central executive is separate from the articulatory loop.
- **L** – This supports the idea of multiple components in STM and the idea of the WMM.

- **E** – Therefore, his brain damage appeared to be restricting his phonological loop and not his visuo-spatial sketchpad.
- **L** – This supports the idea of a separate component for auditory and visual information, as suggested by the WMM.

- **E** – The case of EVR suggests that the idea of a single CE is wrong and there are possibly several different components within our CE.
- **L** – This suggests that the function of the CE is more complex than Baddeley and Hitch had originally suggested.

 A LEVEL ONLY ZONE

 ### P – Another criticism of the WMM comes from…

…evidence using brain-damaged patients.

- **E** – Some of the key evidence for the WMM comes from case studies of individuals with serious brain damage (e.g. KF).
- **E** – There are several problems with using such evidence, for example, individuals may have difficulties in paying attention and therefore simply underperform on certain tasks.
- **L** – This matters because the results of a single case study are difficult, if not impossible, to replicate and difficult to generalise to the general population.

P – A final strength of the WMM comes from…

…evidence for the phonological loop and articulatory process.

- **E** – The PL explains why the word-length effect occurs. People are able to remember short words better than long words because the PL holds information for approximately two seconds and longer words simply don't fit in the PL.
- **E** – Furthermore, the word-length effect disappears if a person is given an articulatory suppression task, as participants are unable to rehearse information.
- **L** – These findings support the idea of a phonological loop and articulatory process in the WMM.

✔ CHOOSE THE RIGHT ANSWER

Which of the following are **not** features of the working memory model?

A	Long-term memory	☐
B	Sensory register	☐
C	Serial position curve	☐
D	Maintenance rehearsal	☐
E	All of the above	☐

Answers on page 272

👁 SPOT THE MISTAKES

Read this student answer to the following exam question: Outline the working memory model. *(4 marks)*

There are **four** mistakes – draw a circle around each.

The working memory model was proposed by Atkinson and Shiffrin to resolve some of the issues found with the multi-store model. It consists of separate stores for acoustic and visual information, which are controlled by the episodic buffer.

The central executive directs the brain's resources to one of three the slave systems, which include the phonological loop and the visuo-spatial sketchpad. The phonological loop contains the articulatory store and phonological store. The visuo-spatial sketchpad contains the visual cache and inner scribe. The purpose of the inner scribe is to store visual information.

Answers on page 272

⚙ APPLYING YOUR KNOWLEDGE (1)

An experiment was conducted to investigate the working memory model.

One group of participants completed one visual and one auditory task at the same time, while the other group complete two visual tasks.

The participants who carried out two visual tasks performed significantly less well than the participants who carried out one visual task and one auditory task.

Use your knowledge of the WMM to explain this finding.

Identify the psychology	Link to the WMM
Condition 1 (one visual and one auditory task)… ➡	*This means that…*
Condition 2 (two visual tasks)… ➡	*This means that…*

Answers on page 272

⚙ APPLYING YOUR KNOWLEDGE (2)

Identify the psychology		Link to WMM
	While writing this revision book, Mr Robinson is able to select pictures for the different pages whilst listening to music at the same time. However, he finds it difficult to talk to his friend while typing. Use your knowledge of the working memory model to explain why Mr Robinson is able to perform the first two tasks at the same time, but finds it difficult to perform the second two tasks at the same time.	

Answers on page 272

KEY TERMS

- Episodic memory
- Procedural memory
- Semantic memory
- Explicit
- Implicit
- Declarative
- Procedural

Possible essay question …

Describe and evaluate types of long-term memory. *(12 marks AS, 16 marks A)*

Other possible exam questions …

+ Explain what is meant by episodic memory. *(6 marks)*
+ Explain what is meant by semantic memory. *(6 marks)*
+ Explain what is meant by procedural memory. *(6 marks)*
+ Explain evidence to support the distinction between episodic and procedural memory. *(6 marks)*

MUST know …

Types of long-term memory (part 1)

Long-term memory is divided into two main types: **explicit** (declarative – knowing that) and **implicit** (procedural – knowing how) memory.

Episodic memories are about knowing that (declarative) and occur as part of a sequence. Episodic memories are concerned with personal experience.

Semantic memories are also about knowing that (declarative). Semantic memories are knowledge about the world which is shared by everyone, rather than a personal 'episodic' experience.

Procedural memory is concerned with skills, such as knowing how to tie a shoelace. It is remembering how to do something, rather than knowing what to do.

 Support for the different types of long-term memory…

…comes from brain scans.

- *E* – Research shows that different areas of the brain are active when using different types of LTM.

 Further support for the different types of long-term memory…

…comes from case studies.

- *E* – The case of patient HM highlights the distinction between procedural and declarative memories. After surgery, patient HM could still form new procedural memories but he was unable to form episodic/semantic memories.

 Additional support for different types of long-term memory…

…comes from patients with Alzheimer's.

- *E* – Hodges and Patterson (2007) found that some patients with Alzheimer's disease retain the ability to form new episodic memories but not semantic memories.

SHOULD know …

Types of long-term memory (part 2): examples

An **episodic** memory might be your memory of a family holiday. Episodic memories have three elements: details of the event, the context and the emotions felt.

Semantic memories related to things, such as the function of objects, or what behaviour is appropriate in a particular situation. They may also be related to abstract concepts such as mathematics and language.

Procedural memories are typically acquired through repetition and practice. We are less aware of these memories as they are automatic, for example, riding a bike.

- *E* – Episodic memory is associated with the hippocampus and temporal lobe, semantic memory also relies on the temporal lobe and procedural memory is associated with the cerebellum.
- *L* – This suggests that the three types of long-term memory are separate and found in different areas of the brain.

- *E* – For example, patient HM was able to draw a figure by looking at its reflection in a mirror, a skill called mirror drawing (procedural memory), however he could not remember learning this skill (episodic/semantic memory).
- *L* – This supports the distinction of procedural and episodic/semantic memories, as different types of long-term memory highlighting the existence of multiple types of long-term memory.

- *E* – Furthermore, Irish *et al.* (2001) found the reverse in Alzheimer's patients, who had poor semantic memories but generally intact episodic memories.
- *L* – This double-disassociation suggests that episodic and semantic memories are separate and that episodic memories may be a gateway to semantic memory, but it is possible for semantic memories to form separately.

 P – However, one criticism of the research investigating LTM is…

…the use of patients with brain damage.

- *E* – It is difficult to conclude from the case of Patient HM the exact parts of the brain that were affected.
- *E* – Damage to a particular area of the brain does not mean that this area is responsible for a particular behaviour.
- *L* – This matters because we are unable to conclude a causal relationship between a particular brain region and type of LTM.

 P – A final criticism of research investigating LTM is…

…the possibility of a fourth type of LTM.

- *E* – Research investigating priming describes how implicit memories influence the response a person makes.
- *E* – Priming is controlled by a brain system separate from the temporal system that supports explicit memory (semantic and episodic) which has led to the suggestion that there is a fourth type of LTM.
- *L* – This suggests that the original theory of LTM is too simplistic and other types of LTM may exist.

✓ CHOOSE THE RIGHT ANSWER

The following concepts relate to long-term memory.

A Episodic memory

B Semantic memory

C Procedural memory

In the table below, write which one of the concepts listed above (**A**, **B** or **C**) matches each of the examples below.

Definition	Concept
A detailed memory of a family holiday to Spain.	
A memory of how to play the piano.	
An understanding of different theoretical models of memory, including the multi-store model and working memory model.	

Answers on page 272

✎ FILL IN THE BOXES

In each box below write one sentence describing an aspect of long-term memory in about 20 words.

In each box below expand the content on the left, writing about another 20 words.

Episodic memory is…
Semantic memory is…
Procedural memory is…

➤

An example of episodic memory is…
An example of semantic memory is…
An example of procedural memory is…

Answers on page 272

✓ A MARKING EXERCISE

Read this student answer to the following exam question:
Explain what is meant by procedural memory. *(6 marks)*

> Long-term memory is divided into two main types: explicit and implicit. One implicit memory is procedural knowledge. An example of procedural knowledge would be the memory of how to tie a shoelace. This type of memory is procedural as we 'know how' to tie a shoelace rather than 'know that'.

This answer is likely to be awarded 3 or 4 out of 6 marks. Why do you think it would be awarded this mark?

Suggest two pieces of information that could be added to improve this answer:

1)

2)

Write an improved answer here…

Answers on page 272

⚙ APPLYING YOUR KNOWLEDGE

Identify the psychology		Link to Clive Wearing

Clive Wearing is a British musician who contracted a virus in 1985 that caused severe amnesia. Since then, he is unable to form new long-term memories, for example, he would not remember visiting his daughter in Australia. However he does remember how to play the piano and sing.
Use your knowledge of long-term memory to explain what type(s) of long-term memory remain intact for Clive and what type(s) is no longer intact.

Answers on page 273

KEY TERMS

- Interference
- Proactive interference (PI)
- Retroactive interference (RI)

Possible essay question ...

Describe and evaluate one explanation for forgetting. *(12 marks AS, 16 marks A)*

Other possible exam questions ...

+ Explain what is meant by the terms *proactive interference* and *retroactive interference*. *(2 marks + 2 marks)*

+ Describe one study that demonstrates that interference may cause forgetting. *(6 marks)*

MUST know ...

Retroactive interference

Retroactive interference (RI) is where learning something new interferes with past learning.

Müller and Pilzecker (1990) demonstrated retroactive interference by giving participants lists of nonsense syllables to learn for six minutes and then, after a retention interval, asking the participants to recall the lists.

Performance was less good when participants were given an intervening task between initial learning and recall. Therefore the intervening task produced RI because the later task interfered with the previously learned material.

 One criticism of research investigating interference is...

...the artificial nature of the tasks.

- **E** – Most of the research investigating interference is laboratory-based and uses artificial lists of words and/or nonsense syllables.

 Another criticism of interference research is that...

...interference only explains some types of forgetting.

- **E** – Critics argue that while interference effects do occur in everyday life, they do not occur very often.

 A final criticism of interference research is ...

...whether interference affects accessibility or availability of memory.

- **E** – Ceraso (1967) found that, if memory was tested again after 24 hours, recognition (accessibility) showed considerable spontaneous recovery, whereas recall (availability) remained the same.

SHOULD know ...

Proactive interference

Proactive interference (PI) is when past learning interferes with the current attempts to learn something new.

Underwood (1957) analysed the findings from a number of studies and found that participants were less able to learn a list of words later in a sequence, in comparison to those presented earlier on.

Furthermore, Underwood found that if participants had to memorise ten or more lists of words, then after 24 hours they only remembered 20%, whereas if they only learned one list, recall was over 70%. These results suggest that PI occurs when learning multiple word lists.

- **E** – Therefore the findings may not relate to everyday uses of memory, which tend not to involve simple word lists.
- **L** – This suggests that the results of interference research lack ecological validity and may not apply to everyday examples of human memory.

- **E** – For example, rather special conditions are required for interference to lead to forgetting – the two memories need to be quite similar.
- **L** – This suggests that interference is a relatively unimportant explanation of everyday forgetting and other theories are required to provide a complete explanation.

- **E** – This shows that interference effects do not cause memories to disappear and the effects are only temporary.
- **L** – This suggests that interference only occurs because memories are temporarily not accessible rather than lost (unavailable).

 P – One strength of interference research is...

...the application to advertising.

- **E** – Danaher *et al.* (2008) found that both recall and recognition of an advertiser's message were impaired when participants were exposed to two advertisements for competing brands in the same week.
- **E** – This demonstrates the effects of interference when people are exposed to multiple competing adverts.
- **L** – This matters because research can potentially save advertisers money and enhance the effectiveness of advertising campaigns.

P – A final criticism of interference research is...

...the evidence of individual differences.

- **E** – Kane and Engle (2000) demonstrated that individuals with greater working memory (WM) spans were less susceptible to proactive interference.
- **E** – The researchers tested this by giving participants three lists of words to learn. Those participants with low working memory spans showed greater proactive interference than those with higher working memory spans.
- **L** – This suggests that interference does not affect everyone equally and individual differences may play an important role in forgetting.

CHOOSE THE RIGHT ANSWER

The following concepts relate to forgetting:

A Interference

B Proactive interference

C Retroactive interference

In the table below, write which one of the concepts listed above (**A**, **B** or **C**) matches each of the examples below.

Definition	Concept
When a person's past learning interferes with their current attempts to learn something new.	
An explanation for forgetting in terms of one memory disrupting the ability to recall another. This is most likely to occur when the two memories have some similarity.	
When a person's current attempts to learn something, interfere with their recall of previously learnt information.	

Answers on page 273

 RESEARCH METHODS (CALCULATIONS)

An experiment was carried out to test the effect of learning similar and dissimilar information.

In Part 1 of the experiment, both groups (A and B) were given a list of 20 male names to remember. In part 2 of the experiment, Group A was given another list of 20 male names and Group B was given a list of 20 different types of fruit.

Both groups (A and B) were then asked to recall as many of the 20 male names from Part 1 of the experiment as they could. The results from the two groups are shown below.

Group A	Group B
5	11
6	15
8	12
7	13
4	19
5	11
6	12
10	15
4	16
5	16
Mean =	Mean =
SD = 1.79	SD = 2.5

(a) Calculate the mean scores for Group A and Group B. Show your calculations for both groups. *(4 marks)*

(b) The psychologist calculated the standard deviation for both groups. Why are the standard deviation scores useful for the experimenter? *(2 marks)*

Answers on page 273

 DRAWING A CONCLUSION

The psychologist replicated the experiment (see the Research Methods activity) and found the following results:

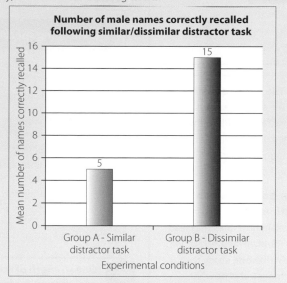

Using your knowledge of forgetting, explain what these results show. *(2 marks)*

Answers on page 273

 A MARKING EXERCISE

Read this student answer to the following exam question: Describe one study that demonstrated that interference may cause forgetting. *(6 marks)*	This answer was awarded 4 out of 6 marks. Why do you think it got this mark?
One study that examined interference was by Müller and Pilzecker (1990). They demonstrated retroactive interference by giving participants lists of nonsense syllables to learn for 6 minutes and then, after a retention interval, asking the participants to recall the lists. They found that performance was less good when participants were given an intervening task with learning and recall.	What is this answer missing to achieve 5 or 6 marks?
	Write the missing section here…

Answers on page 273

KEY TERMS

- Cues
- Retrieval failure
- Encoding specificity principle

Possible essay question …

Describe and evaluate how retrieval failure due to the absence of cues leads to forgetting. *(12 marks AS, 16 marks A)*

Other possible exam questions …

+ Explain how cues may lead to retrieval failure. *(3 marks)*
+ Describe **one** study that demonstrates how the absence of cues may lead to retrieval failure. *(6 marks)*

MUST know …

The encoding specificity principle

Forgetting in LTM is mainly due to **retrieval failure** – the failure to find an item of information because you have insufficient cues.

Tulving and Thomson (1973) proposed the **encoding specificity principle**, the idea that memory is most effective if information that was present at the time of encoding is also available at the time of retrieval.

Tulving and Pearlstone (1966) found that participants recalled 40% of words in a free recall task, in comparison to 60% of words in a cued-recall task, demonstrating the value of retrieval cues.

Retrieval cues can include the environmental context and/or a person's emotional state.

One strength of retrieval failure as an explanation for forgetting is…

…the quantity of research support.

- **E** – A range of laboratory, field and natural experiments support the idea of retrieval failure.

Another strength of retrieval failures as an explanation for forgetting is…

…the application to everyday memory.

- **E** – Abernethy (1940) found that students recalled more information when tested in the same room with the same teacher, in comparison to students tested in a different room with a different teacher.

However, one criticism is that…

…retrieval cues do not always work.

- **E** – In most of the research on retrieval cues, participants are learning word lists. However, everyday learning is far more complex.

SHOULD know …

Context-dependent and state-dependent forgetting

Godden and Baddeley (1975) investigated context-dependent learning. They recruited scuba divers and arranged for them to learn a list of words either on land or underwater. The divers were then tested either on land or underwater. The results revealed the highest recall when the initial context matched the recall environment.

Goodwin *et al.* (1969) demonstrated state-dependent forgetting by asking male volunteers to remember a list of words when they were either drunk or sober. Participants then recalled the list after 24 hours when some were sober and others had to get drunk again. The results revealed that words were best recalled in the same mental state.

- **E** – For example, Tulving and Pearlston (1966) demonstrate the power of retrieval cues and Godden and Baddeley (1975) demonstrate the importance of context-dependent learning.
- **L** – This matters because the evidence has relevance to everyday memory experiences and therefore high levels of ecological validity.

- **E** – This supports the idea of context-dependent learning in everyday memory and suggests that students should revise in the room where they will be taking their exams.
- **L** – This matters because the research provides a strategy for students to enhance their memory and improve their exam results.

- **E** – For example, learning about the multi-store model requires complex associations that are not easily triggered by a single cue.
- **L** – This matters because retrieval cues are unable to explain all types of learning/forgetting.

A LEVEL ONLY EVALUATION

P – One criticism of the encoding specificity principle is that…

…the relationship between encoding and retrieval is correlational.

- **E** – Nairne (2002) has criticised what he calls the 'myth of the encoding–retrieval match'. He claims that the relationship between encoding cues and later retrieval is correlational rather than causal.
- **E** – In other words, the cues do not cause retrieval, they are just associated with retrieval.
- **L** – This matters because a causal relationship between encoding and retrieval cannot be established.

P – One strength of retrieval failure as an explanation for forgetting is the…

…ability to explain interference effects.

- **E** – Tulving and Psotka (1971) found that when participants were given cued recall, the effects of interference disappeared – participants remembered about 70% of the words regardless of how many lists they had been given.
- **E** – This shows that information is there (available) but cannot be retrieved due to interference, as retrieval cues improve subsequent recall.
- **L** – This demonstrates that retrieval failure is a more important explanation of forgetting in comparison to interference.

CHOOSE THE RIGHT ANSWER

Which of the following are examples of retrieval cues?

A A person's emotional state. ☐

B A person's environment. ☐

C A person's social context. ☐

D All of the above. ☐

Answers on page 273

 MATCH THEM UP

Match the key terms and researchers on the left, with the definitions on the right.

Goodwin *et al.* (1969)	Encoding specificity principle
Retrieval cues	Environmental context and/or a person's emotional state
Retrieval failure	Context-dependent learning
Tulving and Thomson (1973)	State-dependent learning
Godden and Baddeley (1975)	The inability to access information that is stored in long-term memory

Answers on page 273

 **RESEARCH ISSUES**

In Godden and Baddeley's (1975) report, they said: "One diver was nearly run over during an underwater experimental session by an ex-army, amphibious DUKW [a type of boat that can also be driven on dry land]." Identify one ethical issue the researchers should have considered in this research.	Suggest how the researcher could deal with this ethical issue. *(3 marks)*

Answers on page 273

⚙ APPLYING YOUR KNOWLEDGE

Identify the psychology		Link to Emmanuel
	Emmanuel spends hours revising at home for a psychology test. Despite his revision, when he enters the psychology room, his mind goes blank and he is unable to remember anything! His teacher suggests that he should revise in the classroom where he will take the exam. Using your knowledge of psychological research, suggest why his teacher's advice might improve his memory. *(4 marks)*	

Answers on page 273

- Eyewitness testimony
- Leading question
- Misleading information
- Post-event discussion

Possible essay question …

Discuss research on the effect of misleading information on the accuracy of eyewitness testimony. *(12 marks AS, 16 marks A)*

Other possible exam questions …

+ Explain what is meant by a leading question. Use an example in your answer. *(3 marks)*

+ Explain how post-event discussion might create inaccuracy in eyewitness testimony. *(3 marks)*

+ Describe one research study related to the effect of misleading information on eyewitness testimony. *(5 marks)*

MUST know …

Loftus and Palmer (1974)

Loftus and Palmer (1974) examined the effect of misleading information by showing 45 students seven films of different traffic accidents. After each film the participants were given a questionnaire. There was one critical question which contained one of five verbs: 'How fast were the cars going when they [contacted / hit / bumped / collided / smashed] each other?'

Loftus and Palmer found that the leading question affected the responses given. For example, participants given the verb smashed reported an average speed of 40.8mph in comparison to participants given the verb contacted who reported an average speed of 31.8mph.

 One strength of Loftus's research come from…

…supporting evidence.

- **E** – Baun et al. (2002) found that misleading information can create inaccurate (false) memories. Participants were exposed to misleading advertising material which contained either Bugs Bunny, Ariel or a control condition.

 One criticism of Loftus's research is…

…the lack of ecological validity.

- **E** – Some researchers argue that laboratory experiments do not represent real life crimes/accidents.

One strength of research investigating eyewitness testimony is…

…the application of the findings to the criminal justice system.

- **E** – Psychological research has been used to warn the justice system of problems with eyewitness identification evidence.

SHOULD know …

Post-event discussion

The memory of an event may also be altered through discussing the event with other people and/or being questioned multiple times.

Conformity effect – Gabbert *et al.* (2003) showed pairs of participants a different video of the same event, so that each participant viewed unique items. Pairs in one condition were encouraged to discuss the event before individually recalling what they had witnessed. 71% of the witnesses who had discussed the event went on to mistakenly recall items from their discussion.

Repeat interviewing – Furthermore, each time an eyewitness is interviewed there is a possibility that the comments from the interviewer will become incorporated into their own recollection of the events.

- **E** – Baun et al. (2002) found that participants who were exposed to misleading advertising materials for Disneyland, later incorporated incorrect information into their original memories. Participants who were exposed to adverts containing Bugs Bunny, later reported shaking hands with this character in their visit to Disneyland, which could not have been possible, as the character belongs to Warner Brothers and not Disney.
- **L** – This demonstrates the power of misleading information which can lead to the creation of false memories.

- **E** – Participants may not take the experiment seriously and they may not be emotionally aroused in the same way that they would be in a real crime/accident.
- **L** – This matters as the results lack ecological validity and don't apply to everyday crimes/accidents.

- **E** – Recent DNA exoneration cases have shown that mistaken eyewitness identification was the largest single factor contributing to the conviction of innocent people (Wells and Olson, 2003).
- **L** – This matters because the research can help ensure that innocent people are not convicted of crimes they did not commit, on the basis of faulty eye-witness evidence.

 P – One criticism of research investigating the accuracy of eyewitness evidence is…

…the individual differences of witnesses.

- **E** – Schacter et al. (1991) found that elderly people have difficulty remembering the source of their information, even though their memory for the information itself is unimpaired.
- **E** – Consequently, they become more prone to the effect of misleading information.
- **L** – This suggests that individual differences, in particular age, are an important factor when examining the reliability of eyewitness accounts.

 P – A final criticism of Loftus and Palmer's (1974) research is…

…the possibility of a response bias.

- **E** – Bekerian and Bowers (1983) found that participants are not susceptible to misleading information if the questions are presented in the same order as the original information.
- **E** – This suggests that the order of questions has a significant effect and that the results of Loftus and Palmer's research may be due to a response bias and not a change in memory.
- **L** – This matters because it provides an alternative explanation to Loftus and Palmer and highlights the importance of question order in police interviews.

CHOOSE THE RIGHT ANSWER

Which of the following is an example of a misleading question?

A How tall was the man who committed the crime? ☐

B Did you see the crime? ☐

C What time did a crime take place? ☐

D How old was the youth who committed the crime? ☐

E All of the above. ☐

Answers on page 273

DRAWING CONCLUSIONS

The graph below shows the findings from the second study by Loftus and Palmer.

'Yes' and 'no' responses to the question about broken glass

Yes ☐
No ☐

(bar graph: Verb condition – Smashed, Hit, Control; Percentage axis 0–50)

State **two** findings and for each one draw a conclusion (state what the finding shows).

Finding 1:

Conclusion 1: This shows that…

Finding 2:

Conclusion 2: This shows that…

Answers on page 273

WRITE YOUR OWN EVALUATION POINT

Select one evaluation point from the page opposite and write a burger (PEEL) paragraph.

Point	
Evidence	
Explain	
Link	

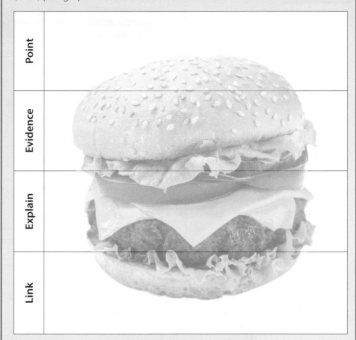

APPLYING YOUR KNOWLEDGE

Identify the psychology		Link to eyewitness accounts
	(image of Space Shuttle launch)	
	On 28 January 1986, the Space Shuttle Challenger exploded 73 seconds into its flight, leading to the deaths of seven crew members. Many people off the coast of Florida witnessed the accident first hand and discussed the accident immediately after and then watched news reports detailing the tragic accident later that day. Psychologists later examined eyewitness accounts. Using your knowledge of psychological research, explain why the eyewitness accounts may have been inaccurate.	

Answers on page 273

KEY TERM

- Anxiety
- Weapon focus effect

Possible essay question …

Discuss research on the effect of anxiety on eyewitness testimony. *(12 marks AS, 16 marks A)*

Other possible exam questions …

+ Explain how anxiety might affect the accuracy of eyewitness testimony. *(3 marks)*
+ Describe **one** research study related to the effect of anxiety on eyewitness testimony. *(5 marks)*

MUST know …

Johnson and Scott (1976)

Johnson and Scott (1976) demonstrated the weapon focus effect by asking participants to sit in a waiting room, where they heard an argument in an adjoining room and then saw a man run through the room carrying either a pen covered in grease (low anxiety condition) or a knife covered in blood (high anxiety, 'weapon focus' condition). Participants were later asked to identify the man from a set of photographs.

They found that the mean accuracy was 49% in the pen condition, compared to 33% in the knife condition, supporting the idea of a **weapon focus effect**.

 One criticism of the weapon focus effect is…

…that the effect may not be caused by anxiety.

- **E** – Pickel (1998) arranged for participants to watch a thief enter a hairdressing salon carrying scissors (high threat, low surprise), a handgun (high threat, high surprise), a wallet (low threat, low surprise) or a whole raw chicken (low threat, high surprise).

 One strength of the weapon focus effect comes from…

…real life studies.

- **E** – Deffenbacher *et al.* (2004) reviewed 34 studies and found that laboratory studies demonstrate that anxiety generally reduced accuracy and that real-life studies are associated with an even greater loss in accuracy.

However, one criticism of the weapon focus effect comes from…

…the results of real-life violent crimes.

- **E** – Halford and Milne (2005) found that victims of violent crimes were more accurate in their recall of crime scene information compared to victims of non-violent crimes.

SHOULD know …

Anxiety has a positive effect on accuracy

However, there is an alternate argument that suggests that high anxiety creates more enduring memories.

Christianson and Hubinette (1993) found evidence of enhanced recall when they questioned 58 real witnesses to bank robberies in Sweden. The witnesses were either victims (bank teller) or bystanders (employee or customer), i.e. high and low anxiety respectively.

The researchers found that all witnesses showed generally good memories for details of the robbery itself (better than 75% accurate recall). Those witnesses who were most anxious (the victims) had the best recall.

- **E** – Identification was least accurate in the high surprise conditions rather than the high threat conditions.
- **L** – This supports the view that the weapon focus effect may be the result of surprise, rather than anxiety.

- **E** – Therefore, the weapon focus effect appears to be the result of anxiety and the higher levels of anxiety found in real life crimes reduce the accuracy of eyewitness accounts even further.
- **L** – This suggests that the results from laboratory studies are reliable, as they are supported by real life studies.

- **E** – Therefore, the effect of anxiety in these violent crimes appears to increase the accuracy of eyewitness testimony.
- **L** – This shows that there is no simple rule about the effect of anxiety on the accuracy of eyewitness testimony.

A LEVEL ONLY ZONE

 P – One criticism of the weapon focus effect is…

…that individual differences may play an important role in accuracy of eyewitness testimony.

- **E** – Bothwell *et al.* (1987) found that participants who were labelled as 'stable' showed rising levels of accuracy as stress levels increased, whereas those labelled as 'neurotic' showed decreasing levels of accuracy as stress levels increased.
- **E** – Therefore, personality characteristics can affect the accuracy of eyewitness testimony.
- **L** – This suggests that one key extraneous variable in many studies of anxiety is personality and this should be taken into consideration when examining the results.

P – A final criticism of the weapon focus effect comes from…

…an alternate theory.

- **E** – Fazey and Hardy (1988) put forward the catastrophe theory which predicts that when physiological arousal increases beyond the optimum level, the inverted-U hypothesis predicts a gradual decrease in performance.
- **E** – Fazey and Hardy observed that in fact there is sometimes a catastrophic decline, which they suggest is due to increased mental anxiety (worry).
- **L** – This suggests an alternate explanation that may offer an explanation of the research findings, especially those of real-life eyewitnesses.

MATCH THEM UP

Match the researchers on the left with the definitions on the right.

Christianson and Hubinette (1993)	Anxiety decreases accuracy of EWT.
Halford and Milne (2005)	Anxiety increases accuracy of EWT.
Pickel (1998)	Surprise decreases accuracy of EWT, not anxiety.
Johnson and Scott (1976)	Violent crimes increase accuracy of EWT.

Answers on page 273

 A MARKING EXERCISE

Read the student answer to the following exam question:

Outline one study that has investigated the effect of anxiety on eyewitness testimony. *(6 marks)*

> Christianson and Hubinette did a study looking at a real-life bank robbery. They interviewed people that were threatened and those who were not directly threatened to see if anxiety affected eyewitness testimony. Those who were directly threatened were more anxious than those not directly threatened.

This answer was awarded 2 out of 6 marks. Why do you think it got this mark?

Suggest **two** pieces of information that could be added to improve this answer:

1 ....

....

2 ....

....

Answers on page 273

 FILL IN THE BOXES

Finish the sentences in columns 2 and 3.

Anxiety reduces the accuracy of EWT	One piece of evidence for this is…	This suggests that…
Anxiety enhances the accuracy of EWT	One piece of evidence for this is…	This suggests that…
Anxiety may sometimes reduce and sometimes enhance the accuracy of EWT	One explanation for this contradiction is…	This suggests that…

Answers on page 274

 SPOT THE MISTAKES

Read this student answer to the following exam question: Describe one research study related to the effect of anxiety on eyewitness testimony. *(5 marks)*

There are **four** mistakes – draw a circle around each.

> Johnson and Scott (1976) investigated the effect of anxiety on eyewitness testimony. Participants were asked to sit in a waiting room where they heard an argument in an adjoining room and then saw a man run through the room carrying either a pen covered in blood (low anxiety condition) or a knife covered in blood (low anxiety, 'weapon focus' condition). Participants were later asked to identify the man from a set of photographs. They found that the man accuracy was 59% in the pen condition, compared to 33% in the knife condition. The results suggest that anxiety reduces the accuracy of eyewitness testimony, as the participants who saw the knife (high anxiety condition) were less accurate in their identifications.

Answers on page 274

KEY TERM

- Cognitive interview

Possible essay question …

Discuss the use of the cognitive interview as a means of improving the accuracy of memory. *(12 marks AS, 16 marks A)*

Other possible exam questions …

+ Identify and explain **two** techniques used in the cognitive interview. *(3 marks + 3 marks)*

+ Explain how a cognitive interview differs from a standard interview. *(4 marks)*

MUST know …

The cognitive interview

Geiselman *et al.* (1984) developed an interviewing technique, the cognitive interview (CI), which has four distinct components.

1. Mental reinstatement of original context – the interviewee is encouraged to mentally recreate the physical and psychological environment of the original incident.

2. Report everything – the interviewee is encouraged to report every single detail of the event, without editing anything out.

3. Change order – the interviewee is asked to consider an alternative timeline of the incident, for example by reversing the order.

4. Change perspective – the interviewee is asked to recall the incident from another perspective.

 One strength of the cognitive interview comes from…

…research support.

- **E** – Köhnken *et al.* (1999) conducted a meta-analysis of 53 studies and found, on average, an increase of 34% in the amount of correct information generated in the CI.

 However, one criticism of the cognitive interview is that the…

…quantity of information is increased not the quality.

- **E** – Köhnken *et al.* (1999) found an 81% increase in the amount of correct information generated, but also a 61% increase in the amount of incorrect information (false positives) when using the enhanced CI.

 Another criticism of the cognitive interview is…

…the time taken and training required for police.

- **E** – Kebbel and Wagstaff report two issues with the CI. Firstly, it requires more time than is often available and secondly, it requires special training.

SHOULD know …

What the interviewer might say…

1. Mental reinstatement of original context – *I would like you to try to think back to the day the event happened. Think about that day … what you had been doing … try and get a picture of it in your mind.*

2. Report everything – *Some people hold back information because they are not quite sure that it is important … Please do not leave anything out.*

3. Change order – *I would like you to tell me what happened from the end to the start.*

4. Change perspective – *Try to recall the incident from the perspective of another person involved in the incident.*

- **E** – However, it must be noted that the effectiveness of the CI may be due to individual elements of the CI rather than the whole process.
- **L** – This suggests that the cognitive interview is an effective technique for increasing the amount of correct information generated.

- **E** – However, the procedure is designed to enhance the quantity (the amount) of correct recall without compromising the quality.
- **L** – This suggests that the cognitive interview is only useful in increasing the quantity of information and that police need to treat all information collected from the CI with caution.

- **E** – Unfortunately, police often use deliberate strategies to limit an interview to save time and many police forces have not provided the necessary training to conduct a CI.
- **L** – This matters because these limitations have prevented the application of the CI to everyday police interviews.

 P – Another criticism of the cognitive interview is…

…the difficulty in establishing the effectiveness of the CI.
- **E** – When the CI is used in the real world it is not just one 'procedure' but a collection of related techniques.
- **E** – For example, the Thames Valley Police use a version that does not include 'changing perspectives'.
- **L** – This matters because it is difficult to conclude which component(s) of the CI are effective and which increase the quality and quantity of information produced.

P – A final criticism of the cognitive interview is…

…the differences found in old vs. young people.
- **E** – Mello and Fisher (1996) found that the CI produced significantly more information for older participants.
- **E** – This may be because older adults are overly cautious about reporting information and the CI places an importance on reporting everything.
- **L** – This matters because it suggests that the CI is more effective for older people, in comparison to younger people.

✓ CHOOSE THE RIGHT ANSWER

Which of the following are features of the cognitive interview? Tick **two** of the boxes.

A Retrieval cues	☐
B Changed perspective	☐
C Reverse order	☐
D Contextual cues	☐

Answers on page 274

🎯 WRITE YOUR OWN EVALUATION POINT

Select one evaluation point from the page opposite and write a burger (PEEL) paragraph.

Point	
Evidence	
Explain	
Link	

💡 DRAWING CONCLUSIONS

A psychologist investigated the effectiveness of the cognitive interview by comparing the mean number of correct/incorrect items recalled for the cognitive and standard interview. The following results were found:

	Cognitive interview	Standard interview
Mean number of correct items recalled	45	32
Mean number of incorrect items recalled	8	8

What do these results suggest about the effectiveness of the cognitive interview? *(4 marks)*

Answers on page 274

⚙ APPLYING YOUR KNOWLEDGE

Using your knowledge of improving the accuracy of eye witness testimony: the cognitive interview, answer the following.

Cognitive interview technique		How it could be used with the students
	During one psychology lesson a man burst into the classroom and demanded to speak to the teacher. He told her that he was very angry about the way she had treated his son and continued shouting until the teacher managed to get him to leave.	
Technique 1		**How it could be used…**
Technique 2	Afterwards the teacher asked the students to write down a description of everything they remember. Suggest how the teacher might use some of the techniques of the cognitive interview to question her students.	**How it could be used…**

Answers on page 274

Anxiety	An unpleasant emotional state that is often accompanied by increased heart rate and rapid breathing, i.e. physiological arousal.
Capacity	This is a measure of how much can be held in memory. It is represented in terms of bits of information, such as number of digits.
Central executive	Monitors and coordinates all other mental functions in working memory.
Coding	(also 'encoding') The way information is changed so that it can be stored in memory. Information enters the brain via the senses (e.g. eyes and ears). It is then stored in various forms, such as visual codes (like a picture), acoustic codes (sounds) or semantic codes (the meaning of the experience).
Cognitive interview	A police technique for interviewing witnesses to a crime, which encourages them to recreate the original context of the crime in order to increase the accessibility of stored information. Because our memory is made up of a network of associations rather than of discrete events, memories are accessed using multiple retrieval strategies.
Cues	These are things that serve as a reminder. They may meaningfully link to the material to be remembered or may not be meaningfully linked, such as environmental cues (a room) or cues related to your mental state (being or sad or drunk).
Duration	A measure of how long a memory lasts before it is no longer available.
Episodic buffer	Receives input from many sources, temporarily stores this information, and then integrates it in order to construct a mental episode of what is being experienced.
Episodic memory	Personal memories of events, such as what you did yesterday or a teacher you liked. This kind of memory includes contextual details plus emotional tone.
Eyewitness testimony	The evidence provided in court by a person who witnessed a crime, with a view to identifying the perpetrator of the crime.
Interference	An explanation for forgetting in terms of one memory disrupting the ability to recall another. This is most likely to occur when the two memories have some similarity.
Leading question	A question that, either by its form or content, suggests to the witness what answer is desired or leads him or her to the desired answer.
Long-term memory (LTM)	Your memory for events that have happened in the past. This lasts anywhere from 2 minutes to 100 years. LTM has potentially unlimited duration and capacity and tends to be coded semantically.
Misleading information	Supplying information that may lead a witness's memory for a crime to be altered.
Multi-store model	An explanation of memory based on three separate memory stores, and how information is transferred between these stores.
Phonological loop	Codes speech sounds in working memory, typically involving maintenance rehearsal (repeating the words over and over again). This is why this component of working memory is referred to as a 'loop'.
Post-event discussion	A conversation between co-witnesses or an interviewer and an eyewitness after a crime has taken place which may contaminate a witness' memory for the event.
Proactive interference (PI)	Past learning interferes with current attempts to learn something.
Procedural memory	Memory for how to do things, for example riding a bicycle or learning how to read. Such memories are automatic as the result of repeated practice.
Retrieval failure	Occurs due to the absence of cues. An explanation for forgetting based on the idea that the issue relates to being able to retrieve a memory that is there (available) but not accessible. Retrieval depends on using cues.
Retroactive interference (RI)	Current attempts to learn something interfere with past learning.
Semantic memory	Shared memories for facts and knowledge. These memories may be concrete, such as knowing that ice is made of water, or abstract, such as mathematical knowledge.
Sensory register	This is the information at the senses – information collected by your eyes, ears, nose, fingers and so on. Information is retained for a very brief period by the sensory registers. We are only able to hold accurate images of sensory information momentarily (less than half a second). The capacity of sensory memory is very large, such as all the cells on the retina of the eye. The method of coding depends on the sense organ involved, e.g. visual for the eyes or acoustic for the ears.
Short-term memory (STM)	Your memory for immediate events. STMs are measured in seconds and minutes rather than hours and days, i.e. a short duration. They disappear unless they are rehearsed. STM also has a limited capacity of about four items or chunks and tends to be coded acoustically. This type of memory is sometimes referred to as working memory.
Visuo-spatial sketchpad	Codes visual information in terms of separate objects as well as the arrangement of these objects in one's visual field.
Working memory model	An explanation of the memory used when working on a task. Each store is qualitatively different.

Topic 1 Short- and long-term memory

Describe and evaluate research that has investigated duration in STM and/or LTM. *(10 marks)*

Peterson & Peterson (1959) investigated the duration of STM, using 24 students. Each participant was presented with a consonant syllable and a three-digit number, for example LXZ 128. They were then asked to recall the consonant syllable at different intervals (3, 6, 9, 12, 15 and 18 seconds). Peterson & Peterson found that on average participants were 90% correct at 3 seconds, but only 2% correct after 18 seconds. This suggests that the duration of STM is approximately 18 seconds.

Bahrick et al. (1975) investigated the duration of LTM, using 400 people of varying ages (17–74), on their memory for former classmates. They found that participants who were tested within 15 years of graduation were 90% accurate. However after 48 years this declined to 70%.

One issues with research investigating STM is that the testing methods are artificial and lack ecological validity. In Peterson & Peterson's study, the participants were required to remember meaningless consonant syllables which is different to the information people try to remember on a day-to-day basis. This matters because we are unable to apply to results of STM research to everyday accounts of memory. However, one strength of research investigating LTM is the high levels of ecological validity. Bahrick's study used real life memories, as the participants matched pictures of former classmates with their names. Therefore, these results reflect our memory for real-life events and can be applied to everyday human memory.

Examiner's comments

This answer has started with a detailed description of research investigating the duration of STM, including the method and results.

In addition, this answer has also outlined the method and results of research investigating the duration of LTM.

Finally, the answer provides two evaluation points which evaluate the weakness of STM research and the strength of LTM research.

Level 4 answer (8–10 marks)

Examiner's comments: AO1: The answer accurately explains all the research, including the method and results section for both Peterson & Peterson (1959) and Bahrick *et al.* (1975). The selection of material for AO1 is appropriate and effectively used.

AO3: The evaluation is thorough and effective and the answer includes two evaluation points with greater depth, using specialist terminology effectively.

Topic 2 The multi-store model of memory

Discuss the multi-store model of memory. Refer to research evidence in your answer. *(16 marks)*

The multi-store model of memory suggests that memory consists of three stores, including: sensory register, short-term memory (STM) and long-term memory (LTM).

Information enters the sensory register, which has a large capacity, as the registers are constantly receiving information. However, most of the information receives no attention and therefore the duration is limited (milliseconds). Information which is attended to, enters the STM and if information is rehearsed in STM this will create a LTM. The LTM has a potentially unlimited duration and capacity.

> The answer has explained the MSM reasonably well, however certain details are missing, for example, the capacity, duration and coding of STM and the process of retrieval.

One strength of the multi-store model comes from supporting laboratory evidence. For example, Miller (1956) found that the duration of STM is 7+/−2 and Bahrick et al. (1975) found that the duration of LTM is approximately 48 years. This matters because the laboratory evidence supports the idea of separate short- and long-term memory stores. Further support for the multi-store models comes from case studies. Scoville and Milner (1985) reported the case of patient HM who could not form new LTMs, although he could remember things from before his surgery. This provides support for the MSM, as Patient HM was unable to transfer information from his STM to LTM but was able to retrieve information from before his surgery, supporting the different processes involved in the MSM.

> The answer has detailed two strengths effectively, using a range of research evidence, as required in this question.

However, the MSM has been criticised for being too simplistic and the working memory model suggests that there are multiple components to short-term memory, including an auditory and visual component. Finally, another criticism of the multi-store models is that long-term memory involves more than just rehearsal. Craik and Lockhart (1972) suggest that long-term memories are created by the depth of processing, rather than just by rehearsing information in short-term memory. This suggests that the process of rehearsal does not fully explain the process of remembering in long-term memory.

> Although two weaknesses have been outlined, the first weakness is not effective and the answer does state why the idea of the MSM being too simplistic is an issue for the model.

Level 3 answer (9–12 marks)

Examiner's comments: AO1: The answer outlines the MSM accurately with reasonable detail, however some key information in relation to short-term memory and the processes involved in the MSM are missing, which prevented the answer from achieving a Level 4.

AO3: The evaluation is mostly reasonable, but not always effective (see above). The answer has included a range of evaluative evidence with reasonable depth, although not all of the points were effective and additional evaluation points could have been included to ensure a broad range of evidence was discussed. The essay was well planned and organised in a clear way.

Topic 3 The working memory model

Discuss the working memory model. Include strengths and limitations in your answer. *(12 marks)*

The working memory model (WMM) was proposed by Baddeley and Hitch (1974) to account for some of the limitations of the multi-store model. In particular, they felt that short-term memory consists of multiple stores and not just one unitary store.

> The answer includes a strong introduction which adds clarity to the structure of the essay.

The central executive controls the WMM and directs attention to one of three slave systems. The phonological loops deal with auditory information and contains the phonological store which holds the words you hear and the articulatory control process which allows for maintenance rehearsal of acoustic information. The visuo-spatial sketchpad (VSS) is used for the planning of spatial tasks. The VSS contains the visual cache which stores visual information and the inner scribe which deals with spatial relationships and stores the arrangement of objects in the visual field.

> The answer has accurately explained all of the components of the WMM in excellent detail, using correct terminology throughout.

Examiner's comments

In 2000, Baddeley added the episodic buffer which is a general store for both visual and acoustic information. The purpose of the episodic buffer is to integrate information from the other three components and send information to long-term memory.

One strength of the working memory model comes from dual task studies. Hitch and Baddeley (1976) found that participants were slower in a dual task study that involved both the central executive and the articulatory loop, in comparison to a task which just required just the articulatory loop. This supports the idea of multiple components within STM and demonstrates a separate central executive and articulatory loop, therefore supporting the WMM. Further support the WMM comes from case studies. Shallice and Warrington (1970) studied a man called KF whose short-term forgetting of auditory information was much greater than his forgetting of visual information. This provides further support to the idea of separate components in STM, indicating a separate component for auditory and visual information.

> The answer has discussed two strengths of the WMM. The evaluation is effective and uses research effectively.

However, one limitation of the WMM is the central executive. Eslinger and Damasio (1985) studied EVR, who had a cerebral tumour removed. Although he performed well on some tests requiring reasoning, he had poor decision-making skills and would spend hours making simple decisions. This suggests that the function of the CE is more complex than Baddeley and Hitch had originally suggested.

> The answer has also discussed a limitation of the WMM. As above, the evaluation is effective and includes research effectively.

Level 4 answer (10–12 marks)

Examiner's comments: AO1: The working memory model has been explained accurately, with an excellent level of detail. All of the components of the working memory model have been outlined, using correct terminology throughout.

AO3: The evaluation is thorough and effective. A broad range of evidence, including both strengths and limitations, has been discussed, with accompanying research to support every point. Specialist terms have been used effectively and the essay is clearly structured.

Topic 4 Types of long-term memory

Explain evidence to support the distinction between episodic and procedural memory. *(6 marks)*

Examiner's comments

One type of evidence which supports the distinction between episodic and procedural memory comes from brain scans. Research has shown that different areas of the brain are active for different LTM tasks. For example, episodic memory is associated with the hippocampus and temporal lobe and procedural memory is associated with the cerebellum. This supports the idea that episodic and procedural memory are found in different areas of the brain and are distinct types of LTM.

> The answer starts by outlining how brain imagining technology supports the distinction between episodic and procedural memory, with excellent detail.

Further support for the distinction between episodic and procedural memory comes from case studies. Following surgery, Patient HM could still form new procedural memories but was unable to form episodic memories. This evidence also supports the distinction between episodic and procedural memories.

> The answer also provides evidence from case studies, however this section could have been developed further to include an example of the types of tasks that Patient HM could and could not perform.

Level 3 answer (4–5 marks)

Note: *This question does not require students to outline the difference between episodic and procedural memory. It requires candidates to explain how different types of evidence (laboratory studies, case studies and brain imagining technology) support the idea that episodic and procedural memories are different (distinct) types of long-term memory.*

Examiner's comments: The answer provides an accurate and generally detailed outlined of the evidence supporting the distinction between episodic and procedural memory. The answer demonstrates clear knowledge and understanding of how the different types of research support the distinction between episodic and procedural memory.

Topic 5 Explanations for forgetting: Interference

Describe and evaluate one explanation for forgetting. *(12 marks)*

One explanation for forgetting is proactive interference, which is when past learning interferes with the current attempts to learn something new.

Underwood (1957) conducted an analysis on research investigating proactive interference and found that participants found it more difficult to learn a list of words later in a sequence than those presented earlier on. In addition, Underwood found that if participants had to memorise 10 or more lists of words, then after 24 hours, they only remembered 20%, whereas if they only learned one list, recall was over 70%. These results clearly demonstrate proactive interference as an explanation for forgetting.

One criticism of proactive interference is that interference can only explain some types of forgetting. Critics argue that interference effects do not occur very often, and require rather specific conditions in order to occur, for example, the two memories need to be quite similar. This suggests that interference is a relatively unimportant explanation of everyday forgetting.

Another criticism of proactive interference is whether interference affects the accessibility of information, or the availability of memory. Ceraso (1967) found that if memory was tested again after 24 hours, recognition (accessibility) showed considerable spontaneous recovery, whereas recall (availability) remained the same. This suggests that interference only occurs because memories are temporarily not accessible rather than lost (unavailable) and so proactive interference is not an explanation of forgetting, but rather accessibility.

However, one strength of proactive interference is its application to advertising. Danaher et al. (2008) found that both recall and recognition of an advertiser's message were impaired when participants were exposed to two advertisements for competing brands within a week, suggesting that interference does occur in everyday life, supporting interference as an explanation for forgetting.

Examiner's comments

The answer starts with a definition of proactive interference to outline the explanation for forgetting this answer will focus on.

The research is explained accurately with a good level of detail and key figures to support the results.

The answer outlines two criticisms and a strength of proactive interference as an explanation for forgetting. The evaluation is thorough and effective with reasonable depth.

Level 4 answer (10–12 marks)

Examiner's comments: AO1: The explanation of proactive interference is accurately explained with a good level of detail. The answer focuses on one explanation (proactive interference) and has selected the correct material and used it effectively.

AO3: The answer includes a broad range of evaluative evidence in reasonable depth and is thorough and effective throughout. Furthermore, most of the evaluation contains research to support the evaluation, while using a range of specialist terms effectively.

Topic 6 Explanations for forgetting: Retrieval failure

Describe one study that demonstrated how the absence of cues may lead to retrieval failure. *(6 marks)*

One study that demonstrates how the absence of cues may lead to retrieval failure was by Godden and Baddeley (1975), who investigated the effect of contextual cues on recall.

Their study used a sample of 18 scuba divers who learned a list of words on land or underwater and were then tested on land or underwater, leading to four experimental conditions: 1) Learning words on land and recalling on land; 2) learning words on land and recalling underwater; 3) learning underwater and recalling underwater; and 4) learning underwater and recalling on land.

Examiner's comments

The answer has outlined the aim of the study and linked the study to the question.

The answer describes the method of the study, including numerous key details, for example, the exact number of participants in the sample and the four experimental conditions.

Examiner's comments

The results revealed that the words learned underwater were best recalled underwater and the words learned on land were best recalled on land. This study demonstrates that the absence of contextual cues can lead to retrieval failure, as the participants who were required to recall words in a different context recalled significantly less than those who recalled words in the same context.

> Finally, the answer outlines the key results of the study and conclusion, linking these to the question.

Level 4 answer (6 marks)

Examiner's comments: The answer provides an accurate and detailed outline of one study (Godden and Baddeley, 1975) that demonstrates how the absence of cues may lead to retrieval failure. Furthermore, the answer demonstrates sound knowledge and understanding, linked to the question.

Topic 7 Accuracy of eyewitness testimony: Misleading information

Discuss research on the effect of misleading information on eyewitness testimony. *(16 marks)*

Examiner's comments

Loftus and Palmer (1974) conducted a study that examined the effect of misleading information on the accuracy of eyewitness testimony. Their sample consisted of 45 students, who each watched seven film clips of different traffic accidents.

After each film the participants were given a questionnaire. The critical question was one that asked the participants about the speed of vehicle, which contained one of five different verbs, for example: 'How fast were the cars going when they [contacted/hit/ bumped/ collided/smashed] each other?'

Loftus and Palmer found that on average participants estimated a speed of 40.8mph when given the verb smashed, in comparison to 31.8mph when given the verb contacted. The results suggest that misleading questions can significantly affect the accuracy of eyewitness testimony.

> The answer provides a detailed outline of one study (Loftus and Palmer, 1974), including the aim, procedure, findings and conclusion.

However, one criticism of Loftus and Palmer's (1974) research is its lack of ecological validity. Some researchers argue that lab experiments do not represent real life cases of crimes/accidents as the participants may not take the experiment seriously and are not likely to be emotionally aroused, as they would be in a real accident. This matters because the results lack ecological validity and do not apply to real-world crimes/accidents.

> The issue of ecological validity, in relation to research on the effect of misleading information, is discussed effectively.

On the other hand, one strength of research investigating misleading information is its application to the criminal justice system. Psychological research has been used to warn the justice system of problems with eyewitness identification evidence and help create new techniques, including the cognitive interview, to ensure that misleading information does not bias eyewitness accounts. This matters because the research can help ensure that innocent people are not convicted of crimes they did not commit, on the basis of faulty eye-witness evidence.

> The practical applications of the research examining the effect of misleading information is discussed with examples.

Loftus and Palmer's research on misleading information has been supported by other studies. Baun *et al.* (2002) found that misleading information can create inaccurate (false) memories. Participants were exposed to misleading advertising material which contained either Bugs Bunny, Ariel or a control condition. Participants in the Bugs Bunny or Ariel conditions were more likely to report having shaken hands with these characters in their visit to Disneyland, which could not have been possible as these characters belong to Warner Brothers and not Disney. This demonstrates the power of misleading information in the creation of false memories.

> The answer includes a second study to support Loftus and Palmer's (1974) research.

A final criticism of research investigating the accuracy of eyewitness evidence is the effect of age. Schacter et al. (1991) found that elderly people have difficulty remembering the source of their information, even though their memory for the information itself is unimpaired. This suggests that individual differences, in particular age, are an important factor when examining the reliability of eyewitness accounts.

The answer includes a final criticism which discusses the effect of individual differences for misleading information.

Level 4 answer (13–16 marks)

Examiner's comments: AO1: The answer discusses two pieces of research, Loftus and Palmer (1974) and Baun *et al.* (2002), accurately. One study is explained in excellent detail, including the aim, procedure, findings and conclusion, while the second study is used to support the first. The selection of material is appropriate for the question.

AO3: The evaluation is generally thorough and effective and the answer includes a broad range of evaluate evidence, with excellent depth, including two strengths and two limitations. A fifth evaluation point could be included to ensure top marks.

Topic 8 Accuracy of eyewitness testimony: Anxiety

Discuss research on the effect of anxiety on eyewitness testimony. *(12 marks)*

Examiner's comments

Johnson and Scott (1976) examined the effect of anxiety on eyewitness testimony, by demonstrating the weapon focus effect. Johnson and Scott asked their participants to sit in a waiting room, where they witnessed one of two situations. In the low anxiety condition, the participants overheard an argument in the adjoining room and then saw a man run through their room carrying a pen covered in grease. In the high anxiety condition, the participants also overheard an argument, but this time the man ran through their room carrying a knife covered in blood.

The answer could have elaborated the introduction and explained the weapon focus effect in more detail.

The method section is detailed and accurate.

The participants were then asked to identify the man from a set of photographs. They found that the accuracy was higher in the pen condition, in comparison to the knife condition.

The results section could include some specific details, for example the percentages in both conditions (49% and 33%), as well as a conclusion.

One criticism of research examining the weapon focus effect is that the effect may not be caused by anxiety. Pickel (1998) also conducted research into the effect of anxiety and found that identification was least accurate in a 'high surprise' rather than 'high threat' condition. This suggests that anxiety may not affect the accuracy of eyewitness testimony, as originally claimed by Johnson and Scott (1976).

Although this evaluation point is generally effective, the method section of Pickel's research could have been elaborated.

However, evidence from real life case studies suggests that anxiety does affect the accuracy of EWT. Deffenbacher et al. (2004) found, from a review of 34 studies, that lab studies in general demonstrate that anxiety leads to reduced accuracy and that real-life studies are associated with an even greater loss in accuracy.

This second evaluation point is accurately explained, but not effective. The answer does not say how the results of Deffenbacher support the idea that anxiety affects the accuracy of EWT.

Level 3 answer (7–9 marks)

Examiner's comments: AO1: The research is generally explained accurately and quite detailed but key details in the results and conclusion are missing from Johnson and Scott's study.

AO3: The evaluation is mostly reasonable, but not always effective. Although there is a range of evaluative evidence, it is presented in limited depth, for example, details of the method are missing from Pickel (1998) and the final evaluation point is not effective, as the answer fails to explain how the results of Deffenbacher support the idea that anxiety affects the accuracy of EWT.

Topic 9 Improving the accuracy of eyewitness testimony: The cognitive interview

Discuss the use of the cognitive interview as a means of improving the accuracy of memory. *(12 marks)*

The cognitive interview was developed to help improve the accuracy of eye witness testimony. Geiselman et al. (1984) developed the cognitive interview (CI) which has four components: 1) Mental reinstatement?. 2) Report everything; 3) Change order, 4) Change perspective.

The cognitive interview has received support from a range of research. Köhnken et al. (1999) conducted a meta-analysis of 53 studies and found, on average, an increase of 34% in the amount of correct information generated in the CI compared with standard interviewing techniques. This suggests that the cognitive interview is an effective technique for increasing the amount of correct information generated.

Furthermore, when the CI is used in the real world it is not just one 'procedure' but a collection of related techniques. For example, the Thames Valley Police use a version that does not include 'changing perspectives'. This matters because it is difficult to conclude which components of the CI are effective and which increase the quality and quantity of information produced.

However, one criticism of the cognitive interview is that the quantity of information is increased but not the quality. Köhnken also found an 81% increase of correct information but also a 61% increase of incorrect information (false positives) when the enhanced CI was used compared to a standard interview. This suggests that the cognitive interview is only useful in increasing the quantity of information and that police need to treat all information collected from CIs with caution.

Examiner's comments

Although the answer outlined the four principles of the CI, they are not explained.

This is an effective evaluation point with excellent detail, including lots of fine detail.

This final criticism is also effective and also contains lots of fine detail.

As this question requires candidates to 'discuss the use' it would have been advisable to include a conclusion summarising the key evaluation points.

Level 3 answer (7–9 marks)

Examiner's comments: AO1: The theories and research are explained accurately although there is a lack of detail in relation to the principles of the CI.

AO2: The evaluation is always thorough and effective and a broad range of evidence has been considered in reasonable depth. There is a good range of specialist terms and the answer is planned in an organised and clear way. A conclusion would have supported the answer and provide clarity to the question.

KEY TERMS

- Attachment
- Caregiver
- Interactional synchrony
- Reciprocity

Possible essay question...

Discuss infant–caregiver interactions. Refer to reciprocity and interactional synchrony in your answer. *(12 marks AS, 16 marks A)*

Other possible exam questions...

+ Outline what is meant by the term *attachment*. *(2 marks)*
+ Describe how psychologists have investigated caregiver–infant interactions in humans. *(3 marks)*
+ Explain what is meant by the term *interactional synchrony* in the context of caregiver–infant interactions. *(2 marks)*
+ Explain what is meant by the term *reciprocity* in the context of caregiver–infant interactions.
+ Outline **one** study of caregiver-infant interactions. *(4 marks)*

MUST know ...

Reciprocity and interactional synchrony

Reciprocity

Research in the 1970s found that infants coordinate their actions with their caregivers. When a baby moves in rhythm with an adult, as if they are taking turns in a conversation, this is known as reciprocity.

Interactional synchrony

Later research discovered a different type of interaction between infants and their caregivers, known as interactional synchrony. This is when a baby mirrors (imitates) the actions of another person, in terms of their facial expressions and body movements. The actions or behaviours move in synchrony – at the same time.

 One criticism of testing infants is...

...their reliability.

- **E** – Infants' mouths are in fairly constant motion and they often stick their tongue out, yawn and smile, which may cause an issue for researchers investigating infant behaviour.

 Another criticism of the research investigating caregiver–infant interactions is...

...the failure to replicate research findings.

- **E** – Recent research by Koepke *et al.* (1983) has failed to replicate the findings of Meltzoff and Moore (1977), suggesting that the original research may be unreliable.

 One strength of examining infant behaviours comes from...

...research investigating intentional behaviour.

- **E** – Recent research examining infant behaviour has shown the infants do not respond to inanimate objects.

SHOULD know ...

Meltzoff and Moore (1977)

Meltzoff and Moore (1977) conducted the first study of interactional synchrony, using a controlled observation.

The study used an adult model who displayed one of three different facial expressions or a hand gesture. A dummy was placed in the infant's mouth during the initial display, to prevent any response. Following the display the dummy was removed and the child's expression was filmed.

The results revealed an association between the infant behaviour and that of the adult model. Later research (Meltzoff and Moore, 1983) revealed the same findings in three-day-old infants, suggesting that interactional synchrony is innate.

- **E** – However, Meltzoff and Moore (1977) measured infant responses by filming infants and asking the observers to judge the infants' behaviour from the video.
- **L** – This increases the internal validity of their findings and suggests that infants do mirror the actions of adults.

- **E** – However, Meltzoff and Moore countered this criticism and said that Koepke et al.'s research was less carefully controlled.
- **L** – This shows that the findings into interactional synchrony are not certain and that infants may not mirror the behaviour and expressions of adults, as originally outlined by Meltzoff and Moore (1977).

- **E** – Abravanel and DeYoung (1991) observed infants interacting with two objects, one simulating tongue movements and the other a mouth opening/closing.
- **L** – They found that infants between 5 and 12 weeks' old made little response to the objects, suggesting that infants do not imitate anything they see and only respond to specific social responses.

A LEVEL ONLY ZONE

 P – One criticism of research investigating caregiver–infant interactions is...

...the effect of individual differences.

- **E** – For example, Isabella *et al.* (1989) found that more strongly attached infant–caregiver pairs, showed greater interactional synchrony.
- **E** – This shows that children will respond to adults differently, depending upon the nature of their attachment.
- **L** – This means that not all children will demonstrate interactional synchrony and that the results of previous research may be unreliable.

P – One strength of the research into interactional synchrony is...

...its application to later adult relationships.

- **E** – Meltzoff (2005) developed the 'like me' hypothesis which explains how infants acquire an understanding of what other people are thinking and feeling.
- **E** – This shows how interactional synchrony might help children to understand the internal mental states of other people, which is fundamental in developing social relationships.
- **L** – This shows the importance of interactional synchrony research to understanding adult social relationships.

✓ CHOOSE THE RIGHT ANSWER

Tick **two** of the boxes below which illustrate interactional synchrony.

A	A child imitates the behaviour of his father and sticks his tongue out.	☐
B	A child responds to his father's smile, by smiling back.	☐
C	A father leans towards his child and the child leans back.	☐
D	A father and child lean towards one another, almost at exactly the same time.	☐

Answers on page 274

📖 RESEARCH ISSUES

Meltzoff and Moore (1977) conducted a controlled observation to investigate interactional synchrony in infants.

Identify **one** ethical issue the researchers would need to consider in this research. Suggest how the researchers could deal with this ethical issue.
(3 marks)

Answers on page 274

◎ WRITE YOUR OWN EVALUATION POINT

Select one evaluation point from the page opposite and write it out in your own words below.

Point	
Evidence	
Explain	
Link	

⚙ APPLYING YOUR KNOWLEDGE

Using your knowledge of caregiver–infant interactions, answer the following:

Proud mother Nathalie was watching her partner, Darren, interacting with their baby daughter, Rebecca. Nathalie thought that it was really sweet how, whenever Darren smiled, Rebecca smiled back. Furthermore, whenever Darren moved his head, Rebecca also moved her head, perfectly in time with each other.

Answers on page 274

Identify the psychology	Link to Darren and baby Rebecca

KEY TERMS

- Multiple attachments
- Primary attachment figure
- Separation anxiety
- Stranger anxiety

Possible essay question...

Describe and evaluate the stages of attachment identified by Schaffer and Emerson. *(12 marks AS, 16 marks A)*

Other possible exam questions...

+ Explain what is meant by the term *multiple attachments*. *(2 marks)*
+ Describe **one** study that investigated the development of attachments. *(6 marks)*
+ Outline the role of the father in the development of attachment. *(6 marks)*

MUST know ...

Stages of attachment

Schaffer and Emerson outlined four stages in the development of attachment.

Stage 1: indiscriminate attachments – at approximately two months old, infants start to show a greater preference for social stimuli, for example, smiling faces rather than inanimate objects.

Stage 2: the beginning of attachment – at four months old, infants can distinguish between familiar and unfamiliar people.

Stage 3: discriminate attachment – at seven months old, infants form one special attachment with their primary attachment figure and show separation anxiety when separated.

Stage 4: multiple attachments – soon after the main attachment is formed, the infant develops a wider circle of multiple attachments.

 One criticism of Schaffer and Emerson's research is...

...the possibility of unreliable data.

- **E** – Some of the mothers examined may have been less sensitive to their infants, but did not report this during the research.

 Another criticism of Shaffer and Emerson's research is...

...the biased sample used.

- **E** – The sample was from a working-class population in the 1960s.

 A final criticism of Schaffer and Emerson's research is...

...the importance placed on the primary attachment figure.

- **E** – The results suggest that infants form one special attachment, known as a monotropic relationship (Bowlby, 1969), and that other relationships are secondary.

SHOULD know ...

The role of the father and multiple attachments

Fathers are far less likely to be primary attachment figures. One theory is that men are not psychologically equipped to form an intense attachment because they lack the emotional sensitivity that women offer.

Heermann *et al.* (1994) found that men are less sensitive to infant cues while other research (Frodi *et al.*, 1978) has found no differences.

However, there are cases where men form secure attachments with their children, as is the case with single (male) parent families.

Fathers have an important role as secondary attachment figures and have a more playful and physically active relationships with their children.

- **E** – This would cause a systematic bias in the results which do not reflect the mother's genuine experiences.
- **L** – This means that the data obtained by Schaffer and Emerson may be unreliable and might not represent mother–infant relationships.

- **E** – Firstly, this means that the sample may not represent other social groups and secondly, the results might not apply today.
- **L** – This means that the biased sample may lack population and historical validity.

- **E** – However, Rutter (1995) argued that all attachments figures are equivalent and are integrated to produce an infant's overall attachment type.
- **L** – This suggests that Schaffer and Emerson may have undervalued the importance of secondary attachments and their role in the development of different attachment types.

A LEVEL ONLY ZONE

 P – Another criticism of Schaffer and Emerson's research comes from...

...cross-cultural research.

- **E** – Sagi *et al.* (1994) found that infants raised in family-based arrangements (individualistic cultures) were twice as close to their mothers, in comparison to those raised in communal environments (collectivist cultures).
- **E** – These results suggest that attachments are culturally specific.
- **L** –Consequently, Schaffer and Emerson's stages of attachment may only apply to individualistic cultures and not collectivist cultures.

P – A final criticism of Schaffer and Emerson's research is...

...the use of stage theories.

- **E** – Stage theories suggest that development occurs in a specific sequence.
- **E** – As a result, development is inflexible and according to Schaffer and Emerson single attachments must come before multiple attachments, which in some situations and cultures may not be correct.
- **L** – This is problematic because these stages become a standard by which families are judged and may be classified as abnormal.

CHOOSE THE RIGHT ANSWER

Jack is a seven-month-old infant who is currently at the discriminate attachment stage. Which of the following behaviours is not usually found at this stage?

A Jack cries when his mother puts him down. ☐

B Jack is easily comforted by a stranger when crying. ☐

C Jack is easily comforted by his mother when crying. ☐

D Jack protests when a stranger attempts to pick him up. ☐

Answers on page 274

DRAWING CONCLUSIONS

Schaffer and Emerson conducted an experiment into the development of attachment by examining the strength of infant attachment (specific attachment) and stranger anxiety.

What **two** conclusions can you draw from the following graph? *(4 marks)*

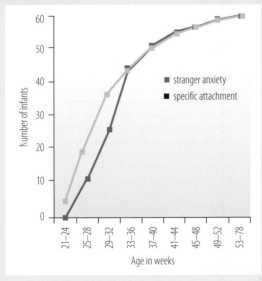

Answers on page 274

A MARKING EXERCISE

Read this student answer to the following exam question:
Outline the role of the father in the development of attachment. *(6 marks)*

Research suggests that fathers are not likely to be a primary attachment figure, because men are unable to form a bond due to their lack of emotional sensitivity. For example, Frodi *et al.* (1994) found that men are not sensitive.

Some men can form secure attachments and often have playful relationships with their children.

- Are there any mistakes in this answer?
- How many critical points has the student made?
- Could they develop their answer, either by adding more information or by elaborating any of their existing points?
- Now rewrite the answer, aiming to achieve 6 marks.

Answers on page 274

MATCH THEM UP

Match the stages of attachment (left) with the key behaviours (right).

Indiscriminate attachments	Infants can now distinguish between familiar and unfamiliar people.
The beginnings of attachment	Infants form one special attachment and start to show stranger anxiety.
Discriminate attachment	After forming one main attachment, the infant develops a wider circle of attachments.
Multiple attachments	Infants start to show a preference for social stimuli, in comparison to inanimate objects.

Answers on page 274

KEY TERM

- Imprinting

Possible essay question…

Describe and evaluate animal studies of attachment. *(12 marks AS, 16 marks A)*

Other possible exam questions…

+ Outline **one** animal study of attachment. In your answer, include what the researchers did and what they found. *(6 marks)*

+ Describe Lorenz's research related to attachment. *(4 marks)*

+ Outline what animal studies have shown about attachment. *(4 marks)*

MUST know …

Lorenz (1935)

Lorenz investigated **imprinting** in baby geese (goslings).

He divided a clutch of gosling eggs into two groups. One group was left with their natural mother, while the other group was placed in an incubator. When the group that was placed in the incubator hatched, the first moving thing they saw was Lorenz and they soon started following him around.

Lorenz marked the two groups (to distinguish them) and placed them together again. Lorenz and their natural mother were present and the goslings quickly divided themselves up, one group following Lorenz and one group following their natural mother.

 One strength of Lorenz's research comes from…

…later research support.

- *E* – Guiton (1966) replicated the findings of Lorenz with leghorn chicks. Guiton found that leghorn chicks, exposed to yellow rubber gloves for feeding, became imprinted on the gloves.

 However, one criticism of Lorenz's research is…

…his concept of 'imprinting'.

- *E* – The original concept of imprinting is that an image is stamped irreversibly on the nervous system. However, it is now believed that imprinting is more flexible.

 One criticism of Harlow's research is…

…the lack of control of the two 'mothers'.

- *E* – The two wire monkeys varied in more ways than just being cloth-covered or not and the two heads were very different. One possibility is that the cloth-covered monkey was more attractive than the bare wire monkey.

SHOULD know …

Harlow (1959)

Harlow created two wire monkeys. One wire mother was wrapped in a soft cloth, while the other was left bare. Eight infant monkeys were examined. For four monkeys the milk bottle was attached to the cloth covered mother, while for the other four it was attached to the bare wire mother. Harlow measured the amount of time each monkey spent with the two different mothers.

All eight monkeys spent most of their time with the cloth-covered monkey.

These findings suggest that infants do not develop an attachment to the 'person' who feeds them, but to the person offering contact comfort.

- *E* – This shows that young animals are not born with a predisposition to imprint to specific type of object, but develop their imprinting behaviour to any moving object within a critical window of development.
- *L* – This supports the findings of Lorenz within a different species and suggests that attachment behaviours are innate, not learnt.

- *E* – For example, Guiton (1966) found that he could reverse the imprinting in chickens who had initially tried to mate with a rubber glove and that after spending time with their own species, they engaged in normal sexual behaviour.
- *L* – This shows that imprinting is no different from other types of learning and the effects are not irreversible, as Lorenz originally proposed.

- *E* – The two different heads might have acted as a confounding variable with the infant monkeys spending more time with the cloth-covered monkey because it was more attractive.
- *L* – This suggests that Harlow's conclusion lacks internal validity, as the two 'mothers' were not appropriately controlled.

A LEVEL ONLY ZONE

 P – **One weakness of animal research is…**

…the issue of generalisation.

- *E* – The aim of animal research is to generalise the conclusions to human behaviour, however humans differ in many ways to animals.
- *E* – However, Harlow's research has been supported by Schaffer and Emerson, who found that infants do not always attach to the person who feeds them.
- *L* – This suggests that the conclusions of animal research should be treated with caution, unless the findings have been replicated in humans.

P – **A final consideration of animal research is..**

…the ethical implications of experimenting on animals.

- *E* – Harlow's research caused lasting emotional harm, as the infant monkeys later found it difficult to form relationships with their peers.
- *E* – However, some psychologists argue that animal research can be justified in terms of the effect it has on our knowledge of attachment and the development of better care for human infants.
- *L* – This suggests that the benefits of animal research outweigh the costs.

CHOOSE THE RIGHT ANSWER

Which of the following statements best describes imprinting?

A An innate tendency to develop a strong bond, during a critical period. ☐

B An ability to attach to the first moving object an infant sees. ☐

C A critical window when attachments form. ☐

D A critical window in which infants learnt to attach. ☐

Answers on page 274

 WRITE YOUR OWN EVALUATION POINT

Complete the burger paragraph below, filling in the blanks.

Point	One weakness of animal research is the issue of _____.
Evidence	The aim of animal research, like Lorenz and Harlow, is to _____ the results/conclusions to _____ behaviour.
Explain	However, Harlow's research has been supported by _____, who found
Link	This suggests

 SPOT THE MISTAKES

Read this student answer to the following question:
Describe Lorenz's research related to attachment. *(4 marks)*

There are **four** mistakes – draw a circle around each.

> Lorenz investigated imprinting in adult geese and divided his goslings into three groups. One group was left with their natural mother, one group was placed in an incubator and one group acted as a control.
>
> The group which hatched in the incubator imprinted onto the first moving object they saw which was Lorenz and started following him around. Lorenz then marked the two groups and placed them together again. All of the goslings started following their natural mother. This suggests that goslings imprint onto the first moving object they see.

Answers on page 274

 A MARKING EXERCISE

Read this student answer to the following exam question:
Describe Lorenz's research related to attachment. *(4 marks)*

> The aim of Lorenz's research was to investigate imprinting in baby geese. He divided a group of goslings into two groups. One was left with their natural mother, while the other was placed in an incubator. When the group in the incubator hatched, the first moving object they saw was Lorenz and they soon started to follow him around, even when he went swimming.

• Are there any mistakes in this answer?
• Has the student outlined the following:
  • Aim
  • Procedure
  • Findings
  • Conclusion

• Now rewrite the answer, ensuring that all four points are included, and aiming to achieve 4 marks.

Answers on page 275

KEY TERMS

- Classical conditioning
- Learning theory
- Operant conditioning
- Social learning theory

Possible essay question...

Describe and evaluate the learning explanation of attachment. *(12 marks AS, 16 marks A)*

Other possible exam questions...

+ Explain the development of attachments using learning theory. *(4 marks)*
+ Explain **one** criticism of the learning theory explanation of attachment. *(4 marks)*
+ Outline research findings which challenge the learning theory of attachment. *(4 marks)*

 Exam tip

When you describe learning theory you MUST be able to apply the principles of conditioning to the development of attachment.

MUST know ...

Classical conditioning

Classical conditioning claims that food is an **unconditioned stimulus (UCS)** which produces an **unconditioned response (UCR)** of pleasure.

During the infant's early weeks, certain things become associated with food because they are present when the infant is fed, most notably the mother, who is referred to as a **neutral stimulus (NS)**.

If a neutral stimulus is associated regularly with the UCS, it will produce the same response as the UCS which is pleasure. At this stage, the NS becomes a **conditioned stimulus (CS)** which produces a **conditioned response (CR)**. Learning theorists called this newly formed stimulus-response 'mother love'.

 One criticism of learning theory is that...

...a lot of the supporting research is based on animals.

- **E** – Learning theory is based on studies with non-human animals, such as Pavlov's research on dogs and Skinner's research on pigeons.

 Another criticism of learning theory is...

...the emphasis placed on food.

- **E** – Research by Harlow (1959) demonstrated that infant rhesus monkeys were most attached to a wire monkey that provided contact comfort and not food.

 However, one strength of learning theory is...

...its explanatory power.

- **E** – According to learning theory, infants do learn through association and reinforcement; however, food may not be the most important reinforcer.

SHOULD know ...

Operant conditioning

Dollar and Miller (1950) offered an explanation of attachment based on operant conditioning and drive reduction theory.

When an infant is hungry, this causes discomfort, so the infant is driven to reduce these unpleasant feelings.

Consequently, when the infant is fed, this discomfort is reduced and the feeding produces feelings of pleasure, known as **positive reinforcement**. The food becomes a primary reinforcer and the person who supplies the food becomes a secondary reinforcer and a source of pleasure in his/her own right. As a result, attachments occur because the child seeks the person who can supply the reward.

- **E** – Behaviourists argue that humans are no different from animals in terms of learning. However, non-behaviourists argue that attachments are far too complex to be explained in such simple terms.
- **L** – This matters because behaviourist explanations may present an oversimplified version of human behaviour and attachment.

- **E** – Learning theory suggests that food is a key element in attachment, whereas research on infant monkeys suggests that food is not the most important factor.
- **L** – This suggests that the learning explanation of attachment is oversimplified and ignores other important factors, such as contact comfort.

- **E** – It is possible that parental attention and responsiveness are important factors that assist in the formation of attachment; however, the basic principles of learning theory are supported.
- **L** – This shows that even though learning theory does not provide a complete explanation of attachment, it still has some value.

A LEVEL ONLY ZONE

 P – Another criticism of learning theory is that...

...drive theory is outdated.

- **E** – Although drive theory was popular in the 1940s, there are many examples of human behaviour that increase discomfort.
- **E** – For example, some people engage in extreme activities, such as bungee jumping, which actually increase discomfort.
- **L** – This suggests that humans are not always motivated to reduce discomfort and that the underlying principles of drive theory are outdated.

 P – A final criticism of learning theory is that...

...that Bowlby's theory may provide a better explanation.

- **E** – Bowlby's theory (see pages 82–83) has many advantages in comparison to learning theory.
- **E** – For example, Bowlby's theory can explain why attachments form, whereas learning theory only explains how attachments form. Furthermore, Bowlby's theory outlines the benefits of attachment, which are not explained through learning theory.
- **L** – This shows that Bowlby's theory provides a more complete explanation of attachment.

✔ CHOOSE THE RIGHT ANSWER

Tick **two** of the boxes below to indicate which of the following statements relate to the learning theory of attachment.

A	Infants become attached to the person who feeds them.	☐
B	Infants are born with an innate tendency to form attachments.	☐
C	Attachments are based on the principles of classical conditioning, operant conditioning and drive reduction theory.	☐
D	Infants form attachments for contact comfort and not food.	☐

Answers on page 275

◉ SPOT THE MISTAKES

Read this student answer to the following exam question:
Explain the development of attachments using learning theory. *(4 marks)*

There are **four** mistakes – draw a circle around each.

According to learning theory, attachments are formed through classical or operant conditioning. Food is a neutral stimulus (NS) which produces an unconditioned response (UCR) of pleasure. During the first few weeks an infant learns to associate the person who feeds them, usually the father, with the pleasure from feeding. Through regular association, the mother becomes a conditioned response (CR), producing a conditioned stimulus (CS). Learning theorists refer to this newly formed stimulus–response as 'mother love' and suggest that attachments occur through feeding.

Answers on page 275

💡 COMPLETE THE DIAGRAM

Match the key terms below with the diagram on the left.

Before conditioning

1.

2.

3.

4.

During conditioning

5.

After conditioning

6.

7.

- Pleasure (UCR)

- No response

- NS is now CS

- Mother (NS)

- Pleasure (CR)

- Food (UCS)

- NS and UCS paired

Answers on page 275

⚙ APPLYING YOUR KNOWLEDGE

Using your knowledge of explanations of attachment: learning theory, answer the following.

Identify the psychology		Link to Sam
	When baby Nathan was born, his father Jon stopped working to stay at home and look after him, while his mother Sophie returned to work.	
	Nathan's mother continues to work full-time and does not have much to do with his care. Now that Nathan is ten months old, he has a particularly close relationship with his father.	
	Use your knowledge of learning theory, explain how Nathan became attached to his father.	

Answers on page 275

KEY TERMS

- Continuity hypothesis
- Critical period
- Internal working model
- Monotropy
- Social releasers

Possible essay question…

Discuss Bowlby's monotropic theory of attachment. *(12 marks AS, 16 marks A)*

Other possible exam questions…

+ Explain what the term *monotropic* means. *(2 marks)*
+ Outline Bowbly's monotropic theory of attachment. *(4 marks)*
+ Briefly outline **one** research study that supports Bowlby's theory of attachment. *(3 marks)*

MUST know …

Bowlby's monotropic attachment theory (1969) of 'how' and 'why' attachments form

Attachments serve an important survival function, as remaining close to an adult aids survival.

According to Bowlby, infants have an innate drive to become attached, which takes place during a **critical period** of three to six months. Infants who do not form an attachment during this time will have difficulty forming an attachment later on.

Babies are born with particular features that elicit caring behaviours from their caregivers, for example smiling and having a 'babyface'. These behaviours are known as **social releasers**, which explain 'how' infants become attached.

Infants form one special emotional bond with their primary attachment relationship, known as **monotropy**.

 One strength of Bowlby's theory comes from…

…early infant behaviours.

- *E* – According to Bowlby, infants become attached during a critical period of three to six months, at the same time human infants start to crawl.

 However, one criticism of Bowlby's theory is…

…the idea of a 'critical period'.

- *E* – Evidence from Rutter *et al.* found that although the idea of a critical period is true to an extent, infants are still able to form an attachment outside this window.

 Another strength of Bowlby's theory comes from…

…research support for 'monotropy'.

- *E* – Prior and Glaser (2006) concluded, that a hierarchical model of attachment, which places emphasis on one central person 'higher' than others, is more likely than multiple attachments.

SHOULD know …

The consequences of attachment

The monotropic relationship provides the infant with a mental representation of relationships, known as an **internal working model**. The internal working model serves two functions: 1) it provides the child with an insight into the caregiver's behaviour and allows the child to influence his/her caregiver's behaviour and 2) it provides a template for all future relationships.

Finally, Bowlby put forward the **continuity hypothesis** which states that an infant's internal working model will influence his/her later adult relationships. Infants who are strongly attached are more likely to have socially and emotionally competent relationships in later life.

- *E* – It is therefore vital that infants form and maintain an attachment during this time, so that their caregivers can protect them.
- *L* – This supports Bowlby's theory and the view that attachments are adaptive.

- *E* – Researchers now use the term 'sensitive period' to illustrate the possibility that infants can still form attachments after six months.
- *L* – This suggests that Bowlby's original idea of a 'critical' period was not accurate and the term 'sensitive' period may be more appropriate.

- *E* – This central person has special significance and contributes to healthy emotional development.
- *L*– This supports Bowlby's concept of monotropy and the idea that one special attachment plays a significance role in emotional development.

 P – Further support for Bowlby's theory comes from …

…the Minnesota parent–child study.

- *E* – Sroufe *et al.* (2005) followed participants from infancy to late adolescence and found continuity between early attachments and later emotional/social behaviour.
- *E* – Individuals who were classified as securely attached in infancy were rated highly for social competence later in childhood. Furthermore, they were less isolated, more popular and more empathetic.
- *L* – This supports Bowlby's continuity hypothesis, as it demonstrates a clear link between early and later attachments.

P – A final criticism of Bowlby's theory comes from…

…the temperament hypothesis.

- *E* – Belsky and Rovine (1987) found that infants between one and three days old who had signs of behavioural instability (were more 'difficult') were later judged to be insecurely attached.
- *E* – This suggests that an infant's innate emotional personality (their 'temperament') may explain their later attachment behaviour.
- *L* – This supports the temperament hypothesis and suggests that Bowlby's monotropic theory may not provide a complete explanation of attachment.

A LEVEL ONLY ZONE

✓ CHOOSE THE RIGHT ANSWER

Tick **two** of the boxes below to indicate which of the following statements relate to Bowlby's theory of attachment.

A Infants are innately programmed to form attachments.	☐
B Attachments must take place during a critical period.	☐
C Infants form attachments based on classical conditioning and operant conditioning.	☐
D Attachments must take place during a sensitive period.	☐

Answers on page 275

An idea 👍

The key elements of Bowlby's theory are:
1 Innate
2 Social releasers
3 Critical period
4 Monotropy
5 Internal working model
6 Continuity hypothesis.

Create a mnemonic with the first letter of each word (I, S, C, M, I, C) to help you remember these key terms.

🧩 MATCH THEM UP

Match the key terms on the left with the definitions on the right.

Continuity hypothesis	The idea that the one relationship that the infant has with his/her primary attachment figure is of special significance in emotional development.
Critical period	The idea that emotionally secure infants go on to be emotionally secure, trusting and socially confident adults.
Internal working model	A social behaviour or characteristic that elicits caregiving and leads to attachment.
Monotropy	A biologically determined period of time, during which certain characteristics can develop. Outside of this time window such development will not be possible.
Social releasers	A mental model of the world which enables individuals to predict and control their environment. In the case of attachment the model relates to a person's expectations about relationships.

Answers on page 275

⚙ APPLYING YOUR KNOWLEDGE

Using your knowledge of explanations of attachment: Bowlby's theory, answer the following.

Shelia takes her newborn daughter Jane to her friend's house. Her friend comments: "Isn't Jane beautiful, with those big blue eyes and her cute round face." Shelia replies: "She might be cute, however she is always crying for my attention."

Explain how Liza has become attached to her mother.

Identify the psychology	Link to Bowlby's theory
	This means that…
	This means that…

Answers on page 275

KEY TERMS

- Insecure-avoidant
- Insecure-resistant
- Secure attachment
- Strange Situation

Possible essay question...

Describe and evaluate the Strange Situation. *(12 marks AS, 16 marks A)*

Other possible exam questions...

+ Identify and explain **one** type of attachment. *(2 marks)*
+ Outline the Strange Situation procedure. *(4 marks)*
+ Explain **one** limitation of using the Strange Situation to investigate attachment. *(3 marks)*
+ Evaluate the Strange Situation as a method for investigating types of attachment. *(4 marks)*
+ Explain how the behaviour of a child showing insecure-resistant attachment would be different from the behaviour of a child showing insecure-avoidant. *(4 marks)*

MUST know ...

The Strange Situation

Ainsworth *et al.* (1971, 78) devised the Strange Situation to see how infants would behave under conditions of mild stress.

The procedure consists of eight episodes, designed to highlight four key behaviours: use of parent as a secure base, stranger anxiety, separation anxiety and reunion behaviours.

The infants are observed using a video recorder or one-way mirror, with their behaviour being recorded every 15 seconds.

Ainsworth combined the data of several studies and identified three main patterns of behaviour which are now referred to as: **secure attachment**, **insecure-avoidant attachment** and **insecure-resistant attachment**.

 One criticism of Ainsworth's analysis comes from...

...later research into attachment.

- **E** – Main and Solomon (1986) analysed over 200 Strange Situation videotapes and put forward a fourth attachment type – insecure-disorganised (Type D).

 One strength of the Strange Situation is...

...the reliability of the observations.

- **E** – Ainsworth *et al.* (1978) found almost perfect inter-observer reliability of .94, suggesting high agreement among the different observers in terms of exploratory behaviour.

 Another strength of the Strange Situation is...

...the application of the research to improving children's lives.

- **E** – The Circle of Security Project teaches caregivers to understand their infants' signals of distress and this project found an increase in the number of infants classified as securely attached (from 32% to 40%).

SHOULD know ...

Types of attachment

Securely attached infants (Type B) use their caregivers as a secure base to explore the environment. They are not likely to cry if their caregiver leaves and show some distress when left with a stranger. When feeling anxious they are easily soothed by their caregivers.

Insecure-avoidant infants (Type A) are happy to explore the environment with or without their caregiver. They show little response to separation and show little or no social interaction and intimacy with others.

Insecure-resistant infants (Type C) seek and resist social interaction with others. They show high levels of separation anxiety and stranger anxiety. When reunited with their caregivers, these children show conflicting behaviours and resist being picked up.

- **E** – These infants don't conform to one of Ainsworth's original attachment types, as they show a very strong attachment behaviour which is often followed by avoidant behaviour.
- **L** – This suggests Ainsworth's original conclusions were too simplistic and do not account for all attachment behaviours.

- **E** – High inter-observer reliability suggests that the observations can be accepted as being reliable and Ainsworth's observations had almost perfect reliability.
- **L** – This suggests that the Strange Situation is a reliable method for examining attachment.

- **E** – Therefore, teaching caregivers to understand their infants can improve and change an infants' attachment type.
- **L** – This supports the research on attachment types, because the application of such research has been used to improve lives.

A LEVEL ONLY ZONE

 P – One criticism of the Strange Situation is...

...the low level of internal validity.

- **E** – Main and Weston (1981) found that children behaved differently in the Strange Situation, depending on which parent they are with.
- **E** – Therefore, the Strange Situation may be measuring an infant's relationship with a particular parent and not a personal characteristic.
- **L** – This suggests that the Strange Situation may lack internal validity as the observation may be measuring individual relationships.

 P – One criticism of Ainsworth's findings comes from...

...research on maternal sensitivity.

- **E** – Raval *et al.* (2001) found low correlations between measures of maternal sensitivity and the strength of attachment. Furthermore, Slade *et al.* (2005) found a greater role for 'maternal reflective functioning'.
- **E** – Reflexive functioning is the ability to understand what someone else is thinking.
- **L** – This suggests that reflective functioning may be a central mechanism in establishing attachment types and not maternal sensitivity.

CHOOSE THE RIGHT ANSWER

Tick **two** of the boxes below to indicate which statements best describe the behaviour of an insecure-avoidant child, in the Strange Situation.

A	The infant is happy to explore the environment without their caregiver.	☐
B	The infant uses their caregiver as a secure base.	☐
C	The infant resists social interaction with others.	☐
D	The infant shows low levels of separation anxiety.	☐

Answers on page 275

RESEARCH ISSUES

A psychologist investigated the relationship between type of attachment in childhood and success in later adult relationships. He published a questionnaire in a local newspaper. The participants were people who read the newspaper, who filled in the questionnaire and sent it to the psychologist. Participants' answers to the questions were used to decide whether they had been securely or insecurely attached as children. The participants who were identified as securely attached children were more likely to have successful adult relationships than those identified as insecurely attached children.

Identify one ethical issue the researcher would need to consider in this research. Suggest how the researcher could deal with this ethical issue. *(3 marks)*

Answers on page 275

COMPLETE THE TABLE

Complete the table below with the key behaviours found for each type of attachment. The possible answers can be found in the final column.

	Secure attachment (Type B)	Insecure-avoidant (Type A)	Insecure-resistant (Type C)	Possible answers...
Willingness to explore				• Low
				• High
				• High
Stranger anxiety				• Low
				• High
				• Moderate
Separation anxiety				• Easy to soothe
				• Distressed
				• Indifferent
Behaviour on reunion with caregiver				• Avoids contact
				• Seeks and rejects
				• Enthusiastic

Answers on page 276

APPLYING YOUR KNOWLEDGE

Using your knowledge of Ainsworth's Strange Situation: types of attachment, answer the following.

Identify the type of attachment		Link to the extract
Ashley	Ashley and Alex are 18 months old. They are observed individually using Ainsworth's Strange Situation. Ashley moves around the room and plays with toys in the corner. She pays little attention to her mother and does not even notice her mother leave the room. She then avoids her mother when she later returns.	
Alex	Alex however does not move around the room and cries intensely when her mother leaves. When her mother returns, she angrily resists being picked up and is difficult to comfort. Use your knowledge of the Strange Situation to suggest Ashley and Alex's attachment type. Link your answer to the extract.	

Answers on page 276

Possible essay question...
Describe and evaluate research on cultural variations in attachment. Refer to evidence in your answer. *(12 marks AS, 16 marks A)*

Other possible exam questions...
+ Describe research by Van IJzendoorn on cultural variations in attachment. *(6 marks)*
+ Explain **one** criticism of research on cultural variations in attachment. *(4 marks)*

 Think

A meta-analysis is where a researcher looks at the findings from a number of different studies and produces a statistic to represent the overall effect.

MUST know ...

Van IJzendoorn and Kroonenberg (1988)

Van IJzendoorn and Kroonenberg conducted a meta-analysis of the findings from 32 studies of attachment behaviour, from eight different countries.

They found that secure attachment was the most common in every country. Insecure-avoidant attachment was the next most common in every country except Israel and Japan, which are two collectivist cultures. In terms of variation within cultures, they found that this was 1.5 times higher than the variation between cultures.

The results suggest that the global pattern of attachment is similar to the US and that secure attachment is the best for healthy social and emotional development.

 One issue with cultural variations in attachment is that...

...similarities may not be innately determined.
- **E** – Van IJzendoorn and Kroonenberg suggest that some cultural similarities might be explained by the media (e.g. TV and books) and not an innate disposition.

 Another issue with cultural variations in attachment is that...

...the findings are based on countries, not cultures.
- **E** – Van IJzendoorn and Sagi (2001) examined attachment in Tokyo and found a similar distribution of attachment types to the Western studies, whereas a more rural sample found an increase in insecure-resistant individuals.

 Furthermore, a criticism of cross-cultural research is that...

...the research 'tools' lack validity.
- **E** – The Strange Situation has certain cultural assumptions that are specific to its country of origin (America). For example, the Strange Situation assumes that 'willingness to explore' is a sign of secure attachment.

SHOULD know ...

Other cultural differences

Grossmann and Grossman (1991) found that German infants are more likely to be insecurely rather than securely attached. This may be the result of German childrearing practices which do not engage in proximity seeking behaviours in the Strange Situation, therefore leading to an insecure classification.

Takahashi (1990) used the Strange Situation with Japanese infants and their mothers and found normal rates of secure attachment but higher rates of insecure-resistant attachment (32%). The Japanese infants were particularly distressed when left alone, which might be the result of different childrearing practices, as Japanese infants are rarely separated from their mothers.

- **E** – The media presents ideas about parenting, so it is possible that children all over the world are exposed to similar parenting, as a result of media and not an innate attachment type.
- **L** – This suggests that the similarities found in Van IJzendoorn and Kroonenberg's research may be the result of a global media culture, rather than innate biological influences.

- **E** – These results highlight the variation within one country and provide support to Van IJzendoorn and Kroonenberg's original claim, that there is more variation within than between cultures.
- **L** – This suggests that cultural variations may not be comparing cultures after all, and that the term 'cultural variations' should be used with caution.

- **E** – These cultural assumptions may not be true of all cultures and research in Japan (Van IJzendoorn and Sagi, 2001) highlights that dependence rather than independence would be a sign of secure attachment.
- **L** – This suggests that the Strange Situation may lack validity in other cultures and could result in the misclassification of attachment types.

 P – Another issue with cross cultural research is...

...the cultural bias of attachment theory.
- **E** – Rothbaum *et al.* (2000) claims that the attachment theory is rooted in American culture.
- **E** – Furthermore, Rothbaum found that Japanese children demonstrate an inhibition of emotional expression and preference to group- rather than self-orientated behaviour.
- **L** – This suggests the high levels of insecure-resistant attachment found in Japanese children, may be the result of a cultural bias in attachment theory.

 P – One strength of cross-cultural research is...

...the development of universal principles of attachment.
- **E** – Posada and Jacobs (2011) note that there is a lot of evidence that supports the idea of underlying principles of attachment.
- **E** – For example, China, Colombia and Germany all support the idea that maternal sensitivity leads to secure attachment.
- **L** – Therefore, even though the expression of maternal sensitivity and behaviours found in securely attached children may vary across cultures, the core concepts are the same.

SPOT THE MISTAKES

Read the student answer to the following exam question:
Explain **one** criticism of research on cultural variations in attachment.
(4 marks)

There are **three** mistakes – draw a circle around each.

> One problem with cultural variations in attachment is that many of
> the results are based on cultures and not individual countries. VanI
> Jzendoorn and Sagi (2001) found a different distribution of attachment in
> Tokyo to Western countries. Furthermore, they also found that more rural
> regions had an increase in insecure-resistant individuals, in comparison
> to less rural regions. This suggests that cultural variations may not be
> comparing cultures but are in fact comparing different countries.

Answers on page 276

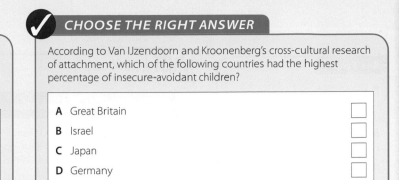 **CHOOSE THE RIGHT ANSWER**

According to Van IJzendoorn and Kroonenberg's cross-cultural research
of attachment, which of the following countries had the highest
percentage of insecure-avoidant children?

A Great Britain ☐

B Israel ☐

C Japan ☐

D Germany ☐

Answers on page 276

 DRAWING A CONCLUSION

A psychologist conducted a meta-analysis of the results of the Strange
Situation studies from different countries. The results are detailed below.

Country	% of each type of attachment		
	Insecure-avoidant (Type A)	Secure (Type B)	Insecure-resistant (Type C)
Country A	9	61	30
Country B	24	63	13
Country C	23	67	4

What does the table show about cultural variations in attachment? *(4 marks)*

Answers on page 276

 APPLYING YOUR KNOWLEDGE

Using your knowledge of cultural variations in attachment, answer the following.

Identify the psychology		Link to Yuna's behaviour…

Yuna comes from a Japanese family. Her parents wish to raise her following Japanese traditions. Yuna took part in a research project where her attachment type was assessed in the Strange Situation.

Explain how Yuna may have reacted in the Strange Situation. *(4 marks)*

Answers on page 276

KEY TERM

■ Deprivation

Possible essay question...

Describe and evaluate Bowlby's theory of maternal deprivation.
(12 marks AS, 16 marks A)

Other possible exam questions...

+ Explain what is meant by maternal deprivation.
  (4 marks)

+ Outline research into maternal deprivation.
  (6 marks)

MUST know ...

Theory of maternal deprivation

Bowlby (1951, 1953) proposed that prolonged emotional deprivation would have long-term consequences on emotional development.

Bowlby placed an important emphasis on maternal care and believed that infants and children need a 'warm, intimate and continuous relationship with a mother (or mother-substitute)' for normal mental health.

Furthermore, according to Bowlby, early childhood separation will only have an effect if it takes place during the critical period of development – before the age of two and a half years old. Therefore, the potential damage can be avoided if suitable emotional care is provided by a mother-substitute.

 One criticism of Bowlby's theory is...

...that emotional separation is ignored.

• **E** – Radke-Yarrow *et al.* (1985) found that 55% of children with severely depressed mothers were insecurely attached, in comparison to 29% of children with non-depressed mothers.

 One strength of Bowlby's theory comes from...

...research support.

• **E** – Bifulco *et al.* (1992) found that women who had experienced separation from their mothers were more likely to experience depression or an anxiety disorder, compared to those who had no experience of separation.

Another strength of Bowlby's theory is...

...the application to childrearing practices.

• **E** – Before Bowlby's research, children were separated from their parents when they spent time in hospital. Furthermore, parents were discouraged from visiting or even forbidden from seeing their children.

SHOULD know ...

Bowlby (1944) – 44 juvenile thieves

Bowlby studied 88 children who were patients at the Child Guidance Clinic in London.

All of the children were emotionally maladjusted. 44 of the children were 'thieves' and the other 44 children were used a control group. Bowlby found that 14 of the thieves showed little sign of affection, shame or sense of responsibility – a group he called 'affectionless psychopaths'.

Bowlby found that 12 out of 14 (86%) affectionless psychopaths experienced frequent early separation from their mothers, in comparison to just 17% of the other thieves. These findings suggest that early childhood separations are linked to affectionless psychopathy.

• **E** – Therefore, even though depressed mothers are physically present, they may be unable to provide suitable emotional care, thus depriving their children.

• **L** – This suggests that psychological separation can also lead to deprivation, in the same way as physical separation.

• **E** – Furthermore, the mental health problems were much greater in those women whose loss occurred before the age of six.

• **L** – This supports Bowlby's idea of a critical period, suggesting that early childhood deprivation can lead to later vulnerability for depression and anxiety disorders.

• **E** – However, Bowlby's work led to major changes in the way children are cared for in hospitals. For example, parents are encouraged to visit their children and there is greater flexibility in terms of visiting hours.

• **L** – This demonstrates the positive application of Bowlby's research to improving childrearing practices in hospitals.

A LEVEL ONLY ZONE

 P – Another criticism of Bowlby's theory is...

...that the individual differences of children are ignored.

• **E** – Bowlby *et al.* (1956) studied 60 children under the age of four who had TB (tuberculosis). These children experienced prolonged separation while in hospital.

• **E** – When the children were assessed in adolescence there were no significant differences in terms of intellectual development.

• **L** – Bowlby suggested that those children who had coped better during their hospitalisation may have been more securely attached and therefore more resilient, suggesting that individual differences may be an important factor when examining the effects of deprivation.

 P – A final criticism of Bowlby is...

...the clarity of his definition of deprivation.

• **E** – Rutter (1981) claimed that Bowlby did not make it clear whether the attachment bond had formed but been broken, or never formed at all.

• **E** – Rutter suggested that there is a distinction between privation (the failure to form an attachment) and deprivation (where an attachment bond is broken).

• **L** – This matters because according to Rutter there is a key distinction between deprivation and privation, and a lack of clarity may affect the validity of research findings.

WRITE YOUR OWN EVALUATION POINT

Complete the evaluation point below by answering the questions in the evidence, explain and link boxes. Try not to refer back to the previous page.

Point	One strength of Bowlby's theory comes from research support.
Evidence	What did Bifulco et al. (1992) find?
Explain	Explain how these results relate to Bowlby's theory.
Link	How does this support the idea of a 'critical period'?

CHOOSE THE RIGHT ANSWER

Tick **two** of the boxes below to indicate which of the following are true in relation to Bowlby's theory of maternal deprivation.

A Maternal deprivation has a short-term effect on emotional development. ☐

B Childhood separation will have a significant effect if it takes place before the age of two and a half years old. ☐

C Maternal deprivation has a long-term effect on emotional development. ☐

D Childhood separation will have no effect during the critical period of development. ☐

Answers on page 276

RESEARCH ISSUES

Bowlby studied 88 children who were patients at the Child Guidance Clinic in London. Bowlby conducted interviews with the parents to find out if the children had experienced early childhood separation.

Identify one issue with the use of interviews that the researcher would need to consider in this research and how the researcher may overcome this issue. *(3 marks)*

Hint: 1) You should state the issue. 2) You should explain why this is an issue. 3) Finally, you should state how the researcher can overcome this issue.

Answers on page 276

APPLYING YOUR KNOWLEDGE

Identify the psychology		Link to Abdul's behaviour
	Abdul's parents both passed away in a car accident when he was six months old, at which point he was placed into care. He was later adopted at five years old, but struggled to form a relationship with his new adoptive parents. His behaviour is sometimes problematic, he is aggressive towards his younger siblings and often gets into trouble at school. Use your knowledge of Bowlby's theory of maternal deprivation to explain Abdul's behaviour. You should refer to research in your answer. *(6 marks)* 	

KEY TERM

■ Institutionalisation

Possible essay question...

Discuss research related to the effects of institutionalisation. *(12 marks AS, 16 marks A)*

Other possible exam questions...

+ Outline **one** study of Romanian orphans. Include details of what the researcher(s) did and what they found. *(6 marks)*

+ Outline the effects of institutionalisation on the development of attachment. *(2 marks)*

MUST know ...

Rutter and Songua-Barke (2010)

Rutter and Sonuga-Barke examined 165 Romanian children who spent their early lives in a Romanian institution. 111 of the children were adopted before the age of two and 54 by the age of four.

Their physical, cognitive and social development was examined using interviews with parents and teachers. Their progress was compared with 52 British children who were adopted before they were six months old.

By the age of four, some of the Romanian children had caught up with the British children. However, those adopted after six months showed significant deficits and signs of disinhibited attachment, highlighting the long-term consequences of institutionalisation.

 One criticism of institutionalisation research is ...

...that individual differences of children may play an important role.

- *E* – Although some research suggests that individuals who do not form an attachment within the sensitive period are unable to recover, this is not true of all children.

 One strength of institutionalisation research is...

...the application of it to improving childrens' lives.

- *E* – The research of Bowlby (see pages 88–89) changed the way that children were looked after so that much more focus was given when children were hospitalised.

 Another strength of institutionalisation research is...

...the value of longitudinal studies.

- *E* – Longitudinal studies take a lot of time and planning; however, the benefits are large.

SHOULD know ...

Effects of institutionalisation

Research has found four key effects of institutionalisation, including:

1 **Physical underdevelopment** – the lack of nourishment and emotional care can lead to deprivation dwarfism.

2 **Intellectual underfunctioning** – emotional deprivation can affect cognitive development.

3 **Disinhibited attachment** – a form of attachment where children treat near-strangers with overfriendliness.

4 **Poor parenting** – research has found (Quinton *et al.*, 1984) that women raised in institutions experience difficulties acting as parents in later life, in comparison to women raised at home.

- *E* – Some children are not strongly affected by institutionalisation and Rutter suggested that some children in institutions might receive special attention, possibly because they smiled more and had some type of attachment experience.
- *L* – This suggests that the findings of institutionalisation research are not universal and some children can recover from the negative effects of institutionalisation.

- *E* – Furthermore, the process of adoption has changed so that mothers who give a baby up for adoption do so within the first week of birth, so that the children can form a secure attachment with their adoptive families.
- *L* – This highlights the benefit of institutionalisation research to improving the lives of children in different ways.

- *E* – Longitudinal studies allow researchers to assess the long-term effects of institutionalisation and whether the effect may disappear after sufficient time with suitable high-quality care.
- *L* – This suggests that the findings of longitudinal studies are a valid representation of the effect of institutionalisation.

A LEVEL ONLY ZONE

 P – One criticism of the Romanian orphan studies is that...

...deprivation is only one factor.

- *E* – The Romanian orphans were faced with much more than emotional deprivation. Their physical conditions were appalling, which may have also impacted their health.
- *E* – The lack of cognitive stimulation may have also affected their cognitive development.
- *L* – This suggests that researchers should be cautious when interpreting the effects of Romanian orphan studies, as there are many factors that could have affected the orphan's development.

P – A final criticism of Romanian orphan studies is that...

...the effects of institutionalisation may disappear over time.

- *E* – Le Mare and Audet found that the physical underdevelopment of children had improved by the age of 11.
- *E* – This suggests that development does continue in these children and that they may not have reached their full potential in the studies conducted so far.
- *b* – This suggests that the effects of institutionalisation may be reversible and that ex-institutional children may just need more time to recover from the negative effects of institutions.

CHOOSE THE RIGHT ANSWER

Tick **two** of the boxes below to indicate which of the following are true in relation to the effects of institutionalisation.

A Emotional deprivation can cause disinhibited attachment. ☐

B Emotional deprivation can lead to deprivation dwarfism. ☐

C Institutionalisation can lead to difficulties in parenting, later in life. ☐

D Intellectual underfunctioning is caused by disinhibited attachment. ☐

Answers on page 276

 MATCH THEM UP

Research has found four key effects of institutionalisation. Match up the key terms on the left, with the effect on the right.

Intellectual underfunctioning	Children in institutional care are usually physically small caused by a lack of emotional care and poor nourishment.
Disinhibited attachment	Children who suffer from emotional deprivation often experience poor cognitive development.
Poor parenting	Children do not discriminate between people they choose as attachment figures. Such children will treat near-strangers with inappropriate familiarity (overfriendliness) and may be attention seeking.
Physical underdevelopment	Research has found (Quinton *et al.*, 1984) that women raised in institutions experience difficulties acting as parents in later life, in comparison to women raised at home.

Answers on page 276

 RESEARCH ISSUES

The scenario in the Applying your knowledge activity below, about Alin, is an example of a case study.

A case study is a detailed study of a single individual, institution or event. Many research methods may be used, such as observations, interviews, psychological tests or experiments. Case studies are often longitudinal, following an individual over an extended period of time.

Identify **one** strength and **one** limitation with the use of a case study in this example. *(4 marks)* | One strength…

One limitation… |

Answers on page 277

⚙ **APPLYING YOUR KNOWLEDGE**

Using your knowledge of Romanian orphan studies: effects on institutionalisation, answer the following:

Research has shown that institutionalisation can have numerous negative effects on children. In the 1990s, many children were found living in awful conditions in Romanian orphanages. Alin lived in one of these orphanages from birth, but was adopted at 18 months old. Alin's development was studied for a number of years and he developed into a healthy young child.

Explain why Alin later developed into a healthy young child. You should refer to psychological research in your answer.

Identify the research	*Link to Alin*
	This shows that…
	This shows that…

Answers on page 276

KEY TERM

- Internal working model

Possible essay question...

Describe and evaluate the influence of early attachment on childhood and adult relationships. In your answer make reference to the role of the internal working model. *(12 marks AS, 16 marks A)*

Other possible exam questions...

+ Explain the role of the internal working model in the development of later relationships. *(4 marks)*

+ Outline **one** study of the influence of early attachment on childhood and adult relationships. *(6 marks)*

+ Evaluate research on the influence of early attachment on childhood and adult relationships. *(4 marks)*

MUST know ...

Hazan and Shaver (1987)

Hazan and Shaver (1987) designed a study to test the **internal working model**.

Hazan and Shaver placed a 'Love Quiz' in the *American Rocky Mountain News* which examined current attachment experiences and attachment history. The questionnaire also asked about attitudes towards love, to assess the internal working model.

620 people responded, 205 men and 415 women. There was a positive correlation between attachment type and love experiences. Securely attached adults described their love experiences as happy, friendly and trusting. In addition, a relationship was found between the conception of love and the internal working model.

 One criticism of attachment research is...

...that the research is correlational.

- *E* – One issue is that the research linking the internal working model with later relationship experiences is correlational and a cause and effect relationship cannot be established.

 Another criticism of attachment research is...

...the reliance on retrospective classification.

- *E* – Studies like Hazan and Shaver rely on adults answering questions about their early lives in order to assess infant attachment.

A final criticism of attachment research is...

...that the theories and findings are deterministic.

- *E* – The research by Hazan and Shaver suggests that very early experiences have a fixed effect on later adult relationships and therefore our adult relationships are determined by early experiences.

SHOULD know ...

Behaviours influenced by the internal working model

There are four key behaviours influenced by the internal working model, including:

1. **Childhood friendships** – are classified as securely attached in infancy score highly for social competency later in childhood.
2. **Poor parenting** – Harlow's research with monkeys demonstrates a link between poor attachment and difficulties with parenting.
3. **Romantic relationships** – Hazan and Shaver found a link between early attachment type and later relationships.
4. **Mental health** – The lack of attachment during the critical period can result in the lack of an internal working model and 'attachment disorder'.

- *E* – It is possible that attachment style and later love styles are caused by another factor – such as the child's temperament.
- *L* – This matters because researchers are unable to conclude that the internal working model determines later relationships, as there may be other factors that cause the differences found.

- *E* – Such recollections may be flawed because our memories of the past are not always accurate and the parents may be inclined to lie.
- *L* – This matters because the research findings may not be valid and therefore longitudinal studies may provide a more accurate representation of early attachment influences.

- *E* – Therefore, a child who is insecurely attached at one year of age is doomed to experience negative relationships as an adult.
- *L* – However, this is not always the case, as Simpson *et al.* (2007) concluded that the research does not suggest that an individual's past unalterably determines the future course of his/her relationships.

 A LEVEL ONLY ZONE

 P – One criticism of attachment research is...

...the low correlations found.

- *E* – Fraley (2002) conducted a review of 27 samples where infants were assessed in infancy and later reassessed (up to 20 years later) and found correlations ranging from .50 to as low as .10.
- *E* – These correlations do not suggest that attachment types are very stable.
- *L* – This matters because correlational research does not show a cause and effect relationship and low correlations indicate that the relationship found is particularly weak/unstable.

P – A final criticism of attachment research comes from...

...alternate explanations.

- *E* – Freeney (1999) suggests that adult attachment patterns may be properties of the relationship, rather than the individual.
- *E* – For example, it is possible that the adult secure relationship causes the adult attachment type.
- *L* – This matters because it is possible that another explanation can account for the findings of early attachment research and the early theories may not be correct.

CHOOSE THE RIGHT ANSWER

Tick **two** of the boxes below to indicate which of the following are true in relation to Hazan and Shaver's (1987) research.

A   Hazan and Shaver collected data through questionnaires. ☐

B   Hazan and Shaver collected data through interviews. ☐

C   No relationship was found between the conception of love and the internal working model. ☐

D   Hazan and Shaver found a correlation between attachment type and love experiences. ☐

Answers on page 277

 RESEARCH ISSUES

Hazan and Shaver placed a 'Love Quiz' in the *American Rocky Mountain News* which examined current attachment experiences and attachment history. The questionnaire also asked about attitudes towards love, to assess the internal working model.

Questionnaires like the 'Love Quiz' can be used to collect quantitative data which is then analysed using statistical tests.

Answers on page 277

Identify **one** strength and **one** limitation of using a questionnaire in this study. *(4 marks)*

 A MARKING EXERCISE

Read this student answer to the following exam question:
Explain the role of the internal working model in the development of later relationships. *(4 marks)*

Research has found that the internal working model has a significant impact on future romantic relationships. For example, Hazan and Shaver found a link between attachment type of later relationships suggesting that the internal working models lays the foundation of future adult relationships.

What mark do you think this would get?
YOUR MARK
AO1
Hint
A hint to help you decide:
How many critical points have been covered?
How much detail is there?
See marking scheme on page 8

What else could you include to improve this answer?

Answers on page 277

 FILL IN THE BOXES

The text below relates to some of the criticisms given on the opposite page.

Fill in the boxes to complete the criticisms and elaborate on them

Childhood friendships…
Securely attached children in infancy score higher in terms of social competence.

Poor parenting…

Romantic relationships…

OPTIONAL: Mental health…

Elaboration…
This was shown in the Minnestoa child-parent study and demonstrates the importance of attachment on childhood friendships.

Answers on page 277

Attachment	An emotional bond between two people. It is a two-way process that endures over time. It leads to certain behaviours such as clinging and proximity-seeking, and serves the function of protecting an infant.
Caregiver	Any person who is providing care for a child, such as a parent, grandparent, sibling, other family member, childminder and so on.
Classical conditioning	Learning through association. A neutral stimulus is consistently paired with an unconditioned stimulus so that it eventually takes on the properties of this stimulus and is able to produce a conditioned response.
Continuity hypothesis	The idea that emotionally secure infants go on to be emotionally secure, trusting and socially confident adults.
Critical period	A biologically determined period of time, during which certain characteristics can develop. Outside of this time window, such development will not be possible.
Cultural variations	The ways that different groups of people vary in terms of their social practices, and the effects these practices have on development and behaviour.
Deprivation	To be deprived is to lose something. In the context of child development, deprivation refers to the loss of emotional care that is normally provided by a primary caregiver.
Imprinting	An innate readiness to develop a strong bond with the mother which takes place during a specific time in development, probably the first few hours after birth/hatching. If it doesn't happen at this time it will probably not happen.
Insecure-avoidant	A type of attachment which describes those children who tend to avoid social interaction and intimacy with others.
Insecure-resistant	A type of attachment which describes those infants who both seek and reject intimacy and social interaction, i.e. resist.
Institutionalisation	The effect of institutional care. The term can be applied widely to the effects of an institution but our concern focuses specifically on how time spent in an institution such as an orphanage can affect the development of children. The possible effects include social, mental and physical underdevelopment. Some of these effects may be irreversible.
Interactional synchrony	When two people interact they tend to mirror what the other is doing in terms of their facial expressions and body movements. This includes imitating emotions as well as behaviours. This is described as synchrony – when two (or more) things move in the same pattern.
Internal working model	A mental model of the world which enables individuals to predict and control their environment. In the case of attachment, the model relates to a person's expectations about relationships.
Learning theory	The name given to a group of explanations (classical and operant conditioning), which explain behaviour in terms of learning rather than any inborn tendencies or higher order thinking.
Monotropy	The idea that the one relationship that the infant has with his/her primary attachment figure is of special significance in emotional development.
Multiple attachment	Having more than one attachment figure.
Operant conditioning	Learning through reinforcement.
Primary attachment figure	The person who has formed the closest bond with a child, demonstrated by the intensity of the relationship. This is usually a child's biological mother, but other people can fulfil the role – an adoptive mother, a father, grandmother and so on. Throughout this chapter when we say 'mother' we are referring to the person who fulfils the role of primary attachment figure.
Reciprocity	Responding to the actions of another with a similar action, where the actions of one partner elicit a response from the other partner. The responses are not necessarily similar, as in interactional synchrony.
Secure attachment	This is a strong and contented attachment of an infant to his or her caregiver, which develops as a result of sensitive responding by the caregiver to the infant's needs. Securely attached infants are comfortable with social interaction and intimacy. Secure attachment is related to healthy subsequent cognitive and emotional development.
Separation anxiety	The distress shown by an infant when separated from his/her caregiver. This is not necessarily the child's biological mother.
Social learning theory	Learning through observing others and imitating behaviours that are rewarded.
Social releasers	A social behaviour or characteristic that elicits caregiving and leads to attachment.
Strange Situation	A controlled observation designed to test attachment security.
Stranger anxiety	The distress shown by an infant when approached or picked up by someone who is unfamiliar.

Topic 1 Caregiver–infant interactions

Discuss infant–caregiver interactions. Refer to reciprocity and interactional synchrony in your answer.
(12 marks)

Examiner's comments

Infancy is the period of a child's life before speech. Psychologists are interested in the interactions between caregivers and infants in terms of non-verbal communication, as such interactions form the basis of later attachments. There are two main types of interaction, known as: reciprocity and interactional synchrony.

> A good introduction outlining the key terms accurately.

Research in the 1970s found that infants coordinate their actions with their caregivers. When a baby moves in rhythm with an adult, as if they are taking turns in a conversation, this is known as reciprocity. Later research discovered a different type of interaction between infants and their caregivers, known as interactional synchrony. This is when a baby mirrors (imitates) the actions of another person, in terms of their facial expressions and body movements. The actions or behaviours move in synchrony – at the same time.

> The answer accurately defines reciprocity and provides an example.

> Furthermore, the answer accurately defines interactional synchrony, while providing a second example.

One issue with testing infant–caregiver interactions, is the reliability of infant expressions. Infants' constantly change their facial expressions and often stick their tongue out, yawn and smile, which may cause an issue for researchers investigating infant–caregiver interactions. This matters because it is difficult to distinguish between infant–caregiver interactions, especially interactional synchrony, and everyday facial expressions.

> The issue of reliability is discussed effectively.

However, one strength of examining infant behaviours comes from research investigating intentional behaviour. Abravanel and DeYoung (1991) observed infants interacting with two objects, one simulating tongue movements and the other a mouth opening/closing. They found that infants between 5 and 12 weeks old, made little response to the inanimate objects, suggesting that infants do not imitate anything they see and only respond to specific social responses. One strength of the research into interactional synchrony is its application to later adult relationships. Interactional synchrony might help children to understand the internal mental states of other people, which is fundamental in developing social relationships.

> Furthermore, the answer outlines research support for examining reciprocity and interactional synchrony.

> This final strength is partially effective, although the answer should link this strength back to the question.

Level 4 answer *(10–12 marks, likely to be the lower end of Level 4)*

Examiner's comments: AO1: The theory of reciprocity and interactional synchrony are explained accurately and in detail. The selection of material is appropriate.
AO3: The evaluation is mostly reasonable but not always effective. The answer includes a broad range of evaluative evidence, although not all of the points are linked back to the question. Finally, the answer incudes a good range of specialist terms and is organised in a clear way.

Topic 2 The development of attachment

Describe one study that investigated the development of attachments. *(6 marks)*

Examiner's comments

Schaffer and Emerson (1964) conducted a study on the development of attachment. Their sample consisted of sixty infants from working-class homes in Glasgow. At the start of the study, the infants ranged from 5 to 23 weeks old, and they were studied until the age of one year. The mothers were visited every four weeks and reported their infant's response to separation.

> The answer describes the procedure of the study, including lots of fine detail.

The results revealed that between 25 and 32 weeks old about 50% of the children showed separation anxiety towards a particular adult, usually their mother, which is known as a specific attachment. Furthermore, the results revealed that by the age of 40 weeks, 80% of the babies had a specific attachment and nearly 30% demonstrated multiple attachments.

> It also describes the results section accurately, with lots of fine detail.

> A conclusion would improve this answer further, to link the results back to the aim of the study.

Level 4 answer *(5–6 marks)*

Examiner's comments: AO1: The answer accurately describes one study examining the development of attachment. The research is detailed and includes fine details from the procedure and results sections. A conclusion should have been included to summarise the results in relation to the aim of the study.

Topic 3 Animal studies of attachment

Describe and evaluate animal studies of attachment. *(12 marks)*

Animal studies have contributed to the understanding of human attachment and two key studies include: Lorenz (1935) and Harlow (1959).

The aim of Lorenz's research was to investigate imprinting in baby geese (goslings). He divided a clutch of gosling eggs into two groups. One group was left with their natural mother, while the other group was placed in an incubator. When the group that was placed in the incubator hatched, the first moving thing they saw was Lorenz and they soon started following him around, a behaviour known as imprinting. Imprinting is a process similar to attachment, as it binds a young animal to a caregiver.

Harlow investigated whether attachment was based on mother love or feeding. He created two wire monkeys. One wire mother was wrapped in a soft cloth, while the other was left bare. Eight infant monkeys were examined. For four monkeys the milk bottle was attached to the cloth covered mother, while for the other four it was attached to the bare wire mother. Harlow measured the amount of time each monkey spent with the two different mothers. All eight monkeys spent most of their time with the cloth-covered monkey. These findings suggest that infants do not develop an attachment to the 'person' who feeds them, but to the person offering contact comfort.

One strength of Lorenz's research comes from later research support. Guiton (1966) replicated the findings of Lorenz with leghorn chicks. They found that leghorn chicks, exposed to yellow rubber gloves for feeding, became imprinted on the gloves. This supports the findings of Lorenz within a different species and suggests that attachment behaviours are innate and not learnt.

One weakness of animal research is the issue of generalisation. The aim of animal research is to generalise the conclusions to human behaviour; however, humans differ in many ways to animals. This suggests that the conclusions of animal research should be treated with caution, unless the findings have been replicated in humans.

A final consideration of animal research is the ethical implications of experimenting on animals. Harlow's research caused lasting emotional harm, as the infant monkeys later found it difficult to form relationships with their peers. However, some psychologists argue that animal research can be justified in terms of the effect it has on our knowledge of attachment and the development of better care for human infants. This suggests that the benefits of animal research may outweigh the costs.

Level 4 answer *(10–12 marks)*

Examiner's comments: AO1: The answer accurately explains animal research, including Lorenz (1935) and Harlow (1959). The research is detailed and appropriately selected for the question. AO3: The evaluation is thorough and effective.

Examiner's comments

The answer has outlined the two key animal studies in attachment.

Lorenz's research is accurately described, with lots of detail.

Harlow's research is also accurately described, with lots of detail.

The first evaluation point is effective, highlighting further research, to support the findings of Lorenz.

The second evaluation point is effective, describing the issue of generalisation.

The third evaluation point is very effective and includes arguments for and against the use of animals in psychological research.
If this was an A-Level 16 mark question, the answer would need to include 4–5 evaluation points.

Topic 4 Explanations of attachment: Learning theory

Describe and evaluate the learning explanation of attachment. *(12 marks)*

Learning explanations of attachment suggest that attachments are learned through classical and/or operant conditioning. According to classical conditioning, children associate the pleasure from food with the person who feeds them and thereby form an attachment. Classical conditioning claims that food is an unconditioned stimulus (UCS) which produces an unconditioned response (UCR) of pleasure. During the infant's early weeks, certain things become associated with food because they are present when the infant is fed, most notably the mother, who is referred to as a neutral stimulus (NS).

If a neutral stimulus is associated regularly with the UCS, it will produce the same response as the UCS which is pleasure. At this stage, the NS becomes a conditioned stimulus (CS) which produces a conditioned response (CR). Learning theorists called this newly formed stimulus-response 'mother love'.

One criticism of learning theory is that the research is based on animals. Learning theory is based on studies with non-human animals, such as Pavlov's research on dogs. This matters because behaviourist explanations may present an oversimplified version of human behaviour and attachment.

Another criticism of learning theory is the emphasis placed on food. Research by Harlow (1959) demonstrates that infant rhesus monkeys were most attached to a wire monkey that provided contact comfort and not food. This suggests that the learning explanation of attachment is oversimplified and ignores other important factors, such as contact comfort.

However, one strength of learning theory is its explanatory power. According to learning theory, infants do learn through association and reinforcement, however food may not be the main reinforcer. This shows that even though learning theory does not provide a complete explanation of attachment, it still has some value.

Examiner's comments

The answer provides a detailed and accurate explanation of classical conditioning, using all of the key terminology correctly.

The first evaluation point is effective, outlining the issue with animal research.

The second evaluation point is also effective, outlining an alternate explanation to learning theory.

The final evaluation point is also effective, outlining a strength of learning theory in terms of explanatory power.

Level 4 answer *(10–12 marks)*

Note: *It is possible to explain the learning explanation of attachment at AS level by describing either classical or operant conditioning in detail. However for A-Level, it is advisable to describe both classical and operant conditioning.*

Examiner's comments: AO1: The answer provides a detailed explanation of the formation of attachment through classical conditioning.
AO3: All the evaluation is thorough and effective and the answer includes a broad range of in depth evaluative evidence. A good range of specialist terms have been used throughout.

Topic 5 Explanations of attachment: Bowlby's theory

Discuss Bowlby's monotropic theory of attachment. *(16 marks)*

According to Bowlby, attachments are adaptive and serve an important survival function. Bowlby's monotropic theory of attachment explains both how and why attachments form.

Bowlby claimed that infants have an innate drive to become attached and that attachment must take place during a critical period of three to six months. In order to help the infant form an attachment, babies are born with certain features/characteristics, known as social releasers, that elicit caring behaviours from their caregivers, for example smiling and having a 'babyface', that facilitate an attachment. In addition, Bowlby claimed that infants form one special emotional bond with their primary attachment relationship, known as monotropy. The monotropic relationship provides the infant with a mental representation of relationships, known as an internal working model which provides the infant with a template for all future relationships, through an internal working model.

One strength of Bowlby's theory is the idea that attachments are adaptive. According to Bowlby, infants become attached during a critical period of three to six months, at the same time human infants start to crawl. It is therefore vital that infants form and maintain an attachment during this time, so that their caregivers can protect them.

Another strength of Bowlby's theory is the concept of 'monotropy'. Prior and Glaser (2006) concluded, from a review of the research, that a hierarchical model of attachment, which places emphasis on one central person 'higher' than others, is more likely than multiple attachments. This supports Bowlby's concept of monotropy and the idea that one special attachment plays a significant role in emotional development.

Further support for Bowlby's theory comes from the Minnesota parent–child study. Sroufe *et al.*, (2005) followed participants from infancy to late adolescence and found continuity between early attachment and later emotional/social behaviour. Individuals who were classified as securely attached in infancy, were rated highly for social competence later in childhood. This supports Bowlby's continuity hypothesis, as it demonstrates a clear link between early and later attachments.

However, one criticism of Bowlby's theory is the idea of a 'critical period'. Rutter et al. found that although the idea of a critical period is true to an extent, infants are still able to form an attachment outside this window. This suggests that Bowlby's original idea of a 'critical' period was not accurate and the term 'sensitive' may be more appropriate.

Examiner's comments

A detailed explanation of how and why attachments are formed according to Bowlby is discussed, including many specialist terms.

A detailed description of the internal working model, with examples, is provided. This final section could have been elaborated to include an example.

The first evaluation point is effective and highlights support from human infant development.

The second evaluation point is also effective and highlight research support for the idea of monotropy.

The third evaluation point highlights research support for the continuity hypothesis and is effectively presented.

Finally, the answer provides a criticism of Bowlby's concept of a critical period, which was redefined by Rutter.

Level 4 answer *(13–16 marks)*

Examiner's comments: AO1: The answer presents a detailed discussion of Bowlby's theory which is accurately explained. It includes all the aspects of the theory presented in a logical sequence. AO3: The evaluation is exceptionally thorough and effective, including a broad range of evaluative points in excellent depth. The essay is planned and structured in an organised and clear way.

Topic 6 Ainsworth's Strange Situation: Types of attachment

Explain how the behaviour of a child showing insecure-resistant attachment would be different from the behaviour of a child showing insecure-avoidant. *(4 marks)*

An insecure-avoidant child would show little response to separation (low separation anxiety), whereas an insecure-resistant child would show high levels of separation anxiety, by acting distressed.

Furthermore, an insecure-avoidant child would avoid contact with their caregiver when reunited, whereas an insecure-resistant child would seek and resist social interaction with their caregiver upon reunion.

Examiner's comments: AO1: The answer clearly outlines two differences in terms of insecure-resistant and insecure-avoidant children, in terms of separation anxiety and reunion behaviours. The answer compares the two attachment types with the use of the phrase 'whereas an insecure-resistant child would…'

Examiner's comments

This answer has compared insecure avoidant and insecure resistant children in terms of separation anxiety and reunion behaviours accurately.

Topic 7 Cultural variations in attachment

Describe and evaluate research on cultural variation in attachment. Refer to evidence in your answer. *(16 marks)*

Van IJzendoorn and Kroonenberg conducted a meta-analysis of the findings from 32 studies of attachment behaviour, from eight different countries. They found that secure attachment was the most common in every country. Insecure-avoidant attachment was the next most common in every country, except Israel and Japan.

Takahashi (1990) used the Strange Situation with Japanese infants and their mothers and found normal rates of secure attachment, but higher rates of insecure-resistant attachment. The Japanese infants were particularly distressed when left alone, which might be the result of different childrearing practices.

One issue with cultural variations in attachment is that the similarities found may not be innately determined. The media presents ideas about parenting, so it is possible that children all over the world are exposed to similar parenting, as a result of media and not an innate attachment type.

Furthermore, another issue with cultural variations in attachment is that the findings are based on countries and not cultures.

In addition, cross cultural research is culturally biased. According to Rothbaum *et al.* (2000) the theory of attachment is rooted in American culture and may not apply to other, non-Western cultures.

However, one strength of cross-cultural research is the development of universal principles of attachment. Posada and Jacobs (2011) note that there is a lot of evidence that supports the idea of underlying principles of attachment. For example, China, Colombia, Germany, Israel, Japan and Norway all support the idea that maternal sensitivity leads to secure attachment.

Level 3 answer (9–12 marks)

Examiner's comments: AO1: The research examining cultural variations in attachment is generally explained accurately and is reasonably detailed. However, key details are missing, including a conclusion from IJzendoorn and Kroonenberg and examples from Takahashi.
AO3: The evaluation is reasonable but not always effective. A range of evaluative evidence has been considered in limited depth. However, most of the points are unsupported.

Examiner's comments

Although the answer has outlined the findings of Van IJzendoorn and Kroonenberg, a conclusion is missing.

The answer has outlined the results and conclusion of Takahashi, however this section could have been elaborated further. How are the childrearing practices different in Japan?

The issue of the media is explained well, however the answer does not say why this is an issue for cultural variations in attachment.

This issue is unsupported. The evaluation point contains no examples or evidence and is not effective in saying why this is an issue for cultural variations in attachment.

This issue is well explained, with appropriate evidence. However, the answer fails to explain why 'cultural bias' poses a problem for cultural variations in attachment.

The final strength is relatively effective, providing a detailed description, evidence and examples. However, again the answer fails to explain why this is a strength for cultural variations in attachment.

Topic 8 Bowlby's theory of maternal deprivation

Describe and evaluate Bowlby's theory of maternal deprivation. *(12 marks)*

Bowlby (1951, 1953) proposed that prolonged emotional deprivation would have long-term consequences in terms of emotional development. He placed an important emphasis on maternal care and believed that infants and children need a 'warm, intimate and continuous relationship with a mother (or mother-substitute)' for normal mental health.

Furthermore, according to Bowlby, early childhood separation will only have an effect if it takes place during the critical period of development – before the age of two and a half years old. Therefore, the potential damage can be avoided if suitable emotional care is provided by a mother-substitute. Finally, Bowlby claimed that the long-term effect of deprivation was emotional maladjustment or even mental health problems, such as depression.

One criticism of Bowlby's theory is that emotional separation is ignored. Radke-Yarrow et al. (1985) found that 55% of children with severely depressed mothers were insecurely attached, in comparison to 29% of children with non-depressed mothers. This suggests that psychological separation can also lead to deprivation, in the same way as physical separation.

One strength of Bowlby's theory comes from research support. Bifulco et al. (1992) found that women who had experienced separation from their mothers were more likely to experience depression or an anxiety disorder compared to those who had no experience of separation. This supports Bowlby's idea of a critical period, suggesting that early childhood deprivation can lead to later vulnerability for depression and anxiety disorders.

Another strength of Bowlby's theory is the application to childrearing practices. Before Bowlby's research, children were separated from their parents when they spent time in hospital. Furthermore, parents were discouraged from visiting or even forbidden from seeing their children. However, Bowlby's work lead to major changes in the way children are cared for in hospitals. For example, parents are encouraged to visit their children and there is greater flexibility in terms of visiting hours.

Examiner's comments

The answer provides an accurate and detailed description of Bowlby's theory of maternal deprivation, including all of the key principles.

The first two evaluation points are effective and provide research support that highlights the strength/limitations of Bowlby's theory.

This evaluation point is reasonably effective, however the answer could elaborate this point further and explain why this application to childrearing practices is a strength.

Level 4 answer *(10–12 marks)*

Note: *This question requires a description of Bowlby's theory of maternal deprivation and not his monotropic attachment theory. Furthermore, the question does not require details of his 1944 study on juvenile thieves.*

Examiner's comments: AO1: Bowlby's theory of maternal deprivation is accurately explained and detailed.
AO3: The evaluation is nearly always thorough and effective. The answer includes a broad range of evaluative evidence in reasonable depth and uses a good range of specialist terms effectively. The essay is planned in an organised and clear way.

Topic 9 Romanian orphan studies: effects of institutionalisation

Outline **one** study of Romanian orphans. Include details of what the researcher(s) did and what they found. *(6 marks)*

Rutter and Sonuga-Barke (2010) conducted a study on Romanian orphans. Their sample consisted of 165 Romanian children who spent their early lives in a Romanian institution. 111 of the children were adopted before the age of two and 54 by the age of four.

Their physical, cognitive and social development was examined using interviews with parents and teachers. Their progress was compared with 52 British children who were adopted before they were six months old. By the age of four, some of the Romanian children had caught up with the British children. However, those adopted after six months showed significant deficits and signs of disinhibited attachment, highlighting the long-term consequences of institutionalisation.

The results suggest that the long-term consequences of institutionalisation are less severe if children are adopted early, however the consequences for those adopted later still remain severe.

Examiner's comments

The method section is accurate and contains lots of fine details.

Details of what the researchers did and what they found is included.

The answer provides a conclusion summarising the findings of the research.

Level 4 answer *(5–6 marks)*

Examiner's comments: AO1: The study of Rutter and Sonuga-Barke (2010) is accurately explained and key details in relation to what the researchers did and what they found are presented clearly.

Topic 10 The influence of early attachment

Discuss research into the influence of childhood on adult relationships. *(12 marks)*

Examiner's comments

Hazan and Shaver (1987) conducted a study to investigate the influence of childhood on later adult relationships, and to test the internal working model. Hazan and Shaver created a questionnaire called the 'Love Quiz' which examined current attachment experiences and attachment history. The questionnaire, which was placed in a local newspaper, also asked about attitudes towards love to assess the internal working model.

> The method section is accurately explained, containing an appropriate level of detail.

620 participants responded to the questionnaire and Hazan and Shaver found a positive correlation between attachment type and love experiences. Securely attached adults described their love experiences as happy, friendly and trusting. In addition, a relationship was found between the conception of love and the internal working model. These results support the idea of an internal working model and demonstrate the influence of childhood, on later adult relationships.

> The results section is detailed and accurate.

However, one issue with Hazan and Shaver's research is that the findings are correlational. Although the 'Love Quiz' found a link between the internal working model and later adult relationships, the researchers were unable to establish a cause and effect relationship. This matters because researchers are unable to conclude that the internal working model determines later relationships, as there may be other factors which cause the differences found.

> Although this is an effective evaluation point, it could have been improved by providing an example of another factor that could influence adult relationships.

Another criticism of attachment research is the reliance on retrospective classification. Studies like Hazan and Shaver rely on adults answering questions about their early lives in order to assess infant attachment. This matters because the research findings may not be valid.

> This evaluation point is reasonably effective. It could be improved by saying why the research findings may not be valid.

A final criticism of attachment research is it is overly deterministic. The research by Hazan and Shaver suggests that very early experiences have a fixed effect on later adult relationships and therefore our adult relationships are determined by early experiences. Therefore, a child who is insecurely attached at one year of age is doomed to experience emotionally unsatisfactory relationships as an adult.

> The final evaluation point has not explained why determinism is an issue. It would be worth noting that many psychologists disagree with determinist theories.

Level 4 answer (10–12 marks)

Examiner's comments: AO1: The research of Hazan and Shaver is explained accurately and is detailed. The material selected is appropriate and tailored to the question.
AO3: The evaluation is generally thorough and effective and includes a broad range of evidence in reasonable depth. The evaluation could be improved by providing further elaboration in places.

KEY TERMS

- Cultural relativism
- Deviation from social norms
- DSM
- Statistical infrequency

Possible essay question…

Outline and evaluate **two** ways of defining abnormality. *(12 marks AS, 16 marks A)*

Other possible exam questions…

+ Outline the statistical infrequency definition of abnormality. *(3 marks)*
+ Outline the deviation from social norms definition of abnormality. *(3 marks)*
+ Evaluate **either** the statistical infrequency definition **or** the deviation from social norms definition of abnormality. *(6 marks)*

MUST know …

Statistical infrequency

This says that abnormal behaviours are those that are extremely rare, that is, those behaviours that are found in very few people.

Normal behaviours are therefore defined as those that are found in the majority of people.

Deviation from social norms

This says that anyone who deviates from socially created norms (or standards of acceptable behaviour) is considered abnormal.

Some social norms, such as not laughing at a funeral, are implicit. Other social norms, such as causing a disorder in public, are policed by laws.

 One limitation of the statistical infrequency definition is that…

…some abnormal behaviour is desirable.

- **E** – For example, very few people have an IQ over 150.

 One limitation of the deviation from social norms definition is…

…that social norms vary over time.

- **E** – For example, homosexuality was considered a mental disorder in DSM.

EVALUATION **A limitation of both the statistical infrequency and deviation from social norms definitions is…**

…that they are culture bound.

- **E** – Classification systems like DSM are based on Western cultures.

SHOULD know …

Statistical infrequency

Women who have their first baby under the age of 20 or over the age of 40 would be defined as abnormal because most women have their first baby later than 20 or earlier than 40.

If most women have their first baby between the ages of 20 and 40, then that is defined as normal.

Deviation from social norms

An example of a social norm is politeness. Impolite people are behaving in a socially deviant way because others find it difficult to interact with them.

Paedophilia is defined as abnormal because it deviates from both an implicit social rule about behaviour and is against the law.

- **E** – The statistical infrequency definition does not distinguish between desirable and undesirable behaviour.
- **L** – This means that we need a way of identifying behaviours that are both infrequent *and* undesirable.

- **E** – However, homosexuality is now considered to be socially acceptable.
- **L** – This means the deviation from social norms definition is based on prevailing social morals and attitudes.

- **E** – However, cultures differ in terms of statistical infrequency and social norms.
- **L** – This means that there are no universal standards or rules for labelling behaviours as abnormal.

A LEVEL ONLY ZONE

 Another limitation of the statistical infrequency definition is that…

…cut-off points are subjectively determined.

- **E** – For example, people disagree on what constitutes an abnormal lack of sleep.
- **E** – However, since this is a symptom of depression, it is important to know where the cut-off point lies for a diagnosis to be made.
- **L** – This means that disagreements about cut-off points make it difficult to define abnormality in terms of statistical infrequency.

 Another limitation of the deviation from social norms definition is that…

…deviance is related to a behaviour's context.

- **E** – For example, wearing few clothes on a beach is normal, but is abnormal at a formal gathering.
- **E** – However, sometimes there is not a clear line between abnormal deviation and harmless eccentricity.
- **L** – This means that social deviance on its own cannot offer a complete definition of abnormality.

CHOOSE THE RIGHT ANSWER

Which **two** of the following are *not* examples of behaviours that deviate from social norms. Tick **two** boxes only.

A Crying at a funeral ☐

B A woman walking around a supermarket in a bikini ☐

C Someone shouting in a library ☐

D A person dancing in a nightclub ☐

E A grown man having a tantrum on the floor ☐

Answers on page 277

 SPOT THE MISTAKES

Read this answer to the following exam question:

Evaluate the statistical infrequency definition of abnormality.

There are **three** mistakes – draw a circle around each.

One strength of the statistical infrequency definition of abnormality is that it is culture-bound. This means that a behaviour that is statistically frequent in one culture may not be statistically infrequent in another. The diagnostic manuals for mental disorders, such as the DSM, are based on non-Western cultures. However, there are cultural differences in what is normal and abnormal. This means that there are universal norms for labelling people as abnormal.

Answers on page 277

 WRITE YOUR OWN EVALUATION POINT

Select **one** evaluation point from the page opposite and write it out in your own words below.

Point	
Evidence	
Explain	
Link	

 MATCH THEM UP

Exam question:

Match the key terms with their definition.

1	Deviation from social norms	**A**	Behaviour cannot be judged properly unless it is viewed in its cultural context.
2	Diagnostic and Statistical Manual of Mental Disorders (DSM)	**B**	Any deviation from unstated rules about how one 'ought' to behave.
3	Statistical infrequency	**C**	A list of behaviours that is used to diagnose mental disorders.
4	Cultural relativism	**D**	Abnormality is defined as those behaviours that are extremely rare.

Answers on page 277

APPLYING YOUR KNOWLEDGE

Using your knowledge of definitions of abnormality, answer the following.

William Buckland (1784-1856) was considered to be a genius for devising a way of introducing gas lighting to Oxford. His IQ has been estimated at over 200. He enjoyed eating bluebottles and moles and, having been shown it by a friend, the embalmed heart of King Louis XIV of France. His favourite drink was bats' urine.

(a) Give **one** definition of abnormality. *(1 mark)*

(b) Use this definition to explain why William Buckland's behaviour might be considered abnormal. *(2 marks)*

(c) Using information contained in the passage above, explain **one** limitation of your chosen definition of abnormality. *(2 marks)*

Answers on page 277

105

KEY TERMS

- Deviation from ideal mental health
- Failure to function adequately

Possible essay question…

Outline and evaluate the failure to function adequately **and** deviation from ideal mental health definitions of abnormality. *(12 marks AS, 16 marks A)*

Other possible exam questions…

+ Explain the 'failure to function adequately' definition of abnormality. *(3 marks)*

+ Explain the 'deviation from ideal mental health' definition of abnormality. *(3 marks)*

+ Evaluate **either** the failure to function adequately definition of abnormality **or** the deviation from ideal mental health definition of abnormality. *(6 marks)*

MUST know …

Failure to function adequately

A person is failing to function adequately if they cannot cope with everyday life.

Not functioning adequately causes distress and suffering for the person and/or may cause distress to others.

If a behaviour is *not* personally distressing or distressing to others, a judgement of abnormality is inappropriate.

Deviation from ideal mental health

Abnormality is defined as deviating from an ideal of positive mental health, defined in terms of Jahoda's (1958) criteria of ideal mental health. Absence of the criteria for positive mental health indicates abnormality and a potential mental disorder.

This definition shares features with the failure to function adequately definition.

 One limitation of the failure to function adequately definition is that…

…some apparently abnormal behaviours can be functional.

- *E* – For example, depression may lead to extra attention for the individual.

 One limitation of the ideal mental health definition is that…

…Jahoda's criteria are unrealistic.

- *E* – Few people satisfy all of the criteria all of the time.

 A limitation of both the failure to function adequately and ideal mental health definitions is that of…

…cultural relativism.

- *E* – For example, both definitions are based on Western cultures' ideals and beliefs.

SHOULD know …

Failure to function adequately

'Functioning' refers to going about day-to-day life, such as going out to work.

Schizophrenia is defined as abnormal because schizophrenic behaviours (e.g. hallucinations, delusions) are distressing to others even if they are not personally distressing.

DSM's assessment of abnormality includes a quantitative measure of functioning.

Deviation from ideal mental health

Jahoda identified six characteristics of ideal mental health including *personal growth and self-actualisation* (having high self-esteem and a strong sense of identity) and *integration* (being able to deal with stressful events).

For example, not being able to cope with stress is abnormal in both definitions.

- *E* – This attention is rewarding and therefore functional, even if generally regarded as abnormal.
- *L* – This means that failure to function adequately is an incomplete definition as it fails to distinguish between behaviours that are dysfunctional and those that have some function for the individual.

- *E* – Therefore, everyone would be described as abnormal to a degree.
- *L* – We need to ask how many of Jahoda's criteria must be absent before someone is judged as abnormal.

- *E* – Applying them to members of non-Western cultures would be inappropriate.
- *L* – This means that both definitions are culture-bound in that they may apply only to individuals in Western cultures.

 Another limitation of the failure to function adequately definition is that…

…someone needs to decide whether this is actually the case.

- *E* – Sometimes people experience personal distress and recognise that their behaviour is undesirable.
- *E* – However, sometimes people are content with their behaviour and it is others who are distressed by it.
- *L* – This means that whether a behaviour is defined as abnormal or not depends on who is making the judgement.

Another limitation of the ideal mental health definition is that…

…it suggests mental health is the same as physical health.

- *E* – In general, physical illnesses have physical causes, which makes them relatively easy to diagnose.
- *E* – However, not all mental disorders have physical causes.
- *L* – This means that it is unlikely we can diagnose mental abnormality in the same way we can diagnose physical abnormality.

CHOOSE THE RIGHT ANSWER

Which **two** of the following are included in Jahoda's six characteristics of ideal mental health? Tick **two** boxes only.

A Fitting into a group ☐

B Integration ☐

C Physical health ☐

D Owning your own house ☐

E Self-actualisation ☐

Answers on page 277

CHOOSE THE RIGHT ANSWER

The following statements are all linked to different definitions of abnormality. Select the **two** statements that describe the failure to function adequately definition of abnormality. Tick **two** boxes only.

A Behaviour that is different from the way most people in society act ☐

B Not achieving self-actualisation ☐

C Not following the standards set by society ☐

D Causing distress or discomfort to others ☐

E Behaviour that interferes with everyday life ☐

F Not being able to resist stress ☐

Answers on page 277

KEY WORDS

Exam question: Outline the failure to function adequately and deviation from ideal mental health definitions of abnormality. *(6 marks)*

On the page opposite, these definitions of abnormality are described for you.

For each definition select **three** key words or phrases.

Failure to function adequately			
Deviation from ideal mental health			

Now try to write an answer to the exam question using your key phrases. Your answer should be between 100–150 words in length.

Answers on page 277

WRITE YOUR OWN EVALUATION POINT

Select an evaluation point about the deviation from ideal mental health definition of abnormality from the page opposite and write it out in your own words below.

Point	
Evidence	
Explain	
Link	

APPLYING YOUR KNOWLEDGE

Using your knowledge of definitions of abnormality, answer the following.

Sandra and Vitaly were having a discussion about the AS Level Psychology course Vitaly was doing. Vitaly told Sandra that he had to study different ways of defining abnormality. Sandra said: "You don't need to study psychology to know what abnormality is. People don't go to clinics because they have some abstract definition of abnormality. They go to clinics because their feelings or behaviours cause them distress or suffering." "Exactly," said Vitaly, "that's one of the definitions we've been studying, but that definition isn't as perfect as you think it is."

(a) Identify the definition of abnormality Sandra was using. *(1 mark)*

(b) Give **one** example of a behaviour that causes people psychological distress or suffering. *(1 mark)*

(c) Vitaly doesn't think Sandra's definition is as perfect as she thinks it is. Explain **one** limitation of the definition of abnormality Sandra was using. *(2 marks)*

Answers on page 277

KEY TERMS

- Depression
- Obsessive compulsive disorder (OCD)
- Phobias

Possible exam questions

+ Outline **one** behavioural and **one** emotional characteristic of phobias. *(2 marks)*
+ Explain the difference between an obsession and a compulsion. *(2 marks)*
+ Outline **two** characteristics of depression. *(2 marks)*

MUST know ...

Phobias

A phobia is an anxiety disorder, and is an irrational fear of a specific object or situation. About 2.6% of the UK population have a clinical phobia.

In adults, the main **emotional** characteristic of a phobia is excessive and unreasonable fear, accompanied by anxiety and panic, which the phobic recognises is disproportionate to the danger posed by the phobic stimulus.

Fear produces the **behavioural** characteristic of avoiding the phobic stimulus, and this interferes with the phobic's usual social and occupational functioning over an extended period of time. Phobics may also 'freeze' or faint in the presence of the phobic stimulus.

A defining **cognitive** characteristic of phobia is irrational thinking about the phobic stimulus and resistance to rational argument about the actual danger it poses.

Obsessive Compulsive Disorder (OCD)

The two components of OCD are recurrent, persistent and intrusive thoughts or impulses (obsessions) and repetitive behaviours (compulsions). The thoughts or impulses are the main **cognitive** characteristic of OCD, and are recognised by sufferers as being excessive or unreasonable.

Because OCD sufferers believe they have no control over the thoughts or impulses, they experience anxiety, and this is the main **emotional** characteristic of OCD. Sufferers also experience embarrassment and shame about their obsessions and compulsions.

A person who is obsessed by a fear of being contaminated by germs may develop compulsive hand-washing behaviour as a way of reducing anxiety. The repetitive behaviour is the main **behavioural** characteristic of OCD. It may be performed overtly (e.g. hand-washing) or covertly (e.g. praying). Sometimes, though, compulsive behaviour is not a response to obsessional thoughts, and people may compulsively avoid certain stimuli.

Depression

Depression is a mood disorder. The main **emotional** characteristic of major depressive disorder is sadness and/or a loss of interest and pleasure in activities a person is normally interested in and takes pleasure from. Other negative emotional characteristics include feelings of despair, low self-esteem, lack of control, and inward- or outward-directed anger.

Behavioural characteristics of depression include difficulties in concentrating, decreased or increased activity patterns, excessive sleep or insomnia, and increased or decreased appetite.

The main **cognitive** characteristics of depression are irrational negative thoughts about the self, the world in general and the future.

CASE study

A case study of phobia

Ms. K reported symptoms that were consistent with a diagnosis of specific phobia with panic features. She experienced overwhelming anxiety on airplanes, at airports and sometimes on other modes of public transportation. Physically, her anxiety would manifest with shortness of breath, accelerated heart rate, bodily warmth and sweating, nausea and muscular tension. Due to her fear of these panic-inducing situations, she had mastered the art of avoidance – not having flown in 12 years, and doing anything in her power to avoid enclosed spaces or public transportation that might somehow remind her of flying on an airplane. Ms. K's fears were so severe at the beginning of her treatment that she could not bring herself to face her airplane phobia. Although her sophisticated avoidance techniques had kept her from experiencing regular periods of panic and anxiety, they had also begun to interfere with her ability to live her life freely and joyfully. Ms. K was unable to travel, which was something she had previously loved to do. In addition, she found herself constantly busy making sure her surroundings were comfortable and within her control. She was using many of her resources simply maintaining a constantly avoidant stance toward her own anxiety. (Adapted from Volpe & Nash, 2012)

A case study of OCD

Shirley K., a 23-year-old housewife, complained of frequent attacks of headaches and dizziness. During the preceding three months, she had been disturbed by recurring thoughts that she might harm her two-year-old son either by stabbing him or choking him. She constantly had to go to his room, touch the boy and feel him breathe in order to reassure herself that he was still alive, otherwise she became unbearably anxious. If she read a report in the daily paper of the murder of a child, she would become agitated, since this reinforced her fear that she, too, might act on her impulse. (Adapted from Goldstein & Palmer, 1975)

A case study of depression

A 55-year-old man has suffered from appetite loss and a 55-pound weight loss over the past six months. His loss of appetite has been accompanied by a burning pain in his chest, back and abdomen, which he is convinced indicates a fatal abdominal cancer. He is withdrawn and isolated, unable to work, uninterested in friends and family, and unresponsive to their attempts to make him feel better. He awakes at 4 a.m. and is unable to fall back asleep. He claims to feel worse in the morning and to improve slightly as the day wears on. He is markedly agitated and speaks of feelings of extreme unworthiness. He says that he would be better off dead and that he welcomes his impending demise from cancer. (Adapted from Spitzer *et al.*, 1981)

CHOOSE THE RIGHT ANSWER

Which **two** of the following are characteristics of phobias? Tick **two** boxes only.

A Repetitive and unconcealed behaviours	☐
B Irrational fears that produce a conscious avoidance of a feared object or situation	☐
C Reduced energy, a sense of tiredness and a wish to sleep all of the time	☐
D In adults, a recognition that fear is excessive or unreasonable	☐
E A loss of interest in usual hobbies and activities	☐

Answers on page 277

 DRAWING CONCLUSIONS

A psychologist compared the rates of phobias, depression, and OCD in three countries. The number of cases per hundred members of the population for the three countries is shown in the table below.

	Phobias	Depression	OCD
Country A	2.7	2.8	2.6
Country B	2.6	2.1	1.5
Country C	0.7	1.4	1.9

(a) Which country has the lowest number of cases of phobias? *(1 mark)*

(b) Which country has the highest number of cases of depression? *(1 mark)*

(c) In which country is the rate of depression twice as high as in Country C? *(1 mark)*

(d) Calculate the mean rate of each disorder in the three countries. Which disorder has the highest mean rate in the three countries? *(2 marks)*

Answers on page 277

 SPOT THE MISTAKES

Read the answer to the following exam question:

Outline an emotional, behaviour and clinical characteristic of phobias. *(3 marks)*

There are **two** mistakes – draw a circle around each.

> The main emotional characteristic of a phobia is a marked and persistent fear of some object or situation. People have rational thoughts about things and are resistant to rational arguments. Phobics avoid the thing they fear and this interferes with their normal routine but not their social activities.

Answers on page 277

 APPLYING YOUR KNOWLEDGE

Using your knowledge of mental disorders, answer the following.

The billionaire Howard Hughes became a recluse and was never seen in public. He insisted that all of his employees wore white gloves when they handled documents that he would later have to touch. His employees were not allowed to look at him, let alone touch him. All of his doors and windows were taped because of the distress he felt about being contaminated by germs. One employee said that she regularly heard him dictating the same phrases over and over again. Hughes said that he wanted to live longer than his parents, and that because everybody carries germs the only way he could do this was by avoiding germs.

Using your knowledge of OCD, identify a cognitive, behavioural and emotional characteristic shown by Howard Hughes in the passage above. *(3 marks)*

Answers on page 278

KEY TERMS

- Biological preparedness
- Classical conditioning
- Diathesis–stress model
- Operant conditioning
- Two-process model

Possible essay question...

Discuss the behavioural approach to explaining phobias. *(12 marks AS, 16 marks A)*

Other possible exam questions...

+ Outline the two-process model as an explanation of phobias. *(4 marks)*

+ Explain the role played by classical conditioning in the development of phobias. *(3 marks)*

+ Give **two** criticisms of the two-process model as an explanation of phobias. *(3 + 3 marks)*

MUST know ...

Mowrer (1947) proposed the two-process model to explain phobias. The first process is classical conditioning. This explains how a phobia is acquired.

If an initially neutral stimulus (NS) is paired with an unconditioned stimulus (UCS) that produces the unconditioned response (UCR) of fear, then the neutral stimulus will become a conditioned stimulus (CS) and produce fear as a conditioned response (CR) whenever it is presented.

The second process is operant conditioning. This explains why phobias are maintained. If fear is lowered by avoiding the phobic stimulus, then avoidance behaviour becomes a negative reinforcer.

 The two-process model is supported by...

...research asking people about their phobias.

- *E* – Sue *et al.* found some people *can* recall a specific event that led to their phobia developing.

 One limitation of the two-process model is that...

...it does not explain the development of all phobias.

- *E* – Some people cannot remember an incident occurring that led to their phobia developing.

Another limitation of the two-process model is that...

...a phobia does not always develop after a traumatic incident.

- *E* – For example, DiNardo *et al.* found that not everyone who is bitten by a dog develops a phobia of dogs.

SHOULD know ...

Watson & Rayner (1920) paired an initially neutral stimulus (a white rat) with an unconditioned stimulus (a loud noise) that produced the unconditioned response of fear in Little Albert. After making this pairing four times, Little Albert produced a conditioned fear response when they showed him the rat on its own. This demonstrated that a fear response to an initially neutral stimulus can be classically conditioned.

If a person was afraid of dogs because they had been bitten by one, the reduction in fear they experienced by avoiding dogs would lead them to continue avoiding them.

- *E* – For example, Sue *et al.* found that agoraphobics are most likely to explain their phobia in terms of a specific event.
- *L* – This shows that classical conditioning can be involved in developing phobias.

- *E* – This suggests different phobias may be the result of different processes.
- *L* – However, Öst says it is possible that such traumatic events did actually happen, but the phobic has forgotten them.

- *E* – The diathesis–stress model says we inherit a genetic vulnerability for developing mental disorders, but a disorder will only manifest itself if triggered by a life event.
- *L* – This suggests a dog bite will only lead to a phobia in people with such a vulnerability.

**A LEVEL ONLY ZONE**

 Phobias have cognitive aspects...

...that cannot be explained in a traditionally behaviourist framework.

- *E* – For example, a person who *thinks* they might die if trapped in a lift might become extremely anxious and this may trigger a phobia about lifts.
- *E* – This shows that irrational thinking is also involved in the development of phobias.
- *L* – This would explain why cognitive therapies can be more successful in treating phobias than behavioural treatments.

 Biological preparedness may be an even better explanation than the two-process model...

...of how phobias develop.

- *E* – Seligman says animals are genetically prepared to learn associations between fear and stimuli that were life-threatening in our evolutionary past, such as snakes.
- *E* – For example, fear is easier to condition to some things (e.g. spiders) than others (e.g. toasters), even though toasters are more dangerous than spiders.
- *L* – This means that behavioural explanations alone cannot explain the development of phobias.

CHOOSE THE RIGHT ANSWER

Which **two** of the following are behavioural explanations for phobias? Tick **two** boxes only.

A	Learning through association	☐
B	Preparedness	☐
C	Learning through reinforcement or punishment	☐
D	Irrational thinking	☐
E	Brain injury	☐

Answers on page 278

 SPOT THE MISTAKES

Read the answer to the following exam question:
Explain the role played by classical conditioning in the development of phobias *(3 marks)*.

There are **three** mistakes – draw a circle around each.

Watson and Rayner proposed the two-process model to explain the development of phobias. Classical conditioning explains how phobias are acquired. If an initially neutral stimulus such as a white rat is paired with unconditioned response (such as a loud noise) then fear occurs. Because the neutral stimulus now produces fear, it has become the conditioned stimulus, and leads to the unconditioned response of fear whenever it is presented.

Answers on page 278

MATCH THEM UP

Match the key terms to the appropriate type of conditioning. There are two key terms for each type of conditioning, and one term will therefore be left over.

1	Learning through association		**A**	Classical conditioning
2	Negative reinforcer			
3	Learning by vicarious reinforcement			
4	Conditioned response		**B**	Operant conditioning
5	Learning through reinforcement or punishment			

Answers on page 278

 DRAWING CONCLUSIONS

The chart below shows the prevalence (number of cases per thousand in a population) of dental fear relative to three other fears.

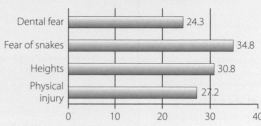

Prevalence of dental fear relative to other fears

Dental fear — 24.3
Fear of snakes — 34.8
Heights — 30.8
Physical injury — 27.2

(a) Which is the modal fear in the chart above? *(1 mark)*

(b) How many extra cases (per thousand) of dental fear would need to occur for it to become the second most common fear in the chart? *(1 mark)*

(c) How many fewer cases of fear of snakes (per thousand) are needed for it to become the least common fear in the chart? *(1 mark)*

(d) What level of measurement is used in the chart? *(1 mark)*

Answers on page 278

 APPLYING YOUR KNOWLEDGE

Using your knowledge of the behavioural approach to explaining phobias, answer the following.

When Stuart was a young boy, his parents bought a Dalmatian puppy for Christmas. One day, the puppy was playing and bit Stuart on the leg. Ever since then, Stuart has been afraid of his parents' dog. Stuart's friend Dave has a Great Dane, but Stuart won't go round to Dave's house because the thought of doing so fills him with fear.

(a) Explain Stuart's behaviour in terms of Mowrer's two-process model. *(4 marks)*

(b) Explain why Stuart is afraid of Dave's Great Dane even though the dog that bit him was a Dalmatian. *(2 marks)*

Answers on page 278

KEY TERMS

- Counterconditioning
- Desensitisation hierarchy
- Flooding
- Reciprocal inhibition
- Symptom substitution
- Systematic desensitisation

Possible essay question…

Describe and evaluate the use of systematic desensitisation **and/or** flooding in the treatment of phobias. *(12 marks AS, 16 marks A)*

Other possible exam questions…

+ Outline how systematic desensitisation is used in the treatment of phobias. You must make reference to relaxation and the use of a hierarchy in your answer. *(4 marks)*

+ Describe flooding as a behavioural approach to the treatment of phobias. *(6 marks)*

+ Compare and contrast systematic desensitisation and flooding as treatments for phobias. *(8 marks)*

MUST know …

Systematic desensitisation (SD) uses counterconditioning to replace fear with relaxation.

Phobics learn a relaxation technique, and then *imagine* scenes with the phobic stimulus. These are rated for anxiety, and a hierarchy from least to most feared is constructed.

The phobic imagines the least feared scene whilst simultaneously relaxing. When no anxiety is experienced, fear has been *desensitised*. The procedure is repeated with the next scene in the hierarchy.

Flooding involves a single exposure to the most feared situation. The phobic learns relaxation techniques, and is then exposed to the actual phobic stimulus or to a virtual reality version of it for two to three hours.

 SD is effective…

…in treating a range of phobias.

- *E* – For example, McGrath *et al.* reported that about 75% of phobics respond to SD.

 Flooding is also effective…

…for those who choose it and stick to it.

- *E* – For example, Craske *et al.* (2008) concluded that flooding and SD were equally effective in treating phobias.

 A strength of both therapies is that…

…they are relatively faster and require less patient effort than other psychotherapies.

- *E* – For example, psychological therapies require willpower.

SHOULD know …

SD is based on 'reciprocal inhibition' – a person cannot simultaneously be relaxed and anxious. Being relaxed inhibits anxiety.

Progressive relaxation techniques enable the phobic to relax 'on command'. In other forms of SD, the phobic is gradually *exposed* to the phobic stimulus rather than imagining it.

The therapist and phobic work through the hierarchy in a *systematic* way until the phobic experiences no anxiety when imagining the most feared scene.

Although intense fear is initially experienced, the fear response is eventually extinguished. When the phobic reports being fully relaxed, therapy is complete and the phobic has been 'cured'.

- *E* – Success appears to lie with actual contact with the feared stimulus.
- *L* – This means that *in vivo* techniques are better than those using pictures or imagining the feared stimulus (*in vitro*).

- *E* – Choy *et al.* agreed that both therapies were effective at reducing the symptoms of phobias.
- *L* – However, they also found that flooding was more effective than SD at treating phobias.

- *E* – This means behavioural therapies can be useful for children and people with learning difficulties.
- *L* – SD can also be self-administered which makes it cheaper than therapist-guided therapies.

A LEVEL ONLY ZONE

 Being able to cope with a phobic stimulus…

…may be more important than being able to be relaxed in its presence.

- *E* – For example, Klein *et al.* found SD and supportive psychotherapy were equally effective in treating social or specific phobias.
- *E* – This suggests that the 'active ingredient' in SD and flooding may be the 'hopeful expectancies' people generate about overcoming their fear.
- *L* – This shows that cognitive factors are much more important than the behavioural approach usually acknowledges.

Removing the symptoms of a phobia…

…does not mean removal of its causes.

- *E* – For example, the symptoms may resurface in another form if the cause remains. This is called symptom substitution.
- *E* – Freud believed the real cause of a phobia is projected on to some other object because the phobia cannot be expressed directly.
- *L* – The psychodynamic approach emphasises the importance of treating the underlying cause of a phobia rather than just concentrating on removing its symptoms.

✓ CHOOSE THE RIGHT ANSWER

Which **two** of the following are involved in flooding? Tick **two** boxes only.

A	A single exposure to the most feared situation	☐
B	Constructing a hierarchy of feared responses	☐
C	Imaging scenes with the phobic stimulus	☐
D	Gradual exposure to feared situations	☐
E	Learning one or more relaxation techniques	☐

Answers on page 278

MATCH THEM UP

Match up the following key terms to their correct definition.

1	Flooding	**A**	A person cannot simultaneously be relaxed and anxious.
2	Systematic desensitisation	**B**	A list of feared situations from least to most fearful stimuli, designed to gradually introduce the phobic to the feared situation.
3	Symptom substitution	**C**	A client is gradually exposed to (or imagines) threatening situations under relaxed conditions until the anxiety reaction is extinguished.
4	Desensitisation hierarchy	**D**	The symptoms of a phobia are removed, but the cause will remain.
5	Reciprocal inhibition	**E**	A client experiences an extreme form of their phobia under relaxed conditions until the anxiety reaction is extinguished.

Answers on page 278

DRAWING CONCLUSIONS

 A researcher conducted a study to test the effectiveness of systematic desensitisation in the treatment of aviophobia (fear of flying). She recorded the percentage of participants who reported that they were still using aeroplanes three years after their treatment and the percentage who were not. She also recorded the percentage of participants who had refused to undergo either systematic desensitisation or flooding when it was offered, and who had to be referred for an alternative form of therapy.

	Systematic desensitisation	Flooding
Percentage still using aeroplanes	41	76
Percentage no longer using aeroplanes	59	24
Percentage who refused therapy when offered	15	37

(a) What do these results suggest about the relative effectiveness of the two forms of therapy? *(1 mark)*

(b) What do the results imply about the usefulness of the desensitisation hierarchy. *(2 marks)*

(c) Explain why the percentage of people refusing the therapies might be higher for one therapy than for the other. *(2 marks)*

Answers on page 278

⚙ APPLYING YOUR KNOWLEDGE (1)

Using your knowledge of the behavioural approach to treating phobias, answer the following.

Andrea has a phobia of speaking in public. She is about to go to university where she knows that part of her course will involve her having to attend seminars and talk about her studies in front of other students. Andrea is so frightened by this prospect that she arranges an appointment with a behaviour therapist who specialises in systematic desensitisation.

Describe how a therapist might use systematic desensitisation to help Andrea overcome her phobia of speaking in public. *(6 marks)*

Answers on page 278

⚙ APPLYING YOUR KNOWLEDGE (2)

Using your knowledge of the behavioural approach to treating phobias, answer the following.

Celine's husband has planned a weekend away sightseeing in Paris. He is very keen to visit the Eiffel Tower and stand at the top admiring the views. Her husband doesn't know it, but Celine has a phobia of heights. This phobia is so bad that she has difficulty in going to her office on the third floor, and she cannot even sit on the top deck of a bus any more. Celine's husband has booked a romantic meal in the restaurant at the top of the Eiffel Tower, and she doesn't want to let him down. A friend suggests she tries flooding to overcome her phobia.

Explain how a therapist might use flooding to help Celine to overcome her phobia. *(6 marks)*

Answers on page 278

KEY TERMS

- ABC model
- Musturbatory thinking
- Negative triad
- Schema

Possible essay question...

Discuss Beck's negative triad **and/or** Ellis's ABC model as a way of explaining depression. *(12 marks AS, 16 marks A)*

Other possible exam questions...

+ Outline Beck's negative triad as a cognitive approach to explaining depression. *(4 marks)*

+ Outline Ellis' ABC model as a cognitive approach to explaining depression. *(4 marks)*

+ Evaluate either Beck's negative triad **or** Ellis' ABC model as an explanation of depression. *(6 marks)*

MUST know ...

Ellis' (1962) ABC model says that when an activating event (A) leads to an irrational belief (B), the consequences of this (C) may be depression.

Musturbatory thinking is the source of irrational beliefs. I *must* be approved of by important people, I *must* do well or I am worthless, and the world *must* give me happiness are the three most important irrational beliefs.

Beck's (1967) model sees depression's roots as lying in traumatic childhood experiences, such as continual parental criticism and/or rejection by others. These experiences lead to negative cognitive schemas developing, such as expecting to fail in situations similar to those present when the schemas were learned. These expectations lead to depression.

 The cognitive approach is supported by...

...research into the link between depression and irrational thinking.

- *E* – Hammen and Kranz (1976) found that depressed participants made more logical errors than non-depressed participants when interpreting written material.

 The cognitive approach is important because...

...of its emphasis on the person.

- *E* – It suggests the person is responsible for their disorder, and can change their thinking.

 The cognitive approach has useful applications...

...to treating depression.

- *E* – For example, both Ellis' and Beck's explanations have been applied to therapy.

SHOULD know ...

Being fired at work (A) might lead to the irrational belief (B) that the company had it in for you, which could lead to the consequence (C) of depression.

People who hold these beliefs may become depressed. For mental healthiness, these 'musts' need to be challenged.

Negative schemas and cognitive biases maintain the negative triad. These concern the self (e.g. 'I'm unattractive'), the world/life experiences (e.g. 'Even my boyfriend left me'), and the future (e.g. 'I'll always be unattractive').

- *E* – However, this does not mean that irrational thinking causes depression as the relationship may be the other way around.
- *L* – Instead, irrational thinking may be the result of being depressed.

- *E* – However, this may lead to the role played by situational factors being overlooked.
- *L* – This means also considering how the client can change their situation to reduce those aspects of their life that might be contributing to their depression.

- *E* – Such therapy has consistently been found to be the best treatment for depression.
- *L* – This means that if depression is treated by challenging irrational thoughts, those thoughts have a role in causing depression.

A LEVEL ONLY ZONE

 One weakness of the cognitive approach is that...

...not all irrational beliefs are 'irrational'.

- E – For example, Alloy and Abrahamson (1979) found that depressed people gave more accurate estimates of the likelihood of disaster than non-depressed people (the 'sadder but wiser' effect).
- E – This suggests that depressive realists tend to see things for what they are, rather than seeing things through rose-coloured glasses.
- L – This means that some 'irrational' beliefs may simply *seem* irrational rather than *be* irrational.

Depression can also be explained in terms of...

...genetic factors and neurotransmitters.

- *E* – For example, studies have found low levels of the neurotransmitter serotonin in depressed people, and a gene related to this is ten times more common in depressed people.
- *E* – Research shows that drug therapies are successful in treating depression.
- *L* – This means that neurotransmitters also play a role in causing depression, and so a diathesis-stress model could be a better approach to take.

CHOOSE THE RIGHT ANSWER

Which **two** of the following are *not* examples of the cognitive approach to explaining depression? Tick **two** boxes only.

A The ABC model	☐
B The two-process model	☐
C The cognitive triad	☐
D Classical conditioning	☐
E Musturbatory thinking	☐

Answers on page 278

 SPOT THE MISTAKES

Read this answer to the following exam question:
Outline Ellis' cognitive approach to explaining depression. *(4 marks)*

There are **four** mistakes – draw a circle around each.

Ellis' cognitive triad says that when an activating event (A) leads to a rational belief (B), the consequences of this (C) may be depression. Musturbatory thinking is the result of irrational beliefs. For example, one of these beliefs is that we must do well otherwise we are worthless. People who hold these kinds of beliefs always become depressed. For mental healthiness, these 'musts' therefore need to be challenged.

Answers on page 278

MATCH THEM UP

Match the key terms to the statement that best describes them.

1	ABC model	**A**	A pessimistic and irrational view of three key elements in a person's belief system.
2	Musturbatory thinking	**B**	Thinking that certain ideas or assumptions must be true for an individual to be happy.
3	Negative triad	**C**	A cognitive approach to understanding mental disorder, focusing on the effects of irrational thinking on behaviour.
4	Schema	**D**	A cognitive framework that helps organise and interpret information in the brain.

Answers on page 278

 APPLYING YOUR KNOWLEDGE (1)

Using your knowledge of the cognitive approach to explaining depression, answer the following.

Boris had a spare ticket for a music concert. Rather than let it go to waste, he thought he'd phone Becky and ask her if she wanted to go with him. "I'd love to, but I'm afraid I can't" said Becky, "I've got loads of psychology homework to do tonight." Boris put the phone down and thought: "These tickets are like gold dust. Becky must really hate me to turn a free ticket down." Boris was so upset he decided not to go to the concert himself.

Using your knowledge of Ellis' cognitive approach, identify the A, B and C in the passage above. *(3 marks)*

Answers on page 278

 APPLYING YOUR KNOWLEDGE (2)

Using your knowledge of the cognitive approach to explaining depression, answer the following.

Simon, an eight-year-old, was the goalkeeper for his village team, which his dad managed. At half-time, the team were losing 5-0 because the opposition were the best team in the county. Simon's dad was shouting and screaming, especially at Simon. "You're to blame for these goals, Simon. If we lose this game it will be all your fault." At school, Simon seemed unhappy, so his PE teacher tried to cheer him up by asking him if he would play in goal for the school team. "Why should I?" said Simon, "You'll only lose if I play".

Using your knowledge of Beck's approach, explain why Simon might be unhappy. *(6 marks)*

Answers on page 278

KEY TERMS

- Cognitive-behavioural therapy
- Empirical disputing
- Irrational thoughts
- Logical disputing
- Pragmatic disputing
- Unconditional positive regard

Possible essay question…

Outline and evaluate a therapy which challenges irrational thoughts as a way of treating depression. *(12 marks AS, 16 marks A)*

Other possible exam questions…

+ Outline **one** way in which cognitive behaviour therapy has been used to treat depression. *(6 marks)*
+ Explain how challenging irrational thoughts can be used to treat depression. *(6 marks)*
+ Evaluate the cognitive approach to treating depression. *(6 marks)*

MUST know …

Ellis' rational emotive behaviour therapy (REBT), a type of cognitive-behavioural therapy (CBT), aims to turn irrational thoughts into rational thoughts, and resolve emotional and behaviour problems.

REBT focuses on challenging or disputing irrational thoughts and replacing them with effective rational beliefs which produce new feelings.

Effective disputing changes self-defeating beliefs into more rational beliefs.

Clients complete homework assignments between therapy sessions, such as asking a person they feared would reject them out on a date.

Therapists provide clients with unconditional positive regard. Another feature is for the client to become more active, since being active leads to rewards that are an antidote to depression.

 A strength of REBT is that is supported by…

…research showing it is an effective therapy.

- **E** – For example, Ellis claimed a 90% success rate with treatment completed in an average of 27 sessions.

 A weakness of CBT is…

…that individual differences influence its effectiveness.

- **E** – Elkin *et al.* found it is less suitable where peoples' irrational beliefs are rigid and resistant to change.

 Research shows that exercise can be beneficial…

…in alleviating depression.

- **E** – Babyak *et al.* found that aerobic exercise, anti-depressant drugs or both together treat depression effectively.

SHOULD know …

Ellis' model was expanded to ABCDEF. D is disputing irrational thoughts and beliefs. E is the effects of disputing and effective attitude to life. F is the new feelings that are produced.

Logical, empirical and pragmatic disputing are ways of challenging irrational thoughts and beliefs and replacing them with more rational thoughts and beliefs.

Catastrophising thoughts are changed to more rational interpretations, which help clients feel better and become more self-accepting.

Homework enables irrational beliefs to be tested against reality and putting new rational beliefs into practice.

An important ingredient of REBT is convincing clients of their value as humans.

- **E** – However, the therapy is not always effective at reducing the symptoms of depression.
- **L** – This suggests that clients do not always put their revised beliefs into action.

- **E** – Ellis believes that some people simply do not want the direct sort of advice that CBT practitioners tend to dispense.
- **L** – This means that CBT is suitable for some people but not others.

- **E** – However, there was significantly lower relapse rates following exercise than drug treatment.
- **L** – This shows that exercise can be beneficial in treating depression.

A LEVEL ONLY ZONE

 CBT is effective but requires effort and commitment…

…from the person undergoing it.

- **E** – For example, Ellis found an average of 27 sessions of REBT were needed for depression to be treated effectively.
- **E** – Cuijpers *et al.* found that CBT is especially effective if it is used in conjunction with drug therapy.
- **L** – This suggests that using CBT and drugs together might help distressed clients who are unable to focus on CBT's demands by helping them cope better.

Different psychological therapies are equally effective…

…at treating mental disorders.

- **E** – For example, Luborsky *et al.* reviewed over 100 studies comparing different therapies and found only small differences between them in terms of their effectiveness.
- **E** – Sloane *et al.* have shown that psychological therapies share many common factors such as being able to talk to a sympathetic person.
- **L** – The lack of difference between psychotherapies might be a result of the commonalities they share.

CHOOSE THE RIGHT ANSWER

Which **two** of the following are features of cognitive-behavioural therapy? Tick **two** boxes only.

A Unconditional positive regard ☐

B Telling the therapist about your dreams ☐

C Remembering your earliest childhood memories ☐

D Challenging irrational thoughts ☐

E Relaxation techniques ☐

Answers on page 278

 RESEARCH ISSUES

A researcher was recruited by a regional hospital trust who wanted to know the most effective form of treatment for depression. She gathered data from therapists working across the region, representing three forms of therapy, CBT (REBT), psychoanalytic therapy and counselling. After six months of receiving therapy, clients were asked to rate (as a percentage) how much they felt they had improved as a result of receiving therapy (see graph, below). The researcher also interviewed each client in order to gather qualitative data on the effects of their therapy.

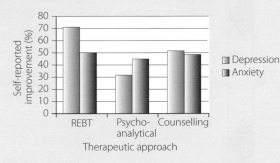

(a) Explain **one** advantage of gaining qualitative data in this study. *(2 marks)*

(b) Explain **two** factors that, unless they were controlled for, would make it difficult to compare the effectiveness of the different types of therapy in this study. *(4 marks)*

(c) State **two** findings from the study and for each draw **one** conclusion (state what the findings show). *(4 marks)*

Answers on page 278

 MATCH THEM UP

Match the researchers to the statement that best describes their research.

1	Luborsky *et al.*	**A**	CBT is less suitable where peoples' irrational beliefs are rigid and resistant to change.
2	Cuijpers *et al.*	**B**	CBT is especially effective if it is used in conjunction with drug therapy.
3	Elkin *et al.*	**C**	Psychological therapies share many common factors such as being able to talk to a sympathetic person.
4	Sloane *et al.*	**D**	Found only small differences between different psychological therapies in terms of their effectiveness.

Answers on page 279

 SPOT THE MISTAKES

Read this answer to the following exam question:
Outline **one** way in which cognitive behaviour therapy has been used to treat depression.

There are **four** mistakes – draw a circle around each.

Ellis' rational emotive behaviour therapy (REBT) aims to turn irrational thoughts into rational thoughts, and resolve emotional and biological problems. The therapy challenges or disputes irrational thoughts, aiming to replace them with rational beliefs that produce new feelings. Clients complete homework assignments between therapy sessions. Homework enables irrational beliefs to be tested against theory and putting new rational beliefs into practice. Conditional regard is given to the client by a therapist, as an important part of REBT is convincing clients of their value as humans. Another feature is for the client to become more passive, since this leads to rewards that are an antidote to depression.

Answers on page 279

 APPLYING YOUR KNOWLEDGE

Although Sophie was a very good student, she told her friends that she felt that she needed to prove her competence all the time. If things didn't go the ways she wanted them to it felt like an absolute disaster to her. Sophie's best friend had told her not to be so silly, but Sophie had reacted to this telling her friend that she felt like she needed everybody to approve of her all the time.

Using your knowledge of CBT, identify **three** irrational thoughts in the above passage and suggest a way in which each of those thoughts could be disputed. *(6 marks)*

Answers on page 279

KEY TERMS

- Caudate nucleus
- Concordance rate
- Dopamine
- Gene
- Neurotransmitters
- Orbitofrontal cortex
- Serotonin

Possible essay question...

Outline and evaluate genetic **and** neural explanations of OCD. *(12 marks AS, 16 marks A)*

Other possible exam questions...

+ Outline genetic **or** neural explanations for OCD. *(4 marks)*

+ Evaluate genetic **or** neural explanations for OCD. *(4 marks)*

MUST know ...

The COMT gene may contribute to OCD. The gene regulates dopamine production.

The SERT gene may also contribute to OCD. This gene creates lower levels of serotonin.

High dopamine levels and low serotonin levels are associated with OCD.

The oribitofrontal cortex (OFC) of the frontal lobes and the caudate nucleus part of the basal ganglia are thought to be abnormal in people with OCD. Serotonin plays a key role in the operation of these structures, whilst dopamine is the basal ganglia's main neurotransmitter. Damage to the caudate nucleus fails to suppress minor 'worry' signals from the OFC, creating a *worry circuit*.

 The role of genetic factors is supported by...

...family studies of OCD.

- *E* – For example, Nestadt *et al.* (2000) found that people with a first-degree relative with OCD are more at risk of developing the disorder.

 Additional support for the role of genetic factors comes from...

...twin studies.

- *E* – For example, Billett *et al.* (1998) found a higher concordance rate for OCD in MZ than DZ twins.

 PET scan studies support the idea of...

...abnormal brain circuits in OCD.

- *E* – People with OCD show heightened OFC activity when their symptoms are active.

SHOULD know ...

One form of this gene is more common in OCD patients, and produces lower COMT gene activity and higher dopamine levels.

A mutation of this gene has been found in two unrelated families where six of the seven members had OCD (Ozaki *et al.*, 2003).

High doses of drugs that enhance dopamine induce stereotypical movements in rats, whilst anti-depressant drugs, which increase serotonin activity, reduce the symptoms of OCD.

Low serotonin levels may cause the areas to malfunction. High dopamine levels lead to overactivity of the basal ganglia.

- *E* – However, families typically share environments as well as genes.
- *L* – This means that environmental factors could also play a part in the development of OCD (the diathesis–stress model).

- *E* – However, the concordance rate for MZ twins is never 100%.
- *L* – This means that environmental factors must also play a role in OCD.

- *E* – The caudate nucleus normally suppresses minor 'worry signals' from the OFC.
- *L* – If the caudate nucleus is damaged, these signals go back to the OFC and cause obsessional thinking.

A LEVEL ONLY ZONE

Studies have demonstrated a genetic link...

...to the abnormalities in brain structure and function found in patients with OCD.

- *E* – People with OCD and their very close relatives have reduced grey matter in key brain regions, including the OFC.
- *E* – This supports the view that anatomical differences are inherited and these may lead to OCD in certain people.
- *L* – Menzies *et al.* (2007) have suggested that brain scans could be used in the future as a way of detecting peoples' risk of developing OCD.

 The two-process model is a psychological alternative to...

...biological explanations of OCD.

- *E* – For example, OCD may be caused by an association between a neutral stimulus and anxiety (classical conditioning) and maintained by anxiety-reducing compulsive behaviours (operant conditioning).
- *E* – Exposure and response prevention (ERP), which prevents people from performing their compulsive behaviour in the presence of the feared stimulus, is effective.
- *L* – OCD may have psychological causes as well as, or instead of, biological causes.

✓ CHOOSE THE RIGHT ANSWER

Which **two** of the following statements about the role of neurotransmitters in OCD are true? Tick **two** boxes only.

A	There is no research evidence for the role of neurotransmitters in OCD	☐
B	The COMT gene regulates serotonin production	☐
C	Low levels of serotonin are associated with OCD	☐
D	The SERT gene regulates dopamine production	☐
E	High levels of dopamine are associated with OCD	☐

Answers on page 279

🧩 MATCH THEM UP

Match the key terms in the left hand column with their definitions in the right hand column.

1	Dopamine	**A**	A sub-cortical brain structure, which is abnormal in people with OCD
2	Serotonin	**B**	A neurotransmitter regulated by the SERT gene
3	Orbitofrontal cortex	**C**	A part of the frontal lobe which is abnormal in people with OCD
4	Caudate nucleus	**D**	A neurotransmitter regulated by the COMT gene

Answers on page 279

🎯 WRITE YOUR OWN EVALUATION POINT

Select **one** evaluation point from the page opposite and write it out in your own words below.

Point	
Evidence	
Explain	
Link	

👁 SPOT THE MISTAKES

Read this answer to the following exam question:

Outline **one** biological explanation for OCD. *(4 marks)*

There are **three** mistakes – draw a circle around each.

One biological explanation for OCD is that it is caused by genetic factors. The SERT gene creates higher levels of serotonin and this may be what causes OCD. Another gene which researchers think is involved in causing OCD is the COMT gene. One variation of this gene is more common in people with OCD. This gene regulates the production of dopamine and produces lower levels of this neurotransmitter. Ozaki *et al.* found that a mutation of the COMT gene was present in two unrelated families where six out of seven of them had OCD.

Answers on page 279

⚙ APPLYING YOUR KNOWLEDGE

Using your knowledge of the biological approaches to explaining OCD, answer the following.

Leon, Andy and Allegra were discussing the biological causes of OCD. "Of course it's genetic," said Leon. "Look at the evidence from family studies. You're five times more likely to develop OCD if you have a first-degree relative who has the disorder. That proves it's genetic." "He's right" said Andy, "twin studies prove it as well. The concordance rate for twins who share the same genes is really high." As confident as Leon and Andy seemed, Allegra wasn't convinced by their arguments.

Explain why Allegra wasn't convinced by Leon and Andy's arguments. *(6 marks)*

Answers on page 279

KEY TERMS

- GABA (gamma-aminobutyric acid)
- Noradrenaline
- Placebo
- Serotonin

Possible essay question...

Outline and evaluate drug therapy as a way of treating OCD. *(12 marks AS, 16 marks A)*

Other possible exam questions...

+ Outline how drug therapy is used to treat OCD. *(4 marks)*
+ Evaluate drug therapy as a biological approach to treating OCD. *(6 marks)*

MUST know ...

Anti-depressants

SSRI anti-depressants (e.g. *Prozac*) are the most commonly used drugs to reduce the anxiety associated with OCD. They block the reuptake of serotonin in the pre-synaptic membrane, increasing serotonin concentration at receptor sites on the post-synaptic membrane.

Tricyclic anti-depressants (e.g. *Anafranil*) block the transporter mechanism that reabsorbs both serotonin and noradrenaline into the pre-synaptic cells that released them.

Anti-anxiety drugs

Benzodiazepine (BZ) anti-anxiety drugs (e.g. *Xanax*) are also used to treat OCD. They enhance the activity of Gamma-aminobutyric acid (GABA), which has a general quietening effect on many brain neurons.

 Using drugs to treat OCD is supported by...

...research that shows they are effective.

- *E* – For example, Soomro *et al.* (2008) found drugs were more effective than placebos in reducing symptoms.

 One strength of drug therapy is that...

...it requires little input or effort from the user.

- *E* – For example, psychological therapies are time consuming.

 One weakness of drug therapy is that...

...all drugs have unpleasant side effects.

- *E* – For example, SSRIs cause nausea, headaches, and insomnia, whilst tricyclics cause hallucinations and an irregular heartbeat.

SHOULD know ...

Anti-depressants

Since low serotonin levels are implicated in the brain's 'worry circuit', increasing serotonin may have the effect of normalising this circuit.

The effect of this is to increase both serotonin and noradrenaline levels. Tricyclics have more side effects than SSRIs, and so are used as a second-line treatment when SSRIs have not been effective.

Anti-anxiety drugs

BZs react with GABA receptors on the outside of the receiving neuron. This makes it harder for the neuron to be stimulated by other neurotransmitters. The neuron's activity is slowed down, and induces feelings of relaxation.

- *E* – However, most of the studies in Soomro *et al.*'s meta-analysis only lasted for three months.
- *L* – This means that we know little about the long-term effectiveness of drugs.

- *E* – They also require the person to attend regular meetings and think about tackling their problem.
- *L* – This means that drug therapies are more economical for the health service.

- *E* – This can lead to the patient choosing to stop taking the drugs.
- *L* – This means that side effects, and the possibility of addiction, limit the usefulness of drugs as treatments for OCD.

A LEVEL ONLY ZONE

Drugs are not a lasting cure...

...for people suffering with OCD.

- *E* – Even though drugs are effective in the short-term, Maina *et al.* (2001) found that patients relapsed within a week if treatment stopped.
- *E* – This suggests that psychological therapies should be tried before drugs are used to treat OCD.
- *L* – Koran *et al.* (2007) have proposed the use of CBT as an alternative to drug therapy.

 The effectiveness of drugs may be exaggerated...

...by a publication bias towards studies showing drugs have a positive effect.

- *E* – For example, Turner *et al.* found that studies showing positive results were more likely to be published in journals.
- *E* – Drug companies have a strong interest in the continuing success of drugs, and fund much of the research into their effectiveness.
- *L* – Selective publication of research may lead doctors to make inappropriate treatment decisions about treating OCD.

CHOOSE THE RIGHT ANSWER

Which **two** of the following are *not* issues with drug therapy? Tick **two** boxes only.

A It can lead to patients becoming addicted to the drugs ☐

B Patients can develop a tolerance to the drug ☐

C We know the long term effects of taking drugs ☐

D It takes a long time for a drug to take effect ☐

E It is possible the research into its effectiveness suffers from publication bias ☐

Answers on page 279

MATCH THEM UP

Match the drug used to treat OCD with the effect that it has on the brain.

1	Tricyclic antidepressants	A	Enhance the activity of GABA
2	SSRI antidepressants	B	Block the mechanism that that reabsorbs serotonin and noradrenaline
3	D-Cycloserine	C	Enhances the transmission of GABA
4	Benzodiazepine anti-anxiety drugs	D	Increases serotonin levels

Answers on page 279

DRAWING CONCLUSIONS

In a study designed to investigate the effectiveness of different kinds of drug therapy, thirty participants with OCD were randomly divided into three groups. The first group were given a course of SSRI drugs. The second group were given tricyclic drugs, and the third group received a placebo. None of the participants were told which group they had been assigned to. A measure was taken of the severity of the participants' symptoms before the study began, and a second measure was taken after three months had elapsed. The lower the score, the more the symptoms were reduced. The results of the study are shown in the table below.

	Mean severity of symptoms before drug therapy began (max. = 100)	Mean severity of symptoms after 3 months of drug therapy (max = 100)
SSRI drugs	70	58
Tricyclic drugs	70	37
Placebo	70	56

State **two** findings from the study and for each finding draw **one** conclusion (state what the findings show). *(4 marks)*

Answers on page 279

RESEARCH ISSUES

A researcher who read about the study described in the Drawing Conclusions activity wrote to the journal in which the findings were published. His complaint was that the study raises a number of ethical issues. Describe **three** ethical issues that the research might have raised. *(6 marks)*

Answers on page 279

APPLYING YOUR KNOWLEDGE

Using your knowledge of the biological approach to treating OCD, answer the following.

Linda, who has recently been diagnosed with OCD, was chatting to Paul and Caroline about getting her condition treated. She told them that she had been prescribed a course of drugs, but couldn't decide whether she wanted to undergo this kind of therapy. "You must!" said Paul, "I can give you three good reasons for drug therapy". "Oh no you mustn't," said Caroline, "I can give you three good reasons against drug therapy!"

(a) Outline **three** reasons Paul might have given Linda for using drug therapy. *(3 marks)*

(b) Outline **three** reasons Caroline might have given Linda for *not* using drug therapy. *(3 marks)*

Answers on page 279

ABC model	Refers to the three components of experience that can be used to judge whether an individual's belief system is distorted. A (activating event) leads to B (belief) and ultimately C (consequences).
Biological preparedness	The view that animals, including humans, are genetically programmed to rapidly learn an association between potentially life threatening stimuli and fear.
Caudate nucleus	A sub-cortical brain structure which sends some signals from the orbitofrontal cortex to the thalami about things that are worrying, such as a potential germ hazard.
Classical conditioning	In classical conditioning, the neutral stimulus (NS) becomes the conditioned stimulus (CS) after the NS is paired with the unconditioned stimulus (UCS). The NS takes on the properties of a CS so it produces a learned or conditioned response (CR).
Cognitive-behavioural therapy	A combination of cognitive therapy (to change dysfunctional *thoughts* and *beliefs*) and behavioural therapy (to change *behaviour* in response to these thoughts and beliefs).
Concordance rate	A measure of similarity between two individuals or sets of individuals on a given trait, usually expressed as a percentage.
Counterconditioning	Being taught a new association that is the opposite of the original association, thus removing the original association.
Cultural relativism	The view that ideas of normal and abnormal behaviour differ from culture to culture.
Depression	A mood disorder where an individual feels sad and/or lacks interest in their usual activities. Further characteristics include irrational negative thoughts, raised or lowered activity levels, and difficulties with concentration, sleep and eating.
Desensitisation hierarchy	In systematic desensitisation therapy, a list of anxiety-provoking situations arranged in order from least to most distressing. Working through these should result in reduced sensitivity to the anxiety-provoking situation.
Deviation from ideal mental health	Abnormality is seen as deviating from an ideal of positive mental health. This includes a positive attitude towards the self and an accurate perception of reality.
Deviation from social norms	Abnormal behaviour is seen as a deviation from unwritten rules about how one 'ought' to behave. Violation of these rules is considered abnormal.
Diathesis-stress model	In the case of certain disorders, individuals inherit a vulnerability for the disorder (diathesis) which develops only if such individuals are exposed to difficult environmental conditions (stress). The greater the underlying vulnerability, the less stress needed to trigger the disorder.
Dopamine	A neurotransmitter involved in the sensation of pleasure. Unusually high levels are associated with schizophrenia.
DSM	(*Diagnostic and Statistical Manual of Mental Disorders*) A manual used to diagnose mental disorders. For each disorder a list of clinical characteristics is given, i.e. the symptoms that should be looked for.
Empirical disputing	Challenging self-defeating beliefs that may not be consistent with reality.
Failure to function adequately	Mentally healthy people are judged as being able to operate within certain acceptable limits. If a behaviour interferes with daily functioning, it may be considered abnormal.
Flooding	A form of behavioural therapy used to treat phobias and other anxiety disorders. A client is exposed to (or imagines) an extreme form of the threatening situation under relaxed conditions until the anxiety reaction is extinguished.
GABA (gamma-aminobutyric acid)	A neurotransmitter that reduces excitement in the nervous system, thus acting as a natural form of anxiety reducer.
Gene	A part of the chromosome of an organism that carries information in the form of DNA.
Logical disputing	Challenging self-defeating beliefs that do not follow logically from the information available.
Irrational thoughts	Dysfunctional or faulty mental activity.
Musturbatory thinking	Thinking that certain ideas or beliefs must be true in order for an individual to be happy.
Negative triad	A cognitive approach to understanding depression, focusing on how negative expectations (schema) about the self, world and future lead to depression.
Neurotransmitters	Chemical substances, such as serotonin or dopamine, that play an important part in the workings of the nervous system by transmitting nerve impulses across a synapse.
Noradrenaline	A neurotransmitter found mainly in areas of the brain that are involved in governing autonomic nervous system activity, e.g. blood pressure or heart rate.
Obsessive compulsive disorder (OCD)	An anxiety disorder where anxiety arises from obsessions (persistent thoughts) and compulsions (behaviours repeated over and over again). Compulsions are a response to obsessions and the person believes the compulsions reduce anxiety.
Operant conditioning	Involves reinforcement. Any behaviour that results in a pleasant consequence is increasingly 'stamped in' (reinforced). It becomes more probable that you will repeat that behaviour in the future. If you do something and it results in an unpleasant consequence (punishment), it becomes less likely that you will repeat that behaviour.

Orbitofrontal cortex	Part of the frontal lobe of the brain that sends 'worry' signals to the thalami via the caudate nucleus.
Phobias	A group of mental disorders characterised by a high level of anxiety in response to a particular stimulus or group of stimuli. The anxiety interferes with normal living.
Placebo	A drug or treatment that contains no active ingredient or therapeutic procedure.
Pragmatic disputing	Emphasising the lack of usefulness of self-defeating beliefs.
Reciprocal inhibition	The view that two incompatible emotions (e.g. being anxious and being relaxed) cannot be experienced simultaneously.
Schema	A cognitive framework that helps organise and interpret information in the brain. A schema helps an individual to make sense of new information.
Serotonin	A neurotransmitter found in the central nervous system. Low levels have been linked to many different behaviours and physiological processes, including aggression, eating disorders and depression.
Statistical infrequency	Abnormality is defined as those behaviours that are extremely rare, i.e. any behaviour that is found in very few people is regarded as abnormal.
Symptom substitution	In behavioural therapy, if the symptoms are removed the cause still remains, and the symptoms will simply resurface, possibly in another form.
Systematic desensitisation	Based on classical conditioning (the behavioural approach), a therapy used to treat phobias and problems involving anxiety. A client is gradually exposed to the threatening stimulus under relaxed conditions until the anxiety is reduced and ultimately extinguished.
Two-process model	A theory that explains the two processes that lead to the development of phobias – they begin through classical conditioning and are maintained through operant conditioning.
Unconditional positive regard	Where the therapist provides respect and appreciation regardless of what the client does and says, facilitating a change in beliefs and attitudes.

Topic 1 Definitions of abnormality

Outline and evaluate **two** ways of defining abnormality. *(16 marks A)*

One way to define abnormality is by seeing if a behaviour is a common one. If a behaviour is done by most people, then it is considered to be a normal behaviour, if it is done by very few people, then it is abnormal behaviour. So, for example, women who have their first baby after the age of forty would be defined as abnormal because most people have their first baby before then.

Another way to define abnormality is by using the 'deviation from social norms' definition. This says that if someone deviates from what society says the right thing to do is, then they are abnormal. For example, social norms say that people should not laugh at a funeral. These are implicit norms because there are no laws which say this. Other social norms are also laws, for example, causing a disturbance in public.

A problem with defining abnormality as statistically infrequent behaviour is that some abnormal behaviour is desirable, for example, having a very high IQ. Statistical infrequency does not take into account the desirability of the abnormal behaviour and, for a good definition of abnormality, we need a way to identify which abnormal behaviour is desirable or not.

Social norms vary over time and this limits the deviation from social norms definition. Until fairly recently, homosexuality was considered to be a mental disorder, according to the DSM. However, society's norms have changed and homosexuality is now considered to be socially acceptable. This means that the deviation from social norms definition is based on society's attitudes, which may not always be true.

Both of these definitions of abnormality are bound by culture. Classification systems, such as the DSM, are based on Western cultures and so the standards and rules they use for labelling behaviours may only be true in Western cultures. Cultures differ in terms of statistical infrequency and social norms and so what may be abnormal in one culture may be completely normal in another. This means that there are no universal standards or rules when it comes to defining abnormality.

Another problem with defining abnormality as statistically infrequent behaviour is that the cut-off points are subjectively determined. Not all people agree on what a normal amount of sleep is, for example. However, since it is a symptom of depression, it is important to know when a normal amount of sleep becomes an abnormal amount of sleep, if we are to make a diagnosis. This means that disagreements about cut-off points make it difficult to define abnormality in this way.

Deviance is related to a behaviour's context, for example, wearing a bikini on a beach is normal, but wearing it to a formal dinner is abnormal. However, this may be harmless eccentricity and not an abnormal deviation, but it is often hard to tell. This limits the deviation from social norms definition because it cannot offer a complete definition of abnormality.

Examiner's comments

An opening paragraph that offers a limited view of the statistical infrequency definition, which lacks detail and specialist terminology.

Appropriate and accurate description of the deviation from social norms approach, although not particularly well-detailed.

The first evaluative paragraph is reasonably clear and effective by looking at the problem of behaviours that are both infrequent *and* desirable.

Evaluation of the deviation from social norms definition follows the PEEL approach although the link back is not particularly clear or effective.

This paragraph also follows the PEEL method, but feels clearer and more effective with a more meaningful link back.

Good point about the difficulties associated with definitions based on statistical infrequency, explained clearly and effectively.

A final paragraph adds a critical point about the eccentricity/abnormality problem. This is reasonably effective but could be better developed.

Level 3 answer (9–12 marks)

Examiner's comments: AO1 Although the descriptive content is accurate and appropriate to the question, it lacks the appropriate level of detail for this sort of question.

AO3 The evaluative content is clearly distinguished from the descriptive material by the use of AO3 only paragraphs. This works well. There are five clear AO3 points that are usually elaborated, but not always.

Topic 2 Definitions of abnormality (continued)

Outline and evaluate the deviation from ideal mental health definition of abnormality. *(12 marks AS)*

Examiner's comments

Jahoda defines abnormality as a deviation from ideal mental health. Absence of the criteria for positive mental health indicates abnormality and a potential mental disorder. From a review of what other people had written about good mental health, she identified six characteristics of ideal mental health. These characteristics enable an individual to feel happy and behave competently. The six are: self-attitudes, which is having high self-esteem; personal growth and self-actualisation, which is the extent to which someone reaches their potential integration, which is being able to cope with stressful situations and autonomy, which is being independent and self-regulating. The final two are having an accurate perception of reality and mastering your environment, which includes the ability to love, function at work and adjust to new situations. If any of these are missing then this indicates abnormality and a potential mental disorder.

> A good opening paragraph, which gives an accurate and detailed account of the deviation from ideal mental health definition. This whole paragraph is AO1, which is an effective way of planning the answer.

Jahoda's criteria are unrealistic, which limits the deviation from ideal mental health as a definition of abnormality. Very few people satisfy all of the criteria all of the time. We also don't know how many of these criteria would need to be absent before someone could be classed as abnormal. Therefore, everyone could be described as abnormal to some degree. If everyone could be described as abnormal under this definition, then it does not help us to determine a genuine difference between normal and abnormal.

> Clear and effective AO3 point; it identifies the criticism, provides elaboration and then draws an appropriate conclusion about the implications of this criticism.

A major problem with the ideal mental health definition of abnormality is that it suggests mental health is the same as physical health. Most of the time, physical illnesses have physical causes which makes them reasonably easy to diagnose. Mental disorders do not always have a physical cause, and are often a result of life experiences. This means that it is not really possible to diagnose mental abnormality in the same way that we diagnose physical abnormality.

> Clear and well-explained AO3 point with an appropriate conclusion makes this an effective piece of evaluation.

The deviation from ideal mental health definition gives us an alternative perspective on mental disorder because it focuses on the positives and not the negatives. It focuses on what is desirable and undesirable, rather than only looking for problems. Jahoda's ideas were not taken up by many metal health professionals, but she clearly had some influence in psychology, for example, in positive psychology.

> An interesting final AO3 point that explains the positive implications of this definition of abnormality.

Level 4 answer (10–12 marks)

Examiner's comments: AO1 Accurate and detailed description of the deviation from ideal mental health definition would clearly be typical of a Level 4 answer.

AO3 Three clear evaluative points that offer an effective critical analysis of this definition. Again, worthy of a Level 4 mark.

Topic 3 Mental disorders

(1) Sybil describes her fear of thunderstorms: 'I dread hearing the weather forecast. As soon as the forecaster says there will be a thunderstorm I go into a panic. I live on my own, but fortunately my sister lives nearby, and so I can go and stay with her. I know that a thunderstorm can't hurt me if I'm inside a house, but as soon as I hear a clap of thunder I run up to the bedroom and hide under the sheets. I put my iPod ear phones on and listen to music very loudly.'

Identify **one** behavioural and **one** emotional characteristic of phobias as shown by Sybil in the above passage. *(2 marks)*

Examiner's comments

One behavioural characteristic shown by Sybil is avoiding hearing a thunderstorm. She runs upstairs and listens to music through her headphones so as to avoid the noise. An emotional characteristic shown by Sybil is the dread she feels whenever she hears a weather forecast and the panic she says she goes into.

> Accurate and probably a little too detailed for a question that only has one mark allocated for each characteristic.

Level 2 answer (2 marks)

Examiner's comments: AO1 Accurate and appropriate answers.

CHAPTER 4   *Annotated answers*

(2) Morag no longer drives a car. Many years ago she was involved in a minor collision with a cyclist. The cyclist wasn't hurt at all, but Morag believes that whenever she drives she will cause an accident in which somebody will be seriously hurt. This worries her so much that the only way she can reduce her fear is by using public transport rather than drive herself.

Explain the difference between an obsession and a compulsion. *(2 marks)*

> Obsessions are recurrent, intrusive thoughts or impulses that are seen as being inappropriate or forbidden. They may be embarrassing for the person who has such thoughts. A compulsion is a behaviour which is carried out to reduce the anxiety cause by obsessional thoughts.
>
> ### Level 2 answer (2 marks)
> **Examiner's comments:** AO1 Accurate and appropriate answer.

Examiner's comments

The middle sentence isn't really needed. Perhaps the word 'whereas' could be used to link the first and last sentences.

(3) Graham had recently failed his driving test. Although he was going to retake it in a month, he felt angry and unhappy. His dad offered to take him for some extra lessons, but Graham had lost interest and said he'd rather just sit in his room. Graham's mum was worried about him. He seemed to spend most of his time in bed and he hardly ever ate any food at the dining table.

Identify **two** characteristics of depression shown in the passage above. *(2 marks)*

> One characteristic is Graham's anger and unhappiness. This is an emotional characteristic and is the most common characteristic seen in depression. Another characteristic is the time Graham spends in bed. Some people with depression sleep much more than usual although others suffer from insomnia. This is a behavioural characteristic.
>
> ### Level 2 answer (2 marks)
> **Examiner's comments:** AO1 Accurate and appropriate answer.

Examiner's comments

We suggest a rough guide of 25 words per mark, but for simple 'identification' programmes such as this, this is too many words and could be simplified.

Topic 4 The behavioural approach to explaining phobias

Discuss the behavioural approach to explaining phobias. *(12 marks AS)*

> Mowrer proposed the two-process model. Classical conditioning says that we learn phobias by association. We associate a neutral stimulus with an unconditioned stimulus, which then leads to a new association being learned. For example, if our unconditioned stimulus is the sound of a metal bar being struck this leads to an unconditioned response of fear. If we pair the unconditioned stimulus with a neutral stimulus of a white rat, then we will learn to associate the sound of the metal bar being struck with the rat. This means that the rat becomes the conditioned stimulus, leading to a conditioned response of fear.
>
> Operant conditioning says that we learn things by reward and punishment. If we do something and we are rewarded for it, we are more likely to repeat the behaviour in the future. However, if we are punished for it, we will be less likely to repeat the behaviour. This theory explains how a phobia is maintained. The avoidance of the phobic stimulus is rewarding and so we are more likely to repeat this avoiding behaviour.
>
> The two-process model is supported by research asking people about their phobias. Some people can recall a specific event that led to their phobia developing. For example, Sue *et al.* found that agoraphobics are most likely to explain their phobia in terms of a specific event. This shows that classical conditioning can be involved in developing phobias.

Examiner's comments

This is a clear and accurate explanation of classical conditioning; its use as an explanation of phobias is also clear and accurate.

Nice concise explanation of operant conditioning and how this might explain the acquisition and maintenance of phobias.

The use of the phrase 'is supported by' is a good way, as here, of making research support effective AO3.

However, one limitation of the two-process model is that it does not explain the development of all phobias. Some people cannot remember an incident occurring that led to their phobia developing. This may be because different phobias may be the result of different processes. Arachnophobics often say that they saw someone else be scared of spiders and this was why they developed the phobia. This shows that neither classical nor operant conditioning can explain the development of all phobias.

Another limitation of the two-process model is that a phobia does not always develop after a traumatic incident. For example, not everyone who experiences a dog bite develops a phobia of dogs. The diathesis stress model says we inherit a genetic vulnerability for developing mental disorders, but this will only become apparent if it is triggered by a life event, such as being bitten by a dog.

Level 4 answer (10–12 marks)

Examiner's comments: AO1 Accurate and detailed description.

AO3 Five good points, clear and effective.

Topic 5 The behavioural approach to treating phobias

Describe and evaluate the use of systematic desensitisation **and/or** flooding in the treatment of phobias. *(12 marks AS)*

Systematic desensitisation (SD) uses counterconditioning to replace fear with relaxation. In this therapy, the phobics learn relaxation techniques which mean that they can relax on command. With the therapist, they imagine scenes with the phobic stimulus and rate them for anxiety, creating a desensitisation hierarchy, from the least to the most feared.

The phobic will start with the least feared scene while relaxing at the same time. When they no longer feel anxious, the fear has been desensitised. They then work their way up the hierarchy towards the most feared scene, one step at a time.

Flooding is a different therapy for treating phobias and it involves a single exposure to the most feared situation. Like systematic desensitisation, the phobic learns relaxation techniques, but then they are exposed to the actual phobic stimulus for two or three hours. If that isn't possible, then they will do this in virtual reality. A person can only be scared for so long and so as their adrenaline levels naturally go down, a new association can be learned between the originally feared stimulus and relaxation.

Research has found that systematic desensitisation is successful for treating a wide range of phobias. McGrath *et al.* reported a 75% success rate, but Choy *et al.* found that actual contact with the phobic stimulus was more effective than simply imagining it. This means that systematic desensitisation is successful in treating phobias.

However, other research has shown that systematic desensitisation may not be as effective for treating phobias that have an underlying evolutionary survival component, such as a fear of the dark. This means that this therapy's effectiveness may depend on what the phobic stimulus is and whether we have learned it through personal experience or not.

Flooding is not always the most effective method of treating phobias as it can be highly traumatic for the client. While they are made aware of this before the therapy begins, this does not mean that they will necessarily be able to cope once the therapy begins. This means that other therapies, such as systematic desensitisation, may be more effective for some people.

Level 4 answer (10–12 marks)

Examiner's comments: AO1 Accurate and well-detailed description of both SD and flooding.

AO3 Clear and effective evaluation, with three points elaborated to an appropriate level of detail.

Examiner's comments

Using alternative explanations, as this student does, is only effective if they are linked to the explanations being evaluated. This is what happens here, so another effective AO3 point.

A limitation is explained and then the diathesis-stress model used to show how a genetic vulnerability might interact with learning to produce a phobia.

Examiner's comments

Good opening paragraph that explains the nature of SD and in particular the important role played by relaxation.

Accurate description of the route through the SD hierarchy. This is sufficiently detailed.

Good, clear and detailed description of flooding. Good use of specialist terminology.

This first AO3 point follows the tried and tested PEEL 'formula', with identification of the main point, followed by evidence, elaboration and a link-back. An effective bit of evaluation.

This point looks at the limitation of SD in the treatment of 'ancient fears'. Clear and informed evaluation.

Another clear and elaborated point, this time evaluating flooding as technique in the treatment of phobias.

Topic 6 The cognitive approach to explaining depression

Discuss Beck's negative triad **and/or** Ellis's ABC model as a way of explaining depression. *(16 marks A)*

Examiner's comments

The cognitive approach explains abnormal behaviour, such as depression, as being a result of irrational thinking. Beck came up with a cognitive explanation for depression, thinking that depressed individuals feel depressed because they do not feel in control and their thinking is biased towards the negative. He said that they have a depressed schema, which they probably got during childhood and this means that they see the world in this way. These negative schemas lead to cognitive biases in thinking, which are where people over-emphasise the negative. The negative triad is made up of three key elements in a person's thinking. They have a negative view of themselves, a negative view of the world and a negative view about the future.

> An accurate and well-detailed description of Beck's negative triad. It is well organised and shows a good use of specialist terminology.

Ellis created the ABC model to explain depression. A is an activating event which happens in someone's life, B is the belief and C is the consequence. The belief can be either rational or irrational but if it is irrational, then it will lead to negative emotions, such as depression. These irrational beliefs come from musturbatory thinking, which means thinking that certain assumptions must be true if someone is to be happy. If you hold these musturbatory thoughts, you are likely to be disappointed or even depressed.

> There is a choice of covering Beck and/ or Ellis. There is a danger, when going for the 'and' option of it being too shallow, but that isn't the case here.

The cognitive approach is supported by research which shows a link between irrational thinking and depression. Hammen and Kranz found that depressed participants made more logical errors than non-depressed participants when interpreting written material. However, this link does not mean we can be sure that irrational thinking causes depression. It may be the other way around, and depression may lead to irrational thinking.

> Research evidence is used effectively to show that support for the cognitive approach. This is elaborated with interpretation of this research support.

One good thing about the cognitive approach as an explanation for depression is that it focuses on the person and it gives them both the responsibility for their disorder and the opportunity to change their thinking. But it also downplays the situational factors, for example, life events or family problems, which might have contributed to the depression. Instead it says that the disorder is all in the person's head and to recover they have to change how they think about the situation, not the situation itself.

> There is effective discussion within the critical point here, showing that despite its good points, there are also limitations of the cognitive approach when explaining depression.

The cognitive approach for depression has useful real-life applications, for example, through the use of therapy. Beck and Ellis' theories have both been used to create therapies, such as CBT. This therapy has been found to be the best treatment for depression, so if depression is successfully treated by challenging irrational thoughts, then irrational thoughts are probably a cause of depression.

> An appropriate way of evaluating an explanation of psychopathology, i.e. that it has led to effective therapies which, in turn lend support to the explanation itself.

One weakness of the cognitive approach as an explanation for depression is that not all irrational beliefs are, in fact, irrational. Alloy and Abrahamson found that depressed people gave more accurate estimates of the likelihood of disaster than non-depressed people. This suggests that depressive realists tend to see things as they are. This means that some 'irrational' beliefs may simply seem irrational rather than be irrational.

> Evaluation is presented in five distinct paragraphs, each one being appropriately elaborated as with this one on 'rational' irrationality.

Depression can also be explained in terms of genetic factors and neurotransmitters. Research has shown that depressed people have lower levels of serotonin than non-depressed people and that drug therapy can be successful in treating depression. This means that neurotransmitters also play a role in causing depression, and so a diathesis-stress model could be a better explanation for depression.

> Biological factors are integrated with cognitive factors by using the diathesis-stress model.

Level 4 answer (13–16 marks)

Examiner's comments: AO1 This answer has covered two approaches accurately and in detail. The level of description is typical of a Level 4 answer.

AO3 Five clear and effective evaluative points. These are mostly aimed at the cognitive approach to explaining depression in general but that's fine here.

Topic 7   The cognitive approach to treating depression

Outline and evaluate a therapy which challenges irrational thoughts as a way of treating depression.
(12 marks AS)

Examiner's comments

One therapy for treating depression is cognitive behavioural therapy (CBT). This therapy is based on the view that the way we think about things has an impact on how we feel about things and the therapy identifies, and challenges, this irrational thinking. Ellis' CBT is known as 'rational emotional behaviour therapy' (REBT) because the therapy resolves behaviour problems, too.

> An opening descriptive paragraph explains how CBT works, although this is a little too general rather than specifically looking at how this works with depression.

REBT focuses on challenging the irrational beliefs that lead to depression and aims to replace them with effective rational beliefs, which produce new feelings. The therapist may question the logic of the thinking, which is known as logical disputing, or they may ask for evidence that this belief is an accurate one (empirical disputing). Throughout the therapy sessions, the therapist will give the client unconditional positive regard, which means that they convince their client of their worth as a human being. This helps the client to feel able to change their beliefs and attitudes.

> Again, some mention of depression, but not specific to the treatment of depression. Things like 'new feelings' and changing 'attitudes' are not specific enough.

After several sessions of CBT, the client can move from catastrophising events to interpreting them more rationally. This means that they become more self-accepting and they feel better. Between therapy sessions, clients are asked to complete homework tasks, which involves testing these irrational beliefs in their own lives and putting new rational beliefs into practice.

> Good clear description of CBT and some (albeit brief) mention of how this might impact on depression.

Research shows that Ellis' REBT was effective in treating people with depression. Ellis himself claimed a 90% success rate over 27 sessions, and when Cuijpers *et al.* reviewed 75 studies, they found that CBT was superior to no treatment, showing that it is an effective method of treating depression.

> Concise, clear and effective AO3 paragraph showing research support for its efficacy.

A weakness of CBT as a therapy for depression is that its effectiveness is influenced by individual differences. Elkin *et al.* found that if people have rigid irrational beliefs and are resistant to change, then CBT is not an effective therapy. Ellis explained a lack of success in therapy as being a problem with suitability and he said that some people do not want a therapist's help. This means that CBT is suitable for some people with depression, but not all.

> Although a more general criticism of CBT, this is still relevant as a critical point on its use in the treatment of depression.

Research shows that exercise can be beneficial in alleviating depression, too. For example, Babyak *et al.* found that anti-depressant drugs, aerobic exercise or both can treat depression effectively. However, the relapse rate was different and people were more likely to relapse following drug treatment than exercise treatment. This shows that behavioural activation can be beneficial in treating depression.

> Not really linked to the use of CBT - therefore only marginally relevant as a criticism of it. This might have been used more effectively, perhaps showing that one is as effective (and less expensive) than the other for some people.

Level 3 answer (7–9 marks)

Examiner's comments: AO1 Tended to be a bit too general but did have some relevance and did offer accurate insights into how CBT works and how it might work with depression.

AO3 Mostly effective, although at times material could have been used in a more explicitly evaluative way. Overall this just about makes Level 3.

Topic 8 The biological approach to explaining OCD

Outline and evaluate genetic **and** neural explanations of OCD *(16 marks A)*

Examiner's comments

It is thought that obsessive compulsive disorder (OCD) may be a genetic disorder. This means that some people inherit specific genes from their parents that are related to the onset of OCD. Two genes have been identified as possibly contributing to OCD. One of these is the COMT gene, which regulates the production of dopamine. One form of the COMT gene has been found to be more common in OCD patients, and in these patients, there is lower activity in the COMT gene and there are higher levels of dopamine.

> Clear and accurate paragraph detailing the role of the COMT gene in OCD, although it might have highlighted why this 'mis-regulation' of dopamine might lead to OCD symptoms.

The other gene that might contribute to OCD is the SERT gene, which affects the way serotonin moves around the brain, which means that people with OCD have less serotonin. Ozaki *et al.* found a mutation of this gene in two unrelated families where six out of seven family members had OCD.

> A little superficial about the role that the SERT gene plays and how this impacts on the development of OCD, although what is here is accurate.

In OCD patients, dopamine is unusually high and we can see compulsive behaviours in rats if we give them too much dopamine. There are, however, lower levels of serotonin in patients with OCD and we can see this when we give antidepressants, which increase serotonin, to people with OCD, their symptoms are reduced.

> The impact of dopamine and serotonin is explained in this paragraph, so links to the first two paragraphs can be made, although this should be more explicit.

Another neural explanation for OCD is brain structure. Damage to the caudate nucleus, which is located in the basil ganglia fails to suppress minor 'worry' signals from the orbitofrontal cortex. This means that a 'worry circuit' is formed, leading to obsessive and compulsive behaviours.

> Good, clear and accurate description of the role of the 'worry circuit'.

One way to test for the role of genetic factors in OCD is to use family studies of OCD and these studies support the idea that genes play a role in OCD. Nestadt *et al.* found that people with a first-degree relative with OCD are more at risk of developing the disorder themselves. The main problem with this research is that families also share environments, so it could be that the environment is the cause of OCD.

> Although this paragraph is probably intended as AO3 evaluation it is mostly written as a description of the research. A 'lead-in' phrase (e.g. 'this is supported by....' would have helped make it more explicitly AO3.

Twin studies also support the role of genetic factors in OCD. Billett *et al.* found MZ twins had a higher concordance rate for OCD than DZ twins. However, because the concordance rate was not 100%, it means that the environment must play a role in the onset of OCD.

> Concise but effective AO3. This identifies the critical point, gives evidence to support it and draws a conclusion from it.

Further support for biological explanations of OCD come from brain scans. These have shown that patients with OCD show heightened activity in their orbitofrontal cortex if the scans are taken while their OCD is active, such as someone with a germ obsession holding a dirty cloth. This shows that obsessional thinking can be caused by damage to the brain circuits.

> Another effective piece of AO3, this time showing support for neurological explanations of OCD through brain scans.

Research shows that there is a genetic link to the abnormalities in brain structure found in patients with OCD. In key brain regions, such as the oribitofrontal cortex, people with OCD have reduced grey matter and so do their very close relatives. Menzies *et al.* suggested that people's risk of developing OCD could be detected by brain scans. This shows that differences in brain structure are inherited and they may lead to OCD in some people.

> This point follows the PEEL route, identifying the point, giving evidence to support it followed by elaboration and a conclusion. This is clear and effective.

An alternative explanation of OCD would be the two-process model, which says that we learn the behaviours associated with OCD. It argues that OCD may be caused by classical conditioning, where an association between a neutral stimulus and anxiety happens. OCD is maintained anxiety-reducing compulsive behaviours, which can be explained by operant conditioning. When people are given exposure and response prevention, and are prevented carrying out their behaviour in front of their feared stimulus, it is effective at reducing the behaviours. This means that OCD may have a psychological cause, either as well as, or instead of a biological cause.

> Quite a lengthy final paragraph that is linked back to biological explanations (fortunately) right at the end. This could have been a little shorter and more explicitly used as an argument against biological explanations alone being the cause of OCD.

Level 4 answer (13–16 marks)

Examiner's comments: AO1 Detailed, accurate and well organised descriptive material would suggest this is a top level answer.

AO3 All AO3 paragraphs are clear and effective and constitute a very good critical evaluation of biological explanations of OCD.

Topic 9 The biological approach to treating OCD

Outline and evaluate drug therapy as a way of treating OCD. *(12 marks AS)*

Examiner's comments

There are two types of drugs that can be used to treat OCD. One of these is an SSRI, which is an antidepressant. These work by acting on the person's serotonin levels. In OCD, serotonin levels are low and so if we give OCD patients drugs that increase serotonin then their behaviour should change, becoming less obsessive or compulsive. SSRIs also reduce the anxiety in OCD. Serotonin reuptake is inhibited by these drugs and so there is more serotonin in the synaptic gap between neurons and so there is an increase in serotonin at the receptor sites.

> This is a reasonably well-detailed description of how SSRIs have been used to treat OCD.

The other drug which is used to treat OCD are tricyclics, which are also antidepressants. These work by acting on both serotonin and noradrenaline and, like SSRIs, inhibit the receptor sites, so more of these neurotransmitters stay in the synaptic gap. As there are more side effects with tricyclics, these drugs are only used when SSRIs are not effective. Instead of antidepressants, OCD is sometimes treated with anti-anxiety medication, such as BZs. These slow down the activity of the central nervous system by reacting with GABA receptors on the outside of the receiving neuron. This makes it harder for the neuron to be stimulated by other neurotransmitters. The neuron's activity is slowed down, and induces feelings of relaxation.

> A detailed AO1 paragraph offering good description of how tricyclics and BZs are used in the treatment of OCD.

Drug therapy is supported by research which shows they are effective in treating OCD. For example, Soomro et al. found drugs were more effective than placebos in reducing symptoms up to three months after treatment. However, this means that we can only know about the short term effectiveness of drug therapy and so we know very little about the long-term effectiveness of drugs.

> This paragraph uses a research study to offer commentary on the effectiveness of drug therapy, and so receives AO3 credit.

One advantage of drug therapy is that it requires little input or effort from the user. Alternative therapies, such as CBT, are expensive, time consuming and require the person with OCD to put a lot of thought and effort into their treatment. Conversely, drug therapy is much quicker and easier, as well as being much more economical for the health service. The main problem with drug therapy, however, is that all drugs have side effects. SSRIs can cause nausea, headaches and insomnia and we know that tricyclics can cause hallucinations, which is why SSRIs are prescribed first. These side effects mean that people may choose to stop taking the drug and so drug therapy may limit the usefulness of drugs as treatments for OCD.

> Two AO3 points are made in this paragraph. They are both relevant, and suitably elaborated. This paragraph shows the benefits of offering 'sustained' evaluation on two evaluative points rather than merely 'bullet-pointing' lots of evaluative points without explaining their importance.

Level 4 answer (10–12 marks)

Examiner's comments: AO1 Competent, well-informed and accurate. There is sufficient detail here to warrant a mark in the top level if the AO3 is of similar quality.

AO3 Fortunately, the AO3 is of similar quality. The evaluative points raised are all relevant, and there is evidence of elaboration. It is this elaboration of the points made that enables this answer to be placed in the top level.

Key Terms

- Empiricism
- Introspection
- Scientific method

Possible essay question …

Outline **one** strength and **one** limitation of the scientific approach in psychology. *(12 marks AS, 16 marks A)*

Other possible exam questions …

+ Explain Wundt's contribution to the development of psychology. *(4 marks)*
+ Outline **one** criticism of Wundt's contribution to psychology. *(3 marks)*
+ Explain what is meant by introspection. *(4 marks)*
+ Outline **two** criticisms of introspection as a method of investigation. *(2 marks each)*
+ Explain the emergence of psychology as a science. *(6 marks)*

MUST know …

Introspection

Wilhelm Wundt was the first person to call himself a psychologist. He believed that the human mind could be studied scientifically, using a technique called **introspection**.

Introspection means 'looking into' and is the process by which a person gains knowledge about their mental and emotional states.

Wundt believed that with appropriate training, mental processes such as memory and perception could be observed systematically. For example, participants would be presented with a stimulus (e.g. a visual image) and asked to provide a description of their inner thought processes. Wundt could then compare these responses, to generate theories of perception.

 One criticism of introspection is…

…the focus on 'nonobservable' behaviour.

- **E** – Wundt's approach required participants to report on their conscious experiences which are unobservable constructs.

 Another criticism of introspection is…

…its lack of accuracy.

- **E** – Nisbett and Wilson (1977) claim that we have little knowledge of what causes or contributes to our behaviours and beliefs.

One strength of the scientific approach is…

…the reliance on objective and systematic methods.

- **E** – Scientific methods rely on a belief in determinism and therefore can establish the cause of behaviour through empirical and replicable methods.

SHOULD know …

The emergence of psychology as a science

Empiricists believe that knowledge comes from observation and experience alone. When empirical methods were applied to the study of human beings by Wundt, psychology began to emerge as a distinct entity.

This new approach – psychology – was based on two major assumptions. Firstly, that all behaviour is 'caused' and secondly, that it is possible to 'predict' behaviour in different conditions. The techniques used to explore these assumptions became known as the scientific method.

The scientific method refers to the use of investigative methods that are **objective, systematic and replicable**.

- **E** – For example, processes like memory and perception are impossible to observe.
- **L** – This matters because Wundt's approach lacks reliability as his results have not been reproduced by other researchers.

- **E** – They found that participants were unaware of the different factors that had been influential in their choice of consumer items, suggesting that we are unable to observe our own thoughts and feelings.
- **L** – This suggests that some of our behaviour and attitudes exist outside of conscious awareness and that introspection would not uncover them.

- **E** – If scientific theories no longer fit the facts, then they can be refined and adjusted to take into account new evidence.
- **L** – Therefore, the scientific approach is self-corrective and new theories will continually emerge.

 One limitation of the scientific approach is that…

…the methods can lack ecological validity.

- **E** – Some psychologists do not believe that all behaviour can be explored through scientific methods.
- **E** – By concentrating on objective and controlled observations, psychologists create contrived situations which lack ecological validity.
- **L** – This matters because human behaviour may be impossible to test scientifically and these methods would therefore be inappropriate.

 However, one strength of introspection is…

…its use in contemporary research.

- **E** – Csikszentmihalyi and Hunter (2003) used introspection as a way of measuring happiness.
- **E** – They found that when teenagers were engaged in a challenging task, they were more upbeat, in comparison to an everyday task.
- **L** – This suggests that introspection has some relevance in contemporary research and is still a useful tool for measuring certain behaviours.

CHOOSE THE RIGHT ANSWER

Which of the following are features of introspection. Tick **two** of the boxes below.

A Introspection is based on the belief that the mind can be studied scientifically. ☐

B Introspection literally means 'to examine'. ☐

C Introspection involves listening to an auditory stimuli, while describing your inner processes. ☐

D Introspection involves viewing a visual stimuli, while describing your inner processes. ☐

Answers on page 280

MATCH THEM UP

Match the key terms on the left with the definitions on the right.

Scientific method	The belief that all knowledge is derived from sensory experience.
Empiricism	The process by which a person gains knowledge about his or her own mental and emotional states.
Introspection	The use of investigative methods that are objective, systematic and replicable.

Answers on page 280

 WRITE YOUR OWN EVALUATION POINT

Select one evaluation point from the page opposite and write a burger (PEEL) paragraph.

Point	
Evidence	
Explain	
Link	

 A MARKING EXERCISE

Read this student answer to the following exam question:

Explain the emergence of psychology as a science. *(6 marks)*

> Psychology is based on two key assumptions. Firstly, that all behaviour is 'caused' and secondly, we can predict a person's behaviour. Psychology is based on scientific methods, for example laboratory experiments.

What mark do you think this would get?

YOUR MARK

AO1

	Hint
	A hint to help you decide:
	How many critical points have been covered?
	How much detail is there?
	See mark scheme on page 8

What else could this person include to improve their answer.

Answers on page 280

KEY TERMS

- Behaviourist
- Classical conditioning
- Operant conditioning
- Punishment
- Reinforcement

Possible essay questions ...

Outline and evaluate the behaviourist approach in psychology. *(12 marks AS, 16 marks A)*

Discuss the contribution of behaviourist psychologists to our understanding of human behaviour. *(12 marks AS, 16 marks A)*

Other possible exam questions ...

+ Explain what is meant by classical and operant conditioning. *(2 marks each)*

+ Outline the main findings of Pavlov's research. *(4 marks)*

+ Explain what is meant by positive and negative reinforcement in operant conditioning. *(2 marks each)*

+ Outline the main findings of Skinner's research. *(4 marks)*

+ Outline **one** strength and **one** limitation of the behaviourist approach. *(6 marks)*

MUST know ...

Classical conditioning

Pavlov discovered the process of **classical conditioning** in his research with dogs.

In Pavlov's original experiment he presented a bell, a **neutral stimulus (NS)**, with food, an **unconditioned stimulus (UCS)**, which led to an **unconditioned response (UCR)** of salivation. During the acquisition phase, the NS is presented shortly before the UCS and after many pairings the NS is able to produce the same response as the UCS. The NS becomes a **conditioned stimulus (CS)** and the response is now called a **conditioned response (CR)**.

Pavlov's experiment demonstrates the learning of innate reflex behaviours in animals.

 One strength of classical conditioning is...

...its application to the treatment of phobias.

- **E** – Classical conditioning has led to the development of systematic desensitisation – a treatment which reduces the anxiety associated with phobias.

 However, one criticism of classical conditioning comes from...

...other theories of learning.

- **E** – Seligman (1970) proposed the concept of preparedness to explain why some relationships are easier to establish than others.

 One strength of operant conditioning is...

...the use of experimental methods.

- **E** – Skinner's research uses controlled conditions to discover the causal relationship between two or more variables.

SHOULD know ...

Operant conditioning

Skinner's theory of **operant conditioning** suggests that the consequences of a behaviour may be positive or negative, and whether or not an organism repeats a particular behaviour depends on the nature of these consequences.

Positive reinforcement occurs when a behaviour produces a consequence that is rewarding for an organism. For example, giving praise to a child after they do something particular well will reinforce their good behaviour.

Negative reinforcement occurs when a behaviour removes an unpleasant consequence. For example, the act of hitting the 'off' button on an alarm clock removes the unpleasant ringing sound.

- **E** – Systematic desensitisation works by using the principles of classical conditioning to replace the learned response (anxiety) with another response (relaxation).
- **L** – This matters because systematic desensitisation is an effective treatment for a range of phobias, including arachnophobia (fear of spiders) and aerophobia (fear of flying).

- **E** – For example, animals are prepared to learn associations that are significant in terms of their survival: a dog will quickly learn to associate the smell of meat with food, however, it is slower to learn the association with the sound of a bell and food.
- **L** – This suggests that species have different capabilities to learn through the process of classical conditioning.

- **E** – Skinner's use of the Skinner box allowed him to manipulate the consequences of the behaviour (the IV) to measure the effect on the rat's behaviour (the DV).
- **L** – This allowed him to establish a cause and effect relationship between positive and negative reinforcement and the likelihood of future behaviour.

 A LEVEL ONLY ZONE ...

 P – One weakness of the behaviourist approach is...

...the reliance on non-human animals.

- **E** – Some psychologists claim that Skinner's reliance on rats and pigeons means that we are unable to draw conclusions in relation to human behaviour.
- **E** – These psychologists argue that humans have free will and that our behaviour is not shaped by classical or operant conditioning.
- **L** – This matters because psychologists may be unable to generalise the findings from animals to humans.

P – A final criticism of the behaviourist approach...

...is that it ignores other psychological explanations.

- **E** – The behaviourist approach ignores cognitive and emotional factors, suggesting that humans are a product of conditioning alone.
- **E** – However, many psychologists argue that human interaction is far more complicated than a simple stimulus-reinforcement relationship.
- **L** – This matters because the behaviourist explanation may not provide a complete explanation of complex human behaviours, for example, 'love'.

MATCH THEM UP

Match the key terms on the left, with the definitions on the right.

Reinforcement	The process by which a neutral stimulus is paired with an unconditioned stimulus, to eventually produce a conditioned response.
Punishment	The process of learning through reinforcement or punishment. If a behaviour is followed by a desirable consequence then that behaviour is more likely to occur again in the future.
Classical conditioning	Where a behaviour is less likely to occur again in the future, because it is followed by an unpleasant consequence.
Operant conditioning	Anything that strengthens a response and increases the likelihood that it will occur again in the future.

Answers on page 280

 COMPLETE THE DIAGRAM

Match the key terms below with the diagrams on the left:

BEFORE CONDITIONING

1   2

3   4

• Bell (NS)

• Food (UCS)

• No response

DURING CONDITIONING

5

• NS is now CS

• NS and UCS paired

AFTER CONDITIONING

6   7

• Salivation (CR)

• Salivation (UCR)

Answers on page 280

 APPLYING YOUR KNOWLEDGE

A behaviourist researcher studying reinforcement carried out a laboratory experiment by placing a pigeon in a puzzle box. The pigeon was able to escape from the box by pecking a red sign which said 'Exit'. However, there was also a green sign which said 'Do NOT press' and each time the pigeon pecked this sign, he received an electric shock.

Each time the pigeon escaped from the box he was given a food treat. The pigeon only pecked the green sign once, and never went near this sign again.

Use your knowledge of operant conditioning to explain the pigeon's behaviour. *(4 marks)*

Identify the psychology	Link to pigeon
	→ *This means that …*
	→ *This means that …*

Answers on page 280

 RESEARCH METHODS (CALCULATIONS)

The behaviourist researcher (in the previous question) noticed that at first the pigeon escaped rather slowly; however, with each attempt made, the time taken to escape decreased. The data from his experiment is shown in the table below.

Attempt	Time taken for the pigeon to escape from the puzzle box (seconds)
1	54
2	45
3	36
4	22
5	15
6	11
7	6

The experimenter chose to calculate the mean time taken. Explain why the mean is an appropriate measure of central tendency for the above data. *(2 marks)*

Calculate the mean time taken for the pigeon to escape from the puzzle box. *(1 mark)*

Calculate the range of scores, in seconds. *(1 mark)*

Answers on page 280

KEY TERMS

- Identification
- Imitation
- Mediational processes
- Modelling
- Social learning theory
- Vicarious reinforcement

Possible essay question ...

Outline and evaluate the social learning approach in psychology. *(12 marks AS, 16 marks A)*

Other possible exam questions ...

+ Explain what is meant by imitation, identification, modelling, vicarious reinforcement and the role of meditational processes. *(2 marks each)*

+ Outline the main findings of Bandura's research into social learning. *(4 marks)*

 Think

SLT takes into account 'thinking' - SLT places emphasis on the role of mediational processes. It is different to other learning approaches, as the observer must form a mental representation of the behaviour and weigh up the probable consequences of the behaviour. Therefore, an individual will only display the learned behaviour if the positive rewards outweigh the negative consequences.

MUST know ...

Social learning theory (Bandura, 1986)

In order for social learning theory (SLT) to take place, someone must '**model**' an attitude or behaviour.

A model provides an example of behaviour that can be observed and later copied.

Imitation is the process of copying an observed behaviour and is more likely to occur when **identification** takes place. Research suggests (Shutts *et al.*, 2010) that children are more likely to identify with and learn from models who are similar to them.

Finally, research has also found (Bandura and Walter, 1963) that children who observe a model receiving rewards are much more likely to imitate their behaviour. This is known as **vicarious reinforcement**.

 One strength of SLT is...

...the application to criminal behaviour.

- *E* – Akers (1998) found that the probability of someone engaging in criminal behaviour increases when they are exposed to models who commit crime.

 Another strength of SLT is...

...the research support for identification.

- *E* – Fox and Bailenson (2009) found that humans are more likely to imitate computer generated 'virtual' humans who were similar to the real participant, in comparison to those who were dissimilar.

EVALUATION **However, one criticism of SLT is...**

...the problem of causality.

- *E* – Siegel and McCormick (2006) argue that young people who possess deviant attitudes and values are more likely to seek out peers with similar attitudes and behaviour, as they are more fun to be with.

SHOULD know ...

Bandura *et al.* (1961)

Bandura *et al.* (1961) conducted an experiment to examine SLT in children.

Children observed an aggressive or non-aggressive adult model and were then tested for imitative learning.

The children who observed the aggressive model imitated a good deal of the aggressive behaviour (both verbal and physical) which was similar to that of the model. None of the children who had observed the non-aggressive model made verbally aggressive remarks.

In addition, in a follow-up study, children who saw the model being rewarded for their aggressive acts were more likely to demonstrate aggression in their own play.

- *E* – Therefore, if an individual identifies with a criminal model and develops an expectation of positive consequences for their own criminal behaviour, they are likely to copy this behaviour.
- *L* – This matters because it allows psychologists to understand and identify factors that lead to criminal behaviour and consequently suggest strategies to reduce crime.

- *E* – Participants who observed a similar virtual model exercising engage in more exercise in the 24 hours following the experiment in comparison to those who viewed dissimilar model exercising.
- *L* – This demonstrates the importance of identification in SLT and suggests that humans are more likely to imitate the behaviour of models who are similar rather than dissimilar.

- *E* – Consequently, it could be argued that humans do not observe and imitate negative (delinquent) behaviours, but those with delinquent attitudes seek out similar peers.
- *L* – This suggests that SLT may not be the cause of delinquent behaviour and other explanations may account for learning of negative behaviours, including crime.

 P – **Another criticism of SLT is...**

...the issue of complexity.

- *E* – SLT explains the development of gender specific behaviour, as a result of gender-specific role models.
- *E* – However, children are exposed to many different influences which interact in a complex way. These include genetic predisposition, media portrayals and so on.
- *L* – This matters because it is difficult to separate the effect of SLT from the many other factors that also influence behaviour.

EVALUATION *P* – **A final strength of SLT is...**

...the application to health campaigns.

- *E* – Andsager *et al.* (2006) found that the perceived similarity to a model in an anti-alcohol advertisement was positively related to the message's effectiveness.
- *E* – Health campaigns try to match characters that model the desired behaviours with the target audience, to increase the level of identification, to bring about greater social learning.
- *L* – This suggests that SLT has had a positive impact on health promotion campaigns.

✓ CHOOSE THE RIGHT ANSWER

Which of the following statements about social learning theory (SLT) is **not** true.

A	SLT only takes place when someone models an attitude.	☐
B	Imitation is when a person copies an observed behaviour.	☐
C	Identification is when a person adopts the attitudes and beliefs of a role model.	☐
D	Vicarious reinforcement takes place when an observer watches someone being rewarded for their behaviour.	☐

Answers on page 280

⚙ APPLYING YOUR KNOWLEDGE (1)

Using your knowledge of social learning theory, answer the following.

Mrs Watkins is a secondary school teacher. She notices that some of the children in her class constantly call out answers without raising their hands, which ruins the learning for other students.

How might Mrs Watkins use vicarious reinforcement to change the behaviour of these children? Explain your answer with reference to both positive reinforcement and punishment *(4 marks)*.

Identify the psychology	Link to Mrs Watkins (Hint: Don't forget the question states 'vicarious').
Positive reinforcement	→ *This means that …*
Punishment	→ *This means that …*

Answers on page 280

🎯 WRITE YOUR OWN EVALUATION POINT

Select one evaluation point from the page opposite and write a burger (PEEL) paragraph.

Point	
Evidence	
Explain	
Link	

⚙ APPLYING YOUR KNOWLEDGE (2)

Using your knowledge of social learning theory, answer the following.

Hint: Use the 'Think' box on page 136 to help you with this question.

Identify the psychology		Link to Joseph
	Joseph has recently started playing golf and is keen to play well.	
	He watches his friend Chris carefully, who hits a fantastic shot, and then tries to copy his shot. He thinks about how Chris was holding the golf club and whether he can do the same.	
	Explain the role of mediational processes in learning. *(4 marks)*	

Answers on page 280

KEY TERMS

- Cognitive
- Cognitive neuroscience
- Computer model
- Inference/Inferring
- Schema
- Theoretical models

Possible essay question ...

Outline and evaluate the cognitive approach in psychology. (*12 marks AS, 16 marks A*)

Other possible exam questions ...

+ Explain what is meant by internal mental processes, schema, theoretical and computer models, and cognitive neuroscience. (*2 marks each*)

+ Outline the use of theoretical and computer models as an explanation of mental processes. (*3 marks each*)

+ Using examples from research, explain the emergence of cognitive neuroscience. (*4 marks*)

+ Outline **two** strengths of the cognitive approach in psychology. (*6 marks*)

+ Outline **two** limitations of the cognitive approach in psychology. (*6 marks*)

MUST know ...

The study of internal mental processes

The cognitive approach recognises that mental processes cannot be studied directly, but must be studied by **inferring** what goes on as a result of measuring behaviour.

A **schema** is a cognitive framework that helps organise and interpret information in the brain. Schemas allow us to take shortcuts when interpreting large amounts of information, but can lead to stereotypes as we make assumptions about people based on incomplete information.

Cognitive psychologists often develop **theoretical models**, for example the multi-store model, to present a pictorial representation of a mental process based on current research.

 One strength of the cognitive approach is...

...its application to the treatment of psychological disorders.

- *E* – The cognitive approach has been used to explain how faulty thinking processes can cause illnesses such a depression.

 Another strength of the cognitive approach is...

...the use of scientific methods.

- *E* – Cognitive psychologists use scientific methods to collect and evaluate evidence.

 However, one criticism of the cognitive approach is that...

...humans are not like computers.

- *E* – The cognitive approach uses computer models to explain human coding and terms such as 'encoding', 'storage' and 'retrieval' are taken directly from the field of computing.

SHOULD know ...

The computer model and emergence of cognitive neuroscience

The development of computers has led to a **computer model** of memory. Information stored on the hard disk is like long-term memory and the computer's RAM (Random Access Memory) is like the working memory.

Cognitive neuroscience – Neuroscientists are now able to study the living brain, using brain imaging technology like positron emission tomography (PET) and functional magnetic resonance imaging (fMRI), to help psychologists understand how the brain supports different cognitive activities and emotions by showing which parts of the brain are active during different tasks.

- *E* – Consequently, the cognitive approach has led to the development of successful treatments, including Cognitive Behavioural Therapy (CBT).
- *L* – This matters because the cognitive approach has improved the lives of many individuals suffering from illnesses like depression.

- *E* – This means that conclusions about the mind are based on far more than common sense and introspection.
- *L* – This matters because the conclusions present a more valid representation of the human mind.

- *E* – However, there is an important distinction between computers and the human mind. For example, computers do not make mistakes, nor do they forget information.
- *L* – This matters because computer models are not an accurate representation of the human mind and should be treated with caution.

 P – Another criticism of the cognitive approach is that...

...it ignores emotion and motivation.

- *E* – Although the cognitive approach can tell us how different cognitive processes take place, it fails to explain why they do.
- *E* – Furthermore, the over-dependence on computer models may explain why the role of emotion and motivation is largely ignored by the cognitive approach.
- *L* – This matters because the human mind is clearly not like a computer, and emotion and motivation are clearly important aspects of human behaviour.

P – A final criticism of the cognitive approach is...

...that the studies often lack ecological validity.

- *E* – Many studies of the cognitive approach tend to use tasks that have little in common with participants' everyday experiences.
- *E* – For example, experiments in memory use artificial test materials that are relatively meaningless in everyday life (e.g. random word lists or digits).
- *L* – Therefore, much of the research in cognitive psychology is said to lack ecological validity, as it fails to reflect real-life behaviour.

✓ CHOOSE THE RIGHT ANSWER

Which of the following is **not** true in relation to the cognitive approach?

A A schema is a cognitive framework to organise and interpret information about the world. ☐

B Theoretical models are used to present a pictorial representation of a mental process. ☐

C Cognitive psychologists make inferences about mental processes, based on observable and measurable behaviour. ☐

D Cognitive neuroscience proves that different cognitive activities are localised in different parts of the brain. ☐

Answers on page 280

MATCH THEM UP

Match the key terms on the left, with the definitions on the right.

Inference/Inferring	Refers to the process of using computer analogies as a representation of human cognition.
Theoretical models	Means reaching a logical conclusion on the basis of evidence and reasoning.
Computer model	A cognitive framework that helps to organise and interpret information in the brain.
Schema	Refers to the process of using a simplified pictorial representation of a particular mental process.

Answers on page 281

DRAWING CONCLUSIONS

A cognitive psychologist conducted a laboratory experiment to how memory works. He gave participants a list of words to recall in one of two conditions.

Condition 1: Eight participants were presented words with pictures.

Condition 2: Eight different participants were presented the same words, without pictures.

The following results were obtained:

Participant	Condition 1 (Words with pictures)	Participant	Condition 2 (Words without pictures)
1	15	9	7
2	14	10	10
3	11	11	4
4	15	12	9
5	8	13	4
6	6	14	6
7	4	15	4
8	15	16	4
Mean		**Mean**	
Standard deviation	4.47	**Standard deviation**	2.29

1 Calculate the mean scores for both conditions. *(2 marks)*

2 Why are the standard deviation scores in the table above useful for cognitive psychologists? *(2 marks)*

Answers on page 281

📖 RESEARCH ISSUES

The experiment above in 'Drawing conclusions' is an example of a laboratory study, where an experiment is carried out in a controlled setting.

Outline one strength and one weakness of studying internal mental processes, like memory, by using laboratory studies. *(3 marks)*

One strength is…

One weakness is…

Answers on page 281

KEY TERMS

- Biological approach
- Evolution
- Gene
- Genotype
- Natural selection
- Neurochemistry
- Phenotype

Possible essay question ...

Outline and evaluate the biological approach in psychology. (*12 marks AS, 16 marks A*)

Other possible exam questions ...

+ Explain what is meant by the terms *genotype* and *phenotype*. (*2 marks + 2 marks*)
+ Outline the influence of genes on behaviour. (*4 marks*)
+ Outline the influence of biological structures and neurochemistry on behaviour. (*4 marks + 4 marks*)
+ Explain the difference between genotype and phenotype. (*3 marks*)
+ Outline the relationship between evolution and behaviour. (*4 marks*)
+ Outline **two** strengths and **two** limitations of the biological approach in psychology. (*3 marks for each*)

! Think

You also need to understand how changes in the population occur over time as a result of **natural selection**.

MUST know ...

The influence of genes and biological structures on behaviour

Genes are inherited from one generation to the next and carry instructions for a particular characteristic (such as intelligence). How these characteristics develop is partly due to the gene and partly due to the environment.

There is an important distinction between **genotype** and **phenotype**. The genotype is the genetic code in the DNA and the phenotype is the physical appearance that results from the inherited information.

Biological structures also play an important role in behaviour. The nervous system carries messages from one part of the body to another using neurons. Many aspects of behaviour are controlled by neurons, including: breathing, eating and sexual behaviour.

 One strength of the biological approach is...

...its use of scientific methods.

- **E** – The biological approach uses experimental methods as its main method of investigation.

 Another strength is...

...its application to the treatment of psychological disorders.

- **E** – Research into the role of neurochemical imbalances in depression has led to the development of drug treatments which correct this imbalance to minimise depressive symptoms.

 However, one criticism of the biological approach is that...

...it is reductionist.

- **E** – Reductionism is the view that human behaviour can be explained by breaking it into its smallest components, such as genes, neurotransmitters and hormones.

SHOULD know ...

The influence of neurochemistry and hormones

Neurotransmitters are electrochemical impulses that transmit messages from one neuron to the next, by travelling across the synapse.

There are different types of neurotransmitters, some of which trigger an impulse (**excitatory**) and some of which stop an impulse from firing (**inhibitory**). Dopamine is an excitatory neurotransmitter associated with drive and motivation, whereas serotonin is an inhibitory neurotransmitter associated with mood. Different levels of neurotransmitters can affect our behaviour.

Finally, **hormones** are chemicals produced by endocrine glands such as the pituitary gland. Hormones are secreted directly into the bloodstream where they travel to their target cells, causing a physiological reaction.

- **E** – Experimental studies take place in highly controlled environments and use sophisticated imaging and recording techniques, including PET and fMRI.
- **L** – Experimental studies are easy to replicate, thus adding validity to the original findings if they can be reproduced.

- **E** – For example, SSRIs (selective serotonin reuptake inhibitors) stop the reuptake of serotonin in the synapse and increase the level of serotonin being absorbed by the post-synaptic neuron, alleviating the symptoms of depression.
- **E** – This matters because the biological approach has helped improve the lives of many sufferers of depression by providing suitable drug treatments.

- **E** – For example, the biological explanation of depression suggests that depression is caused by a low level of serotonin, while ignoring cognitive, emotional and cultural factors.
- **L** – This matters because there are other factors that can contribute to depression and the biological approach ignores all of these other factors.

A LEVEL ONLY ZONE ...

 P – Another criticism of the biological approach is...

...the problem with evolutionary explanations of behaviour.

- **E** – Many human behaviours can be transmitted by both genetic and cultural routes.
- **E** – Furthermore, many patterns of human behaviour have purely cultural origins with no survival or reproductive benefit, for example musical appreciation.
- **L** – This matters because evolutionary explanations are unable to explain behaviours with no survival benefit and therefore do not provide a complete theory of human behaviour.

P – A final criticism of the biological approach is...

...the danger of genetic explanations.

- **E** – Recent research has found a genetic basis for criminal behaviour which has led to concerns about how this information might be used.
- **E** – For example, critics claim that this may lead to genetic screening to identify people at risk of criminality which could lead to discrimination against those people.
- **L** – This matters because individuals may be 'labelled' as criminals because of their genes, when such complex behaviours are far from straightforward.

 **MATCH THEM UP**

Match the key terms on the left with the definitions on the right.

Phenotype	Refers to the change over successive generations of the genetic make-up of a particular population.
Gene	A part of the chromosome of an organism that carries information in the form of DNA.
Neurochemistry	The genetic make-up of an individual. The genotype is a collection of inherited genetic material that is passed from generation to generation.
Evolution	The study of chemical and neural processes associated with the nervous system.
Genotype	The observable characteristics of an individual. This is a consequence of the interaction of the genotype with the environment.

Answers on page 281

SPOT THE MISTAKES

Read this student answer to the following exam question:

Explain the difference between genotype and phenotype. *(3 marks)*

There are **three** mistakes – draw a circle around each.

> Genes are inherited from one generation to the next and carry instructions for a particular characteristic (such as intelligence).
>
> There is an important distinction between genotype and phenotype.
>
> The phenotype refers to the genetic code in the neurotransmitters and the genotype is the physical appears that results from inherited information.

Answers on page 281

✔ **CHOOSE THE RIGHT ANSWER**

Tick **two** of the boxes below to indicate which of the following are true in relation to phenotypes.

A Phenotypes are the result of inheritance. ☐

B Phenotypes are the result of the environment. ☐

C Phenotypes are the result of evolution. ☐

D Phenotypes are the result of neurotransmitters. ☐

Answers on page 281

 APPLYING YOUR KNOWLEDGE

Identify the psychology		*Link to Samuel & Daniel*
	 Samuel and Daniel are identical twins who were separated at birth. When they meet each other at the age of 18 they are surprised by their slight differences in looks and their huge differences in personality. Samuel is much more outgoing than Daniel, who has always been rather shy. Use your knowledge of genotype and phenotype to explain the differences in their personality *(4 marks)*.	

Answers on page 281

KEY TERMS

- Defence mechanisms
- Psychoanalysis
- Psychodynamic
- Unconscious

Possible essay question ...

Outline and evaluate the psychodynamic approach in psychology. *(16 marks)*

Other possible exam questions ...

+ Outline the structure of personality from a psychodynamic perspective. *(4 marks)*

+ Explain **one or more** Freudian defence mechanisms. *(4 marks)*

+ Outline **two** strengths and **two** limitations of the psychodynamic approach in psychology. *(3 marks each)*

MUST know ...

Psychodynamic theories

Psychodynamic theories emphasise:
- change and development in the individual
- unconscious motives and desires
- the importance of early childhood experiences in shaping personality.

Freud's theory of psychoanalysis

The unconscious mind reveals itself through 'Freudian slips', creativity and neurotic symptoms.

Freud described the **structure of personality**, with three parts in conflict:
- The id – impulsive physical appetites including the libido.
- The ego – mediates between the id, the reality of the outside world and the superego.
- The superego – conscience (internalisation of societal rules) and ego-ideal (determined by parental expectations).

Defence mechanisms prevent traumatic memories from becoming conscious and causing anxiety:
- Repression – unconscious blocking of unacceptable thoughts and impulses.
- Denial – refusal to accept reality.
- Displacement – redirecting hostile feelings onto an innocent person or object.

 Psychoanalysis was a pioneering approach to treatment...

...based on case studies rather than introspection.
- **E** – The first to propose psychological treatments for disorders such as depression and anxiety.

 There is empirical evidence supporting...

...aspects of psychodynamic theory.
- **E** – such as unconscious motivations in behaviour, and the defence mechanisms of repression, denial and displacement.

 However, it is gender-biased...

...because Freud was ignorant of female sexuality.
- **E** – He based his theories on male sexual development as the norm, and didn't take account of the differences in female sexuality.

SHOULD know ...

Psychosexual stages

The psychosexual stages emphasise that libido (sexual energy) is the main drive, but is expressed differently at each stage of development.

Stage	Approx age (years)	Description
Oral	0-2	The mouth is the focal point of pleasure (sucking, biting.)
Anal	2-3	Ego development begins, with an awareness of reality and the need to conform. Toilet training is the major issue.
Phallic	3-6	Sexual energy is focused on the genitals. Boys experience the Oedipus complex, a desire to possess their mother and get rid of their father, causing castration anxiety.
Latent	6-12	Mastery of the child's world, repression of the conflicts of earlier stages.
Genital	12+	Fixing of sexual energy in the genitals, culminating in adult sexual relationships.

- **E** – A large-scale review of psychotherapy studies concluded that psychoanalysis produced significant, long-lasting improvements in symptoms.
- **L** – This shows the value of the insights of psychoanalysis and treatments based on them.

- **E** – Although critics claim that psychoanalytic theory is not testable or falsifiable.
- **L** – In fact, many claims of psychoanalysis have been tested experimentally, and are supported by the findings.

- **E** – Later psychoanalysts have criticized Freud's work and developed new theory relating to women's development.
- **L** – The gender bias in Freud's theory is problematic as he treated many female patients, and also because his theories are still very influential.

 Psychoanalysis is also culture-biased...

... may have little relevance to those from non-Western cultures.
- **E** – e.g., in China a person who is depressed or anxious avoids distressing thoughts, rather than being willing to openly discuss.
- **E** – This contrasts with the Western belief that open discussion and insight are always helpful in therapy.
- **L** – Psychoanalysis developed in a Western, middle-class culture so has limitations in its application outside that culture.

Psychoanalysis is a comprehensive theory...

...can be used to explain human behaviour in many fields outside psychology.
- **E** – e.g., in literary criticism, characters can be explored in terms of their unconscious motivations, or as a projection of unconscious aspects of the author's mind.
- **E** – This gives a language and common concepts for interpretation of literature, film and media.
- **L** – This explains the ongoing popularity of Freud's theories.

MATCH THEM UP

Match up the following concepts with their appropriate definitions.

1	Repression	A	The male child wishes to possess his mother
2	Oedipus conflict	B	Disturbing thoughts kept in the unconscious
3	Unconscious mind	C	Protect the conscious mind from anxiety
4	Superego	D	Sexual drive important in development
5	Defence mechanisms	E	Internalisation of societal and parental rules
6	Libido	F	Responsible for most behaviour

Answers on page 281

 ## CHOOSE THE RIGHT ANSWER

The following statements refer to different approaches in psychology. Select **one** statement that describes the psychodynamic approach.

A The mind is an information processor. ☐

B Behaviour is shaped by forces in the environment. ☐

C Behaviour is caused mainly by the unconscious. ☐

D Beliefs about oneself and the world affect behaviour. ☐

Answers on page 281

 ## DRAWING CONCLUSIONS

 A researcher looked at the effectiveness of treatment in two groups of patients suffering from symptoms of depression.

One group received psychoanalytic therapy and the other group received cognitive behavioural therapy, both over a two-year period. These two groups were compared to a control group of patients who received no treatment over the same two-year period.

The graph below shows the percentage of patients who reported a 'significant improvement' in their depressive symptoms at three months, six months and one year.

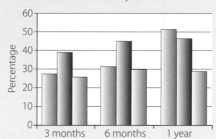

State **two** findings and for each one draw a conclusion (state what the findings show).

Finding 1:

Conclusion 1: This shows that …

Finding 2:

Conclusion 2: This shows that …

Answers on page 281

 ## APPLYING YOUR KNOWLEDGE

Sadie is a 40-year-old woman who has experienced high levels of anxiety since her teenage years. She doesn't remember much about her childhood but she knows it was traumatic and she tries not to think about it. However, her symptoms are now making it impossible to carry out normal everyday tasks like going shopping or meeting friends. She decides to try psychoanalysis after reading about it on the internet.

Using your knowledge of the psychodynamic approach, what might Sadie expect to experience in psychoanalysis? What explanations might a psychoanalyst suggest for her symptoms, and how might the analysis help her? *(6 marks)*

Identify the psychology	Link to Sadie

Answers on page 281

KEY TERMS

- Conditions of worth
- Congruence
- Free will
- Hierarchy of needs
- Humanistic
- Self
- Self-actualisation

Possible essay question ...

Outline and evaluate the humanistic approach in psychology. *(16 marks)*

Other possible exam questions ...

+ Outline Maslow's hierarchy of needs. *(4 marks)*
+ Explain the influence of humanistic psychology on counselling psychology. *(4 marks)*
+ Outline **one** strength and **one** limitation of humanistic psychology. *(3 marks each)*

MUST know ...

Basic assumptions of humanistic psychology

We have free will – the ability to make significant personal choices within biological/societal constraints.

Maslow described a **hierarchy of needs** - people must fulfil each level before moving to the next.

- SELF-ACTUALISATION
- ESTEEM
- LOVE/BELONGING
- SAFETY
- PHYSIOLOGICAL

Conditions of worth are a perception that acceptance from others depends on meeting their expectations.

Research supports Rogers' view that...

... people who experience *conditional* positive regard display more 'false self' behaviour.

- **E** – For example, teenagers who feel they have to fulfil certain conditions to gain their parents' approval frequently dislike themselves.

Maslow's hierarchy applies more broadly...

...to economic development of countries, as well as personal development of individuals.

- **E** – In the early stage of economic development, priority is on physiological and safety needs, such as food and reduction in murder rates.

However, cultural differences exist...

...as shown from cross-cultural studies.

- **E** – For example, a study in China found that belonging took priority over physiological needs, and self-actualisation related to contributions to the community rather than individual development.

SHOULD know ...

Basic assumptions of humanistic psychology

Focus on the self – Rogers claimed that our two basic needs, unconditional positive regard from other people and feelings of self-worth, develop from childhood interactions with parents.

The more similar our self-concept and our ideal self, the greater our psychological health and state of **congruence**. Most people experience some incongruence, and use defence mechanisms to feel less threatened.

The influence on counselling psychology

Rogers believed that people can creatively solve their own problems and become more authentic (true to self). Humanistic therapists provide empathy and unconditional positive regard, facilitating the client in finding self-actualisation.

People who attain self-actualisation are creative and accepting, and have peak experiences of extreme inspiration and ecstasy.

- **E** – Researchers found that adolescents who create a 'false self', pretending to be the sort of person their parents would love, are also more likely to develop depression.
- **L** – This supports 'conditions of worth'; the idea that unconditional positive regard from parents is essential for developing self-worth.

- **E** – Once these basic needs have been met, countries then focus on esteem needs (e.g. women's rights) and self-actualisation (e.g. access to education).
- **L** – This evidence from 88 countries over a 34-year period supports a hierarchy of needs in societies as well as individuals.

- **E** – Many studies confirm that people in Western cultures focus more on personal identity, whereas Chinese, Japanese and Koreans define self-concept in terms of social relationships.
- **L** – Maslow acknowledged that needs may appear in a different order or may be absent altogether. This more flexible hierarchy fits the evidence better.

Humanistic research methods

- **P** – Counselling cannot be tested experimentally due to the rigorous requirements of the experimental method.
- **E** – Rogers was an advocate of non-experimental research methods.
- **E** – Studies have shown personal growth as a result of humanistic counselling, but these do not show that the therapy *caused* the changes.
- **L** – It is, therefore, difficult to evaluate the therapies or theories scientifically.

The humanistic approach is unrealistic...

...with an idealised view of human nature.

- **E** – It assumes that people are inherently growth-oriented, not recognising some people's capacity for self-destructive behaviour.
- **E** – In addition, the humanistic assumption that all problems arise from blocked self-actualisation ignores situational forces in society, such as prejudice and inequality of opportunity.
- **L** – This means that the humanistic approach does not give a full description of human behaviour and development.

MATCH THEM UP

Match up the following concepts with their appropriate definitions.

1	Conditions of worth	**A**	the motivational theory proposed by Maslow
2	Congruence	**B**	the ability to make decisions about how to act
3	Free will	**C**	similarity between the ideal self and self-image
4	Hierarchy of needs	**D**	meeting the expectations of others in order to be accepted
5	Humanistic	**E**	the drive to achieve one's potential
6	Self-actualisation	**F**	the belief that humans have a desire to grow, create and love

Answers on page 281

 CHOOSE THE RIGHT ANSWER

According to Maslow's theory, the highest level of development is the fulfilling of self-actualisation needs, such as creativity, morality and acceptance. Which area of needs forms the level just before self-actualisation? Tick **one** box.

A	Love/belonging	☐
B	Physiological	☐
C	Esteem	☐
D	Safety	☐

Answers on page 281

 SPOT THE MISTAKES

Read this student answer to the following exam question.

Describe the influence of humanistic psychology on counselling. *(4 marks)*

There are **four** mistakes – draw a circle around each.

> Counsellors try to give their clients conditional positive regard, so that they feel accepted. They do this by listening without judgment and offering directive counselling. This results in the client developing more conditions of worth, so that they can be more authentic and true to self. Humanistic counselling is based on the idea that people can solve their own problems with support, and may just need help understanding themselves better so they can move towards the ultimate goal of self-esteem.

Answers on page 281

 APPLYING YOUR KNOWLEDGE

Using your knowledge of humanistic psychology answer the following.

Jasmine has been feeling very low since her relationship breakdown, and has gone to see a counsellor. The counsellor bases her practice on humanistic principles. Explain how the counsellor would try to help Jasmine. *(6 marks)*

Identify the psychology	*Link to Jasmine's counselling*

Answers on page 281

KEY TERMS

- Determinism
- Nature
- Nurture
- Science

Possible essay question …

Compare and contract the biological and behaviourist approaches to psychology. In you answer you should consider the assumptions of each approach, the research methods and therapies associated with them, and their positions in key debates in psychology. *(16 marks)*

Other possible exam questions …

+ Discuss **one or more** differences between the psychodynamic and humanistic approaches to psychology *(5 marks)*

+ Compare the biological and behaviourist approaches to Psychology *(6 marks)*

+ Describe the cognitive approach to psychology. Explain **one or more** similarities between the cognitive approach and social learning theory. *(8 marks)*

 Exam tip

You should be prepared to identify and explain similarities and differences between any pair of the six approaches covered in this chapter.

MUST know …

Determinism

The belief that behaviour is determined by forces such as biology, early experience or rewards. Opposite to this is free will, where the individual is capable of self-determination. Behaviour is, in reality, probably a mixture of the two.

In each approach, behaviour is determined by different factors:

Behaviourist – external forces in the environment (environmental determinism). Consequences of behaviour (reinforcement) determine the likelihood of repeating it.

Social learning – observation of models. Experience determines our vicarious learning, but free will allows us to choose when to apply what we have learnt.

Cognitive – our thought processes determine our behaviour. We have some degree of control.

Biological – physiological and genetic factors, which are outside our control.

Psychodynamic – unconscious factors, largely unknown to us and beyond our control.

Humanistic – our free will, not outside forces or biological predispositions.

Nature and Nurture

Behaviour may be the product of a person's genes (nature) or their experiences (nurture), but is usually a result of an interaction between nature and nurture.

The approaches have different explanations for the origin of behaviour:

Behaviourist – nurture, as behaviour is a consequence of our interactions with our environment.

Social learning – primarily nurture, although the capacity to learn from observation has adaptive value and is therefore innate (nature).

Cognitive – nature and nurture, as we all share innate cognitive processes (nature), but can develop irrational thoughts and beliefs as a result of experiences (nurture).

Biological – primarily nature, as neural and endocrine systems are innate. However, experience may modify these systems (nurture).

Psychodynamic – both nature (unconscious drives and ego conflicts) and nurture (the way we deal with them, which depends on our upbringing).

Humanistic – both nature (drive to self-actualise) and nurture (conditions of worth).

SHOULD know …

Psychology as science

Psychology lies at the intersection of biology, philosophy and sociology, so scientific research methods may not always be appropriate. In the more scientific approaches, high levels of objectivity of laboratory experiments may also mean low ecological validity. The approaches vary in their commitment to scientific methodology:

Behaviourist – positive. A highly objective and experimentally based approach, allowing for accurate measurement and replication.

Social learning – positive. Investigations follow experimental patterns, allowing inferences about cause and effect.

Cognitive – positive to a degree, as most propositions can be tested. However, mental processes cannot be directly observed so models are based on a great deal of inference.

Biological – positive, as factors like neurotransmitters can be studied experimentally.

Psychodynamic – mixed. Largely depends on case studies and subjective interpretation.

Humanistic – largely negative. Argues that scientific research methods are unsuitable for studying complex human experiences.

APPROACH	Basic assumptions
Behaviourist	• External forces in the environment shape our behaviour (i.e. it is determined). • Explanations of behaviour emphasise the role of nurture more than nature. • Behaviourism aligns itself strongly with the scientific method.
Social learning	• Behaviour is learned as a result of the observations of others (i.e. it is determined). • Explanations of behaviour emphasise the role of nurture more than nature. • Social learning aligns itself with the scientific method but research can lack validity.
Cognitive	• Thought processes determine behaviour (i.e. some degree of control over behaviour). • Explanations of behaviour emphasise the role of nature *and* nurture. • Cognitive psychology aligns itself with the scientific method despite some inference.
Biological	• Physiological and/or inherited factors determine behaviour. • Explanations of behaviour emphasise the role of nature more than nurture. • Biological psychology aligns itself strongly with the scientific method.
Psychodynamic	• Unconscious factors beyond our conscious control determine behaviour. • Explanations of behaviour emphasise the role of nature *and* nurture. • Psychodynamic psychology does not really align itself with the scientific method.
Humanistic	• Behaviour is under our conscious control (i.e. we have free will). • Explanations of behaviour emphasise the role of nature *and* nurture. • Humanistic psychology mostly rejects the use of the scientific method.

CHOOSE THE RIGHT ANSWER

Which **one** of the following statements is **false**? Tick **one** box only.

A Humanistic psychology is the least deterministic approach. ☐

B The behaviourist approach is the only one that totally discounts innate factors in behaviour. ☐

C The cognitive approach is based on experimental evidence. ☐

D The biological approach considers behaviour to originate entirely from innate factors (nature). ☐

Answers on page 281

A MARKING EXERCISE

Read this student answer to the following exam question:

Discuss **one or more** differences between the behaviourist and social learning approaches to psychology. *(5 marks)*

> The behaviourist approach believes that all behaviour is learnt by direct experience from the environment, whereas Social Learning Theory (SLT) says we can also learn by watching other people. In behaviourist theory, reinforcement needs to be experienced directly as a consequence of our own behaviour, but SLT includes the possibility of vicarious reinforcement. So behaviourism is deterministic, whereas SLT allows for free will and choices about how to behave.

Task 1 What mark do you think this would get?

YOUR MARK

See marking scheme on page 000.

Task 2 Your turn.

Write an improved answer here.

Answers on page 281

An idea

Make a mind map of the six approaches. Then add on key words for each, relating to determinism, nature/nurture and scientific research methods.

Now you could play a dice game; throw two dice to select two approaches, then flip a coin to select similarities or differences. Then state and elaborate a similarity or difference between these two approaches.

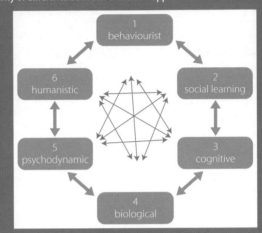

APPLYING YOUR KNOWLEDGE

Alex is determined to carry out a scientific experiment as part of his Extended Project Qualification research. His teacher explains that it is better to start with a research question and then decide on an appropriate research method. However, Alex is not deterred. Suggest an area of psychology that might be appropriate for Alex to study using an experimental method.

Using your knowledge of the different approaches to psychology, what explanations might psychologists give for Alex's determination to carry out an experiment as part of his project? *(6 marks)*

Approach	Explanation of Alex's preference
Behaviourist	
Social learning	
Cognitive	
Biological	
Psychodynamic	
Humanistic	

Answers on page 282

Behaviourist	People who believe that human behaviour can be explained in terms of conditioning, without the need to consider thoughts or feelings.
Biological approach	Views humans as biological organisms and so provides biological explanations for all aspects of psychological functioning.
Classical conditioning	When a neutral stimulus is consistently paired with an unconditioned stimulus so that it eventually takes on the properties of this stimulus and is able to produce a conditioned response.
Cognitive	Mental processes such as perception, memory and reasoning.
Cognitive neuroscience	An area of psychology dedicated to the underlying neural bases of cognitive functions.
Computer model	Refers to the process of using computer analogies as a representation of human cognition.
Conditions of worth	Conditions imposed on an individual's behaviour and development that are considered necessary to earn positive regard from significant others.
Congruence	Similarity between a person's ideal self and self-image. A difference represents a state of incongruence.
Defence mechanisms	Unconscious strategies that protect our conscious mind from anxiety. Defence mechanisms involve a distortion of reality in some way, so that we are better able to cope with a situation.
Determinism	Behaviour is determined by external or internal factors acting upon the individual.
Empiricism	The belief that all knowledge is derived from sensory experience. It is generally characterised by the use of the scientific method in psychology.
Evolution	The change over successive generations of the genetic make-up of a particular population. The central proposition is that the genotype of a population is changeable rather than fixed, and that this change is likely caused by natural selection.
Free will	The ability to act at one's own discretion, i.e. to choose how to behave without being influenced by external forces.
Gene	A part of the chromosome of an organism that carries information in the form of DNA.
Genotype	The genetic make-up of an individual. Inherited genetic material that is passed on, generation to generation.
Hierarchy of needs	The motivational theory proposed by Maslow, often displayed as a pyramid. The most basic needs are at the bottom and higher needs at the top.
Humanistic	The belief that human beings are born with the desire to grow, create and to love, and have the power to direct their own lives.
Identification	A form of influence where an individual adopts an attitude or behaviour because they want to be associated with a particular person or group.
Imitation	The action of using someone or something as a model and copying their behaviour.
Inference/Inferring	Reaching a logical conclusion on the basis of evidence and reasoning.
Introspection	The process by which a person gains knowledge about his or her own mental and emotional states as a result of the examination or observation of their conscious thoughts and feelings.
Mediational processes	The internal mental processes between environmental stimuli and the response made by an individual to those stimuli.
Modelling	A form of learning where individuals learn a particular behaviour by observing another individual performing that behaviour.
Natural selection	The process by which inherited characteristics that enhance an individual's reproductive success (or 'fitness') are passed on to the next generation, and so become more widespread in the population over time.
Nature	Behaviour is a product of innate (genetic) factors.
Neurochemistry	The study of chemical and neural processes associated with the nervous system.
Nurture	Behaviour is a product of environmental influences.
Operant conditioning	Learning through reinforcement or punishment. If a behaviour is followed by a desirable consequence then that behaviour is more likely to occur again in the future.
Phenotype	The observable characteristics of an individual. This is a consequence of the interaction of the genotype with the environment.
Psychoanalysis	A term used to describe the personality theory and therapy associated with Sigmund Freud.
Psychodynamic	Any theory emphasising change and development in the individual, particularly where 'drive' is central in development.
Punishment	Involves the application of an unpleasant consequence following a behaviour, with the result that the behaviour is less likely to occur again in the future.
Reinforcement	A term used to refer to anything that strengthens a response and increases the likelihood that it will occur again.

Schema	A cognitive framework that helps to organise and interpret information in the brain. Schemas help an individual to make sense of new information.
Science	A systematic approach to creating knowledge, using the scientific method.
Scientific method	The use of investigative methods that are objective, systematic and replicable, and the formulation, testing and modification of hypotheses based on these methods.
Self	Our personal identity, used synonymously with the terms 'self-image' and 'self-concept'.
Self-actualisation	A term used by Rogers to mean the drive to realise one's true potential. Maslow used it to describe the final stage of his hierarchy of needs.
Social learning theory	Learning through observing others and imitating behaviours that are rewarded.
Theoretical models	In cognitive psychology, models are simplified, usually pictorial, representations of a particular mental process based on current research evidence.
Unconscious	The part of the human mind that contains repressed thoughts and memories, as well as primitive desires and impulses that have not been allowed to enter conscious awareness.
Vicarious reinforcement	Learning that is not a result of direct reinforcement of behaviour, but through observing someone else being reinforced for that behaviour.

Topic 1 The origins of psychology

Explain Wundt's contribution to the development of psychology. *(6 marks)*

Examiner's comments

Wundt was the first person to be called a 'psychologist' and contributed to the development of psychology by moving from philosophical roots to controlled scientific research. He established the first psychology laboratory in Germany where he promoted the used of introspection as a way of studying internal mental processes.

> The answer starts with an outline of who Wundt is and his method 'introspection'.

Introspection means 'looking into' and is the systematic analysis of a person's own conscious experience. Wundt believed that with appropriate training, mental processes such as memory and perception could be studied scientifically and this paved the way for later controlled research and the study of internal mental processes by cognitive psychologists.

> The answer then provides a detailed description of introspection and highlights the contribution of introspection to the development of psychology.

Level 3 answer (5-6 marks)

Examiner's comments: AO1: The answer provides clear knowledge of Wundt's role in the development of psychology and is very accurate and detailed. The answer uses specialist terminology throughout and is clear and organised.

Topic 2 The behaviourist approach

Outline and evaluate the behavourist approach in psychology. *(12 marks)*

Examiner's comments

The behaviourist approach believes that human behaviour can be explained in terms of learning, known as conditioning. There are two main types of conditioning: classical and operant.

> The answer includes a short introduction, highlighting the key theories.

Pavlov discovered the process of classical conditioning in his research with dogs. In Pavlov's original experiment he presented a bell, a neutral stimulus (NS), with food, an unconditioned stimulus (UCS), which led to an unconditioned response (UCR) of salivation. Through repeated pairings, the NS becomes a conditioned stimulus (CS) and the response, salivation, becomes a conditioned response (CR). Pavlov's experiment demonstrates the learning of innate reflex behaviours in animals.

> Classical conditioning is explained accurately, with specialist terminology used throughout.

Operant conditioning suggest that the consequences of a behaviour may be positive or negative and whether or not an organism repeats a particular behaviour depends on the nature of these consequences. Positive reinforcement occurs when a behaviour produces a consequence that is rewarding for an organism, whereas negative reinforcement occurs when a behaviour removes an unpleasant consequence.

> Operant conditioning is explained accurately, although the answer could have elaborated on positive and negative reinforcement by providing examples.

One strength of the behaviourist approach is its application to the treatment of phobias. Classical conditioning has led to the development of systematic desensitisation – a treatment that reduces the anxiety associated with phobias. This matters because systematic desensitisation is an effective treatment for a range of phobias and demonstrates the utility of the behaviourist approach.

> The answer highlights a strength of the behaviourist approach in psychology, demonstrating its application to the treatment of phobias.

In addition, one strength of operant conditioning is its use of controlled scientific methods. Skinner's research on rats and pigeons used controlled conditions to discover the causal relationship between two or more variables. This allowed him to establish a cause and effect relationship between positive and negative reinforcement and the likelihood of future behaviour.

> The answer also highlights a strength of the operant conditioning and the use of controlled experimental methods.

However, one weakness of the behaviourist approach is the reliance on non-human animals. Some psychologists claim that Skinner's reliance on rats and pigeons and Pavlov's research on dogs, means that we are unable to draw conclusions in relation to human behaviour. This matters because psychologists may be unable to generalise the findings from animals to humans, therefore limiting the application of this approach.

> Finally, the answer also discusses a weakness of the behaviourist approach and the overreliance on animal research. All three evaluation points are thorough and effective.

Level 4 answer (10–12 marks)

Examiner's comments: AO1: The behaviourist theories of classical and operant conditioning are explained accurately with excellent detail. The answer could have elaborated on the description of operant conditioning, by providing examples of positive and negative reinforcement.
AO3: The evaluation is always thorough and effective and a broad range of evaluative evidence has been explored in reasonable depth.

Topic 3 Social learning theory

Outline and evaluate the social learning approach in psychology. *(16 marks)*

Examiner's comments

According to social learning theory (SLT), learning takes place through observing others and imitating behaviours that are rewarded. In order for SLT to take place, someone must model an attitude or behaviour. If a model's attitude or behaviour is observed, it may later be copied, especially if the behaviour is rewarded. If a person observes a model receiving a reward, they are likely to copy their behaviour, because they are learning from the reinforcement they receive, a process known as vicarious reinforcement. When a person copies an observed behaviour, imitation is said to have taken place. Finally, research suggests (Shutts et al., 2010) that children are more likely to identify with and learn from models who are similar to them.

> Although the term *identify* has been used, the answer should define the term identification, as it has only been briefly mentioned in this answer.

SLT is different to the behaviourist approach as it also takes into account 'thinking'. SLT places emphasis on the role of mediational processes, as the observer must form a mental representation of the behaviour and weigh up the probably consequences of the behaviour.

One strength of SLT is the research support for identification. Fox and Bailenson (2009) found that humans are more likely to imitate computer generated 'virtual' humans who were similar to the real participant, in comparison to those who were dissimilar. This demonstrates the importance of identification in SLT and suggests that humans are more likely to imitate the behaviour of models who are similar rather than dissimilar.

> The answer describes research support for SLT accurately providing an effective evaluation of identification.

However, one issue with SLT is the problem of causality. Siegel and McCormick (2006) argue that young people who possess deviant attitudes and values are more likely to seek out peers with similar attitudes and behaviour, as they are more fun to be with.

> The issues of causality has been explained well, however the evaluation point is not effective, as the answer has not explained why this is an issue for the social learning approach.

Another strength of SLT is its application to criminal behaviour. Akers (1998) found that the probability of someone engaging in criminal behaviour increased when they are exposed to models who commit crime. This matters because it allows psychologists to understand and identify factors which lead to criminal behaviour.

> The final strength, highlights the application of SLT to criminal behaviour and is effectively written.

Level 3 answer (9–12 marks)

Examiner's comments: AO1: The theory of SLT has been explained accurately and is reasonably detailed. However, certain key terms, including identification, could have been defined to add clarify. Furthermore, the answer could have outlined key research by Bandura *et al.* (1961) to support the social learning approach.

AO3: The evaluation is mostly reasonable but not always effective, for example, the issue of causality has been explained well, but the answer fails to state why this is an issue for the social learning approach. Other points could have been included, for example, how SLT can explain the development of gender specific behaviours. Overall, the essay has a clear and organised structure.

Topic 4 The cognitive approach

Outline and evaluate the cognitive approach in psychology. *(12 marks)*

The cognitive approach focuses on how people perceive, store, manipulate and interpret information through processes like perception and memory. The cognitive approach acknowledges that mental processes, like memory, cannot be studied directly.

Cognitive psychologists often develop models to help us understand and represent different cognitive processes. There are two types of models: theoretical models, for example, the multi-store model, which presents a pictorial representation of memory and computer models.

Another cognitive theory is idea of schemas. A schema is a cognitive framework that helps organise and interpret information in the brain. Schemas allow us to take shortcuts when interpreting large amounts of information.

One strength of the cognitive approach is its application to the treatment of psychological disorders. The cognitive approach has been used to explain how faulty thinking processes can cause illnesses such a depression, leading to the development of treatments like Cognitive Behaviour Therapy (CBT). This matters because the cognitive approach has improved the lives of many individuals suffering from illnesses like depression.

Another strength of the cognitive approach is the use of scientific methods. Cognitive psychologists use scientific methods to collect and evaluate evidence. However, one criticism of the cognitive approach is that humans are not like computers and the approach ignores emotion and motivation which are important in explaining human behaviour.

Level 3 answer (7–9 marks, likely to be the lower end of Level 3)

Examiner's comments: AO1: The cognitive approach is explained accurately and in detail. However, the idea of computer models requires elaboration or an example to improve this explanation.

AO3: The evaluation is only effective some of the time; however, there is a range of evaluative evidence in limited depth and the answer includes specialist terms appropriately.

Examiner's comments

The answer provides a good introduction outlining the key assumptions. However, the answer could have been developed to say why internal mental processes cannot be studied directly.

Theoretical models are accurately explained, with the use of an example. There is little detail in relation to computer models, and an example or elaboration is required here. The idea of schemas is accurately outlined.

The first evaluation point is thorough and effective, highlighting the application of the cognitive approach to the treatment of depression.

The final two evaluation points are reasonable points, but neither are elaborated or effective. Examples are required to elaborate on these answers and the answer should say why these points are a strength or criticism of the cognitive approach.

Topic 5 The biological approach

Outline the influence of biological structures and neurochemistry on behaviour. *(4 marks + 4 marks)*

Biological structures play an important role in behaviour. The nervous system carries messages from one part of the body to another using neurons. Furthermore, the brain is divided into two halves, known as hemispheres with each hemisphere divided into four different parts, known as lobes. Each lobe has a different influence on behaviour.

Neurotransmitters are electrochemical impulses that transmit messages from one neuron to the next, by travelling across the synapse. There are different types of neurotransmitters, some of which trigger an impulse (excitatory) and some of which stop and impulse from firing (inhibitory). The neurotransmitters serotonin is an inhibitory neurotransmitter associated with mood; serotonin can influence behaviour and has been associated with psychological disorders such as depression.

Examiner's comments

The answer has outlined biological structures well, but the influence on behaviour is limited. The answer should include an example of how the different lobes in the brain influence behaviour.

The answer has outlined the influence of neurotransmitters effectively. An example of how a specific neurotransmitter influences behaviour has been accurately explained.

Level 3 answer (5–6 marks)

Note: *This question can be treated as two four mark questions: outline the influence of biological structures (4 marks) and outline the influence on neurochemistry on behaviour (4 marks). Each part of the answer requires an example explicitly linked to the influence on behaviour.*

Examiner's comments: AO1: The answer has accurately outlined biological structures and neurochemistry. However, the answer has not explained how biological structures influence behaviour, but has explained the effect of neurotransmitters effectively, with an example.

Topic 6 The psychodynamic approach

Outline and evaluate the psychodynamic approach in psychology. *(16 marks)*

Examiner's comments

> 6 marks are available for A01 and 10 for A03, so you should aim to balance your essay with a bit more evaluation than description.

Psychodynamic approaches have certain features in common. They emphasise that individuals are able to change and develop, and they are driven by unconscious motivations. Early childhood experiences are really important and can cause problems later on.

> The opening paragraph gives a good introduction to psychodynamic theories generally.

Freud's theory is a psychodynamic approach. He invented psychoanalysis, and a lot of theories about the unconscious. There are three things I am going to explain, the structure of personality, the defence mechanisms, and the psychosexual stages.

> This paragraph doesn't say anything – don't waste time saying what you are going to say, or listing ideas without elaborating them.

According to Freud, the personality is made up of the id, the ego and the superego. They are in conflict with each other so we have defence mechanisms to defend us from this conflict. Defence mechanisms include repression, where the thoughts and memories are pushed down into the unconscious, and denial, where people refuse to accept reality. For example, an alcoholic who refuses to admit they have a problem.

> The structure of the personality is not elaborated. A list does not get much credit. The defence mechanisms are better explained, with an appropriate example.

The psychosexual stages are oral, anal, phallic and genital stages of development. The main drive in development is sexual energy, and little boys have an Oedipus complex when they want to sexually possess their mother and kill their father. That is the phallic stage. It causes conflict which the child has to repress.

> No elaboration of the meanings of the stages. The phallic stage has a reasonable level of elaboration, which is accurate.

The theories are quite weird and don't make much sense, but have become quite popular for explaining things like books and films. There is evidence that people do have unconscious motivations (we aren't always aware of the reasons we do things). And the defence mechanisms, repression and denial, do seem to be true. So there is evidence that supports some of Freud's theory. But actually it is very hard to test it, and critics say that it can't be tested so it is not scientific.

> Personal opinion about Freud's theories does not add anything to an essay.
>
> The very brief point about popularity is not elaborated. This is a different point from the evidence, and should be a separate paragraph.
>
> Good discussion of evidence and whether it is scientific.

Freud was very sexist and based his theory on male sexuality, because he didn't understand women. This means that it doesn't make sense for women as they don't have the Oedipus complex.

> Reasonable evaluation point, but it doesn't explain why this is a problem for women or for the theory.

Also his theory is culture biased because he based it on his middle class clients in Vienna. There is evidence that people have different priorities in Eastern cultures like China, where they don't necessarily want to talk about their problems like depression, and they would rather avoid it. This means his theory doesn't apply in other cultures.

> Effective evaluation point.

So overall his theories do have some evidence to back them up, and people have benefitted from psychoanalysis, but it is a limited theory because it is gender and culture biased.

> Final paragraph touches on practical applications, but otherwise adds nothing.

Level 3 answer (9–12 marks)

Examiner's comments: Overall, some points are well elaborated but some are very brief and list-like. Mostly accurate understanding of psychodynamic and good use of some technical terms.

Topic 7 Humanistic psychology

Outline and evaluate the humanistic approach in psychology. *(16 marks)*

Examiner's comments

Humanistic psychology was developed by Maslow and Rogers. Maslow described a hierarchy of needs, and said that people must fulfull each level before moving up to the next one. At the bottom, the most basic needs are biological – food, water, sex, etc. Then come safety needs, which include shelter, resources and employment. Next is the need for love and belonging, from family and a sexual partner. After that comes the need for esteem, which means self-esteem and also being respected by other people. Finally, if all these have been achieved, people can aim for self-actualisation, which includes creativity, spirituality and acceptance of the world as it is. This is a rare achievement and people who reach this often have amazing spiritual experiences where they are at one with the world.

> The first paragraph gives a very clear explanation of Maslow's theory, well elaborated and organised logically.

There is some evidence that people go through this hierarchy of needs, and even countries do in their economic development. However, people may go through the levels in a different order and in some countries people don't value self-actualisation in the same way. For example, in China people value contributions to the community rather than individual achievement of personal goals.

> A03 – evidence mentioned about people, and about countries, but no elaboration. Reasonable discussion of cultural differences but this could be better linked back to how it affects the theory.
>
> As there are two separate theorists, it makes sense to evaluate each separately like this.

Rogers had a slightly different view, and just looked at two basic needs, the need for unconditional positive regard from other people, and the need for self-worth. Both of these come from good relationships with supportive parents, and later with friends and partners. He also developed the idea of congruence, which is when your self-concept (the way you think you actually are) and your ideal self (the way you'd like to be) match up well – this is a healthy state to be in. Most people have some incongruence and use defence mechanisms to stop them feeling bad.

> Clear explanation of Rogers' theory – more A01.

Humanistic psychology has had a big influence on counselling psychology, and counsellors often use Rogers' ideas of unconditional positive regard and try to help the client work towards self-actualisation. This means it is a useful theory with real-world applications.

> Application to counselling is used as A03 here as it is well linked to practical applications.

However, it is hard to test the effectiveness of counselling as it can't be done scientifically as an experiment. People do seem to benefit from counselling, but you can't tell whether they would have got better anyway. So it is not a very scientific approach.

> This is then evaluated and linked to an issue with the relationship between humanistic psychology and scientific evidence, which is simply expressed but accurate.

It does support free will, as it says we can make decisions for ourselves, rather than our behaviour being determined by our biology or experiences.

> This return to free will at the end is very brief and the mention of biology or experiences could have been elaborated to make a contrast with other approaches, which would have been a higher level evaluation point.

Level 3 answer (9–12 marks)

Examiner's comments: A01: Overall, the A01 is much more effective than the A03.

A03: This essay has become unbalanced in favour of A01, when it should have more A03 than A01, to reflect the mark allocation.

Topic 8 Comparison of approaches

Describe the cognitive approach to psychology. Explain **one or more** similarities between the cognitive approach and social learning theory. *(8 marks)*

In the cognitive approach, the mind is thought of as an information processor, like a computer. Its processes like attention, decision making and memory can't be observed directly but can be inferred from the behavioural outcomes – things we do or say. So experiments can be done to investigate how information is processed. Researchers can then develop models, such as the working memory model, which are theories that fit the current research evidence.

Cognitive psychology is based on experimental research, so it is a very scientific approach as experiments allow researchers to draw conclusions about cause and effect. Similarly, social learning theory (SLT) is based on experimental investigations.

Both approaches allow for individual free will, as we can choose how to behave, although SLT has some deterministic aspects, as our experiences of vicarious learning affect what behaviours are available for us to choose from. For example, if you've never seen someone hitting another person it may never occur to you to hit someone. Similarly, the cognitive approach has some degree of determinism as our thought processes may be fixed and so we can't necessarily control them and make different choices. For example, if our schema says that people always shout when they are angry, then it might be difficult to choose not to do the same.

Level 4 answer (7–8 marks)

Examiner's comments: This is very clearly explained with appropriate examples for each approach, showing how there is a tension between determinism and free will in both approaches.

Overall, a Level 4 answer with plenty of material for 8 marks, clearly expressed.

You should pay attention to the marks available and don't just write everything you know, as this will take up too much time in the exam. To use your time efficiently means writing enough but not too much for each question. In A level, there is a weighting towards A02 or A03 in extended writing, so make sure you take more time evaluating (or in this case comparing) than describing, in proportion to the marks available.

Examiner's comments

This is a good summary of the cognitive approach, which is plenty for 3 marks of A01. The example of a model is useful to illustrate how the scientific process works in cognitive psychology – this is then picked up in the A03 section.

First similarity, brief but accurate, and the similarity is clearly signposted.

For 'one or more' questions, it is a good idea to cover one aspect in depth and one more superficially – the 1 ½ rule. In this case, determinism/free will is covered in more detail than the scientific approach.

This is very clearly explained with appropriate examples for each approach, showing how there is a tension between determinism and free will in both approaches.

KEY TERMS

- Autonomic nervous system (ANS)
- Brain
- Central nervous system (CNS)
- Peripheral nervous system
- Somatic nervous system
- Spinal cord

Possible essay question...

(This question would be based on a stem, and requires application of psychology.)

Outline the structure of the nervous system, and explain what is happening in Sophie's nervous system to produce this sequence of responses. *(12 marks)*

Other possible exam questions...

+ Outline the role of the central nervous system. *(4 marks)*

+ Identify the **two** divisions of the autonomic nervous system. *(2 marks)*

+ Identify the **two** components of the central nervous system. *(2 marks)*

+ Outline the role of the somatic nervous system. *(4 marks)*

+ Outline the role of the autonomic nervous system. *(4 marks)*

MUST know ...

The central nervous system (CNS)

- Comprised of the **brain** and **spinal cord**
- Controls behaviour and regulates physiological processes
- Receives information from the sensory receptors in the sense organs via sensory neurons
- Sends messages to effector organs (muscles and glands) via motor neurons
- Simple reflexes are relayed via the **spinal cord** without brain involvement

The brain has four main areas:

- The cerebrum (left and right cerebral hemispheres)
- The cerebellum (balance and coordination)
- The diencephalon
- The brain stem (regulates autonomic functions like breathing, heartbeat and swallowing)

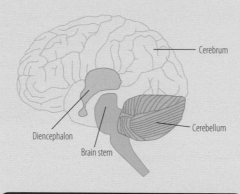

Cerebrum

Cerebellum

Diencephalon

Brain stem

The peripheral nervous system

All other nerves in the body, including:

1. The somatic nervous system, made up of sensory neurons and motor neurons

2. The autonomic nervous system which controls involuntary bodily functions such as heartbeat and digestion

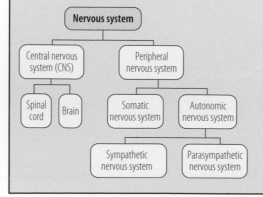

SHOULD know ...

The central nervous system

The cerebrum is made up of right and left cerebral hemispheres which are connected by the corpus callosum. They have four lobes each, which have specialist functions, eg:

- Frontal lobe (thought and speech production)
- Occipital lobe (visual processing)

The diencephalon is made up of:

- The thalamus (relay of impulses from sensory neurons)
- The hypothalamus (regulates body temperature and other homeostatic functions, links to the endocrine system via the pituitary gland)

The peripheral nervous system

The autonomic nervous system has two branches that tend to have opposite effects on organs:

1. The sympathetic nervous system

- Fight or flight, emergency responses
- Noradrenaline is the main neurotransmitter
- Increases heart rate, dilates blood vessels and pupils, slows down non-emergency processes like digestion

2. The parasympathetic nervous system

- Rest and digest response
- Acetylcholine is the main neurotransmitter
- Slows heartbeat, reduces blood pressure, restores digestive processes to normal

MATCH THEM UP

Match up the division of the nervous system with its function.

1	Sympathetic nervous system	A	Calm and restore: rest and digest
2	Central nervous system	B	Carries sensory and motor signals to and from the CNS
3	Autonomic nervous system	C	Emergency response: fight or flight
4	Somatic nervous system	D	Controls involuntary body functions
5	Parasympathetic nervous system	E	Relays nerve impulses from CNS to the rest of the body, and from body to CNS
6	Peripheral nervous system	F	Controls behaviour and physiological processes

Answers on page 282

 SPOT THE MISTAKES

Read this student answer to the following exam question:

Outline the role of the autonomic nervous system. *(4 marks)*

There are **five** mistakes – draw a circle around each.

> The autonomic nervous system allows you to carry out conscious activities. It includes two divisions, the sympathetic and non-sympathetic branches. The sympathetic nervous system tends to stimulate organs like the heart, sweat glands and digestive system. The neurotransmitter acetylcholine is mainly involved in this branch, and it is concerned with response to emergency situations. The para-sympathetic branch helps to restore a normal physiological state after the emergency has passed, and is known as the rest and refresh system.

Answers on page 282

 APPLYING YOUR KNOWLEDGE

Using your knowledge of the nervous system, answer the following.

Sophie has a spider phobia. She is calmly eating breakfast when she suddenly spots an enormous spider walking across the table towards her, and she becomes very tense and alert, her heart beating rapidly and her breathing becoming rapid and shallow. She starts to sweat and feels sick. Luckily her kind sister Charlotte is not afraid of spiders, and picks it up and removes it. Gradually Sophie calms down and she is able to continue with her breakfast. Explain what is happening in Sophie's body to produce this sequence of responses. *(8 marks)*

Identify the psychology	Link to Sophie

Answers on page 282

 An idea
On a separate piece of paper draw out the diagram of the divisions of the nervous system and try labelling it from memory. For each part, add one or two key words about its functions.

Possible essay question...

Explain the nature of synaptic transmission, and evaluate changes in neurochemistry of the brain as an explanation of behaviour. *(12 marks)*

Other possible exam questions...

+ Explain what is meant by sensory, relay and motor neurons. *(2 marks each)*

+ Explain the nature of synaptic transmission. *(6 marks)*

+ Explain what is meant by excitation and inhibition in synaptic transmission. *(2 marks each)*

+ Explain the role of excitatory and inhibitory neurotransmitters. *(3 marks each)*

★ Exam tip

You will never be asked more than 6 marks' worth of description. 6 marks' worth is about 150 words.

❗ Think

What do you know about different drug therapies for OCD and depression, and how they affect levels of neurotransmitters? See page 120.

MUST know ...

The structure and function of neurons

Sensory neurons carry nerve impulses from sensory receptors to the CNS.

Relay neurons connect sensory and motor neurons, and are found in the CNS. They are also known as interneurons.

Motor neurons have long axons which carry nerve impulses to muscles, triggering muscle contraction.

The **nerve impulse** travels along the axon in the form of an electrical signal called an action potential.

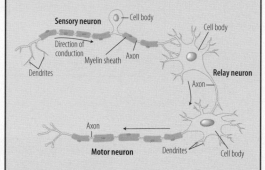

Synaptic transmission

The nerve impulse crosses the synaptic gap between the pre-synaptic and post-synaptic neuron with the help of neurotransmitters.

- The arrival of an action potential at the end of the axon triggers the release of neurotransmitter molecules from synaptic vesicles into the synaptic gap, by exocytosis.

- These neurotransmitter molecules diffuse across the gap and bind to specialised receptors in the membrane of the post-synaptic neuron, where they trigger a new action potential.

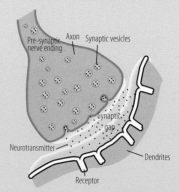

Excitatory and inhibitory neurotransmitters

Neurotransmitters can have different effects when they bind to the receptor on the post-synaptic neuron. The total effect determines whether an impulse is produced in the next neuron.

SHOULD know ...

The structure and function of neurons

- Neurons receive a signal via their dendrites from other neurons or from sensory receptors, and pass it on via their axon.

- The axon is covered in an insulating layer called the myelin sheath, which allows nerve impulses to travel along it more rapidly.

Synaptic transmission

Neurotransmitters are removed from the synaptic gap by:

- reuptake into the presynaptic neuron, for recycling

- breakdown by enzymes.

Some psychoactive drugs affect the rate of reuptake or breakdown of neurotransmitters, for example, SSRIs.

Excitatory and inhibitory neurotransmitters

Excitatory neurotransmitters:

- cause an excitatory post-synaptic potential (EPSP), making the postsynaptic neuron more likely to fire

- include acetylcholine and noradrenaline.

Inhibitory neurotransmitters:

- cause an inhibitory postsynaptic potential (IPSP), making the postsynaptic neuron less likely to fire

- include serotonin and GABA.

The summation of EPSP and IPSP inputs determines whether or not an action potential is produced, or how frequently the neuron will fire.

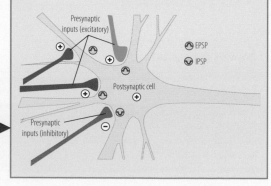

COMPLETE THE DIAGRAM

Select the correct labels for this diagram of a sensory neuron.

Sensory neuron

Direction of conduction

	A	B	C	D
Axon	☐	☐	☐	☐
Synapse	☐	☐	☐	☐
Dendrites	☐	☐	☐	☐
Nucleus	☐	☐	☐	☐
Cell body	☐	☐	☐	☐
Myelin sheath	☐	☐	☐	☐

Answers on page 282

CHOOSE THE RIGHT ANSWER

Which **one** of the following is only found within the central nervous system?

A Synapse ☐

B Sensory neuron ☐

C Relay neuron ☐

D Motor neuron ☐

Answers on page 282

DRAWING CONCLUSIONS

Researchers wanted to find out how much oxygen is used during different mental tasks. They used two groups of participants, who each carried out two conditions of the experiment. The first group were maths A level students, and the second group had failed maths GCSE. In the first condition, participants were asked to relax physically and focus on a screen displaying a landscape picture. In the second condition, they were asked to relax physically while performing some complex calculations, which appeared on the screen. The table below shows the mean oxygen consumption during the task by participants in each condition.

Table 1: Mean oxygen consumption by students carrying out each task (units per hour)

	Maths A level students	Students who failed maths GCSE
Condition 1	55	53
Condition 2	62	76

What does the table show about oxygen consumption during different tasks?

Finding:

Draw a conclusion: This suggests that …

Second finding:

Draw a conclusion: This suggests that …

Answers on page 282

APPLYING YOUR KNOWLEDGE

Researchers tested synaptic transmission in slices of rat brain. They stimulated different combinations of presynaptic neurons, and found that an action potential was sometimes produced, but not always. Use your knowledge of excitatory and inhibitory neurotransmitters to explain this finding. *(6 marks)*

Identify the psychology	Link to this study

Answers on page 282

KEY TERMS

- Endocrine glands
- Endocrine system
- Hormones
- Pituitary gland

Possible essay question...

Outline the functions of the endocrine system, and discuss the role of the endocrine system in behaviour. (12 marks)

Other possible exam questions...

+ Outline the functions of the endocrine system. (6 marks)
+ Explain the relationship between endocrine glands and hormones. (4 marks)
+ Outline the role of **one** endocrine gland and **one** hormone that it produces. (4 marks)

MUST know ...

Glands and hormones

Endocrine glands produce and secrete hormones into the bloodstream.

Each gland in the endocrine system produces specific hormones.

Hormones

- are the body's chemical messengers
- are released by endocrine glands into the bloodstream, where they circulate around the whole body
- bind to specific receptor molecules on the surface of target cells, stimulating a response in the target cells.

The pituitary gland...

...is controlled by the hypothalamus, a region of the brain that receives information via the nervous system and regulates many body functions.

The pituitary is the 'master gland', releasing hormones which control many other endocrine glands.

The anterior (front) pituitary releases ACTH as a response to stress, and also produces luteinising hormone (LH) and follicle-stimulating hormone (FSH).

- The posterior (back) pituitary releases oxytocin.

The adrenal glands

- Sit on top of the two kidneys.
- The adrenal cortex produces cortisol, which regulates important cardiovascular and anti-inflammatory functions in the body.
- The adrenal medulla releases adrenaline and noradrenaline, which prepare the body for fight or flight.

SHOULD know ...

Glands and hormones...

...are self-regulated by negative feedback, like a thermostat in the heating system of a house. This is called homeostasis. For example:

- The hypothalamus releases corticotrophin-releasing hormone (CRH).
- This stimulates the pituitary to release adenocorticotrophic hormone (ACTH).
- This in turn stimulates release of hormones from the adrenal cortex, such as cortisol.
- The increase in blood concentration of cortisol affects the hypothalamus and the pituitary, slowing down the release of CRH and ACTH.
- This ensures levels of hormone circulating in the blood are kept stable.

Pituitary hormones...

...have different effects in males and females.

In females, LH and FSH stimulate the ovaries to produce oestrogen and progesterone, whereas in males, they stimulate the testes to produce testosterone and sperm.

In females, oxytocin stimulates contraction of the uterus in childbirth, and is involved in mother-infant bonding. It has important effects on the brain and behaviour of males too, for example in sexual behaviour and reduction of anxiety.

The adrenal glands

Cortisol production is increased in response to stress. If cortisol level is low, the individual has low blood pressure, poor immune function and an inability to deal with stress.

Adrenaline helps the body to respond to acute stress by increasing heart rate and blood flow to the muscles and brain, and encouraging the breakdown of glycogen into glucose to provide energy.

Noradrenaline constricts the blood vessels, causing blood pressure to increase.

 ### Feedback and the pituitary-adrenal system

The hypothalamus and pituitary gland have special receptors that monitor circulating cortisol levels.

They can respond to increased cortisol in the blood by reducing secretion of CRF and ACTH, so cortisol levels return to normal.

This limits the potentially damaging effect of cortisol on the body.

 ### However...

...this system may not always work.

- **E** – Some researchers believe that this feedback system may break down when individuals are exposed to long-term stress.
- **E** – Research has found that the longer an individual is exposed to stress, the more adverse the effects are.
- **L** – This might explain why individuals in stressful jobs or stressful relationships suffer more stress-related illness.

MATCH THEM UP

Match up the hormone with the endocrine gland that produces it.

1	Testosterone		**A**	Ovaries
2	Oestrogen		**B**	Pituitary
3	Cortisol		**C**	Hypothalamus
4	ACTH		**D**	Adrenal cortex
5	CRH		**E**	Adrenal medulla
6	Noradrenaline		**F**	Testes

Answers on page 282

SPOT THE MISTAKES

Read this student answer to the following exam question.

Outline the role of **one** endocrine gland and of **one** hormone that it produces. *(4 marks)*

There are **four** mistakes – draw a circle around each.

> The pituitary gland stimulates the hypothalamus to produce
> hormones. The pituitary gland produces ACTH which targets the
> adrenal medulla, as part of the stress response. It also sends
> messages to the ovaries to make them release follicle stimulating
> hormone, oestrogen and progesterone. In males, it secretes
> testosterone which acts on the testes to make them produce sperm.

Answers on page 282

FILL IN THE BOXES

In each box below write one sentence describing an aspect of the endocrine system in about 20 words.

In each box below expand the content on the left, writing about another 20 words.

Endocrine glands are…	Endocrine glands are regulated by…
An example of an endocrine gland is…	This gland is controlled by…
Hormones are…	Hormones can affect the brain and behaviour by…
An example of a hormone is…	This hormone affects…

Answers on page 282

APPLYING YOUR KNOWLEDGE

Sandra has recently been diagnosed with Cushing's disease, which is caused by a tumour in the pituitary gland. Her symptoms include high blood pressure, fatigue and anxiety. She also finds that cuts and insect bites take a long time to heal. Using your knowledge of the hormones produced by the pituitary gland, explain Sandra's symptoms. *(6 marks)*

Identify the psychology	Link to Sandra

Answers on page 282

KEY TERMS

- Fight-or-flight response
- HPA axis

Possible essay question...

Discuss the fight-or-flight response to stress. *(12 marks AS, 16 marks A)*

Outline and evaluate the role of the fight-or-flight response. *(12 marks AS, 16 marks A)*

Other possible exam questions...

+ Explain what is meant by the term **fight or flight response**. *(2 marks)*

+ Outline the fight-or-flight response. *(6 marks)*

+ Outline the role of adrenaline in the fight-or-flight response. *(3 marks)*

MUST know ...

The fight-or-flight response to stress...

...enables us to react quickly to life-threatening situations.

Response to acute (sudden) stressors

- The hypothalamus activates the acute response via the **sympathetic nervous system** (SNS).
- The SNS sends a signal to the adrenal medulla.
- The adrenal medulla releases adrenaline into the bloodstream.
- **Adrenaline** causes increases in heart rate, breathing and blood pressure, so more oxygen reaches the heart and muscles. It also triggers release of glucose into the blood to supply energy, but inhibits digestion during the emergency.
- When the threat has passed, the **parasympathetic nervous system** restores heart rate and blood pressure to normal, and allows digestion to restart.

 ### However, there can be negative effects...

...on the body.

- *E* – Long-term increase in blood pressure can damage the blood vessels and lead to heart disease.

 ### But the 'tend and befriend' response...

...may be a more characteristic coping pattern for females (Taylor *et al.*).

- *E* – As women's stress responses evolved to enable them to be the primary caregiver of children, a fight-or-flight response would put children in danger.

 ### Another criticism is that...

...most animals and humans initially 'freeze' in response to a threat (Gray).

- *E* – This enables them to assess the threat before responding.

SHOULD know ...

The amygdala and hypothalamus

The stress response is triggered by the amygdala, an area of the brain which associates sensory inputs (sights, sounds, and smells) with emotions like fear and anger. The amygdala sends a distress signal to the hypothalamus.

Response to chronic (ongoing) stressors

If the threat is ongoing, the **HPA axis** kicks in.

H – The hypothalamus releases CRH into the bloodstream.

P – The pituitary gland responds to CRH and releases ACTH.

A – The adrenal cortex is stimulated by ACTH to release cortisol.

Cortisol helps the person to deal with stress by:

- reducing sensitivity to pain
- giving a quick burst of energy.

Cortisol also has a negative feedback effect on the hypothalamus and pituitary (see previous spread).

- *E* – In addition, too much cortisol suppresses the immune response.
- *L* – This increases the likelihood that the person will become ill.

- *E* – This difference could be linked to the release of the hormone oxytocin in caregivers, which decreases anxiety and reduces the fight-or-flight response.
- *L* – This means that there may be a genetic basis to sex differences in responses to stress.

- *E* – Adrenaline and cortisol promote this hyper-vigilant state, where the individual is alert to danger, focusing attention on relevant sensory inputs.
- *L* – This gives adaptive advantages, as we are able to choose the best response to particular threats.

A LEVEL ONLY ZONE

 ### Male aggressive responses

- *P* – There is evidence of a genetic basis for gender differences in the fight-or-flight response.
- *E* – Lee and Harley found that the SRY gene, found on the male Y chromosome, promotes development of male aggression.
- *E* – This might prime males to release more adrenaline when threatened.
- *L* – This adds further explanation to the different response of females, who do not have a Y chromosome.

Cooperative behaviour under stress

- *P* – Von Dawans *et al.* challenged the fight-or-flight response, observing that people often cooperate during crises like the 9/11 terrorist attacks in New York.
- *E* – Acute stress can increase friendly behaviour, even in men.
- *E* – Humans' social, mutually protective behaviour has contributed to our success as a species.
- *L* – Human behaviour in response to stress may depend on social/cultural factors, not just biologically determined responses.

MATCH THEM UP

1	ACTH	A	Slows down heart rate and decreases blood pressure
2	Adrenaline	B	Causes pituitary gland to release ACTH
3	Cortisol	C	Boosts the supply of oxygen and glucose to the brain and muscles
4	CRH	D	Associated with the 'tend and befriend' response to stress
5	Parasympathetic nervous system	E	Hormone involved in chronic stress
6	Oxytocin	F	Activates adrenal cortex to release cortisol

Answers on page 282

CHOOSE THE RIGHT ANSWER

Tick **two** of the boxes to indicate which of the following are part of the fight-or-flight response to acute stress.

A Cortisol ☐
B The pituitary gland ☐
C Adrenaline ☐
D The adrenal medulla ☐

Answers on page 282

COMPLETE THE DIAGRAM

Fill in the flow chart summarising the acute and chronic responses to stress.

CHRONIC STRESS — Hypothalamus — ACUTE STRESS

Answers on page 282

APPLYING YOUR KNOWLEDGE

Karl and Karla are walking down the street on a Saturday night when they come face to face with a large, aggressive-looking group of teenagers. Karl's muscles tense, and he approaches them, making a loud, challenging statement and raising his fists. Karla, on the other hand, stops very still and becomes pale and starts shaking uncontrollably. Using your knowledge of the fight-or-flight response, explain Karl and Karla's behaviour in this threatening situation. *(12 marks)*

Identify the psychology	Link to Karl and Karla's behaviour

Answers on page 282

163

KEY TERMS

- Broca's area
- Localisation of function
- Motor cortex
- Somatosensory cortex
- Wernicke's area

Possible essay question...

Discuss localisation of function in the human brain. *(16 marks)*

Other possible exam questions...

+ Explain what is meant by the term *localisation of function*. *(2 marks)*
+ Outline the nature of the motor centre in the brain. *(3 marks)*
+ Outline the role of the somatosensory centre in the brain. *(3 marks)*
+ Outline the role of the visual centre in the brain. *(3 marks)*
+ Outline the role of the auditory centre in the brain. *(3 marks)*
+ Explain the role of Broca's and Wernicke's areas. *(3 marks each)*

! Think

What problems might there be in using evidence about localisation of function from patients with brain lesions? Think about reliability and ethical considerations.

MUST know ...

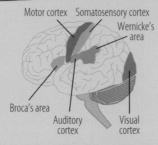

Motor cortex · Somatosensory cortex · Wernicke's area · Broca's area · Auditory cortex · Visual cortex

Visual centres

A nerve impulse from the retina is transmitted via the optic nerve to the thalamus, which relays it to the visual cortex in the occipital lobes. Input from the left of the visual field transfers to the visual cortex in the right hemisphere, and vice versa.

Auditory centres

Nerve impulses from the cochlea travel via the auditory nerve to the brain stem, for basic decoding, then continues via the thalamus to the auditory cortex, where the sound is interpreted.

EVALUATION
Support for localisation comes from...

...studies of patients with aphasia due to lesions.

- *E* – Broca researched nine patients with similar speech deficits, and found they all had lesions in a particular part of their left frontal lobe.

EVALUATION
One problem with this study is...

...that lesions often affect several brain areas.

- *E* – Dronkers *et al.* examined the preserved brains of two of Broca's patients using MRI, and found other areas were damaged, not just Broca's area.

EVALUATION
Communication between brain areas...

...may be more important than localisation.

- *E* – If the connecting neurons between different brain areas are damaged, this can result in loss of function.

SHOULD know ...

Motor and somatosensory areas

These are next to each other, along the precentral and postcentral gyri.

The somatosensory cortex processes sensory information from the skin, which it maps to different body regions.

The motor cortex sends nerve impulses to the muscles, with different parts of the motor cortex controlling different parts of the body.

The information relating to each half of the body is processed in the opposite hemisphere of the brain.

Language centres

Broca's area, in the posterior part of the left frontal lobe, near to the motor region which controls the mouth and vocal cords, is involved in speech production.

Wernicke's area is in the posterior portion of the left frontal lobe, near the auditory cortex. It is involved with speech comprehension.

- *E* – In addition, Wernicke researched patients who could still speak but had problems understanding language. He found they all had lesions in a similar area in the left temporal lobe.
- *L* – This shows that there are specific areas in the brain that are specialised for language production and comprehension.

- *E* – In fact, lesions that only affect Broca's area generally only result in temporary speech disruption.
- *L* – This suggests that language involves networks of brain regions, not just a few specific areas.

- *E* – Dejerine described a case in which the loss of ability to read resulted from damage to neurons connecting the visual cortex and Wernicke's area.
- *L* – This suggests that complex behaviours, like reading, involve impulses being passed around the brain through a network of neurons.

EVALUATION
Equipotentiality

- *P* – Lashley believed that, if a brain area was damaged, other intact areas of cortex could take over their function.
- *E* – The effect of brain damage would depend on its extent rather than its location.
- *E* – This is supported by the discovery that people can regain some cognitive abilities after brain damage (see section on Plasticity).
- *L* – This supports the idea that basic motor and sensory functions are localised, but higher mental functions are not.

EVALUATION
Individual differences in language areas

- *P* – Patterns of activation of brain areas during language tasks vary between individuals.
- *E* – For example, Bavelier *et al.* observed activation in the right temporal lobe as well as the left frontal, temporal and occipital lobes during silent reading.
- *E* – Other studies have shown that women, who use language more than men, have larger Broca's and Wernicke's areas.
- *L* – This suggests that localisation of function may develop differently depending on use.

CHOOSE THE RIGHT ANSWER

Which of the following areas of the brain is being defined in each of the examples below? Choose one area of the brain that matches each function and write A, B, C or D in the box next to it.

A Broca's area

B Motor area

C Somatosensory area

D Wernicke's area

(i) Area of the brain responsible for the production of speech. ☐

(ii) Area of the brain responsible for comprehension of speech. ☐

(iii) Area of the brain responsible for processing inputs from touch. ☐

Answers on page 283

 RESEARCH ACTIVITY

A neurologist was investigating a very frustrated patient who had lost his ability to speak after a stroke. The neurologist decided she would like to publish the details in a case study.

Identify **one** ethical issue the neurologist should consider in publishing this case study. Suggest how she could deal with this ethical issue.

Ethical issues:	How to deal with this issue:

Answers on page 283

 APPLYING YOUR KNOWLEDGE

The neurologist observed that her patient, Lionel, seemed to be experiencing a familiar pattern of difficulties. He appeared to be able to understand speech, and could make vocal sounds, but could not express any intelligible words. He was also unable to write down what he wanted to say.

Using your knowledge of localisation of function in the brain, suggest which area(s) of the brain may have been damaged by this patient's stroke. *(8 marks)*

Identify the psychology	Link to Lionel's problems

Answers on page 283

An idea 👍

On a piece of paper, draw some rough outlines of the side view of the brain. Then close this spread, and try to mark on the location of the somatosensory cortex, motor cortex, visual and auditory centres, Broca's and Wernicke's areas. Then recall the function of each and add key words to your diagram.

Now open your book and check your diagram. Keep repeating this until you can label the diagram without hesitation.

KEY TERMS

- Hemispheric lateralisation
- Split-brain research

Possible essay question...

Outline and evaluate research into lateralisation and/or the split brain. *(16 marks)*

Other possible exam questions...

+ Explain the nature of lateralisation in the brain. *(6 marks)*

+ Outline the findings of split-brain research. *(6 marks)*

+ Explain what is meant by the terms lateralisation and split-brain research. *(2 marks each)*

MUST know ...

Hemispheric lateralisation

Each hemisphere has functional specialisations.

- The left hemisphere is dominant for language and speech.
- The right hemisphere specialises in visuo-motor tasks.

The two hemispheres are connected by bundles of nerve fibres such as the corpus callosum, through which they exchange information.

Split-brain research

To treat severe epilepsy, surgeons would sometimes cut the nerve fibres of the corpus callosum. This would prevent seizures from affecting both halves of the brain.

These 'split-brain' patients were researched to explore how each half of the brain would respond to visual inputs when unable to communicate with the other hemisphere.

 Split-brain research has limitations...

... as patients who have had this procedure are rare.

- **E** – The procedure is rarely carried out nowadays, and many studies only included a few participants, or even just one.

 However, lateralisation is not fixed...

... but changes with age for many types of tasks.

- **E** – Healthy older adults have less lateralisation of function, using both hemispheres more as they get older.

 Language may not be restricted to the left hemisphere...

...but differs between individuals.

- **E** – Right-handed people generally develop their language centres in the left hemisphere, but left-handed people may have them on either side, or both.

SHOULD know ...

Hemispheric lateralisation

Paul Broca reported that damage in a particular area of the left hemisphere led to language deficits, yet damage to the equivalent area of the right hemisphere did not.

The connection via the corpus callosum means that we are still able to talk about things perceived by the right hemisphere (e.g. face recognition).

Key Study: Sperry and Gazzaniga (1967)

How? They studied split-brain patients. They presented information to either the left or right visual field, and asked patients to respond verbally or using one of their hands.

Showed? If a picture is shown to the left visual field, this information is processed by the right hemisphere, but it cannot respond verbally as it has no language centre. The left hemisphere does not receive the information and therefore cannot talk about it, despite having a language centre.

- **E** – These patients may have had underlying physical disorders, or there may have been some intact nerve fibres remaining.
- **L** – This means the results of studies are not always replicated, and it may be unwise to draw general conclusions from them.

- **E** – Szaflarski *et al.* found that language lateralisation increased during childhood and adolescence, but decreased steadily after age 25.
- **L** – This suggests that older people's brains recruit both hemispheres to increase their processing power, perhaps to compensate for age-related cognitive decline.

- **E** – For this reason, neurosurgeons find out which hemisphere is dominant and contains language centres in an individual patient before carrying out treatments like ECT (electro-convulsive therapy), in order to minimise cognitive side effects.
- **L** – This means we shouldn't generalise or make assumptions about the lateralisation of language centres in individuals.

 The purpose of lateralisation is unclear

- **P** – Lateralisation is assumed to increase neural processing capacity.
- **E** – However, there is little empirical evidence of any functional advantage of lateralisation in humans.
- **E** – Lateralisation enables chickens to be better at performing two tasks simultaneously (finding food and watching for predators).
- **L** – This suggests that lateralisation of function may enhance efficiency when carrying out simultaneous but different tasks.

 Split-brain patients may develop new abilities

- **E** – For example, a patient known as J.W. developed the capacity to speak about information presented to either hemisphere.
- **E** – This shows that his lateralisation was not fixed.
- **L** – This supports the idea that lateralisation is determined by use and the brain can adapt to new requirements.

APPLYING YOUR KNOWLEDGE

B.L. is a split-brain patient, whose corpus callosum was severed surgically in order to treat her severe epilepsy. When a picture of a cat is presented to her left visual field, and a lion to her right visual field, she says she has seen a lion. However, when she is asked to pick a matching card using her left hand, she picks the picture of the cat.

Explain this using your knowledge of lateralisation of function in the brain. *(12 marks)*

Identify the psychology	Link to B.L.

Answers on page 283

 CHOOSE THE RIGHT ANSWER

Which **one** of the following statements about lateralisation is false? Tick one box only.

A The left hemisphere is generally dominant for language. ☐

B Information from the right visual field is processed by the left hemisphere. ☐

C The motor cortex in the right hemisphere controls muscles of the left half of the body. ☐

D Facial recognition generally takes place in the left hemisphere. ☐

Answers on page 283

 A MARKING EXERCISE

Read this student answer to the following exam question.

(a) Split brain patients show unusual behaviour when tested in experiments. Briefly explain how unusual behaviour in split brain patients could be tested in an experiment. *(2 marks)*	The patient could be shown pictures on a screen. They then have to say what they've seen.
(b) Briefly evaluate research using split brain patients to investigate hemispheric lateralisation. *(4 marks)*	The research has been carried out on a very small sample of individuals, as not many have split brains, so findings should not be generalised. The people who had split brain surgery may have had other brain changes caused by the drugs they'd been taking to treat their epilepsy. The control group would not, so wouldn't be a valid control.

How many marks do you think they would get? How could you improve these answers.

Your mark:

Your mark:

Answers on page 283

 DRAWING CONCLUSIONS

In a study of hemispheric dominance, normal participants were played recordings of different word lists through headphones, so that each ear received a different list of ten words. They were then asked to recall as many words as possible.

The table shows how many words from each list were accurately recalled by the participants.

Participant	1	2	3	4	5	6	7	8	9	10
Words heard by left ear	3	9	6	8	5	0	2	10	7	3
Words heard by right ear	7	2	4	0	1	7	6	1	2	4

What percentage of participants remembered more words heard in their left ear?

Answers on page 283

A LEVEL ONLY ZONE

KEY TERMS

- Brain plasticity
- Functional recovery

Possible essay question...

Outline and evaluate the evidence for plasticity and/ or functional recovery after trauma. *(16 marks)*

Other possible exam questions...

+ Explain what is meant by the term plasticity of the brain. *(2 marks)*

+ Outline evidence for plasticity in the brain. *(6 marks)*

+ Outline evidence for functional recovery after trauma. *(6 marks)*

MUST know ...

Plasticity

The brain continues to create new neural pathways and alter existing ones as a result of **experience**. The brain can develop new connections and prune away weak ones.

For example, playing video games results in new synaptic connections in brain areas involved in spatial recognition, strategic planning, working memory and motor performance.

Functional recovery after trauma

When brain cells are damaged, as they are during a stroke, other parts sometimes take over their functions.

This can happen by **neural unmasking**, in which dormant synapses can be reactivated when they receive more neural input than previously.

Animal studies support plasticity...

...in response to an enriched environment.

- **E** – Kemperman found that rats kept in complex environments developed more new neurons than rats kept in lab cages.

London taxi drivers also demonstrate plasticity.

- **E** – Maguire *et al.* measured the grey matter in taxi drivers brains using MRI scanning, and found a positive correlation between the size of their posterior hippocampus and how long they had worked as a taxi driver.

Stem cells have helped rats...

...to recover from traumatic brain injury (TBI).

- **E** – In a controlled experiment, rats given transplants of stem cells into their brains developed more neuron-like cells in the area of the injury than control rats.

SHOULD know ...

Plasticity

There is a gradual decline in cognitive function with age, but even 60-year-olds still have brain plasticity, and can increase their grey matter in the visual cortex when taught a new skill, such as juggling.

Davidson *et al.* found that experienced meditators (Tibetan monks) produced more gamma brainwaves than student volunteers, indicating that meditation causes permanent changes.

Functional recovery after trauma

Stem cells implanted into the brain may help to treat brain damage, by:

- directly replacing damaged cells
- secreting growth factors that 'rescue' injured cells
- forming a neural network linking uninjured areas with the damaged brain region.

- **E** – In particular, they showed an increase in neurons in the hippocampus, which is associated with learning and navigation.
- **L** – This supports the idea that the number of new neurons can change in adult animals in response to environmental stimulation.

- **E** – This was a way of operationalising their navigational experience.
- **L** – So it seems that the more navigational experience the drivers had, the larger their posterior hippocampus had become, supporting plasticity in response to experience.

- **E** – Also, stem cells were observed to have migrated to the area of injury.
- **L** – This suggests that stem cells could be actively involved in recovery from TBI, at least in rats.

 Functional plasticity reduces with age...

...so adults may need to develop compensatory behavioural strategies to deal with cognitive deficits, such as writing lists or seeking social support.

- **E** – However, adults can still show functional recovery with intense retraining and extensive practice.
- **L** – But the capacity for neural reorganisation is much greater in children than adults.

 Patients with college level educational attainment...

...are much more likely to recover well after TBI.

- **E** – Schneider *et al.* retrospectively examined data from the US TBI Database.
- **E** – Nearly 40% of patients with college level education achieved disability-free recovery after a year, compared to less than 10% of patients who left school early.
- **L** – The researchers concluded that 'cognitive reserve' could be a factor in neural adaptation during recovery from TBI.

DRAWING CONCLUSIONS (1)

The hippocampus is a brain structure involved with memory. Maguire used MRI scans to measure the volume of the hippocampus of taxi drivers. The scattergraph shows data from a similar study.

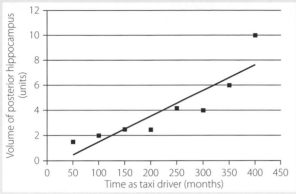

- Describe the relationship between the volume of the posterior hippocampus and the time spent as a taxi driver.

Findings:

- What does this suggest about plasticity in this part of the brain?

Conclusions:

Answers on page 283

 SPOT THE MISTAKES

Read this student answer to the following exam question.

What is meant by the terms 'plasticity' and 'functional recovery' of the brain? *(2 + 2 marks)*

> The brain is able to change by developing new synaptic connections and pathways. This is called plasticity. For example, playing video games kills brain cells. Even if some parts of the brain are destroyed by trauma, they can re-grow. This is called functional recovery.

What mark would you give this answer?

My mark:

Write an improved answer.

Answers on page 283

 DRAWING CONCLUSIONS (2)

Below are some data from the US Traumatic Brain Injury systems database.

Total no of patients	Patients with DFR	*DFR = disability free recovery after 1 year
769	214	

What percentage of the total number of patients achieved DFR?

The table below shows the relationship between DFR and years of education.

Years of education	≥16	12–15	≤12
% DFR	39.2	30.8	9.7

Display these findings on an appropriate graph.

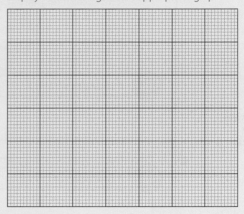

What do they show about the relationship between educational attainment and functional recovery?

Answers on page 283

 WRITE YOUR OWN EVALUATION POINT

Select one evaluation point from the page opposite and write it in your own words below.

Point	
Evidence	
Explain	
Link	

Key Terms

- Electroencephalogram (EEG)
- Event-related potential (ERP)
- Functional magnetic resonance imaging (fMRI)
- Post-mortem examinations

Possible essay questions...

Describe and evaluate ways of investigating localisation of function within the brain. *(12 marks)*

Discuss the use of functional magnetic resonance imaging as a way of studying the brain. Refer to other scanning techniques as part of your discussion. *(16 marks)*

Other possible exam questions...

(A 'stem' describing a study could be given here) …

+ Compare **two** ways of studying the brain, and explain which might be most useful for investigating this patient's difficulties. *(6 marks)*

+ Outline **one** strength and **one** limitation of … (any of the four ways of studying the brain could be given). *(6 marks)*

MUST know …

Post-mortem examinations

If a researcher suspects that a patient's behavioural changes were caused by brain damage, they may look for abnormalities after the person dies. For example, Broca observed patients' speech difficulties, and found lesions in the brain post-mortem.

Scanning techniques

Functional magnetic resonance imaging (fMRI) measures changes in blood flow, indicating increased neural activity, in particular brain areas.

Electroencephalograms (EEG) measure electrical activity in the brain via electrodes placed on the scalp. EEGs show brainwaves over time.

Event-related potentials (ERPs) are very small voltage changes triggered by specific stimuli.

 A strength of fMRI is…

…it is non-invasive
- **E** – so it can be used to measure activity in the living brain without causing harm.

 A limitation of fMRI is…

…it is not measuring neural activity directly
- **E** – so findings can be misinterpreted.

 A strength of EEG is…

…it records brain activity in real time
- **E** – so researchers can monitor responses to tasks.

 A limitation of EEG is…

…it can't detect activity in deeper brain regions.
- **E** – such as the hippocampus.

 A strength of ERP is…

…they provide a continuous measure of processing in response to a stimulus.
- **E** – This gives quantitative experimental data.

 A limitation of ERP is…

…require many repetitions to gain meaningful data
- **E** – so they can address simple questions.

 A strength of post-mortems is…

…brain tissue can be examined in detail
- **E** – and deeper structures can be investigated.

 A limitation of post-mortems is…

…use of drugs and age may affect brain tissue
- **E** – so there are many confounding variables.

SHOULD know …

Post-mortem examinations

HM's brain has been extensively investigated post-mortem, confirming damage to his hippocampus related to his inability to store new memories. Post-mortem studies have also identified brain abnormalities in schizophrenia and depression.

Scanning techniques

fMRI images are useful for identifying which areas of the brain are involved in particular mental activities.

EEG patterns in patients with epilepsy show spikes of electrical activity. Alzheimer's patients often show overall slowing of electrical activity.

Sensory ERPs occur in the first 100ms after the stimulus; cognitive ERPs are generated later.v

Another strength of fMRI is…

…it is more objective than relying on verbal reports of psychological processes
- **E** – useful for studying non-verbal phenomena.

Another limitation of fMRI is…

…it overlooks the networked nature of brain activity
- **E** – may be more important than localised activity.

Another strength of EEG is…

…it is useful for clinical diagnosis.
- **E** – e.g., epileptic seizures give characteristic EEG spikes.

Another limitation of EEG is…

…it can't pinpoint the exact source of activity
- **E** – as electrodes detect electrical activity from overlapping areas.

Another strength of ERP is…

…they can measure brain responses without the need for behavioural response or speech.
- **E** – Researchers can 'covertly' monitor responses.

Another limitation is that they only record…

…voltage changes in superficial brain areas
- **E** – so only events in the neocortex are measurable.

Another strength of post-mortems is that…

…changes in neurotransmitter levels can be measured
- **E** – e.g., abnormalities associated with schizophrenia.

Another limitation of post-mortems is…

…only retrospective data can be collected.
- **E** – It is too late to test cognitive function.

MATCH THEM UP

Match up the technique with its advantages.

1	fMRI	**A**	Measures brain's response to a stimulus
2	EEG	**B**	Detailed examination of brain tissue, anatomy and neurochemistry
3	ERP	**C**	Non-invasive, no radiation, measures pattern of activity of living brain
4	Post-mortem examinations	**D**	Records brain activity over time, can detect epilepsy

Answers on page 283

RESEARCH ISSUES

Identify one ethical issue with the use of H.M.'s brain after death, and explain how this issue might have been dealt with.

Answers on page 283

KEY WORDS

Exam question: Discuss the use of functional magnetic resonance imaging as a way of studying the brain. Refer to other scanning techniques as part of your discussion. *(16 marks)*

Select key words or phrases to fill in the table.

fMRI technique			
Strengths			
Limitations			
Another technique			
Advantages			
Disadvantages			

APPLYING YOUR KNOWLEDGE

Flora has been experiencing seizures, which started with short blank periods, but recently she has become unconscious and fallen to the ground during a seizure. Her GP referred her to a neurologist for investigation. What technique would be most appropriate for examining Flora's brain, and why? What limitations might there be to this method of investigation? *(8 marks)*

Identify the psychology	Link to Flora's investigations

Answers on page 283

KEY TERMS

- Circadian rhythm
- Sleep-wake cycle

Possible essay question...

Discuss the role of circadian rhythms in human behaviour. (16 marks)

Other possible exam questions...

+ What is meant by the term, *circadian rhythm*? (2 marks)
+ Give **one** example of a circadian rhythm. (2 marks)
+ Outline **one** research study that has investigated circadian rhythms. (4 marks)

MUST know ...

The nature of circadian rhythms

Biological rhythms lasting about 24 hours adapt the body to meet the demands of the day/night cycle.

The **sleep-wake cycle** is controlled by the suprachiasmatic nucleus (SCN) in the hypothalamus. The strongest sleep drive is usually between 2–4 am and 1–3 pm. This sleepiness is more intense if we are sleep deprived.

This 'free-running' internal circadian 'clock' maintains a cycle of 24–25 hours even in the absence of external cues. It is disrupted by major changes in sleep schedules, such as jet travel or shift work.

 Evidence for a 'free-running' circadian rhythm...

...comes from studies by the French cave explorer Michel Siffre.

- *E* –During six months in a cave in Texas with no daylight, clocks or radio, his circadian rhythm settled to just over 24 hours, but with some dramatic variations.

 There are individual differences...

...in circadian rhythms.

- *E* –The cycle length can vary from 13 to 65 hours.

 However, earlier studies suffered...

...as they assumed that dim artificial light would not affect circadian rhythms.

SHOULD know ...

The nature of circadian rhythms

Environmental light levels cause neural signals to be sent to the SCN, so that the circadian rhythm can be synchronised with daylight hours. This is photoentrainment.

The homeostatic drive for sleep increases gradually throughout the day, as we use up energy in activity.

Other circadian rhythms

Core body temperature is lowest (about 36°C) around 4:30 am, and highest (about 38°C) around 6 pm. It also dips between 2 pm and 4 pm.

Hormone production also follows a circadian rhythm. For example, melatonin production by the pineal gland peaks during the hours of darkness, promoting sleepiness.

- *E* –At age 60, his circadian rhythm had slowed down, sometimes stretching to 48 hours.
- *L* – This shows that the circadian rhythm is not dependent on light or social cues and can vary with age.

- *E* – Also, 'morning people' prefer to rise early and go to bed early, whereas 'evening people' prefer to wake and go to bed later.
- *L* – So individuals seem to have innate differences in their cycle length and onset.

- *E* – Czeizler *et al.* altered participants' circadian rhythms down to 22 hours and up to 28 hours using dim artificial light alone.
- *L* – This weakens the evidence of earlier studies.

 Chronotherapeutics

- *P* –A real world application of circadian rhythms is chronotherapeutics – the study of how timing affects drug treatments.
- *E* – To be most effective, drugs need to be released into the body at the optimal time.
- *E* – For example, the risk of heart attack is greatest in the early morning.
- *L* – This has prompted the development of novel drug delivery systems so that the drug is released into the bloodstream during the vulnerable period.

 Temperature may be more important...

... than light in setting the body clock.

- *E* – It seems the SCN transforms information about light levels into neural messages that set the body's temperature.
- *E* – Buhr *et al.* found that fluctuations in body temperature cause tissues to become active or inactive.
- *L* – So, although the SCN responds to light, the circadian fluctuation of body temperature may actually control the other biological rhythms.

MATCH THEM UP

Match up the term with its elaboration.

1	Homeostatic drive	**A**	is affected by daylight
2	Sleep drive	**B**	tends to be about 24–25 hours, though it can vary between 13 and 65 hours in different individuals
3	Sleep-wake cycle	**C**	is strongest between 2–4 am and 1–3 pm
4	Melatonin	**D**	causes an increasing need for sleep through the day
5	Free-running circadian rhythm	**E**	is produced by the pineal gland in the brain in response to darkness

Answers on page 283

CHOOSE THE RIGHT ANSWER

Which **two** of the following terms can be applied to the sleep-wake cycle?

A Lateralisation ☐

B Circadian rhythm ☐

C Infradian rhythm ☐

D Endogenous ☐

Answers on page 283

APPLYING YOUR KNOWLEDGE (1)

Katie and Jack have moved in together, and found that they have very different sleep patterns. Katie likes to go to sleep by 10 pm and wakes about 6 am, often going for a run before breakfast. Jack, however, prefers to stay up until 1 or 2 am, and sleeps until 10 am.

Referring to psychological research, how can you explain this difference, and what advice would you give Katie and Jack if they want to see more of each other? *(8 marks)*

Identify the psychology	Link to Katie and Jack's sleep incompatibility

Answers on page 283

APPLYING YOUR KNOWLEDGE (2)

Researchers measured body temperatures at two hourly intervals during a 24 hour period, for a group of participants. The table below shows the means and standard deviations of these measurements.

Time	00:00	2:00	4:00	6:00	8:00	10:00	12:00	14:00	16:00	18:00	20:00	22:00	24:00
Mean body temperature °C	36.5	36.6	36.0	36.9	37.2	37.3	37.7	36.8	37.5	38.1	37.9	37.1	36.5
Standard deviation	0.7	0.3	0.6	1.5	1.8	0.4	0.2	0.5	0.7	1.1	1.9	1.7	0.8

Draw an appropriate graph of the mean body temperatures. *(6 marks)*

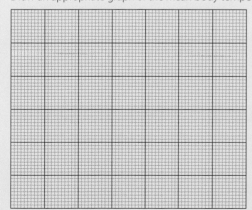

Comment on what the findings show about the circadian rhythm for body temperature. *(4 marks)*

Finding 1	
Conclusion 1	
Finding 2	
Conclusion 2	
Finding 3	
Conclusion 3	

Answers on page 283

KEY TERMS

- Infradian rhythms
- Ultradian rhythms

Possible essay question…
Outline and evaluate evidence for infradian and/or ultradian rhythms. *(16 marks)*

Other possible exam questions…

+ Explain what is mean by the terms *infradian rhythm* and *ultradian rhythm*. *(2 marks each)*

+ Give **one** example of an infradian rhythm and **one** example of an ultradian rhythm. *(2 marks each)*

MUST know …

Ultradian rhythms

Cycles lasting less than 24 hours, such as the **sleep stages**. Sleep involves a repeating cycle of 90–100 minutes, with five stages including REM (rapid eye movement) sleep.

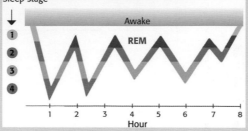

The ultradian rhythm of sleep

This 90-minute rhythm continues during the day as the **basic rest activity cycle** (BRAC).

Infradian rhythms

Cycles with a duration longer than 24 hours, for example the **female menstrual cycle**. This can vary between 23 days and 36 days, but averages 28 days. It is regulated by hormones and ovulation takes place roughly half way through the cycle.

 Research support for the BRAC…

…comes from studies of elite performers.

- **E** – Ericsson found that elite violinists generally practice for 90 minutes at a time, and often nap between practice sessions.

 Individual differences in sleep patterns…

…may be biologically determined.

- **E** – Tucker *et al.* found large differences between individuals' sleep patterns, which were consistent over 11 nights in a controlled sleep lab.

The menstrual cycle can also…

…be controlled by exogenous cues.

- **E** – When several women of childbearing age live together and do not take oral contraceptives, their menstrual cycles tend to synchronise.

SHOULD know …

Ultradian rhythms

Each of the five **sleep stages** shows a characteristic EEG pattern. During deep sleep, brainwaves slow and breathing and heart rate decrease. During REM sleep the EEG pattern resembles waking brainwaves and dreams occur.

The **BRAC** involves periods of alertness alternating with periods of physiological fatigue and low concentration.

Infradian rhythms

There may also be weekly **infradian rhythms**, with changes in hormone levels and blood pressure at weekends.

Annual rhythms can be seen in seasonal variations in mood, increased rates of heart attacks in winter, and a peak of deaths in January.

- **E** –Ericsson found the same pattern among other musicians, athletes, chess players and writers.
- **L** – This supports the existence of a 90-minute ultradian cycle of alertness and fatigue.

- **E** – Individuals also responded very differently to 36-hour periods of sleep deprivation.
- **L** – This suggests that sleep patterns may be at least partially determined by genes.

- **E** – Russell *et al.* applied daily sweat samples from one group of women to the upper lips of women in a separate group, and their menstrual cycles become synchronised.
- **L** – This suggests that a woman's menstrual cycle can be regulated by pheromones from other women as well as her own pituitary hormones.

 The menstrual cycle affects mate choice

- **P** – Around ovulation, women prefer more 'masculinised' faces.
- **E** – These may represent 'good genes' for short-term liaisons, with more likelihood of conception.
- **E** – In contrast, women generally prefer 'slightly feminised' male faces when picking a partner for a long-term relationship, as they may represent kindness and cooperation.
- **L** – This shows how a hormonally controlled rhythm may also impact behaviour.

 Belief in lunar rhythms

- **P** – Many people believe that the moon affects aspects of human behaviour.
- **E** – For example, many midwives believe that more babies are born during a full moon, but statistics do not support this.
- **E** – Also, many mental health professionals believe the full moon influences psychopathology, but there is no evidence.
- **L** – This shows that perceptions of infradian rhythms may be purely subjective.

CHOOSE THE RIGHT ANSWER

The female menstrual cycle is an example of a biological rhythm. Which type of rhythm describes it?

A Circadian ☐

B Infradian ☐

C Ultradian ☐

Answers on page 283

An idea

On paper, draw a chart showing the different time scales of biological rhythms.

Mark on examples of each.

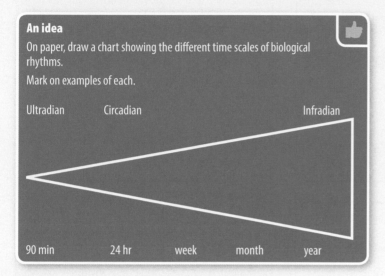

Ultradian   Circadian   Infradian

90 min   24 hr   week   month   year

SPOT THE MISTAKES

Read this student answer to the following exam question:

Outline infradian and/or ultradian rhythms. *(6 marks)*

There are **seven** mistakes – draw a circle around each one.

Biological rhythms that are longer than 24 hours are known as ultradian. For example, the female menstrual cycle is exactly 28 days and is controlled by the orbit of the moon. Ovulation occurs about half way through the cycle when progesterone levels peak.

In addition, human health follows annual rhythms. Some people become severely depressed in the winter, and most deaths occur in December.

Sleep consists of four stages which make up an ultradian rhythm, including NREM sleep which is when most dreaming occurs.

This cycle repeats every hour through the night.

Answers on page 283

APPLYING YOUR KNOWLEDGE

Mr Walker, the Principal of Moody College, is considering changing the college timetable to benefit students' concentration levels. What advice would you give him, based on your knowledge of ultradian rhythms?

(12 marks)

Identify the psychology	Advice to Mr Walker

Answers on page 283

KEY TERMS

- Endogenous pacemakers
- Exogenous zeitgebers

Possible essay question...

Outline and evaluate the effect of endogenous pacemakers and exogenous zeitgebers on the sleep-wake cycle. *(16 marks)*

Other possible exam questions...

+ Explain what is meant by the terms *endogenous pacemaker* and *exogenous zeitgeber*. *(2 marks)*

+ Outline findings of research into the effect of exogenous zeitgebers on the sleep-wake cycle. *(6 marks)*

MUST know ...

Endogenous pacemakers

These are internal biological clocks in the brain.

The **suprachiasmatic nucleus** (SCN) in the hypothalamus acts as the 'master clock', controlling other pacemakers in the body. It receives information about light levels via the optic nerve which keeps the SCN's circadian rhythm synchronised with daylight.

The SCN sends signals to the **pineal gland**, which produces the hormone melatonin at night.

Exogenous zeitgebers

These are environmental events which affect the biological clock.

Light resets the biological clock each day, keeping it on a 24-hour cycle.

We are also influenced by **social cues** from the activity of people around us.

 Animal studies support...

...the role of the SCN as an endogenous pacemaker.

- **E** – SCN neurons from hamsters bred to have abnormally short circadian rhythms were transplanted into normal hamsters, which then displayed the abnormal rhythm too.

 However, body rhythms...

...can become out of step with each other.

- **E** – For example, Folkard studied a student who spent 25 days in a lab without daylight. Her core temperature rhythm stayed at 24 hours but her sleep-wake cycle extended to 30 hours.

The role of melanopsin...

...is supported by studies of blind people.

- **E** – Most blind people who still have some light perception have normally entrained circadian rhythms.

SHOULD know ...

Endogenous pacemakers

Neurons in the **SCN** spontaneously synchronise with each other. They have links with other brain regions controlling sleep and arousal, and with peripheral pacemakers. There is also a neural pathway connecting the SCN with the pineal gland.

Melatonin from the **pineal gland** inhibits brain mechanisms that promote wakefulness, and so induces sleep.

Exogenous zeitgebers

Specialised light-detecting cells in the retina contain melanopsin. They gauge brightness and send signals to the SCN to set the daily clock. This system works in most blind people too, even in the absence of rods and cones or visual perception.

- **E** – Further confirmation came in the reverse experiment, when SCN neurons from normal hamsters were transplanted into the abnormal hamsters. They then changed to a normal 24-hour circadian pattern.
- **L** – This supports the importance of the SCN in regulating the 24-hour circadian rhythm.

- **E** – This much longer sleep-wake cycle shows the importance of exogenous zeitgebers in regulating sleep patterns.
- **L** – This experiment also shows that the SCN 'master clock' does not have total control of other biological rhythms.

- **E** – Some blind people who totally lack visual perception, and have no functioning rods and cones, still entrain their circadian rhythm to daylight.
- **L** – This suggests that the pathway from retinal cells containing melanopsin to the SCN is still intact in these individuals.

 Using light exposure to avoid jet lag

- **P** – Burgess *et al.* exposed volunteers to light treatments in order to shift their sleep-wake cycles.
- **E** – Participants' sleep patterns and melatonin levels were monitored in a lab.
- **E** – Participants who had been exposed to bright light felt sleepy two hours earlier in the evening and woke two hours earlier in the morning.
- **L** – This shows that circadian rhythms can be shifted by light exposure.

 Artifical light as a zeitgeber

- **P** – Vetter *et al.* used 'warm' or 'blue-enriched' artificial lights, and monitored volunteers' sleep patterns.
- **E** – The blue-enriched light is more similar to daylight.
- **E** – Volunteers living in the 'warm' light shifted their sleep patterns with sunrise (which changed by 42 minutes during the five-week period) whereas those in the 'blue-enriched' condition stayed synchronised to office hours.
- **L** – This shows that the spectral composition of light affects its role as an external zeitgeber.

✓ CHOOSE THE RIGHT ANSWER

Which **two** of the following can function as exogenous zeitgebers? Tick the boxes.

A Suprachiasmatic nucleus ☐

B Light ☐

C Social cues ☐

D Pineal gland ☐

Answers on page 283

📖 RESEARCH ISSUES

A researcher wanted to investigate children's sleep patterns and their sensitivity to light. She decided to carry out a field experiment, monitoring the children's sleep in their own homes using an electronic activity monitor worn on their wrist. Half of the children were given thin curtains which let the daylight in, and the other half were given blackout blinds. They were asked to follow normal bedtime routines and were monitored for a week.

• Identify **one** ethical issue the researcher should consider in this research. Suggest how the researcher could deal with this ethical issue. *(3 marks)*

• Explain **one** problem with the design of this study and suggest ways of dealing with this problem. *(4 marks)*

Answers on page 283

✓ A MARKING EXERCISE

Read this student answer to the following exam question:

Claire works night shifts as a nurse. She finds it difficult to sleep during the day, and struggles to stay alert during her shift, especially when it is quiet on the ward. Using your knowledge of endogenous pacemakers and/or exogenous zeitgebers, explain why Claire is experiencing sleep difficulties. *(6 marks)*

Clare has a conflict between the circadian rhythm originating from her endogenous pacemakers and exogenous zeitgebers. As she is working nights, her pineal gland, which responds to light, will be producing melatonin during the night. This would normally make her sleepy during dark periods. However, if she works in a bright environment the pineal gland will actually be responding to the input of artificial light via her eyes, so this would not be so much of a problem. She will also be receiving social cues (an exogenous zeitgeber) such as interaction with colleagues and patients, as long as there are things going on. But during quiet periods on the ward she won't be getting these social cues so may feel sleepy

How many marks would you give this answer?

Your mark:

Write an improved answer.

Answers on page 284

⚙ APPLYING YOUR KNOWLEDGE

James lives in the UK, but has to travel to Chicago for a week every three months for his work. When he returns home, the six-hour time difference makes it hard for him to get to sleep at night, and it generally takes him a week to recover normal sleep patterns. What advice could you give James to help him adjust to the time changes more quickly? *(6 marks)*

Identify the psychology	Advice to James

Answers on page 283

Aphasia	An impaired ability to understand (receptive aphasia) or produce (productive aphasia) speech as a result of brain damage.
Auditory cortex	The area in the temporal lobes of the brain where auditory information from the ears is processed.
Autonomic nervous system	Controls the body's involuntary activities such as heartbeat and digestion. It is not under conscious control, and is divided into sympathetic and parasympathetic branches.
Brain	The part of the central nervous system that is responsible for coordinating responses to sensory input, conscious thought, and autonomic activities.
Brain plasticity	The brain's ability to modify its own structure and function as a result of experience.
Broca's area	An area in the frontal lobe, usually in the left hemisphere, which is critical for speech production.
Central nervous system (CNS)	Comprises the brain and spinal cord. The spinal cord can relay simple reflex responses without the involvement of the brain.
Circadian rhythm	A pattern of behaviour that occurs or recurs approximately every 24 hours.
Electroencephalogram (EEG)	A method of recording changes in the electrical activity of the brain using electrodes attached to the scalp.
Endocrine glands	Specialised groups of cells that produce and secrete hormones.
Endocrine system	A network of glands around the body that manufacture and secrete hormones.
Endogenous pacemakers	Mechanisms within the body that govern the internal, biological bodily rhythms.
Equipotentiality	A theory that the effect of brain damage would be determined by the extent of damage rather than its location, as intact areas of cortex could take up any function.
Event-related potential (ERP)	A technique that takes raw EEG data and uses it to investigate cognitive processing of a specific event. It achieves this by averaging multiple readings in order to filter out all brain activity that is not related to the appearance of the stimulus.
Exogenous zeitgebers	Environmental cues, such as light, that help to regulate the biological clock.
Fight-or-flight response	A sequence of nervous and endocrine responses that enables the body to prepare for defending or attacking (fight) or running away to safety (flight).
Frontal lobes	The lobes at the front of the cerebral hemispheres, which contain high level processing areas.
Functional magnetic resonance imaging (fMRI)	A technique for measuring brain activity which works by detecting changes in blood oxygenation and flow that indicate increased neural activity.
Functional recovery	The recovery of mental abilities that have been compromised as a result of brain injury or neurodegenerative disease.
Hemispheric lateralisation	The fact that some mental processes in the brain are mainly located in either the left or right hemisphere.
Hormones	The body's chemical messengers. They travel through the bloodstream and affect many responses in the body and the brain by binding to receptors on target cells.
HPA axis	The sequence of nervous and endocrine responses to stress, involving the hypothalamus, pituitary and adrenal cortex.
Infradian rhythms	Body rhythms with a duration of over 24 hours: may be weekly, monthly or yearly.
Localisation of function	The principle that different cognitive processses have specific locations within the brain.
Motor cortex	An area in the frontal lobe of the brain (the precentral gyrus) dedicated to generating voluntary movements of the muscles.
Motor neurons	Carry nerve impulses from the CNS to muscles, where they control muscle contraction.
Neurotransmitters	Chemical substances that transmit a nerve impulse across a synapse.
Occipital lobes	The lobes at the back of the cerebral hemispheres, where the visual cortex is located.
Peripheral nervous system	All of the nerves that are outside the CNS. It carries signals from the CNS to the body and from the body to the CNS.
Pituitary gland	The 'master gland' that influences the release of hormones from other endocrine glands.
Post-mortem examinations	Examining the brains of people who have shown particular psychological abnormalities prior to their death in an attempt to establish the possible neurobiological cause for this behaviour.
Relay neurons	The most common type of neuron in the CNS. Communicates between sensory and motor neurons.
Sensory neurons	Carry nerve impulses from sensory receptors to the CNS.
Sleep-wake cycle	Alternating states of sleep and waking that are dependent on the 24-hour circadian cycle.
Somatic nervous system	The part of the peripheral nervous system that carries sensory information from sense organs to the CNS, and motor information from CNS to effector organs.

Somatosensory cortex	A region in the parietal lobe of the brain (the postcentral gyrus) responsible for processing sensory information from the skin, including sensations of touch, pressure, pain and temperature.
Spinal cord	A bundle of nerve fibres enclosed within the spinal column that connects nearly all parts of the body with the brain.
Split-brain research	Studies of individuals whose cerebral hemispheres have been surgically separated, by the severing of the corpus callosum.
Synapse	The conjunction of the end of the axon of one neuron and the dendrite or cell body of another.
Synaptic transmission	The process by which a nerve impulse crosses the synaptic gap from the presynaptic neuron to the postsynaptic neuron.
Temporal lobes	The lobes at the side of the cerebral hemispsheres, where the auditory cortex is located.
Ultradian rhythms	Cycles lasting less than 24 hours, such as the cycle of sleep stages that repeats every 90–100 minutes through the night.
Visual cortex	An area in the occipital lobe of the brain that processes visual information from the retina.
Wernicke's area	An area in the left temporal lobe that is vital for understanding language.

Topic 1 The nervous system

> Sophie has a spider phobia. She is calmly eating breakfast when she suddenly spots an enormous spider walking across the table towards her, and she becomes very tense and alert, her heart beating rapidly and her breathing becoming rapid and shallow. She starts to sweat and feels sick. Luckily her kind sister Charlotte is not afraid of spiders, and picks it up and removes it. Gradually Sophie calms down and she is able to continue with her breakfast.

Outline the structure of the nervous system, and explain what is happening in Sophie's nervous system to produce this sequence of responses. *(12 marks)*

Examiner's comments
6 marks available for A01 and 6 marks for A02

> As this is an application question, it is vital to read the stem carefully so you are thinking of incorporating key points from the stem Highlight the phrases that link to relevant psychology, such as 'heart beating rapidly', 'feels sick' etc.

The nervous system consists of the central nervous system (CNS) and the peripheral nervous system. The CNS is the brain and spinal cord. The brain controls behaviour and physiological process in the body, and the spinal cord is a big bundle of nerve fibres inside the spine, which connects it to the peripheral nervous system.

> This is a reasonable explanation of the basic structure. There is no detail about the structure of the brain.

The peripheral nervous system is all the nerve cells or neurons that go all over the body. Some control automatic bodily functions and some are involved in senses and in controlling muscles, which we can consciously control.

> This student appears to have forgotten some of the key terms, such as autonomic nervous system, somatic nervous system, involuntary bodily functions, sensory and motor neurons. However, the functions are correctly explained.

Within the automatic part is the sympathetic nervous system and the parasympathetic nervous system. They have different functions and different neurotransmitters are involved.

> This paragraph doesn't really add much, except for naming the SNS and PNS. This could have been elaborated.

When Sophie sees the spider, her eyes send a signal to her brain. She recognises it as a spider and because of her phobia she immediately feels terrified. This makes her hypothalamus (in her brain) send a signal to the sympathetic nervous system. This gets adrenaline going in her blood which makes her heart rate increase and her breathing speeds up.

> This is correct, but misses out the role of the amygdala in associating the stimulus with an emotional response (fear). There is correct identification of the hypothalamus here, and good linking to the stem.

Once her sister had got rid of the spider, Sophie's parasympathetic nervous system comes into action and this slows down her heartbeat again.

> There is no mention of the effect of the SNS and PNS on digestion, which could have linked to the stem 'feels sick'.

She should get some therapy for her phobia. This could be systematic desensitisation or flooding, which would make her sit in a room with a lot of spiders until she didn't feel scared any more.

> This final paragraph is irrelevant. Keep reading the question as you write, so you don't go off track.

Level 3 answer (7–9 marks)

Examiner's comments: Overall, correct information but a bit thin in places; in particular, this answer does not make full use of the application opportunities (A02). More detail could have been included about the brain or the peripheral nervous system too, although it wouldn't be necessary to cover both in this essay.

Topic 2 Neurons and synaptic transmission

Explain the nature of synaptic transmission, and evaluate changes in neurochemistry of the brain as an explanation of behaviour. *(12 marks)*

Neurotransmitters are chemicals that carry a nerve signal across the synaptic gap. They are released by the pre-synaptic neuron and diffuse across the gap to the post-synaptic neuron. When they get there, they fix onto receptors and start up a nerve signal in the next neuron.

There are many different neurotransmitters and some of them actually stop the next neuron from firing instead. The different inputs add up to decide whether the neuron fires or not. These are called IPSP and EPSP neurotransmitters. They can be serotonin, noradrenaline, dopamine, GABA and many other different chemicals.

Once the neurotransmitter has done its job, it has to be removed and sometimes it is broken down by enzymes, and sometimes it is taken back into the original neuron for recycling. Some drugs can affect how this happens.

If someone is depressed or has OCD they may have low levels of serotonin in their brain. This means they are not very good at transmitting signals using this particular neurotransmitter. SSRIs are used to treat this, which stop the serotonin getting taken back into the neuron (reuptake), so there is more serotonin around in the synapse. This keeps it doing its job of stimulating the next neuron to fire. This shows how a change in neurochemistry, serotonin, can explain a change in behaviour, depression. Taking SSRIs also changes the neurochemistry and helps to treat depression and anxiety, which supports neurochemistry as an explanation of behaviour.

However, drugs are not a permanent cure as they only make people better while they still take them, they don't change the underlying problem. People relapse if they stop taking the drugs.

Also this is part of the biological approach that is reductionist. It doesn't take into account other explanations of behaviour like wrong thinking or social learning theory.

Level 3 answer (7–9 marks)

Examiner's comments: This evaluation could focus on general points about the biological approach, application of knowledge about neurotransmitters in treating disorders, or specific treatments aimed at changing neurochemistry in the brain such as anti-depressants and anti-anxiety drugs.

Examiner's comments

6 marks available for AO1 and 6 marks for AO3

A good start.

This paragraph is a bit confused. It would have been better to explain IPSPs and EPSPs, and their relevant neurotransmitters, and then say how spatial or temporal summation of inputs determines if an action potential is produced.

This is correct although more technical terms could have been used.

This is a good explanation of the action of SSRIs and linked well to the question, with explanations of how the neurotransmitter change in depression affects behaviour, and also how SSRIs act via changing neurochemistry.

This evaluation point is not relevant to the question.

Reductionism could be used to evaluate neurochemistry as an explanation of behaviour, but this paragraph is very brief. Reductionism needed to be explained and actually thinking and learning operate via neurotransmitters too, so this point is not a valid criticism.

Topic 3 The endocrine system

Outline the functions of the endocrine system, and discuss the role of the endocrine system in behaviour. *(12 marks)*

The endocrine system is made up of glands that produce hormones. These are chemical messengers that go into the bloodstream and are carried around the body in the blood. When they reach a target organ, they can bind onto receptors and trigger a response in the receptors.

Hormones from the endocrine system control many processes in the body, and are involved in many aspects of behaviour as they also affect the brain. For example, in the fight-or-flight response to stress there are hormones such as adrenaline. This makes us alert when we face a threat, by changing things in our body like increasing heart rate and breathing so we get more oxygen to our brain and muscles. And in the response to chronic stress there are even more hormones, such as ACTH and cortisol. This shows how hormones are involved with behaviour.

The endocrine system is self-regulating, so if a hormone level goes up then that gives feedback to the endocrine glands that produced it, and they stop making so much, so the hormone level stays stable.

The pituitary gland is near the brain and is controlled by the hypothalamus, which is part of the brain. The pituitary is known as the master gland as it controls many other endocrine glands. It makes ACTH, which triggers the adrenal cortex to make cortisol. It also controls the testes to make testosterone.

Testosterone also affects behaviour. There is research evidence for this. A Canadian ice hockey team had testosterone surges whenever they played at home, showing that their hormone levels are involved in their defensive behaviour.

There are practical applications for the role of the endocrine system in behaviour, for example people may be given hormone treatments to control their behaviour. Also it is a very scientific approach but it is reductionist as it explains behaviour in terms of biology and ignores social and cognitive factors.

Level 3 answer (7–9 marks)

Examiner's comments: Overall a level 3 answer. A01 better than A03.

The discussion could draw on specific functions such as the hormones involved in the fight-or-flight response, or general points evaluating the biological approach, as long as these are linked to the role of the endocrine system. It would also be possible to discuss the limitations of the endocrine system as an explanation of behaviour, and refer to other explanations from the biological approach or other approaches.

Examiner's comments

6 marks available for A01 and 6 marks for A03.

A01. Good straightforward explanation, although some confusion about receptors.

A03 – well linked back to the role of the endocrine system in behaviour. There could have been more detail about the behavioural effects of the stress hormones.

A01, correct but an example would have been useful here.

A further A03 link to behaviour, using research evidence to support the link.

An attempt at evaluation but the use of hormone treatments is very vague. A very brief mention of two other evaluation points without any explanation.

Topic 4 The fight-or-flight response

Discuss the fight-or-flight response to stress. *(12 marks)*

We need to be able to respond quickly to threats, and this has evolved to help us survive in a dangerous world, by fighting off attackers or running away to save our lives. This evolved because it helps individuals to survive and reproduce, so it gives an adaptive advantage and genes for a fight-or-flight response then got passed on to the children. So it is a very useful response.

When we see something threatening, like a Rottweiler about to attack, the amygdala in the brain sends a signal to the hypothalamus to say that we are scared. The hypothalamus then triggers the fight-or-flight response, via the sympathetic nervous system. This signals to the adrenal medulla, which is an endocrine gland and produces adrenaline. Adrenaline has many effects on the body and basically gets us ready for fight-or-flight by making our heartbeat and our breathing speed up so we get more oxygen in our muscles, ready for action. Also it makes glucose go into our blood again ready for springing into action.

Obviously this has advantages that it helps us to survive, but unfortunately the fight-or-flight response can also have bad effects as it increases blood pressure which can be a health risk.

There are criticisms of the whole idea of the fight-or-flight response, as actually many animals and people freeze when they are in danger rather than fighting or running away. This may keep them safe by 'playing dead' or it may just give them time to analyse the situation properly before rushing into a reaction.

Also women tend to react differently, as they make friends when they are stressed. This might also have a basis in evolution as fighting or running away could put their children at risk and traditionally women would have been looking after the babies. So women may not have so much of a fight-or-flight response, and this could be linked to their different hormones.

Level 4 answer (10–12 marks)

Examiner's comments: Altogether, a clearly explained, accurate and thoroughly evaluated essay.

Examiner's comments

6 marks available for A01 and 6 for A03. If this was in an A level paper it could be a 16-mark version with 6 marks for A01 and 10 for A03.

This starts out with an interesting A03 introductory paragraph which actually dives straight into an explanation of the purpose of this response, and an evolutionary explanation.

This is a clear and contextualised explanation of the fight-or-flight response which works well. A01

A03 – a disadvantage of the response.

A03 – a discussion of an alternative response to threat.

A03 another alternative response to threat, nicely linked back to the evolutionary explanation for this biological response.

Topic 5 Localisation of function – A level only zone

Discuss localisation of function in the human brain. *(16 marks)*

The brain has different structures within it that have different functions, for example the brain stem regulates autonomic functions in the body like heartbeat, breathing and swallowing. The cerebellum is involved with coordination and balance. And the hypothalamus is a very small structure in the middle of the brain with a very important function of communicating with the endocrine system, mainly via the pituitary gland.

As well as these separate structures, the cerebral hemispheres have areas of localised function within them. The visual cortex is at the back of the cerebral hemispheres, and each one receives signals from the opposite eye. The auditory cortex receives information from the ears and it is at the side of the head. Near to this is the language centre of Wernicke's area, which processes language for comprehension. This is just in the left front lobe. Also in the left front lobe but a bit further forward is Broca's area which is involved in speech production. This is near to the motor region that controls the mouth. At the top of the brain are the motor regions that control muscle movements, and the somatosensory area that receives information from the touch receptors in the skin.

The idea about localisation of function first came from studies of patients with brain damage caused by strokes. Broca's area is named after Broca, who studied patients who all had damage in a similar area and had lost the power of speech. Wernicke's area similarly is named after Wernicke, whose patients could still speak but couldn't understand speech, and didn't make much sense. This shows that there are specific areas in the brain which are specialised for speech functions.

However, this evidence could have problems as Broca and Wernicke were only able to study their patients' brains after they had died, and strokes actually affect larger areas of the brain not just a specific area each time. In fact another researcher looked at some of Broca's patients preserved brains using MRI scans, and found that they had damage to larger areas. Also it seems that if the damage only affects Broca's area itself it only causes a temporary effect on speech. This shows it might be damage to networks that affects function, not just small areas.

More evidence that networks matter comes from a case where a patient lost the ability to read, and their brain damage turned out to be in a part that connects the visual cortex to Wernicke's area. This supports the idea that complex functions like reading involve a whole network of areas, not just a small area of the brain.

Another criticism of the idea of localisation comes from individual differences, as people have activation in different areas when they do the same task. And people can often recover some function after brain damage, by different parts of the brain taking over (plasticity).

Level 3 answer (top end) (9–12 marks)

Examiner's comments: Overall, a clear essay with a very logical structure and argument leading towards a conclusion in the last-but-one paragraph. Some of the description is a bit thin, so this is at the borderline between level 3 and 4.

Examiner's comments

6 marks available for A01, 10 marks for A03

This is an effective use of knowledge of larger brain structures and how they relate to different functions of the brain.

A clear, accurate paragraph of A01 describing localisation in the cerebral cortex. There is limited identification of the lobes in which the different areas as situated, but the student clearly has a visual image of the brain which they are using to describe the locations. The functions are simply described, without the pathways being explained, but the material is connected together into a concise, readable description.

A03 evidence for Broca's and Wernicke's areas. Well linked.

This evidence is successfully evaluated with later evidence from MRI scans, leading into a broader view of functional networks

Evidence for functional networks relating to a specific function. Again well linked.

A couple of brief criticisms, not unpacked but relevant still. This doesn't really add much to the evaluation.

Topic 6 Lateralisation and split-brain research – A level only zone

Outline and evaluate research into lateralisation and/or the split brain. *(16 marks)*

Broca studied lateralisation in the nineteenth century when he did post-mortems on patients who had brain damage. He found that damage in an area of the left hemisphere (now called Broca's area) led to speech problems, whereas damage to the matching area in the right hemisphere didn't.

However, this research depended on patients who had suffered from strokes and so they might have had other damage as well. And because he was only able to look at their brains after they were dead, there may have been further problems that caused their death. So it does not give reliable evidence about living brains.

In the twentieth century, surgeons would sometimes treat severe epilepsy by cutting the nerve fibres that connect the two halves of the brain, in the corpus callosum. These people were called split-brain patients and they were then tested experimentally by Sperry and Gazzaniga. They showed the patients pictures in their right or left visual field, and asked them to say what they saw, or choose a matching picture with their hand. They found that it was as if the patients had two separate brains. What they saw with their left visual field is processed by their right visual cortex, and as this had no connections to the left hemisphere where the language centres were, they weren't able to say it, but they could choose a matching picture with their left hand because this is operated by the right hemisphere motor cortex. On the other hand, the right visual field sent the image to the left visual cortex and they could say what they saw as the language centre is in the left hemisphere. Other researchers did the same thing with playing different words through headphones to each ear.

This research is criticized now as not all the patients showed the same results. Some of them may have recovered some function (plasticity) or their language centres may have been in different places because of individual differences. Also they may have had damage from their epilepsy or from the drugs they took for many years. And also there are other fibres that connect the hemispheres, and it is not clear whether all of them were cut. Maybe there were still some connections and some information could leak through in the patients who didn't have the same findings.

There were not many split-brain patients, and this treatment isn't done any more so researchers can't replicate the studies, so they lack reliability and we should be cautious in generalising from them.

Level 3 answer (9–12 marks)

Examiner's comments: Overall, a clear essay. A bit too much A01 at the expense of A03, but the evaluation points are well used to support an argument and well organised.

Examiner's comments

6 marks available for A01 and 10 for AO3

The question asks for a discussion of research, so it is a good idea to start straight away with a description of some research.

This is then evaluated, with several good criticisms being made here.

This essay is organised by time order, which makes it flow logically and tell a good story. Split brain research is well described here although it could be more concise – it is quite a wordy explanation, which means it takes up time and space. Remember to keep your A01 tight as you need more A03 in an A level essay.

The student has a good understanding of lateralisation, which is described in the context of research, so addresses the questions.

There are some excellent evaluation points here, clearly expressed. The whole paragraph is introduced as criticism of the research, and adds various points that contribute to this.

This is another good point, linked well to explain how it affects our conclusions from split brain research.

Topic 7 Plasticity and functional recovery of the brain – A level only zone

Outline and evaluate the evidence for plasticity and/or functional recovery after trauma. *(16 marks)*

Examiner's comments

It used to be thought that the adult brain couldn't grow and develop, but now we know that the structure of the brain changes as we practise particular skills, which is called plasticity, and also it can often recover function after trauma.

> This introductory paragraph just introduces the terms and doesn't outline any evidence, so it is really a waste of time.

The neurons are constantly making new synaptic connections and building new pathways, which is how we learn from experience. For example, even old people can increase the amount of neurons and connections in their visual cortex if they learn a new skill like juggling. And playing video games actually builds more connections in many areas of the brain to do with working memory, hand-eye coordination etc. So our brains change as a result of experience, which is plasticity. After trauma, which is brain damage, like a stroke, sometimes nearby parts of the brain can take over the functions of the damaged areas. This is called functional recovery. Again, new connections and networks are formed.

> This is a useful connection of evidence of plasticity in response to different learning experiences, well linked.

> This is very brief and doesn't refer to any evidence, so doesn't answer the question.

There is evidence of brain plasticity from animal studies. Kemperman kept rats in different environments; those with more stimulation developed more neurons, especially in their hippocampus, showing that animals can develop new neurons as a result of more stimulation.

> Now we have some evidence: an A03 point. However, the findings are not compared with the control group. And there is no explanation of the sort of enriched environment that might affect the hippocampus.

There is also evidence that this happens in humans too. Maguire measured taxi drivers' brains using MRI scanning, and found that their hippocampus got larger if they spent longer driving the taxi. This shows that more experience navigating around increases the size of the hippocampus.

> Not quite – this was a correlational finding, so we can't conclude causality. Be careful how you express findings of correlational studies, e.g. 'the longer they had worked as taxi drivers, the larger their posterior hippocampus'. Also different areas of the hippocampus had different changes, so this needs to be specifically the posterior hippocampus.

There is evidence supporting functional recovery from trauma in rats as well. Some rats were given brain injuries, then their brains were injected with stem cells. Some of the stem cells migrated to the area of the injury, so this shows that stem cells may be involved in recovery from brain damage. This suggest a practical application as it may be possible to develop stem cell treatments to help people recover from brain injuries or strokes.

> This is a clear and useful A03 point, with the addition of practical application of stem cell research.

Level 3 answer (9–12 marks)

Examiner's comments: Overall, mostly accurate, some loss of focus, mostly clear and organised.

Topic 8 Ways of studying the brain – A level only zone

Discuss the use of functional magnetic resonance imaging as a way of studying the brain. Refer to other scanning techniques as part of your discussion. *(16 marks)*

Examiner's comments

6 marks available for A01, 10 for A03

Functional magnetic resonance imaging (fMRI) is a way of studying the living brain. It measures the blood flow in different parts of the brain, and the results appear as a map of the brain with different parts in different colours depending on how much blood flow they had. If the brain cells in a particular area are more active, they will be using up more oxygen for respiration, so they will need more blood. So we can conclude that areas that are 'lit up' are the active ones.

> This is a high quality A01 explanation of fMRI, and what conclusions we can draw from it.

The advantage of fMRI is that it can be used to see the brain activity when people are doing cognitive tasks, and compared with control tasks like resting with their eyes shut. Then we can conclude that the difference in active brain areas is due to the task.

> A03 is clear and concise.

fMRI is non-invasive, so it doesn't cause any harm, which is an advantage over some older types of scanning that used radiation to map brain activity. A limitation of fMRI is that you can't actually tell what people are thinking about, and it measures brain activity indirectly so it's not necessarily showing what you think it is. Another limitation is that networks of brain areas may be more important than activity of separate localised areas, and fMRI doesn't show how the areas are connected up.

> More A03 but without details of older types of scanning, or what the problem is with using radiation. Two brief points, no detail or elaboration.

> This point is better elaborated.

Other scanning techniques include EEG and ERP. EEG uses electrodes on the scalp to measure brain activity, and is good for diagnosing epilepsy. However, it only shows activity in the surface areas of the brain, not parts that are deeper. ERP is similar but can measure brain responses to particular tasks, which is useful for experiments. Again it only measure brain activity from surface areas, not deeper ones.

> As required, there is an attempt to describe two other scanning techniques, but these are just briefly described and evaluated separately. The question was asking for them to be included in a discussion on fMRI, which needed direct comparison of the similarities or differences of the techniques.

Post mortems can also be used to find out more about the brain, and they were the only way of doing this for Broca and Wernicke. They both discovered things about brain function by doing post mortems on patients who had lost particular speech functions, and so they could connect the problem with the area of brain damage. It is still used now, and researchers can also measure levels of neurotransmitters in the dead brain tissue.

> This paragraph is irrelevant, as post-mortem examination is not a scanning technique. Read the question carefully!

Level 3 answer (lower end) (9–12 marks)

Examiner's comments: Overall, a good explanation and good evaluation of fMRI, but not compared effectively with other scanning techniques.

Topic 9 Circadian rhythms – A level only zone

Discuss the role of circadian rhythms in human behaviour. *(16 marks)*

Circadian rhythms are biological cycles that last about 24 hours. They are driven by the endogenous pacemaker in the brain, the suprachiasmatic nucleus (SCN), which is located in the hypothalamus. This is affected by light so it can be kept in sync with day and night. This is called photoentrainment. Circadian rhythms include the sleep-wake cycle, and body temperature and hormone production patterns, which follow a circadian rhythm, too. I will focus on the sleep-wake cycle, as it is the most familiar and obviously affects our behaviour.

Examiner's comments

6 marks available for A01, 10 for A03

> Good A01 paragraph with correct terminology. Final sentence is unnecessary – most familiar to whom?

The sleep-wake cycle lasts about 24 hours to fit in with day and night, but can actually be longer than this. A man who lived in a cave for months found that his sleep-wake cycle was generally more than 24 hours. Sleep studies in a sleep lab have found that there are individual differences in the length of the sleep cycle, and the sleep-wake cycle can vary between individuals from about 13 to 60 hours. Some people are 'morning people' who like to wake up early, and other people are 'evening people' who prefer to stay up late, but this can change with age. Sleep cycles can be affected by changing time zone when travelling.

> This is being used as A01. It is a series of unconnected statements and doesn't have any sense of direction or linking. Try to use connecting words to make your argument flow, and if you are using studies as discussion points (A03) then you need to flag this up.

There are two things that make us sleepy, one is the sleep drive that gives us dips of sleepiness at about 2–4am and 1–3pm. This is controlled by the SCN, in the hypothalamus, which produces a hormone, melatonin, which makes us sleepy. The other is the homeostatic drive to sleep that just makes us get more sleepy through the day, as we need to sleep to restore energy levels. This affects human behaviour by making us want to sleep at night, and to have a nap in the afternoon if possible because of the afternoon dip.

> Mostly accurate description of the sleep drive. However, some inaccuracy here. Melatonin is actually produced in the pineal gland which is controlled by the SCN. And the homeostatic drive operates through any waking period, such as a night shift, not just through the day. This paragraph seems a bit repetitive.

Sleep cycles are affected by light, and it was thought that only natural light or bright artificial light would have this effect. Some studies in sleep labs used dim artificial light assuming it would not affect sleep cycles. But Czeizler used dim artificial light to alter people's circadian rhythms down to 22 hours and up to 28 hours so this assumption may be false.

> Good discussion point (A03), with use of research evidence.

Level 3 answer (9–12 marks)

Examiner's comments: Overall, this essay is a bit unbalanced. There are points that could have been used as A03 but were not linked into a discussion. It is mostly clear and accurate.

Topic 10 Ultradian and infradian rhythms – A level only zone

Outline and evaluate evidence for infradian and/or ultradian rhythms. *(16 marks)*

Ultradian rhythms are natural body rhythms that are shorter than 24 hours, such as the stages of sleep. There is evidence from sleep research that the five stages of sleep generally fit roughly onto a 90-minute cycle that repeats through the night. Each stage, such as REM (rapid eye movement) sleep and Non-REM sleep, has typical EEG patterns. However, the patterns are not always identical and they do show individual differences. In a sleep lab study, individuals' sleep patterns were consistent over a ten-day period but different from each other. Sleep labs are able to control conditions so this has good validity. This shows that the particular sleep patterns of each individual may be genetically determined.

Even in the day, there is a 90-minute cycle of alertness alternating with fatigue and poor concentration. This is called the Basic Rest Activity Cycle (BRAC). Ericsson studied professional musicians and found that they tend to follow this pattern, with 90-minute practise periods alternating with a break or a nap. Many other musicians, athletes and chess players have the same ultradian pattern too. This means that there is strong support for the BRAC in different groups of people who choose how to spend their time, although it may not be the same in people who have fixed working hours.

Infradian rhythms have a cycle that is longer than 24 hours. These include the female menstrual cycle, which follows a roughly 28-day cycle, although it can vary from this in different individuals. It is regulated by oestrogen and progesterone, hormones that are produced by the pituitary gland, and ovulation takes place just after an oestrogen peak roughly half way through the cycle. As well as this endogenous regulation, there is some evidence of impact from exogenous factors. When women live together, like girls in a boarding school or nuns, their cycles tend to become synchronised with each other. In order to find to how this works, Russell put sweat samples from one group of women onto the top lips of women living in a separate group, so they would smell the sweat. Their menstrual cycles became synchronised with the first group, which suggests that there is a chemical in the sweat that triggers this effect. This is called a pheromone. This is evidence that infradian rhythms may have an interaction between endogenous and exogenous control.

The menstrual cycle has interesting effects on female psychology. For example, it is found that around ovulation women prefer more 'masculinised' faces, whereas at other times they would choose a more 'feminised' face. The suggestion is that a masculinised face represents healthy genes to be passed on to children at the time when there is an egg available for fertilisation, whereas the feminised face represents a better bet for a long-term partner, as they may be kinder and more cooperative. This would support an evolutionary explanation of the effect of hormones on female mate choice, as these choices would maximise survival off offspring.

Level 4 answer (13–16 marks)

Examiner's comments: This student has chosen to make a logical argument, addressing ultradian rhythms first, then infradian rhythms. Evaluation of the evidence fits fluently within this analysis rather than being broken up, and this addresses the question very effectively.

Examiner's comments

6 marks available for A01, 10 for A03

A clear first paragraph with a good conclusion to the point, and evaluation of the evidence.

Clear outline of the BRAC with supporting evidence, and evaluation of the evidence.

This paragraph is quite long, and might have been better broken up. However, it explains the menstrual cycle effectively and uses research evidence to support this too.

The final paragraph gives an interesting application of the evolutionary approach, and is clearly argued.

Altogether, a thorough and clear discussion.

Topic 11 Endogenous pacemakers and exogenous zeitgebers – A level only zone

Outline and evaluate the effect of endogenous pacemakers and exogenous zeitgebers on the sleep-wake cycle. *(16 marks)*

The sleep-wake cycle is a circadian rhythm that means that we generally sleep at night and wake up in the day. It is controlled by endogenous pacemakers (internal body clocks) and is also influenced by exogenous zeitgebers (factors in the outside environment). This makes it possible to keep the 24-hour rhythm synchronised with day and night, and to adjust to changes like with jet travel. This is called entrainment.

The internal clock is the suprachiasmatic nucleus (SCN), which is in the hypothalamus. It sends nerve signals to the pineal gland, which produces the hormone melatonin at night time. The SCN contains neurons that spontaneously synchronise with each other and control other pacemakers in the body, as well as linking to brain areas associated with sleep and arousal. Also the melatonin affects areas of the brain that make you wake up, so it actually makes you sleep.

The internal clock keeps its own free-running circadian rhythm going, although this can vary from the 24 hours, as shown by research in caves or sleep labs where there is no external light to reset the body clock. In that situation, people's sleep cycles can become shorter or longer, and individuals seem to have their own typical sleep-wake cycle.

The SCN is also affected by external factors, the exogenous zeitgebers. The main one is light. Light enters the eye and is sensed by special cells containing melanopsin in the retina that send a signal to the SCN. This works even in blind people, who aren't aware of the light, as long as they still have these special cells.

Animal studies support the role of the SCN as an endogenous pacemaker. There were some hamsters that were bred to have an abnormally short circadian rhythm. When their SCN neurons were put into normal hamsters, their rhythm also became shortened. And the other way round, when the SCN neurons from normal hamsters were put into the abnormal ones, they also went back to a normal 24-hour circadian rhythm. This supports the role of the SCN as an endogenous pacemaker.

Light can be used artificially to change people's body clocks, which has useful practical applications for shift workers and people who travel internationally. It depends on the colour of the light, as shown by Vetter who used artificial lights with a warm natural colour or a blue tint. The participants in the warm light became synchronised with daylight over a five-week period, whereas the blue light didn't have that effect. This experiment shows that the colour of light affects its ability to work as an external zeitgeber.

Level 4 answer (13–16 marks)

Examiner's comments: Overall, a clear line of argument with appropriate selection of material, and mostly accurate.

Examiner's comments

Good first paragraph explaining the concepts and the connection between them, and using correct terminology.

This is another good paragraph with clear explanation and logical structure.

Research evidence brought in to support variation in circadian rhythms A03.

Outline of an exogenous zeitgeber, light. A good choice as it links well with the explanation of the interaction at the level of the brain.

A clear explanation of this research study, supporting the role of the SCN. The first and last sentences are almost identical, which is a bit dull to read. Try to introduce a point by linking from the previous paragraph when possible, then use the last sentence to link back to the original question. For example, 'This means that there is clear experimental evidence for the SCN's involvement with circadian rhythm like the sleep-wake cycle.

This final paragraph attempts to use a further research study to support a practical application to benefit people who need to shift their body clock. There is a slight error in describing the warm light as natural, but the point is still clear and useful in the argument.

KEY TERMS

- Aims
- Debriefing
- Ethical issues
- Experiment
- Extraneous variable
- Hypothesis
- Independent variable (IV)
- Dependent variable (DV)
- Informed consent
- Operationalise
- Standardised procedures

Possible exam questions…

+ Identify the key features of an experiment. *(2 marks)*
+ Explain the difference between the aims of a study and a hypothesis. *(2 marks)*
+ Explain what is meant by operationalisation. *(2 marks)*
+ Explain why standardisation is important in research procedures. *(2 marks)*

★ Important

In this chapter we have not always followed the PEEL rule because many of the evaluation questions are only worth 2 marks (see possible questions above).

MUST know …

About experiments

Psychological investigations begin with an **aim**, which may be:

- an intention, e.g. 'to investigate the effect of TV on the work a student produces', or
- a research question; 'does noise affect the quality of work?'

The **independent variable** (IV) is directly manipulated by the experimenter. The different values of the IV are known as the experimental **conditions**.

The **dependent variable** (DV) is measured to see how the change in the IV has affected it.

This leads to a **hypothesis**: a testable statement of what you expect to find.

Standardised procedures ensure that each participant does exactly the same thing within each condition. They may include standardised instructions – the instructions given to participants to tell them how to perform the task.

The procedure should also include:

- consideration of **ethical issues** and how to deal with them
- obtaining **informed consent** from participants
- **debriefing participants** after the experiment.

Informed consent ensures all participants know what they are expected to do and have the opportunity to refuse to take part.

Debriefing is a post-research interview designed to inform participants of the true nature of the study, particularly if deception was involved, and to restore them to the psychological state they were in at the start of the study. They should also be given the right to withdraw their data if they wish to.

SHOULD know …

About experiments

In an experiment, the IV is deliberately changed to see if there is any effect on the DV. This permits us to draw causal conclusions – conclusions about cause and effect.

The hypothesis should be fully **operationalised**, i.e. the variables should be defined in a way that they can easily be measured or tested. A concept such as 'educational attainment' needs to be specified more clearly if we are going to investigate it. For example, it might be operationalised as 'GCSE grade in Maths'.

A good hypothesis includes the two (or more) levels of the IV, e.g. 'Students who do a memory task with the TV on produce work that gets fewer marks than those who do the same task without the TV on.'

Extraneous variables (EVs) should be identified and controlled before the experiment begins. These are any variable, other than the IV itself, which may potentially affect the DV. If EVs are not controlled they may become confounding variables, which affect the validity of the findings.

Ethical issues concern questions of right and wrong. They arise in research where there are conflicting sets of values between researchers and participants concerning the goals, procedures or outcomes of a research study.

Debriefing is not an ethical issue; it is a means of dealing with ethical issues. It may also be used to gain useful feedback about the procedures in the study.

✓ CHOOSE THE RIGHT ANSWER

Which **two** of the following are directional hypotheses? Tick **two** boxes only.

A People who are hot are more aggressive than people who are cold. ☐

B To investigate the effect of temperature on aggression. ☐

C Men and women are different in terms of their aggression scores. ☐

D Drinking through a straw is better than not drinking through a straw. ☐

Answers on page 284

A MARKING EXERCISE

Read the student answers to the following exam question, given below:

An experiment was conducted where participants completed a test in a very hot room or a cool room to demonstrate the effect of temperature on aggression levels. Aggressiveness was assessed by a researcher and each participant was given an aggression score.

Identify the operationalised independent variable and the operationalised dependent variable in this study. *(2 marks + 2 marks)*

Kerry's answer

The operationalised independent variable is room temperature and the operationalised dependent variable is aggression.

Megan's answer

The operationalised independent variable is temperature and the operationalised dependent variable is the difference in aggression between the participants.

Rohan's answer

The operationalised independent variable is the room temperature (hot or cool) and the operationalised dependent variable is the aggression score.

For each answer there are 2 marks available. Write the marks you would give each answer in the table below.

	Mark for IV out of 2	Mark for DV out of 2
Kerry		
Megan		
Rohan		

Answers on page 284

⚙ APPLYING YOUR KNOWLEDGE

A researcher becomes interested in the effects of simple rewards on children's ability to do well on school tests. The researcher intends to conduct a laboratory experiment to investigate this. He invites 30 children to his laboratory and gives them a general knowledge test. Beforehand he tells half of the children that he will give them £1 as a reward for doing the test. Afterwards he compares the children's scores on the test.

Answer the following questions:

(a) What is the aim of this study? *(2 marks)*

(b) Identify the operationalised independent variable and the operationalised dependent variable in this study. *(2 marks + 2 marks)*

(c) Write a hypothesis for this study. *(2 marks)*

(d) Is your hypothesis directional or non-directional? *(1 mark)*

(e) Identify one possible extraneous variable in this study. Explain how this extraneous variable could have affected the results of this experiment. *(1 mark + 3 marks)*

(f) With reference to this study, explain one strength and one limitation of lab experiments. *(2 marks + 2 marks)*

Answers on page 284

An idea 👍

Make a pack of flashcards of Research Methods key terms. Add to the pack as you work your way through this chapter of the Revision and Exam Companion. Keep testing yourself on the definitions, and try matching the cards up in different ways. This will help you to make connections in your memory between similar concepts, and to be clear about the differences between similar ideas, such as:

Aim	Hypothesis	Research question
IV	DV	EV
Directional hypothesis	Non-directional hypothesis	Operationalised hypothesis
Briefing	Debriefing	Informed consent
Standardised procedure	Standardised instructions	
Investigation	Experiment	

See page 194 for an explanation of directional and non-directional hypotheses.

Key Terms

- Confounding variable
- Control
- External validity
- Ecological validity
- Population validity
- Historical validity
- Extraneous variables
- Internal validity
- Mundane realism
- Validity

Possible exam questions...

+ Give an example of a confounding variable in the context of this study. *(2 marks)*

+ Explain why it is important to control extraneous variables in a study. *(2 marks)*

+ Distinguish between extraneous variables and confounding variables. *(2 marks)*

! Think

The assumptions behind a theory can also be criticised in terms of validity. How might this apply to Freud's Psychodynamic theory? (A level only)

MUST know ...

There is an inevitable trade-off between control and realism in psychological research.

Laboratory experiments have the greatest control, and allow conclusions about cause-and-effect relationships, but findings in this artificial context may not be generalisable to real life situations.

On the other hand, studies in everyday settings lack control of extraneous variables, so the findings may be meaningless.

Control

Uncontrolled extraneous variables may affect the DV in an experiment, becoming confounding variables. These could include factors like time of day, noise and distractions.

Realism

The aim of psychological research is to find out how people behave in 'real life'. Studies in artificial settings may lack mundane realism, so the results may not apply to behaviour in the real world.

Validity

This refers to how genuine an observed effect is.

Internal validity is the degree to which a researcher tested what they intended to test.

External validity is the extent to which the findings from particular research participants can be generalised to other people and situations. It includes:

- **Ecological validity** – can the research findings be generalised to real life?
- **Population validity** – can the findings from this sample of participants be generalised to all people (different ages/ genders/ cultural backgrounds)?
- **Historical validity** – can the results of an old study be generalised to people's behaviour today?

SHOULD know ...

Control

Differences between individuals in different conditions of an experiment also act as extraneous variables, which may make it difficult to detect an effect of the IV on the DV.

Generalisation

Researchers hope to be able to generalise the findings of a study beyond the research setting. This may not be possible if aspects of the study lack realism, or are unique to the particular research setting. For example:

- The materials used in the study (film clips, written scenarios)
- The environment of the study, particularly if participants are aware they are being studied
- The sample of participants is limited (American students)

These factors can limit generalisability of the findings.

Validity

To gain high internal validity, researchers should consider:

- whether the IV produced the change in the DV, or whether a confounding variable may have affected the results
- whether the researcher actually tested what they intended to test (For example, was the participant actually paying attention?)
- whether the study possessed (or lacked) mundane realism.

Testing involves:
1. Writing a hypothesis.
2. Designing a study to test the hypothesis.
3. Collecting data.
4. Analysing results.
5. Questioning the validity of the study.
6. Drawing conclusions.

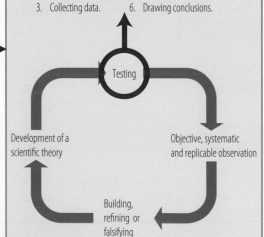

The scientific process

MATCH THEM UP

Match up the experiment with the validity issue.

1	I test some drinks on ten five-year olds then conclude that "9 out of 10 people prefer hot chocolate to coffee"	**A**	Internal validity
2	I give a class a memory test using a word list, with half the class sitting and half standing, then say "People remember things better when they are sitting down than standing up"	**B**	Historical validity
3	I want to compare males' and females' memories, so I get them to listen to a story and write it down, and I count how many words they have written as a measure of memory.	**C**	Ecological validity
4	I read some classic research about women's colour preferences and make recommendations to a paint company based on these findings.	**D**	Population validity

Answers on page 284

 APPLYING YOUR KNOWLEDGE (2)

Ainsworth developed the Strange Situation to assess the nature of children's attachment to their primary caregiver. This procedure uses controlled observation of a caregiver and infant interacting in a research room. Comment on the validity of the findings of research based on the Strange Situation. *(4 marks)*

Answers on page 284

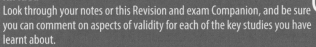 **An idea**

Look through your notes or this Revision and exam Companion, and be sure you can comment on aspects of validity for each of the key studies you have learnt about.
Then identify examples of studies that are:
· High in internal validity
· Low in internal validity
· High in external validity
· Low in external validity

 APPLYING YOUR KNOWLEDGE (1)

Read the item below and then answer the questions that follow.

A psychologist wanted to compare the effectiveness of different memory improvement strategies in learning French vocabulary. The participants are children from a local school. One group of students use strategy A and the other group use strategy B. They are asked to learn lists of French words, and are tested on their recall the next day.

The results are shown in the table.

	Mean number of words remembered correctly	**Standard deviation**
Strategy A	12	1.9
Strategy B	14	3.8

(i) What conclusion could the psychologist draw about the effect of type of memory strategy on the number of words correctly recalled? Refer to both the mean scores and standard deviations as part of your answer. *[4 marks]*

(ii) Sketch a graph to show the difference in average scores between the two conditions. *[4 marks]*

(iii) Explain **two** reasons why the results from this study may lack validity. *[4 marks]*

Answers on page 284

KEY TERMS

- Confederate
- Directional hypothesis
- Non-directional hypothesis
- Pilot study

Possible exam questions...

(These are generally paired with a 'stem' describing a study)

+ Explain why a researcher would conduct a pilot study. *(2 marks)*

+ Briefly explain how a pilot study would be conducted. *(2 marks)*

+ Explain why a researcher would choose to use a non-directional hypothesis rather than a directional hypothesis. *(2 marks)*

 Exam tip

Exam questions about pilot studies rarely ask you to explain what a pilot study is – you are more likely to be asked how a researcher would conduct one or why a researcher might conduct a pilot study. Make sure you deal with 'how' or 'why' in such questions.

 Think

Tip: in any exam question that describes an experiment, start by identifying:

- The IV
- The DV
- The hypothesis (and whether it is directional or non-directional)

MUST know ...

Directional and non-directional hypotheses

A **directional hypothesis** states the expected direction of the results. For example:

- People who do homework without the TV on produce *better* results than those who do homework with the TV on.
- People who have plenty of sleep get *higher* marks in class tests than those who don't.

A **non-directional hypothesis** states that there is a difference between the two conditions, but does not state the direction of the difference.

- People who do homework with the TV on produce *different* results from those who do homework with no TV on.
- Lack of sleep *affects* performance in class tests.

Pilot studies

A pilot study is a small-scale trial run of a research design, to check all aspects of the procedure and change some if necessary. These could include:

- The instructions to participants (Are they clear? Did participants understand what they had to do?)
- The timings (Too long or too short?)
- The materials used (Did participants have any difficulties understanding them? Were there too many tasks or questions, leading to boredom or fatigue?)
- Whether participants had guessed the purpose of the study.

Confederates

Sometimes a researcher has to use another person to play a role in an investigation. They are part of the research set-up rather than a participant.

SHOULD know ...

Directional and non-directional hypotheses

To fully operationalise the hypothesis on the left, you would need to give the operationalised IV and DV. So the second example becomes:

- People who have an average of eight hours or more sleep per night over a period of one month have lower results in class tests than people with a lower average sleep duration.

A directional hypothesis can be used when past research (theory or studies) suggests that the findings will go in a particular direction. If there is no relevant past research, or findings are contradictory, then a non-directional hypothesis should be used.

Pilot studies

If a researcher tries out the research design using a few typical participants, they can see what needs to be adjusted without having invested a large amount of time and money in a full-scale study.

The results of a pilot study are irrelevant. However, carrying out a pilot study and making appropriate changes to the procedure can improve the validity and reliability of the findings of the main study.

Confederates

For example, Milgram's study on obedience used confederates to play the roles of the experimenter and the learner. In Asch's study on conformity the confederates pretended to be other participants.

MATCH THEM UP

Match the examples with the related key terms.

1	Younger people have better memories than older people.	A	Research question
2	To see if blondes have more fun than brunettes.	B	Aim
3	Do people who sleep with a teddy bear sleep longer than people who don't?	C	Directional hypothesis
4	Positive expectations lead to differences in performance.	D	Directional hypothesis
5	Men with beards are more attractive.	E	Non-directional hypothesis
6	Lack of sleep may affect schoolwork.	F	Non-directional hypothesis

Answers on page 284

 CHOOSE THE RIGHT ANSWER

If researchers do not have evidence of previous research findings in the area they wish to study, they should use:

A A pilot study ☐

B A directional hypothesis ☐

C A correlational analysis ☐

D A non-directional hypothesis ☐

Answers on page 284

 A MARKING EXERCISE

Read the student answers to the following exam question, given below:

A researcher is investigating the hypothesis that people given a list of emotionally charged words recall fewer correctly than participants given a list of emotionally neutral words. Suggest why the researcher might carry out a pilot study for this investigation. *(2 marks)*.

A The researcher would select all of the participants for the experiment, and give them a few words to try to learn first. They would then decide how many words should be included in the actual experiment.

B The researcher wants to save time and money by checking the procedure before carrying it out on all his participants.

C The researcher wants to check that the participants understand all the words. If they don't, then the word lists can be changed before the actual experiment is carried out.

How many marks would you give each answer?

A	
B	
C	

Answers on page 284

 FILL IN THE BOXES

Look through some of the key studies in the memory chapter, and identify the IV and DV, then try writing directional and non-directional hypotheses for each. Also think about what aspects of the procedure could have been checked in a pilot study.

Study	IV	DV	Directional hypothesis	Non-directional hypothesis	What to check in a pilot study

KEY TERMS

- Counterbalancing
- Experimental design
- Independent groups design
- Matched pairs design
- Order effect
- Random allocation
- Repeated measures design

Possible exam questions...

(These are generally paired with a 'stem' describing a study)

+ Explain what is meant by *independent measures design*. *(2 marks)*

+ Identify the experimental design used in this study. *(2 marks)*

+ Explain **one** advantage and **one** limitation of using this experimental design in this study. *(2 marks + 2 marks)*

Exam tip

Exam questions often ask you to identify the experimental design used in a particular study. When students see the phrase 'experimental design' in an exam question they often can't remember what 'experimental design' means. Here's one way to remember – in the middle of the word 'experimental' are the letters RIM, which stand for Repeated, Independent and Matched pairs.

MUST know ...

Repeated measures design

Every participant carries out each condition of the experiment (all levels of the IV). The performance (DV) of each participant on the two tests can be compared.

Independent groups design

Each group of participants does one condition of the experiment, and the performance of the two groups is compared.

Matched pairs design

Two groups of participants are used, but pairs are matched on key characteristics believed to affect performance on the DV. For each pair, one member is randomly allocated to each condition. The procedure then continues as for independent groups.

Limitations of repeated measures design

- Order effects, such as practice (that may improve performance), boredom or fatigue effects (that may worsen performance).
- Participants may guess the purpose of the experiment, affecting their performance in the second condition.

Limitations of independent groups design

- Participant variables (individual differences) cannot be controlled, and are a confounding variable.
- More participants are required than a repeated measures design.

Limitations of matched pairs design

- It is very time-consuming and difficult to match people on key variables, and requires participants to be selected from a large pool.
- Only known variables can be matched, and there are likely to be other relevant variables that were not known about but still affect the DV.

SHOULD know ...

Counterbalancing

To deal with order effects in a repeated measure design, researchers can ensure that each condition is tested first or second in equal amounts. For example,

- half of the participants carry out condition A then B, and the other half do B then A
- alternatively, all participants take part in each condition twice: ABBA.

Matched pairs design

It is important to match on characteristics that could affect the DV. For example, age or gender may be relevant to some studies, but this decision must be based on evidence.

Dealing with the limitations

- Researchers may use two different but equivalent tests to reduce practice effects.
- Counterbalancing is the main way of dealing with order effects.
- A cover story can help to prevent participants guessing the aims of the study.

Dealing with the limitations

- Randomly allocating participants to conditions helps to distribute participant variables evenly (in theory).

Dealing with the limitations

- Restrict the number of variables to match, to make it easier.
- Conduct a pilot study to explore which key variables may be important to match.

Strengths of each experimental design

The limitations of one design are often the strengths of another.

For example, one limitation of repeated measures is that participants do better in the second condition because of a practice effect.

Therefore, one strength of independent measures and matched pairs designs is that they avoid order effects because each participant only does one condition.

Identify two strengths for each design

Repeated measures:

Independent groups:

Matched pairs:

MATCH THEM UP

Match the key term with the definition.

1	Participant variable	**A**	Same participants in both conditions
2	Repeated measures	**B**	Two groups, unpaired participants
3	Independent groups	**C**	Used in independent groups design
4	Order effect	**D**	Two groups where participants are paired
5	Matched pairs	**E**	A problem in independent groups design
6	Random allocation	**F**	A problem in repeated measures design

Answers on page 284

CHOOSE THE RIGHT ANSWER

Which **three** of the following statements relates to a repeated measures experimental design?

Tick **three** boxes.

A All participants are tested twice. ☐

B Participants are allocated to separate groups. ☐

C Participants are matched on key characteristics. ☐

D Participants may guess the aims of the study. ☐

E This design may lead to order effects. ☐

F Participant effects are not controlled. ☐

Answers on page 284

APPLYING YOUR KNOWLEDGE (1)

A study investigates the effect of coffee on reaction time by testing each participant twice – at the start of the experiment and again after they have drunk a cup of coffee.

Explain two reasons why it was more appropriate to use a repeated measures design than an independent groups design. *(2 marks + 2 marks)*

Reason 1:

Reason 2:

Answers on page 284

APPLYING YOUR KNOWLEDGE (2)

A researcher wants to conduct an experiment to investigate differences between people who are left- and right-handed. One area of interest is creativity. The researcher intends to assess creativity using a test.

Answer the following questions:

A Explain why this is an independent groups design. *(2 marks)*

B Explain why a repeated measures design would be unsuitable to use in this experiment. *(3 marks)*

C Explain **one** strength and **one** limitation of using an independent groups design. *(2 marks + 2 marks)*

D Write a non-directional hypothesis for this experiment. *(2 marks)*

Answers on page 284

KEY TERMS

- Field experiment
- Laboratory experiment

Possible exam questions...

(These are generally paired with a 'stem' describing a study.)

+ Explain what is meant by a *laboratory experiment*. *(2 marks)*

+ Explain **one** limitation of a field experiment. *(2 marks)*

+ Suggest **one** reason why the researchers decided to use a field experiment rather than a laboratory experiment. *(2 marks)*

+ Discuss laboratory and field experiments, referring to examples of each. *(6 marks)*

MUST know ...

All experiments involve the manipulation of the IV while trying to keep all other variables constant. The DV is measured. We can conclude that the change in the IV has caused the change in the DV.

Laboratory experiments

These are carried out in a special environment where variables can be controlled. Participants are aware that they are taking part in a study.

Field experiments

These are carried out in a more natural environment. The IV is still deliberately manipulated by the researcher. Participants are usually unaware that they are participating in an experiment.

 A strength of laboratory experiments is that...

...they are high in internal validity

- **E** – because variables are tightly controlled, so we can be more certain that any change in the DV is due to the IV.

 A strength of field experiments is that...

...that they are in a more natural setting

- **E** – so participants are less likely to respond to cues in their environment.

There is a balancing act...

...between control and ecological validity

- **E** – as lab experiments have better control at the expense of mundane realism, and field experiments may be more like everyday life, but lose control of variables.

SHOULD know ...

Laboratory experiments

Participants may alter their behaviour as they know it is being recorded. In addition, the laboratory environment and the materials used may be quite unlike everyday life.

Not all laboratory studies are laboratory experiments; they could be observations, natural experiments or quasi-experiments.

Field experiments

Participants' behaviour may be more natural.

Not all field studies are experiments; the IV must be manipulated by the experimenter.

Some experiments may be carried out in a laboratory environment, but the purpose of the study is so well concealed that participants are behaving quite naturally, so the study is more like a field experiment.

However, a limitation of laboratory experiments is...

...low ecological validity.

- **E** – This is because
  - the setting is low in mundane realism
  - the participants know they are in a study
  - the IV or DV may be operationalised in ways that don't represent everyday life.

However, a limitation of field experiments is...

...there is less control of extraneous variables.

- **E** – This means they may be lower in internal validity than a laboratory experiment.
- **E** – Also, participants in a field experiment may be unaware that they are being studied and it is difficult to debrief them afterwards.
- **L** – This means there are more ethical issues with field experiments than laboratory experiments.

CHOOSE THE RIGHT ANSWER

Which **one** of the following statements is **not** true of field experiments? Tick **one** box only.

A They tend to have lower internal validity than a laboratory experiment	☐
B They tend to have higher ecological validity than a laboratory experiment	☐
C The IV is naturally occurring	☐
D They are carried out in a natural environment	☐

Answers on page 284

RESEARCH ISSUES

Bickman tested the effects of perceived authority on obedience in a field experiment.

Confederates dressed in a jacket and tie, a milkman's uniform or as a guard, and made requests to passers-by; for example, asking them to pick up some litter or to give someone money for a parking meter. Participants obeyed most when the confederate was dressed as a guard. This study shows that we are more likely to obey someone who looks like they have authority than someone who does not.

Identify **one** ethical issue the researcher should consider in this research. Suggest how he could deal with this issue.

Answers on page 284

APPLYING YOUR KNOWLEDGE

Find key studies in each chapter of this book, and answer the following questions:

1. Identify the IV and DV. *(2 marks)*

2. Was the task required of participants contrived? *(1 mark)*

3. Was the study conducted in a natural setting? *(1 mark)*

4. Was the setting high or low in mundane realism? *(1 mark)*

5. Did the participants know they were being studied? *(1 mark)*

6. Were the participants brought into a special situation, or did the experimenter go to them? *(1 mark)*

7. What relevant variables might not have been controlled? *(1 mark)*

8. Do you think this was a lab or field experiment? *(1 mark)*

FILL IN THE BOXES

From the activity above, you should be able to identify two classic laboratory experiments and a field experiment. Complete the table below:

	What study was it?	IV	DV	Uncontrolled variables	Task	Setting	Were participants aware?
Lab experiment 1							
Lab experiment 2							
Field experiment							

Answers on page 284

KEY TERMS

- Natural experiment
- Quasi-experiment

Possible exam questions ...

(These are generally paired with a 'stem' describing a study.)

+ Explain what is meant by a quasi-experiment. *(2 marks)*
+ Explain why this is a natural experiment. *(2 marks)*
+ Describe a limitation of natural experiments. *(2 marks)*
+ Discuss the use of natural experiments in psychological research, giving examples in your answer. *(6 marks)*

MUST know ...

Natural experiment

A natural experiment is conducted when it is not possible, for ethical or practical reasons, to deliberately manipulate an IV - the IV is naturally occurring. It may take place in a laboratory. The DV is measured, but only tentative conclusions can be drawn about the IV's effect on the DV, as the IV was not deliberately manipulated and participants were not randomly allocated to conditions.

Quasi-experiment

In a quasi-experiment the IV is also naturally occurring – it is a naturally existing difference between people, for example gender. Again, causal conclusions must be tentative.

 The IV is not directly manipulated...

...in natural or quasi-experiments

- *E* – so we cannot be sure that any change in the DV is caused by the IV.

 Participants are not randomly allocated...

...to the conditions.

- *E* – This means there may be biases in the different groups of participants.

 The sample may be unique...

...in that participants have particular characteristics.

- *E* – This would give the study low population validity.

SHOULD know ...

Natural experiment

For example, a study of the effect of institutionalisation on children, in which the two groups were adopted before or after six months of age. The DV could be tested in a lab, e.g. IQ or behaviour in the Strange Situation.

Quasi-experiment

The IV could be measured by psychological testing, for example groups of people with internal or external locus of control. This is a personal attribute of the individuals, not something that was manipulated by researchers. Participants' responses in a situation would then be the DV measured in the quasi-experiment.

- *E* – There may have been uncontrolled confounding variables
- *L* – so conclusions about cause and effect must be tentative.

- *E* – There may be other variables that vary systematically with the IV, but are not controlled.
- *L* – They would become confounding variables, giving a different cause for the change in the DV.

- *E* – For example, Charlton *et al.* carried out a longitudinal natural experiment on the island of St Helena. They measured the effect of introducing TV on children's behaviour. However, the people in St Helena were a particular pro-social community which may explain why TV didn't affect their behaviour.
- *L* – This means the findings can't be generalised to other groups.

 A LEVEL ONLY ZONE ...

 Natural experiments...

...allow psychologists to research 'real' problems

- *E* – for example, the effects of a disaster on health
- *E* – where the IV already exists.
- *L* – This gives high levels of mundane realism and ecological validity.

Studies comparing older and younger people...

...are quasi-experiments.

- *E* – Age is a 'condition' of the individual and cannot be artificially manipulated.
- *E* – However, other variables may also covary with age, such as cognitive decline or dementia.
- *L* – This means that the conclusion cannot simply relate age to the difference in the DV.

MATCH THEM UP

Match the experiment type with the correct description.

1	A natural experiment	A	The IV is manipulated by the experimenter and it takes place in a natural environment.
2	A laboratory experiment	B	The IV occurs naturally and is a characteristic of the individuals.
3	A field experiment	C	The IV is manipulated by the researcher and it takes place in a controlled environment.
4	A quasi-experiment	D	Groups belonging to different conditions of the IV are compared, and they could be asked to do things in a laboratory.

Answers on page 285

✓ CHOOSE THE RIGHT ANSWER

People who score high on the authoritarian personality scale are compared with people low on the authoritarian personality scale in terms of how willing they are to obey orders in a Milgram-type study.

Which type of experiment is this? Tick **one** box.

A Laboratory experiment ☐
B Field experiment ☐
C Natural experiment ☐
D Quasi-experiment ☐

Answers on page 285

⚙ APPLYING YOUR KNOWLEDGE

A study investigates the anti-social effects of TV by monitoring whether people who watch a lot of TV (more than five hours a day) are more aggressive than those who don't. Their aggression levels are measured by asking friends and family to rate them on a scale.

(a) Identify the IV and DV. *(2 marks)*.

(b) Identify whether it is a laboratory, field, natural or quasi-experiment. *(1 mark)*

(c) Explain your decision. *(2 marks)*

(d) Explain why you think the study would have high or low validity. *(2 marks)*.

Answers on page 285

FILL IN THE BOXES

Complete the summary table comparing different types of experiment.

	Strength 1	Strength 2	Limitation 1	Limitation 2
Lab experiment				
Field experiment				
Natural experiment				
Quasi-experiment				

KEY TERMS

- Demand characteristics
- Investigator effect

Possible exam questions...

(These are generally paired with a 'stem' describing a study.)

+ Explain what is meant by *demand characteristics*. *(2 marks)*
+ Explain how a researcher might avoid investigator effects in this study. *(2 marks)*

 Exam tip

The only specialist terms used on this spread that are in the specification are *demand characteristics* and *investigator effects*. This means that exam questions can only use these terms. The other terms may be useful for you when discussing research methods or critically evaluating research studies.

MUST know ...

Demand characteristics

Cues that make participants unconsciously aware of the aims of a study or help them work out what the researcher expects to find. The situation creates expectations and participants do not behave as they would usually. Thus, demand characteristics may act as a confounding variable.

Investigator effects

Any cues from an investigator that encourage certain behaviours in the participant, and which might lead to a fulfilment of the investigator's expectations. For example, investigators may be more encouraging to one group of participants, or may ask leading questions. Investigator effects may act as a confounding variable.

 Single blind design can help...

...to deal with demand characteristics.

- **E** – In a single blind design, the participant is not aware of the research aims or which condition of the experiment they are in.

 Double blind design is even better...

...at reducing demand characteristics.

- **E** – In a double blind design both the participant and the person conducting the experiment are 'blind' to the aims or hypotheses.

 Experimental realism ensures...

...that the situation appears genuine to participants.

- **E** – If the events appear natural and realistic the participant will behave more naturally.

SHOULD know ...

Demand characteristics

Participants generally want to be helpful, and can therefore behave over-cooperatively. However, some participants deliberately try to spoil an experiment – the 'screw you' effect.

People taking part in studies are known as 'participants' to reflect that they are actively involved, searching for cues about meaning and expected behaviour in a situation. In early psychological research they were known as 'subjects', which implied passivity and powerlessness.

Investigator effects

These may include direct effects (as a result of the investigator interacting with the participant) and indirect effects (as a consequence of the way the investigator designed the study).

- **E** – This prevents the participant from responding to cues about the aims or expectations of the experiment
- **L** – so they should behave more naturally.

- **E** – Ideally the person conducting the experiment will also be unaware of which participants are in which group or condition.
- **L** – This means the investigator is less likely to produce cues about their expectations.

- **E** – If the participant is sufficiently engaged in the task, they are not paying attention to the fact that they are being observed.
- **L** – This also reduces demand characteristics.

 A LEVEL ONLY ZONE ...

 Participant variables are not the same as participant effects

- **E** – Participant variables are the characteristics of individual participants, which act as extraneous variables in an independent groups design.
- **E** – For example, age, intelligence, motivation, etc.
- **E** – whereas participant effects refer to the behaviour of participants in response to an experimental situation.
- **L** – Participant variables can be controlled by a repeated measures or matched pairs design (matching for relevant characteristics).

Situational variables...

...are aspects of the research situation that affect participants' behaviour.

- **E** – For example, order effects such as practice or fatigue.
- **E** – These can also become confounding if they vary systematically with the IV, for example if one group are all tested in the morning and another group are all tested in the afternoon.
- **L** – Then the change in the DV may be due to the EV rather than the IV.

MATCH THEM UP

Match up the term with the definition.

1	Demand characteristics	**A**	Characteristics of the participant in a research study
2	Investigator effects	**B**	A study in which the participant is not aware of which condition they are in
3	Participant variables	**C**	Aspects of the research situation itself which may affect participants' behaviour
4	Situational variables	**D**	Cues given by the experimenter that influence participants' behaviour
5	Single blind design	**E**	Neither experimenter nor participant are aware of which condition participants are in
6	Double blind design	**F**	Cues that lead participants to behave as they think they are expected to

Answers on page 285

 CHOOSE THE RIGHT ANSWER

Which **one** of the following is an effect of demand characteristics? Tick **one** box.

A Participants may be harmed by the experiment ☐

B The experimenter makes unreasonable demands on the participants ☐

C Participants may change their behaviour to match what they think is expected ☐

D The experimenter may behave differently towards participants with particular characteristics ☐

Answers on page 285

 APPLYING YOUR KNOWLEDGE

In a pilot study, Orne and his colleagues asked a number of casual acquaintances whether they would do the experimenter a favour; when they agreed, they were asked to perform five push-ups. Their response tended to be amazement, incredulity and the question "Why?" Another similar group of individuals were asked whether they would take part in an experiment of brief duration. When they agreed to do so, they too were asked to perform five push-ups. Their typical response was "Where?'"

Explain why this difference may have occurred.

Identify the psychology	Link to Orne's research

Answers on page 285

 DRAWING CONCLUSIONS

A study into teacher's expectations was carried out by Rosenthal in the 1960s. He randomly allocated children to two groups, and told their teachers that one group had been found to score high for 'intellectual blooming', and should be expected to show great increases in intelligence during the coming year. Children's IQ scores (a measure of intelligence) were tested at the beginning and the end of the year. The findings are shown in the table below.

	Mean gains in IQ during the year	
Grade	**'normal' group**	**'high score for intellectual blooming potential' group**
1	12	27.4
2	7	16.5
3	5	5

a. Draw a bar chart to display these findings. *(3 marks)*

b. What conclusions can you draw about the effect of teachers' expectations on the children's learning? *(3 marks)*

Conclusion 1:

Conclusion 2:

Conclusion 3:

Answers on page 285

KEY TERMS

- Bias
- Generalisation
- Opportunity sample
- Population
- Random sample
- Sampling
- Stratified sample
- Systematic sample
- Volunteer bias
- Volunteer sample

Possible exam questions…

(These are generally paired with a 'stem' describing a study.)

+ Identify the sampling method in a study and explain a limitation of this method. *(3 marks)*
+ Explain how bias is a problem in opportunity sampling. *(2 marks)*
+ Explain what is meant by *generalisation*. *(2 marks)*

★ Exam tip

About 10% of your marks in the exams will come from questions relating to mathematical concepts. These include the principles of sampling as applied to scientific data, for example explaining how a random or stratified sample could be obtained from a population.

MUST know …

Populations and samples

The population is the group of individuals the researcher is interested in; they select a smaller sample to study, e.g. 20–30 participants.

Opportunity sample
People are recruited because of convenience or availability.

Random sample
Each person in the population has an equal chance of being selected. Selection involves:

- The lottery method – put all names in a hat, and select the number required.
- Random number generators – number everyone, computer picks numbers randomly.

Volunteer sample
Advertise on the internet or a noticeboard or in a newspaper.

 Opportunity sampling…

…is the easiest method
- ***E*** – so takes less time to find a sample than other methods.

Random sampling…

…is unbiased
- ***E*** – as all members of the population have an equal chance of being selected.

Stratified sampling…

…is likely to be more representative than other methods
- ***E*** – because there is a proportional representation of subgroups.

Systematic sampling…

…is unbiased
- ***E*** – as participants are objectively selected.

 Volunteer sampling…

…gives access to a variety of participants
- ***E*** – so may be more representative than an opportunity sample.

SHOULD know …

Populations and samples

Ideally the sample will be representative of the population so that generalisations can be made. Most studies use opportunity or volunteer sampling.

Stratified sample
Subgroups within the population are identified (e.g. age groups or genders). Participants are obtained from each group in proportion to their occurrence in the population, using random selection.

Systematic sample
Uses a predetermined system to select participants, such as every twentieth in a list.

- ***E*** – However, the sample is inevitably biased.
- ***L*** – This means the findings may lack population validity.

- ***E*** – However, it requires a list of names of all members of the population, from which a random selection is recruited.
- ***L*** – This may take some time.

- ***E*** – However, subgroups must be identified, participants randomly selected from subgroups, then contacted.
- ***L*** – This is very time-consuming.

- ***E*** – However, it is not actually random unless you select a person from the list randomly to begin the counting from.

- ***E*** – However, participants may be highly motivated, or short of money, or have extra time on their hands.
- ***L*** – This leads to volunteer bias.

 **A LEVEL ONLY**

 Sample bias is inevitable

- ***E*** – For example, an opportunity sample only represents people who are easily available to the researcher.
- ***E*** – People who volunteer to take part in research are likely to differ from other members of the population in potentially important ways.
- ***L*** – This distorts or biases the data they produce.

 Participants must be willing…

…to take part in research..
- ***E*** – Whatever the sampling method, some participants may refuse to take part or may withdraw.
- ***E*** – This is another reason bias is often unavoidable.
- ***E*** – However, this sampling bias can be avoided in field experiments if participants are unaware they are being studied, and don't have the opportunity to withdraw.

MATCH THEM UP

The table below lists the three main methods used to select participants.

Underneath the table are descriptions of the sampling methods used in various studies. Place the letters A–F next to the appropriate sampling method.

Sampling method	Matching description
Opportunity sample	
Volunteer sample	
Random sample	

A A study is conducted in a primary school. Only ten participants are needed. All the names in the school are put in a hat and ten names are drawn out.

B Some psychology students advertise for participants by putting a notice on the school noticeboard.

C A psychology class do an experiment in class and the participants are the class members.

D Opinions on smoking are collected by interviewing people in a town centre.

E People fill in a questionnaire in a magazine and the data is used in a psychology study.

F Participants for a child health study are selected by using computer generated numbers to pick 100 names from a list of the babies born in the UK in the week beginning 1 January 2013.

Answers on page 285

A MARKING EXERCISE

Student answers to the following question are given below:

A study used opportunity sampling. Evaluate the choice of this sampling technique. *(3 marks)*

What marks would you give the following answers?

Dylan's answer

Opportunity sampling can create a bias as the types of people who are available will vary depending on the time and place. However, opportunity sampling is often good because it doesn't involve a long process or special criteria for how to choose participants.

Carrie's answer

Opportunity sampling allows you to take advantage of whoever is available to the researcher at the time. This means there is a high chance of bias and low population validity therefore this may not be representative data.

Charlotte's answer

Opportunity sampling is a good technique because everyone has an equal chance of being in the research. However, it may be biased and participants may not be aware that they are being studied.

Student	Mark
Dylan	
Carrie	
Charlotte	

Answers on page 285

SPOT THE MISTAKES

Read the text below.

There are **four** mistakes – draw a circle round each.

Psychologists need to select participants for their research studies. One way to do this is by using a voluntary sample. This means you ask people if they want to take part. Such a sample is likely to be unbiased. Another technique that can be used is the random sample. To do this you identify your main population and then put all the names in a machine like they use for the lottery and randomly select the number you require. A third method is the opportunity sample. The people who are chosen are the ones most willing.

Answers on page 285

APPLYING YOUR KNOWLEDGE

A psychologist plans to study the use of mobile phones by adults. The psychologist selects 30 participants for the study and divides them into two groups: heavy users (more than three calls per day) and light users (three calls or fewer per day). All participants are rated for friendliness to test the hypothesis that heavy users are more friendly than light users.

Answer the following questions:

(a) Identify a suitable method to use for selecting your sample and explain how this sample would be obtained. *(1 mark + 2 marks)*

(b) Identify one strength of using this sampling technique in this study. *(2 marks)*

(c) Identify the experimental design. *(1 mark)*

(d) Identify the operationalised independent variable (IV) in this study. *(2 marks)*

(e) Explain why this is a natural experiment. *(2 marks)*

Answers on page 285

See page 196 for an explanation of experimental design.

KEY TERMS

- Confidentiality
- Deception
- Informed consent
- Privacy
- Protection from harm
- Right to withdraw

Possible essay question …

Discuss ethical issues in the design and conduct of psychological students. Refer to examples of studies in your answer. (12 marks AS, 16 marks A)

Other possible exam questions …

(These are generally paired with a 'stem' describing a study.)

+ One ethical issue is 'protection from harm'. Explain situations where apparent harm might be considered acceptable. (4 marks)

+ Identify **one** other ethical issue in psychological research and explain why it is an issue. (2 marks)

+ Discuss the role of the British Psychological Society's code of ethics. (8 marks)

MUST know …

Ethical issues…

…are conflicts between:

- what the researcher wants to do in order to conduct useful and meaningful research, and
- the rights of participants.

All research must be conducted in an ethically appropriate way, including student research.

Informed consent…

…means telling participants the true aim of a study and what is going to happen, so they can make an informed decision about participating. They should be aware of any potential risks or benefits.

Deception…

…can be necessary to avoid demand characteristics. However, there is a difference between withholding some details of the research aims (acceptable) and deliberately giving false information (less acceptable).

The right to withdraw…

…is important if participants feel distressed during a study, particularly if they were not fully informed. Participants should not lose any payments or rewards by withdrawing.

Protection from harm

Research is considered acceptable if the risk of harm (physical or psychological) is no greater than a participant would be likely to experience in ordinary life, and they leave the study in the same state they arrived in.

Confidentiality…

…is a legal right for participants. Personal data can only be recorded in such a way that the participants cannot be identified.

Privacy

People would not expect to be observed by others in certain situations, such as their own homes, whereas in public places (like a park) being observed would not feel so invasive.

SHOULD know …

The BPS

The British Psychological Society (BPS) identifies four ethical principles for researchers:

1. Respect for the dignity of people
2. Competence – high standards of professional work
3. Responsibility – to clients and the public
4. Integrity – honest research and reporting

Informed consent

Researchers may not want to reveal the true aims of a study because it could change the way the participants behave.

Researchers cannot always predict the risks or benefits of taking part in a study.

Deception…

…can lead people to see psychologists as untrustworthy, and contravenes the right to informed consent. However, much of the deception in research is minor and harmless, and participants would have little reason to refuse to take part.

The right to withdraw

If participants do leave during the study the sample will become biased, as those who remain may be more compliant or hardy.

Protection from harm…

…is difficult to guarantee as studies addressing some important questions may involve a degree of distress or embarrassment, and outcomes may be hard to predict.

Confidentiality…

…can also be difficult to protect, as researchers wish to publish the findings. They can guarantee anonymity, but it may be possible to identify details of participants from their particular characteristics in a small target population.

Privacy

Researchers may need to study participants without their awareness, which could be seen as an invasion of privacy.

MATCH THEM UP

Match up the ethical issue with the example.

1	Informed consent	**A**	Being able to stop participating in a study if you feel uncomfortable.
2	Deception	**B**	Understanding the purpose of a study and agreeing to take part.
3	Protection from harm	**C**	Withholding key information about a study.
4	Lack of privacy	**D**	Invading a person's personal space.
5	Right to withdraw	**E**	Not making someone feel embarrassed or anxious.

Answers on page 285

An idea 👍

Look through your notes and try to identify studies that are examples of each of the ethical issues, so you could refer to them in a discussion question.

Informed consent	
Deception	
Right to withdraw	
Protection from harm	
Confidentiality	
Privacy	

✓ **CHOOSE THE RIGHT ANSWER**

Which **one** of the ethical principles in psychological research can be an issue for researchers, as it can result in a biased sample? Tick **one** box.

A	The right to confidentiality	☐
B	The right to withdraw	☐
C	The right to protection from harm	☐
D	Informed consent	☐

Answers on page 285

 APPLYING YOUR KNOWLEDGE

In the Stanford Prison Experiment the researchers took great care to gain informed consent. However, the participants did not know the amount of psychological distress that would be caused by participating.

Discuss how the issue of psychological harm could have been dealt with more effectively in this study. *(6 marks)*

Answers on page 285

KEY TERMS

- Cost-benefit analysis
- Debriefing
- Ethical guidelines (code of conduct)
- Ethics committee
- Presumptive consent

Possible essay question...

Discuss how psychologists deal with ethical issues in psychological research. Refer to examples of research studies in your answer. *(12 marks AS, 16 marks A)*

Other possible exam questions ...

(These are generally paired with a 'stem' describing a study.)

+ Explain why deception can be an issue in social psychological research. *(3 marks)*

+ How can researchers ensure that any deception in this study is dealt with in accordance with ethical guidelines? *(3 marks)*

+ Explain the role of an ethics committee in psychological research. *(4 marks)*

MUST know ...

Strategies to deal with ethical issues

The BPS 'Code of Ethics and Conduct' and the 'Code of Human Research Ethics' (BPS, 2014) give **ethical guidelines** on which behaviours are acceptable and how to deal with ethical dilemmas.

A **cost-benefit analysis** attempts to judge the research in terms of its costs and benefits to the participants themselves and to society as a whole.

Ethics committees in research institutions must approve any study before it can go ahead, considering how researchers intend to deal with ethical issues and weighing up costs and benefits.

Advice, not punishment – the codes use the word 'should' rather than 'must' to reinforce the advisory nature of the documents.

Dealing with specific ethical issues

Informed consent – participants sign a consent form and are offered the right to withdraw. Presumptive consent could be used instead.

Deception – must be approved by an ethics committee after considering costs to participants and benefits to society. Participants must be fully debriefed and have the opportunity to discuss any concerns and withdraw their data.

Right to withdraw – participants should be informed at the beginning of the study that they can withdraw at any time without losing any benefits.

Protection from harm – the study should be stopped if harm is suspected.

Confidentiality – researchers should use numbers or false names for participants.

Privacy – do not study anyone without their informed consent, unless it is public behaviour in a public place.

SHOULD know ...

Strategies to deal with ethical issues

The BPS code of ethics offers **guidelines** such as:

- Deception is inappropriate if participants become angry or distressed when they are debriefed.
- How to safeguard children and vulnerable adults.
- If harm or unusual discomfort may occur, the investigator must obtain approval from independent advisors and fully informed consent from participants.

Advice, not punishment – 'The role of these codes is primarily to guide researchers rather than punish them for non-compliance.

Dealing with specific ethical issues

These approaches have limitations:

Informed consent – if participants are given full information this may invalidate the study. Even if they have been fully informed, do they really understand what they have agreed to? Presumptive consent assumes that people can imagine the scenario and their responses accurately, which may not be the case.

Deception – cost-benefit decisions are flawed because the outcomes are not evident until after the study. Debriefing can't undo any harm to participants.

Right to withdraw – participants may feel they shouldn't withdraw because it might spoil the study.

Protection from harm – harm may only become apparent later.

Confidentiality – it may be possible to identify participants via details of location, etc.

Privacy – it is not universally agreed what constitutes a public place.

A LEVEL ONLY ZONE ...

 Ethical guidelines

- *P* – A 'rules and sanctions' approach has limitations, as it is impossible to cover every situation that a researcher may encounter.
- *E* – Also, rules tend to absolve researchers of responsibility, as they can simply claim "I followed the guidelines so my research is acceptable".
- *E* – The Canadian approach is different, encouraging debate around hypothetical dilemmas.
- *L* – This encourages psychologists to engage deeply with ethical issues, rather than just following rules.

 The problem with a cost-benefit analysis approach is that...

...it is difficult to predict the costs and benefits before conducting a study.
- *E* – In fact, they are difficult to assess and quantify even after a study.
- *E* – Diana Baumrind argued that this approach could even legitimise unethical practices, such as deception and harm, provided the benefits are high enough.
- *L* – This means that cost-benefit analysis simply exchanges one set of dilemmas for another.

CHOOSE THE RIGHT ANSWER

According to the BPS code of ethics and conduct, which criteria should be met for deception to be acceptable in psychological research? Tick all of the boxes that apply.

A If agreed by an ethics committee after full cost-benefit analysis ☐

B If it is essential for the research study to be able to obtain valid results ☐

C If participants could be harmed or distressed in the research ☐

D If participants are fully debriefed afterwards, and given the opportunity to withdraw their data and express any objections ☐

Answers on page 285

An idea 👍

Look back at the six studies you identified on the previous spread, and on a separate piece of paper, consider how a researcher might deal with the ethical issues in each case.
(3 marks each)

 A MARKING EXERCISE

Student answers to the following question are given below:

Identify one ethical issue. Explain how a psychologist could deal with this issues. *(1 mark + 3 marks)*

What mark would you give each answer?

Ahmed's answer

One issue is confidentiality. Don't identify the participants. Don't use photographs or names in published research. Names of people and/or places should be changed.

Christian's answer

One issue is confidentiality. The researcher used 100 adults. To fix confidentiality the research could use fake names in the data. The researcher could also just use numbers or statistics.

Student	Mark
Ahmed	
Christian	

Answers on page 285

 APPLYING YOUR KNOWLEDGE

A researcher is studying age and eyewitness testimony. She shows participants a recording of a robbery. She asks them to report back a week later for a further study but doesn't tell them she is going to test their recall. At this second session she shows participants some photographs and asks them to identify the robber and one of the victims. There are two groups of participants: children aged 6–10 years old and adults aged 30–40 years old.

Answer the following questions.

(a) Identify two ethical issues associated with this study. Suggest how psychologists could deal with each of these issues.
(1 mark + 1 mark + 3 marks + 3 marks)

(b) Aside from ethical issues, explain one problem with conducting research with children. *(2 marks)*

(c) Explain the purpose of the BPS Code of Ethics. *(3 marks)*

The results of the study are displayed in the table below.

	Mean number of correct identifications	Standard deviation
Children	0.83	0.57
Adults	1.23	0.81

(d) Explain what is meant by the mean. *(2 marks)*

(e) What do the data in the table show about the differences between children's and adults' accuracy as eyewitnesses? *(2 marks)*

Answers on page 285

See page 224 for an explanation of mean and standard deviation.

KEY TERMS

- Controlled observation
- Covert observation
- Inter-observer reliability
- Naturalistic observation
- Non-participant observation
- Observer bias
- Overt observation
- Participant observation

Possible exam questions...

(These are generally paired with a 'stem' describing a study.)

+ Explain what is meant by *participant observation*. *(2 marks)*

+ Explain the difference between a naturalistic observation and a controlled observation. *(4 marks)*

+ Identify and explain **one** ethical issue relating to covert observations. *(2 marks)*

+ Give **one** limitation and **one** strength of using non-participant observation as a method of collecting data. *(2 marks + 2 marks)*

MUST know ...

Types of observation

In a **naturalistic observation**, behaviour is studied in a natural situation, and the researcher does not interfere with what is happening.

In a **controlled observation**, some aspects of the environment are organised by the researcher, enabling them to investigate the effects of particular objects or situations on behaviour.

In an **overt observation** participants are aware that they are being observed. This is likely to affect the validity of findings as it will affect behaviour.

A **covert observation** takes place without participants' awareness.

In **non-participant observation** the observer watches from a distance and does not interact with participants.

In **participant observation** the observer joins the group being observed, either overtly or covertly.

 Observational studies may have high validity...

...because they record people's actual behaviour, not just their intentions.

- **E** – They can also capture unexpected behaviour.

 Naturalistic observations...

...are high in ecological validity, especially if participants are unaware that they are being observed.

- **E** – However, other variables are not controlled, so may influence behaviour.

Ethical issues...

...arise in covert observations, whether in public or in a participant observation where the observer has become part of the group without their knowledge.

- **E** – As participants are unaware they are being observed, they cannot give or withhold consent.

SHOULD know ...

Types of observation

A **naturalistic observation** could be used in an experiment to measure the dependent variable; it is a technique for gathering data rather than a separate research method.

The control of variables in a **controlled observation** reduces the 'naturalness' of the environment and of the behaviour being studied.

Researchers carrying out **overt observation** try to be as unobtrusive as possible, and may be hidden behind a one-way mirror.

In a **covert observation**, participants may be informed afterwards.

If two or more observers record behaviour, then **inter-observer reliability** can be calculated. More than 80% consistency between their data indicates a high level of reliability.

- **E** – However, it is difficult for observers to be objective; what they observe is distorted by their expectations, and only observable behaviour (actions and speech) are recorded, not thoughts or motivations.
- **L** – This means that observer bias and interpretation of behaviour can affect the internal validity of the findings.

- **E** – On the other hand, controlled observations enable control of the environment so observers can focus on specific behaviours
- **L** – but this is at the cost of ecological validity as the situation may feel unnatural to participants.

- **E** – In addition, the researcher must take care not to invade people's privacy while observing them.
- **L** – The observer can sometimes seek retrospective consent, but it is not always possible to follow up people who have been observed in a public place.

MATCH THEM UP

Match up the observation type with the explanation.

1	Naturalistic observation	**A**	An observation carried out in an everyday setting
2	Controlled observation	**B**	Observing people without their knowledge
3	Overt observation	**C**	The observer is separate from the people being observed
4	Covert observation	**D**	Observations made by someone who is also taking part in the activity being observed
5	Participant observation	**E**	Observation where participants are aware that their behaviour is being studied
6	Non-participant observation	**F**	An investigation in which behaviour is observed but under conditions where certain variables have been organised by the researcher

Answers on page 286

 RESEARCH ISSUES

A researcher is interested in what young people talk about. He sits in a pub and records the conversations he hears. Identify one ethical issue the researcher would need to consider in this research. Suggest how the researcher could deal with this ethical issue. *(3 marks)*

Answers on page 286

 FILL IN THE BOXES

Identify validity issues with each type of observation, and fill in the table.

For example, do they have high or low ecological validity; high or low internal validity? Think about observer bias and demand characteristics.

	Covert	Overt
Participant observation		
Non-participant observation		

Answers on page 286

 APPLYING YOUR KNOWLEDGE

In each of the studies described below, decide whether the study involved observations that were:

(a) naturalistic or controlled (1 mark)

(b) overt or covert (1 mark)

(c) participant or non-participant (1 mark)

(d) ethically acceptable (explain your answer) (2 marks).

Study A Ainsworth studied infant attachment patterns using the Strange Situation (see page 84). Infants and a caregiver were placed in a room with a pre-determined and fixed set of toys.

They were observed through a one-way mirror so that the infants wouldn't be disturbed by the observer's presence. Caregivers gave informed consent.

Study B Ainsworth also studied 26 mothers and their infants who lived in six villages in Uganda. She observed the mothers in their own homes interacting as they normally would with their infants.

Study C One study observed boys and girls aged three to five years during their free-play periods at nursery school, without the children's awareness. The researchers classified activities as male, female or neutral and recorded how playmates responded. The researchers found that children generally reinforced peers for sex-appropriate play and were quick to criticise sex-inappropriate play (Lamb and Roopnarine, 1979).

Study D Moore spent weeks walking round New York, writing down everything he heard and uncovering some interesting exchanges between people he observed.

Study E Rosenhan conducted a classic study on insanity. Sane individuals pretended to hear voices and were admitted to mental hospitals. While in hospital they noted down the behaviour of the staff in the institution and the patients.

Answers on page 286

Key Terms

Key Terms

- Behavioural categories
- Event sampling
- Sampling
- Structured observation
- Time sampling

Possible exam question ...

(These are generally paired with a 'stem' describing a study.)

+ Describe how the researcher could carry out an observational study of aggression in children in a nursery school. *(6 marks)*

+ Explain how behavioural categories are used in observational research. *(3 marks)*

+ Suggest suitable behavioural categories and sampling methods for this study. *(4 marks)*

! Think

Make sure you are clear about the different uses of the term 'sampling' – for procedures in observational studies, as on this page, and also for selecting participants (see page 204).

MUST know ...

Unstructured observations

The researcher records all relevant behaviour, but without a system. This may be useful in a novel situation to decide what behaviours could be more systematically recorded.

Structured observations

Once researchers have decided which behaviours are relevant and observable, they can plan a structured observation using behavioural categories and sampling procedures.

Behavioural categories

Behaviours must be operationalised by breaking them down into categories which are:

- Objective – not requiring interpretation
- Comprehensive – covering all possible component behaviours, without an 'other' box
- Mutually exclusive – each behaviour must fit in only one category

Sampling procedures

The observer should ideally record every instance of a behaviour. However, if the behaviours are very frequent this become impossible so sampling enables observers to calculate an estimate of the frequency of the behaviour.

SHOULD know ...

Limitations of unstructured observations

There may be too much to record. The behaviours recorded are likely to be those that were most noticeable to the observer, which may not be the most important or relevant.

Benefits of structured observations

These enable observations to be more objective and rigorous.

Behavioural categories

For example, infant behaviour could include components such as smiling, crying, and sleeping.

Facial expressions have been coded by Ekman into a 64-component system, the Facial Action Coding System (FACS). This includes items such as blink, lip droop, eyes up, and outer brow raise, and it takes extensive training to recognise each component.

Sampling procedures

- **Event sampling** – counting the number of times a certain behaviour occurs in a target individual in a period of time. For example, counting how many times a person smiles in ten minutes
- **Time sampling** – noting what a target individual is doing every 30 seconds (or an appropriate time interval), by ticking behavioural categories on a check list.

APPLYING YOUR KNOWLEDGE (1)

A psychologist observed ten infants using the Strange Situation technique.

Answer the following questions:

(a) Identify two behavioural categories used in this technique. *(2 marks)*

(b) Identify one limitation of using observational techniques. *(2 marks)*

(c) Give one strength of conducting an observational study in a laboratory setting. *(2 marks)*

Answers on page 286

APPLYING YOUR KNOWLEDGE (2)

A research team investigated peer relations in children. They planned to observe children in their day care environment and assess their social development. To conduct the observations they selected behavioural categories, one of which was 'argues with other children'.

Answer the following questions:

(a) Suggest one other relevant behavioural category the psychologist could select. *(1 mark)*

(b) Explain how content analysis could be carried out on the data collected. *(3 marks)*

(c) Explain one or more possible limitations of this investigation. *(4 marks)*

Answers on page 286

See page 220 for an explanation of content analysis.

CHOOSE THE RIGHT ANSWER

A researcher decided to observe a sloth at the zoo over a two hour period, and record all its behaviour. What kind of observation was the researcher using?

A Time sampling

B Event sampling

C Structured observation

D Unstructured observation

Answers on page 286

DRAWING CONCLUSIONS

A researcher was interested in prosocial behaviour. She carried out a structured observation of six children, three girls and three boys, who were playing in single-sex groups. The children were filmed and the video recording was analysed.

The researchers recorded the behaviour for each child every 2 seconds over a 30 second period. A second researcher carried out the same procedure. Each table below compares the observations by the two observers at each time point. For example, at one time point, observer 1 recorded that the girl was smiling, and observer 2 thought she was receiving a toy. This is indicated by the highlighted cell. (Note: 'face' means the child turns to face another child).

Girls		Observer 2						
		Smile	Laugh	Give	Receive	Look	Face	Totals
Observer 1	**Smile**	5	2		1	2		10
	Laugh		4			1		5
	Give			5				5
	Receive				2			2
	Look					22	7	29
	Face		1			5	29	35
	Totals	5	6	6	3	30	36	86

Boys		Observer 2						
		Smile	Laugh	Give	Receive	Look	Face	Totals
Observer 1	**Smile**							0
	Laugh							0
	Give							0
	Receive							0
	Look					28	3	31
	Face					3	66	69
	Totals	0	0	0	0	31	69	100

a) Name three behavioural categories used in this study. *(1 mark)*

b) Which sampling procedure did the researchers use? *(1 mark)*

c) Why did she also collect results from a second observer? *(1 marks)*

d) Comment on the similarity or difference between the scores of the two observers. *(2 marks)*

e) What conclusions can be drawn from this study about the girls' and boys' prosocial behaviour when playing? *(3 marks)*

Answers on page 286

KEY TERMS

- Interview
- Interviewer bias
- Questionnaire
- Social desirability bias
- Structured interview
- Unstructured interview

Possible exam questions...

(These are generally paired with a 'stem' describing a study.)

+ Explain what is meant by *self-report techniques*. (2 marks)
+ Explain the difference between a structured and an unstructured interview. (3 marks)
+ Give **one** limitation of using a questionnaire rather than a structured interview to collect data. (2 marks)

⭐ Exam tip

When giving the difference between questionnaire and an interview, it is important to compare in terms of the same thing. For example, you could point out that… *'Questions are always predetermined (i.e. structured) in a questionnaire, whereas interviews can either be structured or unstructured, where new questions are developed during the course of the interview.'*

MUST know ...

Questionnaires

A pre-determined set of written questions which can permit a researcher to find out what people think and feel.

Questionnaires can be used to collect quantitative data which is then analysed using statistical tests, or qualitative data which gives deeper insight into individuals' experiences.

 See page 228 for an explanation of qualitative and quantitative data

Structured interview

A structured interview also has pre-determined questions. The interviewer reads out the questions and the interviewee replies. There is no deviation from the written questions.

Unstructured interview

The interviewer may begin with general aims and a few starting questions, but the conversation develops depending on the answers given.

Self-report techniques allow access...

…to people's thoughts, feelings and attitudes.

- *E* – But sometimes people don't know what they think or can't express their thoughts clearly, so their responses lack validity.

Questionnaires can easily be distributed...

…to a large number of people, quickly and cheaply.

- *E* – This enables a researcher to collect data from a large sample of people.

Interviewer's expectations...

…can influence the answers the interviewee gives.

- *E* – This is called **interviewer bias**, a form of investigator effect.

SHOULD know ...

Questionnaires...

…can be an objective and scientific way of conducting research, if they are well designed.

The questionnaire may be a research method, providing data to answer a research question. Alternatively, it may be part of an experimental study, for example to identify two groups of participants with different beliefs (the IV) in order to explore their responses (the DV).

A structured interview...

…is similar to a questionnaire but is delivered face-to-face or over the telephone.

An unstructured interview...

…is also known as a *clinical interview,* as doctors may follow a similar format.

- *E* – The key limitation is that people may not be truthful, as they answer in a way that presents them in a good light.
- *L* – This is called social desirability bias, and distorts the findings of many self-report studies.

- *E* – In addition, people may be more willing to reveal personal information than they would in an interview situation, as it is more impersonal.
- *L* – This reduces social desirability bias.

- *E* – Interviewer bias may be unconscious, with expectations communicated non-verbally through tone of voice, length of pause, etc.
- *L* – To avoid interviewer bias, interviewers must be trained to ask the questions in a neutral and consistent way.

A LEVEL ONLY ZONE ...

Sample bias is likely to occur...

…in all self-report techniques ….

- *E* – as participants must be willing and able to spend time filling in the questionnaire or answering the questions.
- *E* – This means that the sample may not be representative of the population,
- *L* – and this limits generalisability of the findings.

Interview data...

…can be easier to analyse from a structured interview

- *E* – because the questions are standardised, so data is more objective.
- *E* – However, in an unstructured interview the interviewer tailors the questions to specific responses,
- *L* – so it is possible to obtain more detailed information and deeper insights into individuals feelings, thoughts and experiences.

✓ CHOOSE THE RIGHT ANSWER

Which of the following does **not** affect data collected using self-report techniques?

A	Social desirability bias	☐
B	Observer bias	☐
C	Interviewer bias	☐
D	Sample bias	☐

Answers on page 286

📖 RESEARCH ISSUES

Explain two possible ethical issues that might arise when using questionnaires in research on failure to form attachment. *(4 marks)*

Issue 1:	
Issue 2:	

Answers on page 286

💡 DRAWING CONCLUSIONS

A research study explored the number of attachments that teenage children had. The children were asked the following question: 'If you were seriously injured and in hospital, who would you most like to be there to comfort you? You are allowed to identify more than one person'.

The percentage for each kind of answer is shown below.

Identified three or more people	33%
Identified two people	26%
Identified one person	41%

What do these findings show about teenagers' attachments?

Finding:

Conclusion: This shows that . . .

Answers on page 286

⚙ APPLYING YOUR KNOWLEDGE

A psychologist conducted a study of day care experiences, using a questionnaire with children aged 10–18 who had attended day care.

Answer the following questions:

(a) Explain why the psychologist might want to carry out a pilot study before the main study. *(2 marks)*

(b) For this study, explain **one** strength of collecting information using a questionnaire. *(3 marks)*

(c) The researcher wonders if it might be better to use an interview instead of a questionnaire. Explain why an interview might be better. *(3 marks)*

Answers on page 286

KEY TERMS

- Closed questions
- Open questions
- Qualitative data
- Quantitative data

Possible exam questions...

(These are generally paired with a 'stem' describing a study.)

+ Identify and explain **two** issues that are important in questionnaire construction. *(2 marks + 2 marks)*

+ Identify and explain **two** issues that are important in the design of interviews. *(2 marks + 2 marks)*

+ Explain the difference between closed and open questions. Use examples in your answer. *(4 marks)*

+ Give **one** strength of using closed questions in an interview. *(3 marks)*

MUST know ...

Questionnaire construction

Questions need to take into consideration:

- **Clarity** – avoid ambiguity, double negatives and double-barrelled questions.
- **Bias** – avoid leading questions, and try to reduce social desirability bias.
- **Analysis** – closed questions give data that is easier to analyse, but respondents may be forced to select answers that don't represent their true thoughts. Open questions may be more revealing but are difficult to analyse.

Design of interviews

The same factors as above should be considered. Also:

- The interview must be **recorded**, by note-taking or audio or video recording.
- The interviewer should use **listening skills**, such as non-verbal communication, warmth and encouragement.

 Open questions allow respondents to expand...

...on their answers. For example, "What factors contribute to making work stressful?" Both questionnaires and interviews can use open questions.

- **E** – This gives qualitative data, which can be rich, detailed and sometimes unexpected.

Closed questions have a limited range...

...of responses. They can include Likert scales, forced choice questions, or other tick-box questions. Closed questions can also be used in questionnaires or interviews.

- **E** – These produce quantitative data, which can be summarised and analysed using graphs and statistics.

SHOULD know ...

Writing good questions

A questionnaire may contain a mixture of closed and open questions, with filler questions – irrelevant questions to distract respondents from the true aim of the survey, and reduce demand characteristics.

The sequence may start with easier questions to reduce anxiety.

A sample of participants must be selected.

The questions can be tested in a pilot study, and refined if necessary.

Questioning skills...

...are important in unstructured interviews.

The interviewer should be careful not to probe too much, which can seem aggressive, and should give the respondent time to think.

- **E** – However, respondents who are less literate may find open questions difficult, and many people only give brief answers.
- **L** – The data is therefore difficult to summarise, but analysis involves looking for patterns or themes in order to draw conclusions about the behaviour being studied.

- **E** – However, respondents may be forced to choose answers that don't represent their true thoughts, or may select 'don't know'. People also tend to respond positively – an acquiescence bias.
- **L** – This means the data may lack validity.

A LEVEL ONLY ZONE ...

Psychological tests...

...are a set of tasks that measure some aspect of human behaviour,

- **E** – for example, IQ tests (measuring intelligence), personality tests, mood scales, attitude scales, and aptitude scales (measuring particular abilities such as numeracy).
- **E** – They often involve filling in questionnaires. The data is then analysed by a psychologist to produce a profile or score.
- **L** – They are not really self-report techniques, but many of the same considerations are relevant.

Ceiling and floor effects

- **P** – If all the questions in a test are too easy, then everyone will do well. This is called a ceiling effect.
- **E** – Conversely, if all the questions are too hard, most people will score very low – a floor effect.
- **L** – It is important, therefore, to include a range of questions of different difficulties, and to test out the questions in a pilot study.

MATCH THEM UP

Match up the question type with the evaluation point.

1	Open questions in a questionnaire	A	Participants can be prompted to expand by the researcher
2	Open questions in an interview	B	Give quantitative data which is easy to analyse statistically
3	Closed questions in a questionnaire	C	Participants may not write very much
4	Forced choice questions	D	Help to reduce demand characteristics
5	Filler questions	E	May not allow participants to express their real thoughts
6	Ambiguous questions	F	Cause confusion and reduce validity of the answers

Answers on page 286

✓ **CHOOSE THE RIGHT ANSWER**

Which of the following is **always** true of interviews? Tick **one** box.

A	They produce qualitative data	☐
B	They produce quantitative data	☐
C	The interviewer has to make notes	☐
D	The data has to be analysed	☐

Answers on page 286

⚙ **APPLYING YOUR KNOWLEDGE**

You have been asked to construct questions for an interview about people's attitudes towards smoking.

a. Write **one** closed question and **one** open question for this interview. *(2 marks + 2 marks)*

b. When asking questions about smoking attitudes, what factors might be important in an interviewer's behaviour? *(4 marks)*

c. An interviewer should avoid using leading questions. Give an example of a leading question that the interviewer should avoid in this interview. *(1 mark)*

Answers on page 286

 DRAWING CONCLUSIONS

The table below shows how Jess has answered on a self-report scale for the personality trait of Excitement Seeking (taken from the IPIP online resource)

Excitement Seeking Scale	Strongly disagree	Disagree	Disagree somewhat	Neutral	Agree somewhat	Agree	Strongly agree
	1	2	3	4	5	6	7
1. I love action						X	
2. I enjoy being reckless			X				
3. I tend to seek adventure				X			
4. I am willing to try anything once						X	
5. I enjoy being part of a loud crowd							X
6. I would never go hang gliding or bungee jumping			X				
7. I act wild and crazy		X					
8. I tend to seek danger			X				
9. I dislike loud music		X					
10. I love excitement						X	

(a) Calculate Jess's Excitement Seeking score, which is the mean of the scores for each item. Notice that items **6** and **9** are negatively oriented to avoid acquiescence effects, which means that on these two items you have to subtract Jess's scores from 8 first, so 1 becomes 7, 2 becomes 6, etc. *(2 marks)*

(b) The mean Excitement Seeking score for a group of students was 5.8. How does Jess compare with this group? *(2 marks)*

Answers on page 286

KEY TERMS

- Co-variable
- Continuous variable
- Correlation
- Correlation coefficient
- Curvilinear correlation
- Intervening variable
- Linear correlation
- Scattergram
- Significance

Possible exam questions...

(These are generally paired with a 'stem' describing a study.)

+ Explain what is meant by a *zero correlation*. *(2 marks)*
+ Explain the difference between experiments and correlations. *(4 marks)*
+ A research study produced a negative correlation between two co-variables. Explain what this means. *(2 marks)*

⭐ Exam tip

When you are asked to evaluate a study or a research method, make sure you include context from the details you have been given in the question stem. This is essential for getting full marks.

MUST know ...

Correlations

A correlation is a systematic association between two **continuous variables**.

Studies using correlational analysis are known as **correlational studies**.

The results can be displayed on a **scattergram**, where each point plotted shows the values of the two variables for one individual.

A **correlational hypothesis** states the expected association between the co-variables:

- positive correlation – as one increases, the other increases
- negative correlation – as one increases, the other decreases
- zero correlation - no association
- a correlation - unspecified direction (non-directional hypothesis)

EVALUATION — *One strength of correlational analysis...*

...is that it can be used when it is not possible to manipulate a variable.

- *E* – This contrasts with an experiment, where the investigator manipulates the IV in order to observe the effect on the DV.

EVALUATION — *Correlation does not imply causation*

- *E* – There may be **intervening variables** that explain the association between the co-variables. Alternatively, the causal relationship may be the opposite of what it seems.

EVALUATION — *Validity should still be considered...*

...in a correlational study.

- *E* – For example, the generalisability of the sample, the operationalisation of variables. These issues would affect external (population) validity and internal validity.

SHOULD know ...

Correlation coefficient

A number between -1 and +1 which tells us how closely the co-variables are related. A perfect positive correlation would be +1, and perfect negative correlation would be -1.

A strong correlation has a correlation coefficient closer to +1 or -1 and a weak correlation is nearer to zero.

The statistical significance of the correlation depends on the number of participants. This can be analysed using tables of significance. (See A level Year 2 book)

- *E* – Correlations can therefore be used to investigate trends in data.
- *L* – But this means that no conclusion can be made about one co-variable causing another in a correlational study.

- *E* – For example, a correlation between attendance and exam results may have other explanations, such as personal circumstances or motivation to succeed. We cannot conclude that increasing attendance would improve results.
- *L* – This means that further investigation would need to be carried out to find out if the relationship is causal.

- *E* – Correlational studies can often be easily replicated,
- *L* – so findings can be confirmed, and causality can be explored further using experimental or longitudinal methods.

A LEVEL ONLY ZONE

EVALUATION — Linear and curvilinear correlation

- *P* – Linear correlations produce a scattergram with values lying on a straight line.
- *E* – However, a curvilinear correlation is also possible.
- *E* – This is a consistent relationship between two variables, which changes as one variable increases, for example the relationship between stress and performance.
- *L* – This requires a different sort of statistical significance testing, to see how closely the data fit a curve rather than a straight line.

EVALUATION — A curvilinear correlation

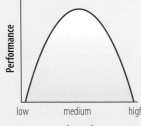

The Yerkes-Dodson effect. Arousal is positively correlated with performance at low levels of arousal, but negatively correlated at higher levels of arousal.

MATCH THEM UP

Match up the terms with their descriptions.

1	Positive correlation	**A**	Bottom left to top right
2	Negative correlation	**B**	A number that expresses the strength of a correlation
3	Zero correlation	**C**	All dots close together in a line
4	Correlation coefficient	**D**	Random scatter
5	Scattergram	**E**	Top left to bottom right
6	Strong correlation	**F**	Graph showing correlational data

Answers on page 286

 DRAWING CONCLUSIONS

A study looked at the behaviour of pairs of twins to see how similar they are.

Each twin was rated for aggressiveness on a scale of 1 to 10. The results are displayed in the table below.

Twin 1:	8	6	4	5	2	8	9	6	7
Twin 2:	6	5	8	6	5	4	7	5	7

(a) How many people were tested in this study?

(b) Draw an appropriate scattergram to display this data.

Correctly label the scattergram.

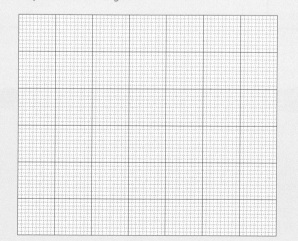

(c) What does this graph show about the twins' aggression?

Answers on page 286

 APPLYING YOUR KNOWLEDGE

A research study looks at the relationship between hours spent in day care per week and aggressiveness. The study finds a positive correlation.

Answer the following questions:

(a) Suggest how you might operationalise aggressiveness. *(2 marks)*

(b) Write an appropriate non-directional hypothesis for this study. *(2 marks)*

(c) One newspaper claimed that the results showed time in day care caused aggressiveness. Explain why this claim may be untrue. *(3 marks)*

(d) Explain **one** strength of using a correlational analysis in this study. *(3 marks)*

Answers on page 287

 RESEARCH ISSUES

Explain why it would be appropriate for the researcher to use a pilot study in this research above. *(4 marks)*

Hint

When a question includes the phrase 'in this study' or 'in this research', you must refer to details of the study in your answer.

Answers on page 287

KEY TERMS

- Case study
- Content analysis
- Effect size
- Meta-analysis
- Review

Possible exam questions...

(These are generally paired with a 'stem' describing a study.)

+ Explain **one** limitation of a meta-analysis. *(2 marks)*
+ Evaluate the use of a case study in this research. *(4 marks)*

MUST know ...

Meta-analysis

Review studies use databases of published research to search for studies addressing a particular aim or hypothesis.

A **meta-analysis** then assesses trends in the data and evaluates the **effect size** across all of the studies, using statistical analysis.

Multi-method approach

Some studies don't neatly fit any category of research methods, but are simply investigations of particular situations: for example, Milgram's study of obedience.

Many published studies use a combination of research methods. For example, Schaffer and Emerson's study of attachment (see page 76) used naturalistic observation, interviews and rating scales, but also included an experimental element.

Other research techniques

A **longitudinal study** of an individual or group can observe long-term effects such as treatments or aging.

A **cross-sectional study** compares groups at the same point in time, for example 20-year-olds and 50-year-olds in 2015.

 Meta-analysis can increase the validity...

...of conclusions, as they are based on a wider sample of participants.

- *E* – So, an overall conclusion can be drawn, even if the original studies produced contradictory results.

SHOULD know ...

A level only – Case studies

The detailed study of a single individual, institution or event. Many research methods may be used, such as observation, interview (of the person themselves or their family and friends), psychological tests or experiments. Case studies are often longitudinal, following an individual over an extended period of time.

A level only – Content analysis

A form of indirect observation by analysing a sample of artefacts produced by people, such as TV programmes, articles, adverts, songs, paintings, etc. It aims to systematically describe the content, often tallying coding units (themes or behavioural categories) to transform qualitative into quantitative data.

Other research techniques

In **cross-cultural studies**, researchers compare samples from different cultures in a kind of natural experiment. For example, the IV could be child-rearing practices in different cultures, and the DV is a particular behaviour such as attachment.

Role play (such as Zimbardo's prison simulation study) is a form of controlled observation.

- *E* – However, the research designs of the original studies may vary considerably, so they may not be truly comparable.
- *L* – This means that conclusions are not always valid.

A LEVEL ONLY ZONE ...

 Case studies offer rich, in-depth data...

...describing complex interactions of factors in an individual or an event.

- *E* – They are also valuable for investigating rare cases or situations that could not be generated experimentally for ethical reasons.
- *E* – However, case studies are often unique, and data is gathered retrospectively (e.g. after brain damage), so we do not know what abnormalities were already present.
- *L* – This makes the findings difficult to generalise.

 Content analysis is based on observations...

...of real communications such as books, newspapers, and videos.

- *E* – If these sources can also be accessed by other researchers then findings can be replicated.
- *E* – But different observers may interpret the meanings of material and the behavioural categories or coding systems differently, due to observer bias.
- *L* – Therefore, content analysis has high ecological validity, but may lack reliability and internal validity.

MATCH THEM UP

Match up the terms with their definitions

1	Lab experiment	**A**	The relationship between continuous variables are analysed.
2	Field experiment	**B**	A study where the researcher does not interfere in any way.
3	Natural experiment	**C**	Experiment conducted in an everyday setting where the experimenter controls the IV.
4	Study using correlational analysis	**D**	Using observations of behaviour made indirectly.
5	Observation	**E**	Study with IV and DV, in a contrived environment with high level of control.
6	Naturalistic observation	**F**	A study where behaviour is recorded by watching or listening to what people do.
7	Controlled observation	**G**	A self-report technique with a predetermined set of questions in written form.
8	Content analysis	**H**	A detailed study of one individual, group or event.
9	Questionnaire	**I**	Study with an IV and DV, researcher makes use of an IV that is not controlled by the researcher.
10	Interview	**J**	A self-report technique where questions are delivered by another person who may respond if needed.
11	Case study	**K**	A study using observational techniques where the researcher controls some aspects of the environment.

Answers on page 287

 APPLYING YOUR KNOWLEDGE (1)

The effects of privation were investigated by looking at one institution in Eastern Europe where orphaned children were looked after. Answer the following questions:

(a) Aside from interviewing the staff at the institution, describe one other technique that might be used as part of this case study. *(2 marks)*

(b) In order to conduct this study the researchers had to select just one institution in Eastern Europe. Describe a sampling method they might have used to select this institution. *(2 marks)*

Answers on page 287

 RESEARCH ISSUES

A psychologist plans to conduct research on the effects of adoption. To do this he is going to do a case study of a woman who was adopted as a child.

How could the psychologist maintain confidentiality when reporting this case study? *(3 marks)*

Answers on page 287

 APPLYING YOUR KNOWLEDGE (2)

A university psychology department is asked to conduct a case study of the 2011 riots in London.

Answer the following questions:

(a) Psychologists use a range of techniques to gather information in case studies. Outline **one** technique that the psychologists could use in this case study. *(2 marks)*

(b) Apart from ethical issues, explain **one or more** limitations that may be a problem in this case study. *(4 marks)*

(c) Explain **one** strength of studying this behaviour by using a case study. *(2 marks)*

Answers on page 287

- Fraction, percentage, ratio
- Order of magnitude
- Significant figures
- Standard form (or scientific notation)

Possible exam questions...

(Mathematical questions will form part of longer research methods questions or part of the questions in other sections.)

+ What percentage of children showed secure attachment in this study? Give your answer to an appropriate number of significant figures. *(3 marks)*
+ What fraction of students felt confident about their maths ability? *(2 marks)*

Exam tip

You will be allowed to use a calculator in the exam – just make sure you have one.

Make sure you show all the stages of your working as there will be marks for this as well as for the correct answer.

MUST know ...

Mathematical requirements in the specification

10% of the marks in the AS and A level exams are related to mathematical skills. These include arithmetic, handling data, simple algebra (see Year 2 book) and graphs.

Some basic arithmetic

A **fraction** expresses part of a whole number. For example, if there are 120 participants in a study and 40 are in condition A, this is $\frac{40}{120}$.

This can be simplified to $\frac{1}{3}$ as top and bottom of the fraction can be divided by 40.

A **percentage** is a fraction out of 100.

So 5% means $\frac{5}{100}$ or $\frac{1}{20}$.

As a **decimal** this would be 0.05.

To change a fraction to a percentage, first divide the top by the bottom using a calculator to make a decimal. Then multiply by 100.

For example, in an EWT experiment 13 participants matched a face correctly, and 27 did not. What percentage chose the correct face?

The total number of participants is 13 + 27 = 40.

$\frac{13}{40} = 0.325 = 32.5\%$.

Ratios show how much there is of one thing compared to another thing. For example, if the ratio of insecurely (type A) to securely (type B) attached infants is 2:3, that means out of every 5 children, 2 are type A and 3 are type B. So out of 50 children there will be 20 type A and 30 type B.

SHOULD know ...

More arithmetic

It is a good idea to **estimate** the result of a calculation, to check your answer makes sense. You can do this by rounding and by checking whether a result should be smaller (if you have divided) or larger (if you have multiplied) than the starting numbers.

However, if you multiply by a number less than 1, the result will be smaller. For example, $24 \times 0.5 = 12$.

You may be asked to round a number to 2 or 3 **significant figures**. The rest of the digits are then replaced by zeros. You must consider whether to round up or down. So, for example, the fraction $\frac{19}{36}$ is 52.7777778% as a percentage. This can be rounded to 52.8% to 3 significant figures (sf), or 53% to 2 sf, or even 50% to 1 sf.

With very large or very small numbers we can put them into **standard form**. This enables us to compare their **order of magnitude**.

For example, 8,600,000,000 is 8.6×10^9. The 9 represents how many places the number has moved in relation to the decimal point (we have divided by 10^9 or 1000,000,000).

0.0045 is 4.5×10^{-3} (as we have multiplied by 10^3 or 1000).

5.8×10^3 is less than 2.1×10^4 because it is a lower order of magnitude. ($5.8 \times 10^3 = 5,800$ and $2.1 \times 10^4 = 21,000$)

Useful mathematical symbols:

= and ~	< and <<	> and >>	≤	∝
Equal and approximately equal	Less than and much less than	More than and much more than	Less than or equal to	Proportional to

MATCH THEM UP

Match up the fraction with the correct decimal and percentage.

$\frac{1}{10}$	0.1875	4%
$\frac{1}{25}$	0.125	50%
$\frac{3}{16}$	0.1	18.75%
$\frac{1}{8}$	0.5	12.5%
$\frac{1}{2}$	0.55 (to 2 sf)	55% (to 2 sf)
$\frac{83}{150}$	0.04	10%

Answers on page 287

APPLYING YOUR KNOWLEDGE (1)

A psychologist carried out an observation of baby monkeys with their mothers and aunts. She filmed the baby interacting with each adult separately for ten minutes. She then used a time sampling technique to record the frequencies of different behaviours by the baby. Her findings are shown in the table below.

	Gripping adult	Suckling	Being groomed by adult	Total
Mother	11	8	1	20
Aunt	5	0	15	20
Total	16	8	16	40

a) In what percentage of the total observations was the baby suckling? Show your calculations. *(2 marks)*

b) In what fraction of total observations was the baby being groomed? *(2 marks)*

c) What was the frequency of time sampling used by the researcher? *(1 mark)*

Answers on page 287

An idea
Use GCSE Maths Revision websites to practise any arithmetic you found difficult on this page. The more you practise, the quicker and more accurate you will get.

APPLYING YOUR KNOWLEDGE (2)

a) Give $\frac{3}{8}$ as a percentage. Give your answer to two significant figures. *(2 marks)*

b) Explain what the following expression means, where n is the number of girls, and m is the number of boys: $n < m$. *(1 mark)*

c) Express 0.02 as a fraction. *(1 mark)*

d) A researcher wants to divide 4,526 by 42. Estimate what the result would be, explaining how you arrived at your answer. *(2 marks)*

e) If there are 36 participants divided into four groups, how many will be in each group? *(1 mark)*

f) In the AS Psychology exam, there are two exam papers of 72 marks each. At least 25% of the marks will relate to Research Methods. How many marks will this be altogether? *(2 marks)*

g) In the A level Psychology exam, there are three exam papers of 96 marks each. At least 10% of the marks will require mathematical skills. How many marks will this be altogether? Give your answer to two significant figures. *(2 marks)*

Answers on page 287

KEY TERMS

- Descriptive statistics
- Mean
- Measure of central tendency
- Measure of dispersion
- Median
- Mode
- Quantitative data
- Range
- Standard deviation

Possible exam questions …

(These are generally paired with a 'stem' describing a study.)

+ Choose a suitable measure of central tendency for this data and explain how to calculate it. *(1 mark + 2 marks)*

+ Explain **one** advantage and **one** limitation of using the mean to work out the central tendency of a data set. *(2 marks + 2 marks)*

+ Name **one** measure of dispersion that the researcher could have used to describe the data, and justify your answer. *(2 marks)*

★ Exam tip

You won't be asked to calculate standard deviation in the exam, but should be able to explain it.

MUST know …

Quantitative (numerical) data can be summarised in terms of its central tendency and dispersion, to identify trends in the data. These are **descriptive statistics.**

Measures of central tendency…

…are averages, which describe the centre of a set of data.

Mean - add up all the values and divide by the number of items.

Median - the middle value in an ordered list. For an even number of items, the median is the mean of the central two.

Mode - the most common data item or category. A data set may be bi-modal.

Measures of dispersion…

…describe the spread of the data.

The **range** is the difference between the top and bottom values in a data set, plus one.

The **standard deviation** is the average distance of each data item from the mean.

 The mean is the most sensitive…

…measure of central tendency, because it takes into account all data values.

- **E** – However, this means that it can be distorted by extreme values.

 In contrast, the median is not affected…

…by extreme scores.

- **E** – But it is not as 'sensitive' as the mean because it ignores all the data except the middle.

The mode can be used for nominal data…

…unlike the mean and median.

- **E** – This is because it is only possible to state the most popular category.

SHOULD know …

Levels of measurement (NOIR)

Nominal data are in categories that do not have any particular order, e.g. grouping people by their favourite pet.

Ordinal data can be ranked in order but are not on a regular scale, e.g. the order of preference of pets.

Interval data are measured using units of equal intervals, e.g. temperature. Psychological scales can also be treated as interval data.

Ratio data has a true zero point, e.g. age.

Measures of central tendency and dispersion

Mean – can only be used with ratio and interval level data.

Median – can be used with ratio, interval and ordinal data.

Range – add 1 to the difference between top and bottom values because they may have been rounded; e.g. a bottom number of 3 could represent a true value of 2.5, and a top number of 15 could really be 15.5 giving a range of (15 − 3 + 1) = 13.

- **E** – It cannot be used with nominal data, or with data that has discrete values such as average number of legs (1.999?)
- **L** – so it is not always representative of the data as a whole, and should always be considered alongside the standard deviation.

- **E** – It can be used for ordinal (ranked) data, when an arithmetic mean does not make sense.
- **L** – This means it can be used to describe a variety of data sets, including skewed data and non-normal distributions (see Topic 19).

- **E** – It can also be useful for discrete data, such as the most common number of legs.
- **L** – However, it is not useful if there are several modes in a data set.

A LEVEL ONLY

The range is easy to calculate…

…but is affected by extreme values.

- **E** – It also fails to take account of the distribution of the data.
- **E** – For example, whether the values are closely grouped around the mean or more spread out.
- **L** – But it has to be used with ordinal data or with highly skewed data.

The standard deviation is very sensitive…

…as it takes into account all the values

- **E** – but, like the mean, it is affected by extreme values.
- **E** – It is also unsuitable for highly skewed distributions.
- **L** – It is best used, together with the mean, to describe interval or ratio data, which is normally distributed.

 See page 226 for an explanation of skewed distribution

MATCH THEM UP

Match up the following concepts with their appropriate definitions.

1	Quantitative	A	Spread of data around the mean
2	Qualitative	B	A measure of central tendency making use of all the data
3	Central tendency	C	Numerical data
4	Mean	D	Middle value of an ordered list
5	Median	E	Difference between highest and lowest
6	Mode	F	The most frequent
7	Dispersion	G	Data that expresses meanings
8	Range	H	Averages
9	Standard deviation	I	Spread of data

Answers on page 287

 KEY WORDS

For each definition select two key words or phrases to help you remember the meaning. The first one has been done for you.

Quantitative	Numbers	How much
Qualitative		
Mean		
Median		
Mode		
Range		
Standard deviation		

DRAWING CONCLUSIONS 1

A psychologist conducted a study about working memory. The participants in Group A were asked to carry out two visual tasks at the same time. Group B participants were asked to carry out a visual task and a verbal task at the same time. The results are shown in the graph below.

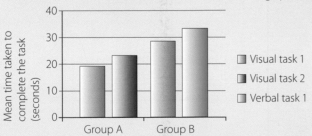

What does the graph show about working memory?

One finding:

Draw a conclusion: This suggests that . . .

Second finding:

Draw a conclusion: This suggests that . . .

Answers on page 287

 APPLYING YOUR KNOWLEDGE

The data from a laboratory experiment are shown in the table below. A student is given a series of similar puzzles to solve, and the time taken to solve the puzzle is measured in seconds.

Attempt	Time taken for student to solve a puzzle
1	72
2	67
3	61
4	55
5	56
6	34
7	39
8	43

a) Calculate the mean time taken for the student to solve the puzzle. Show your calculations. Give your answer to 3 significant figures. *(2 marks)*

b) Choose a suitable measure of dispersion for this data, and explain your choice. *(2 marks)*

c) Draw a graph of this data. *(3 marks)*

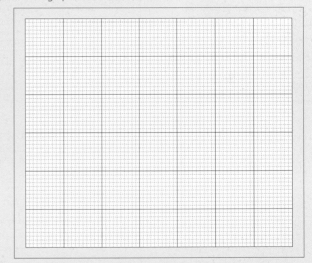

d) What conclusions can you draw about how this student's ability to solve the puzzle changed? Suggest reasons for this change. *(3 marks)*

Answers on page 287

KEY TERMS

- Bar chart
- Histogram
- Negative skewed distribution
- Normal distribution
- Positive skewed distribution
- Skewed distribution

Possible exam questions...

(These are generally paired with a 'stem' describing a study.)

+ Describe the characteristics of a normal distribution. *(2 marks)*

+ Explain how the mean differs from the mode in a negatively skewed distribution. *(2 marks)*

+ Display this data in graphical form. *(4 marks)*

★ Exam tip

You should be able to select the appropriate graph for a set of data, and plot it accurately, labelling axes precisely. Use shading rather than colour, as the papers are scanned in black and white. And don't forget a key.

MUST know ...

Display of quantitative data

Tables and graphs should:
- have a short but informative title
- use operationalised variables as titles for columns (in a table) or axes (on a graph).

Tables can display raw data, but usually display summaries – measures of central tendency and dispersion for the groups or conditions.

Bar charts display discrete (discontinuous) or nominal (category) data. The spaces between the bars indicate the lack of

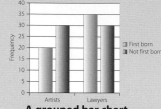

A grouped bar chart

continuity of the IV, which is on the horizontal axis. The vertical axis is for scores (the DV) or frequencies.

Histograms are used for continuous data, and the bars should therefore be touching. The vertical axis should start from zero:

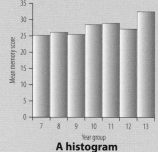

A histogram

Frequency polygons display the same data as frequency histograms, but are better for comparing two or more sets of data as the bars are replaced by dots that are joined with a line:

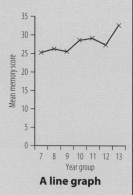

A frequency polygon

Line graphs have continuous data on both axes, and can be used for time series:

Scattergrams are used for correlational analysis (see page 218):

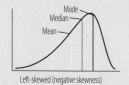

A line graph

SHOULD know ...

Data distributions

In a large data set, the frequency distribution will approximate to a curve.

The **normal distribution** is a bell-shaped curve. Many human characteristics are normally distributed, such as height and intelligence.

- Mean, median and mode are all at the exact mid-point.
- The distribution is symmetrical.
- The dispersion of data follows a predictable pattern, so that 68.26% of people fall within one standard deviation of the mean (half each side). Only 4.56% are more than 2 standard deviations from the mean. This distribution underlies the concept of the statistical deviation model of abnormality (see page 104).

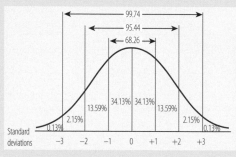

In a **skewed distribution** the scores are not distributed symmetrically around the mean.

In a **positive skewed distribution**, a few high extreme high scores have a strong effect on the mean, which will therefore be higher than the median and mode.

In a **negative skewed distribution**, the bulk of the scores are high, e.g. if an exam was too easy (a ceiling effect) but a few extreme low scores skew the mean to the left of the median and mode.

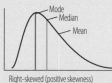

Left-skewed (negative skewness)   Right-skewed (positive skewness)

MATCH THEM UP

Match up the graphs with their purposes.

1	Bar chart	**A**	Can be used to display a series of results over a period of time
2	Histogram	**B**	A distribution in which the mode is to the right of the mean
3	Frequency polygon	**C**	Graph to display frequencies of continuous data, useful for comparing two sets of data
4	Line graph	**D**	A distribution with most values to the left and a long tail to the right
5	Scattergram	**E**	Graph to display frequencies of continuous data, with touching bars
6	Normal distribution	**F**	A symmetrical bell-shaped frequency distribution
7	Positively skewed distribution	**G**	Graph to display category data
8	Negatively skewed distribution	**H**	Displays findings of a correlational study

Answers on page 287

 CHOOSE THE RIGHT ANSWER

In the population of 1,000 people, the mean standardised score for IQ is 100 and the standard deviation is 15.

Which of the following statements is incorrect? Tick **one** box.

A	All of the scores are between 85 and 115	☐
B	Less than five people are likely to have an IQ above 145	☐
C	Half of the population have scores above 100	☐
D	The most common score (mode) is 100	☐

Answers on page 287

 DRAWING CONCLUSIONS

A day care study followed children over a period of ten years, testing each child's social development every two years. The mean social development scores for children in day care and home care are shown in graph below.

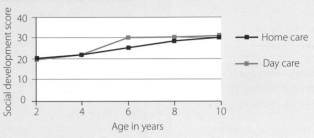

What does the graph show about the effects of day care on social development?

One finding:
Draw a conclusion: This suggests that . . .
Second finding:
Draw a conclusion: This suggests that . . .

Answers on page 287

 APPLYING YOUR KNOWLEDGE

Identify which type of graph is appropriate for each of these data sets:

Data representing:	Appropriate graph
A Mean number of words recalled in each condition in a memory experiment	
B Frequency of behaviours in each category in a naturalistic observation (e. g. children playing)	
C Participants' stress scores and illness scores obtained from questionnaires	
D The number of participants who score 0–5, 6–10, 11–15, and 16–20 in a recall test	
E Data comparing the number of male and female students who spend 1 hr, 2 hrs, 3 hrs, etc. on private study each week	

Answers on page 287

KEY TERMS

- Primary data
- Qualitative data
- Quantitative data
- Secondary data

Possible exam questions...

(These are generally paired with a 'stem' describing a study.)

+ Explain what is meant by quantitative data. Give examples in your answer. *(3 marks)*

+ Give **one** strength of producing qualitative data in a questionnaire. *(2 marks)*

+ Distinguish between primary and secondary data. *(3 marks)*

+ Suggest a question that could be used in this study to obtain qualitative data. *(2 marks)*

★ Exam tip

You need to learn the definitions and be able to give examples, but always read the questions carefully as they may ask for slightly different things; identifying types of data in a study, giving strengths or limitations, etc.

MUST know ...

Quantitative and qualitative data

Quantitative data measures behaviour numerically, and can be collected from:

- the DV in an experiment
- closed questions in questionnaires and interviews.

Qualitative data is non-numerical data, such as words, pictures or videos. It comes from:

- open questions
- descriptions of behaviour
- collected material such as articles, books, photos, web forum discussions.

Primary and secondary data

Primary data is collected directly, first-hand, by the researcher, specifically to address the aims and hypothesis of the study.

Secondary data is information gathered for a different purpose or by another researcher. It could include government statistics or health records.

 Quantitative data are easy to analyse...

- **E** – ...using descriptive statistics and statistical tests.

 On the other hand, qualitative data...

- **E** – provide rich, descriptive details of participants' experiences.

SHOULD know ...

Quantitative and qualitative data

Qualitative data can be turned into quantitative data by tallying behavioural categories in an observational study, or coding categories in a content analysis.

Qualitative and quantitative data can both be used to explore people's thoughts and feelings.

Primary and secondary data

Primary data can be collected using a research method such as an experiment, observation or questionnaire. The researcher designs the study, gains ethical approval, pilots the study, recruits and tests participants, analyses the data and draws conclusions.

Secondary data is used in review studies and meta-analyses, and often in correlational studies.

- **E** – However, this may oversimplify reality,
- **L** – leading to meaningless conclusions.

- **E** – This can produce unexpected insights into thoughts and behaviour,
- **L** – but this makes it harder to analyse qualitative data and draw conclusions.

A LEVEL ONLY ZONE

 Primary data is collected specifically...

...to meet the aims and hypotheses of a study.

- **E** – This means that the researcher has high control over the type, quality and quantity of data collected.
- **E** – However, data collection is time-consuming and often expensive.
- **L** – So studies must be very carefully designed and carried out to ensure useful data is collected.

 Secondary data is much simpler to access...

...because someone else has gone to the trouble of collecting it.

- **E** – If statistical tests have already been carried out, the researcher knows whether findings are significant.
- **E** – However, variables may have been differently operationalised, or procedures may vary.
- **L** – This means that secondary data may not fit the needs of a new study, or may not be valid for comparison with similar data from other studies.

CHOOSE AN ANSWER

A researcher is analysing data from a mental health database to investigate the effectiveness of treatments for depression. The data gives symptom scores obtained from patients' responses to a questionnaire survey. Which type of data is this? Tick **two** boxes.

A Primary data ☐

B Secondary data ☐

C Quantitative data ☐

D Qualitative data ☐

Answers on page 287

An idea 👍

Look through this revision book and identify studies that use primary or secondary data, and qualitative or quantitative data. Complete the table below with examples.

	Primary data	**Secondary data**
Qualitative data		
Quantitative data		

🔑 KEY WORDS

For each kind of data select two key words or phrases to help you remember the meaning. The first one has been done for you.

Quantitative	Numbers	How much
Qualitative		
Primary		
Secondary		
Nominal		
Ordinal		
Interval		
Ratio		

See page 224 for an explanation of levels of measurement of data (NOIR)

APPLYING YOUR KNOWLEDGE

A researcher wishes to investigate children's aggressive behaviour when playing together in small groups, using an observational technique. Her hypothesis is that boys play more aggressively than girls. She obtains ten-minute video recordings of the children playing.

(a) Suggest how she could use this material to obtain:

  i) qualitative data *(3 marks)*

  ii) quantitative data. *(3 marks)*

b) Evaluate the use of each type of data in this study, and suggest which will best address her hypothesis. *(6 marks)*

Answers on page 287

KEY TERMS

- Calculated value
- Critical value
- Descriptive statistics
- Inferential statistics
- Level of significance
- One-tailed test
- Probability (*p*)
- Sign test
- Significance
- Table of critical values
- Test statistic
- Two-tailed test

Possible exam questions…

(These are generally paired with a 'stem' describing a study)…

+ Explain when a sign test is used. *(3 marks)*

+ Use a sign test to test the significance of these results. *(4 marks)*

+ Explain what the letter *N* stands for in relation to statistical tests. *(1 mark)*

MUST know …

Inferential statistics test the probability (*p*) that a particular set of data could have occurred by chance. They establish significance: whether the differences or associations we have observed in our sample are likely to be true in the population as a whole.

The sign test…

…can be used to test significance in paired or related data (repeated measures or matched pairs design).

1. State the hypothesis.

2. For each pair of data, add a sign column (+ or – depending on which item in the pair is greater). If there is no difference between a pair of scores, leave blank.

3. Find the **calculated value** of the test statistic, *S*, which is the frequency of the less frequent sign.

4. Find the **critical value** of *S* from the **table of critical values**, where *N* = total number of scores (ignoring blank rows), and choosing a one- or two-tailed test and a **level of significance** of $p < 0.05$ or $p < 0.01$.

5. Compare the calculated value with the critical value, following the instruction below the table, to see if the difference is **significant**. Then decide whether the result is in the expected direction, so whether the hypothesis can be accepted.

▼ Table of critical values of *S*.

Level of significance for a one-tailed test	0.05	0.01
Level of significance for a two-tailed test	0.10	0.02
N		
5	0	
6	0	0
7	0	0
8	1	0
9	1	1
10	1	1
11	2	1
12	2	2
13	3	2
14	3	2
15	3	3
16	4	3
17	4	4
18	5	4
19	5	4
20	5	5
25	7	7
30	10	9
35	12	11

Calculated value of *S* must be EQUAL TO or LESS THAN the critical value in this table for significance to be shown.

SHOULD know …

Inferential statistical tests account for sampling error (random error), but not sample bias, which is a problem of the research design.

The sign test

A directional hypothesis requires a one-tailed test. A non-directional hypothesis requires a two-tailed test.

If the **calculated value** is less than or equal to the **critical value**, then the result is **significant**.

At a **level of significance** of $p < 0.05$, there is less than 5% probability that the results are due to chance and not a real effect.

At a level of significance of $p < 0.01$ there is a 1% chance of this happening. This would be a more stringent test, which would be suitable for testing drug treatments.

Example:
Table of results for a natural experiment measuring people's happiness scores before and after a holiday.

Participant	Happiness score before	Happiness score after	Difference (after–before)	Sign
1	6	7	1	+
2	3	4	1	+
3	4	6	2	+
4	8	6	−2	−
5	5	7	2	+
6	7	5	−2	−
7	5	7	2	+
8	5	8	3	+
9	4	7	3	+
10	8	5	−3	−
11	4	4	0	
12	8	9	1	+
13	6	7	1	+
14	5	6	1	+

- The hypothesis is that people are happier after a holiday than before. This is directional, so a one-tailed test is needed.

- The calculated value of $S = 3$
- $N = 13$ (1 score omitted).
- The critical value of $S = 3$ as well, so the result is significant.
- There were more pluses than minuses, which fits our hypothesis, so we can accept the hypothesis.

The conclusion is: The calculated value of *S* (3) is equal to the critical value of *S* (3) ($N = 13$, $p < 0.05$, one-tailed), so the results are significant. The null hypothesis can be rejected and the experimental hypothesis can be accepted.

MATCH THEM UP

Match up the terms with their definitions.

1	One-tailed test	**A**	The test statistic for a particular data set
2	Two-tailed test	**B**	Used for a non-directional hypothesis
3	Critical value	**C**	Describe or summarise the findings
4	Calculated value	**D**	Used for a directional hypothesis
5	Descriptive statistics	**E**	Test significance of the findings
6	Inferential statistics	**F**	The test statistic read from the table

Answers on page 287

 CHOOSE THE RIGHT ANSWER

In a repeated measures experiment, a student used the sign test to test his directional hypothesis. He calculated a test statistic, $S = 6$. There were 20 participants but for two of them the scores were the same in both conditions of the experiment. Use the table of critical values on the facing page to decide what the student can conclude. Tick **one** box.

A The result is significant, and the hypothesis is supported ☐

B The result is significant, and the hypothesis is not supported ☐

C The result is not significant, and the hypothesis is not supported ☐

D Not enough information is given ☐

Answers on page 287

 APPLYING YOUR KNOWLEDGE (1)

A slimming club wanted to find out whether their programme worked. They recorded the weights of ten members of the club when they first joined, and after three months. Use the sign test to work out whether the programme was effective for these members. *(4 marks)*

Slimming club member	Starting weight	Weight after three months	Difference	Sign
Jan	80	74		
Julie	125	102		
Jess	113	114		
Josie	108	87		
Jodie	96	82		
Jenny	78	78		
Joe	102	94		
Jeff	124	125		
June	97	75		
Jade	122	94		

1. Hypothesis:
Is this directional or non-directional?

2. (Complete the sign column)
3. Calculated value of $S =$

4. $N =$
Critical value of $S =$

5. Is this significant?
If so, does the difference go in the predicted direction?
Can the hypothesis be accepted on the basis of this test?

Answers on page 287

 APPLYING YOUR KNOWLEDGE (2)

a. What descriptive statistics would be suitable to describe the data in (1) above? (2 marks)

b. Calculate a suitable measure of central tendency. Show your working. *(3 marks)*

c. What might you now conclude about the effectiveness of the slimming programme? *(2 marks)*

d. Looking back at the original data, how can you explain this? *(2 marks)*

e. Would you recommend people to join this club? Give a reason for your answer. *(2 marks)*

Answers on page 288

KEY TERM

- Peer review

Possible exam questions...

(These are generally paired with a 'stem' describing a study.)

+ Explain why peer review is essential to the scientific process. *(3 marks)*
+ Discuss the purpose of peer review. *(6 marks)*
+ Explain **two** criticisms of peer review. *(2 marks + 2 marks)*

 Exam tip

If you are asked to discuss the purpose of peer review, you will not get any credit for describing the **process** of peer review. You could briefly describe the **purpose** of peer review, but focus mainly on evaluating the **strengths and limitations** of peer review and to what extent it achieves its purposes.

MUST know ...

The role of peer review

The **scientific process** (see page 192) has developed to ensure that scientific discoveries are reliable, and includes the requirement for peer review of articles before publication.

Peer review (also called 'refereeing') is the assessment of scientific work by others who are experts in the same field. The aim is to ensure that published research is of high quality.

 Peer review in psychology is essential...

...to establish the validity of published research.

- ***E*** – In the 1950s Burt published research into IQs in twins, which now appears to have been fraudulent. This is a problem as educational policy was based on his findings.

 However, finding an expert may be difficult...

...because the field of research may be new or small.

- ***E*** – This means that the reviewers don't really understand the research, and may accept poor quality research, or may be biased towards prestigious researchers.

Publication bias is a problem...

...as journals prefer to publish positive results, and avoid publishing replications, although these are essential for establishing reliability of findings.

- ***E*** – This is known as the 'file drawer' phenomenon, where less significant findings remain unpublished in the researcher's filing cabinet.

SHOULD know ...

The role of peer review

The purposes of peer review are:

- Responsible allocation of research funding by government and charitable bodies
- Preventing incorrect data entering the public domain via publication
- Assessing the research quality rating of university departments

- ***E*** – In addition, a recent anonymous survey of psychologists indicates that the majority have used questionable research practices, and 1% admitted to falsifying data. These practices result in a lack of trust for published research.
- ***L*** – Peer review aims to stop this happening, to the benefit of scientists and society.

- ***E*** – This also means it may be difficult to find a journal to publish controversial findings or theories that contradict existing ideas.
- ***L*** – So peer review may actually be assessing the acceptability rather than the validity of a new finding.

- ***E*** – This publication bias creates a misperception of the facts.
- ***L*** – This means that reviews and meta-analyses also become biased as they can only examine published data.

A LEVEL ONLY ZONE

 Reviewers are usually anonymous...

...so that they can be honest and objective.

- ***E*** – But reviewers can often work out who the researcher is, and may be in direct competition with them for research grants and jobs.
- ***E*** – So reviewers may not be very objective, and may try to bury rival research.
- ***L*** – Some journals now favour open reviewing, where the author and reviewers know each other's identity.

 Once research is published...

...it remains in the public domain.

- ***E*** – If errors or fraud are subsequently found, the journal may publish a retraction, but readers may not be aware of this.
- ***E*** – So subsequent research or policy decisions may be based on poor research.
- ***L*** – This underlines the importance of vigilance by scientists to ensure their work is high quality, and to communicate clearly with the public and policymakers.

KEY WORDS

Exam question: Discuss the purpose of peer review *(6 marks)*

Complete the table by selecting key words to summarise a brief explanation of the purpose, and **three** evaluation points to answer this question:

The purpose		
A strength		
A problem		
Another problem		

CHOOSE THE RIGHT ANSWER

A researcher sends her article to a journal for publication, and before making a decision about publication, the journal sends it to referees for peer review.

Which of these is **not** a purpose of peer review? Tick **one** box.

A To ensure that the research methodology is clear and unambiguous ☐

B To check the conclusions are valid, based on the statistical analysis of the findings ☐

C To decide whether the findings are novel, important and add to knowledge of a field ☐

D To ensure that ethical procedures were followed in the study ☐

Answers on page 288

RESEARCH ISSUES

Suggest three reasons why a research paper might be rejected for publication after peer review. *(3 marks)*

A future researcher decides to undertake a review of existing research in an area. How will her meta-analysis be affected by the rejection of some research in the area? *(4 marks)*

Why the paper was rejected	How this affects the meta-analysis

Answers on page 288

APPLYING YOUR KNOWLEDGE

Imagine that you have been sent Freud's research (page 142) to peer review. What issues might you comment on? *(2 marks + 2 marks + 2 marks)*

Issues	Why they would be a problem for publication	What suggestions you would make to Freud to improve his research

Answers on page 288

KEY TERM

- heuristic
- reciprocity

Possible exam questions...

+ Outline one example of how psychological research has been used to benefit the economy. *(3 marks)*
+ Discuss the implications of psychological research for the economy. *(6 marks)*

Exam tip

You could be asked about economic benefits in relation to any area of psychology, so practise thinking about these, making sure you can explain how they benefit society economically. You could also be asked to select an area and explain how it benefits the economy, so have one up your sleeve.

MUST know ...

Economic psychology...

...is also called 'behavioural economics'. Researchers investigate the social, cognitive and emotional factors in economic decisions.

Irrational thinking has been extensively researched by Kahneman, who was awarded the Nobel prize for economics in 2002. For example:

- The **availability heuristic** – people overestimate the likelihood of events such as a plane accident, because they are more easily remembered when making a probability judgement, due to media stories.
- The **framing effect** – people's decisions differ depending on whether a choice is presented as a gain or a loss.

These insights have changed many aspects of life, e.g. juries, business and tax collection.

People are also influenced by **reciprocity**, or the idea of fairness. For example, the message on a government website: 'If you needed an organ transplant, would you have one?' led to an increase in donors.

Psychology has benefitted society...

...by applying understandings of social psychology to the real world.

- *E* – For example, a campaign to reduce drink driving used social norms to change people's attitudes.

Memory research has improved EWT...

...by introducing the cognitive interview.

- *E* – Cognitive interviewing has improved the amount of accurate information collected.

Attachment theory has influenced...

...childcare policy,

- *E* – as we now understand the importance of emotional care in early childhood development.

SHOULD know ...

Economic psychology...

Tverksy and Kahneman tested the framing effect experimentally, asking participants to select a treatment for a deadly disease affecting 600 people. Two groups were told different facts about the treatments:

	Treatment	Told:	Choice:
Group 1	A	200 saved	72%
	B	1/3 chance all saved, 2/3 chance no one saved	28%
Group 2	C	400 deaths	22%
	D	1/3 chance no one dies, 2/3 chance all die	78%

The only difference between A and C, and between B and D, is the way they are framed, as lives saved or lives lost. The results show that framing irrationally affected people's choices.

- *E* – However, this approach is limited to tasks where behaviour is moderated by social criteria.
- *L* – This can lead to positive social changes that will benefit the economy.

- *E* – This ensures that police and court times is used efficiently.
- *L* – This results in economic benefits as it reduces the expense of wrongful arrests.

- *E* – UNICEF: TH 'deprivation that stems from lack of care and nurture...can have just as detrimental an effect on brain development as lack of food.'
- *L* – This has led to health care policies which improve children's chances, helping them to become more economically independent.

Mental health policies have economic implications

- *E* – Mental health care costs around £22.5 billion a year in England, and there are also huge indirect costs via the impact on the criminal justice system, lost employment, etc.
- *E* – Treatments vary in their cost implications; for example, drug treatments may be much more cost-effective than psychotherapy for some disorders.
- *L* – Therefore, evidence-based decisions help to reduce costs.

Neuroscience is revolutionising...

...our understanding of the human brain.

- *E* – For example, the development of 'smart' machines with artificial intelligence, which can interact more effectively with people.
- *E* – In addition, our understanding of the biopsychology of disorders such as dementia may lead to better treatment and prevention.
- *L* – These insights all have the potential to lead to economic benefits for society.

✓ CHOOSE THE RIGHT ANSWER

The UK Government Behavioural Insights Team (the Nudge Unit) has recommended that doctors' surgeries should display the percentage of appointments attended, rather than the percentage of missed appointments. For example, '85% of patients attended their appointments last month.'

Which behavioural explanation is this recommendation based on? Tick **one** box.

A Availability heuristic ☐

B Conformity ☐

C The framing effect ☐

D Reciprocity ☐

Answers on page 288

📖 RESEARCH ISSUES

The Nudge Unit has successfully increased the payment of car taxes, increased attendance at adult literacy classes, and improved police diversity by using behavioural insights. These changes have economic benefits to society. Discuss ethical issues associated with appointing psychologists and economists to influence citizens in this way. *(5 marks)*

Answers on page 288

⚙ APPLYING YOUR KNOWLEDGE

Explain how the following areas of psychological research have led to economic benefits.

Area of psychology	Theory/research finding	Economic benefits
Conformity		
Minority influence		
Memory		
The behavioural approach to phobias		
The cognitive approach to depression		
The biological approach to OCD		
Social learning theory		
Brain plasticity		
Brain scanning techniques		

💡 DRAWING CONCLUSIONS

Draw a bar chart of the findings of Tverksy and Kahneman's study into framing effects. *(6 marks)*

What conclusion can be drawn from these findings? *(4 marks)*

Answers on page 288

Aims	A statement of what the researcher intends to find out in an investigation.
Bar chart	A graph used to represent the frequencies of nominal (category) or discrete (discontinuous) data.
Behavioural categories	A way of operationalising behaviour by defining specific, objective, mutually exclusive observable components.
Bias	A systematic distortion.
Calculated value	The value of a test statistic calculated for a particular data set.
Case study	A detailed study of a single individual, institution or event.
Closed questions	Questions that have a predetermined set of answers from which respondents select one. Tend to produce quantitative data.
Content analysis	A kind of observational study in which behaviour is observed indirectly in written or verbal material such as interviews, conversations, books, diaries or TV programmes.
Co-variables	The two measured variables in a correlational analysis. They must be continuous.
Confederate	An individual in a study who is not a real participant and has been instructed how to behave by the investigator.
Confidentiality	Concerns the communication of personal information and the trust that the information will be protected.
Confounding variable	A variable in a study which is not the IV but which also affects the DV.
Continuous variable	A variable that can take on any value within a certain range.
Control	The extent to which any variable is held constant or regulated by a researcher.
Controlled observation	A form of investigation in which behaviour is observed under conditions where certain variables have been organised by the researcher.
Correlation	Determining the extent of an association between two variables. The co-variables may not be linked at all (zero correlation) or may both increase together (positive correlation), or as one variable increases the other decreases (negative correlation).
Correlation coefficient	A number between -1 and +1 that describes the strength of the association between two co-variables in a correlational analysis.
Cost-benefit analysis	A systematic approach to estimating the negative and positive impact of any research.
Counterbalancing	Used to overcome order effects when using a repeated measures experimental design. Ensures that each condition is tested first or second in equal amounts.
Covert observations	Observing people without their knowledge. Knowing that behaviour is being observed is likely to alter a participant's behaviour.
Critical value	In an inferential test, the value of the test statistic that must be reached to show significance.
Curvilinear correlation	A non-linear relationship between co-variables, that does not fall on a straight line.
Debriefing	A post-research interview designed to inform participants of the true nature of the study and to restore them to the physical and psychological state they were in at the start of the study.
Deception	A participant is not told the true aim of the study and thus cannot give truly informed consent.
Demand characteristics	A cue that makes participants unconsciously aware of the aims of a study or causes them to change their behaviour to match what they think is expected.
Descriptive statistics	A way of summarising a data set using measures of central tendency and dispersion.
Directional hypothesis	States the direction of the predicted difference between the two conditions or two groups of participants.
Effect size	A measure of the strength of the relationship between two variables.
Ethical guidelines (code of conduct)	A set of principles designed to help professionals behave honestly and with integrity.
Ethical issues	Concern questions of right and wrong. They arise in research where there are conflicting sets of values between researchers and participants.
Ethics committee	A group of people within a research institution that must approve a study before it begins.
Event sampling	An observational technique in which a count is kept of the number of times a certain behaviour occurs.
Experiment	A research method in which causal conclusions can be drawn because an independent variable is deliberately manipulated to observe the effect on the dependent variable.

Experimental design	A set of procedures used to control the influence of factors such as participant variables in an experiment. How the participants are allocated to the different conditions of the IV.
External validity	The degree to which a research finding can be generalised to other settings (ecological validity); to other groups of people (population validity); over time (historical validity).
Extraneous variable	Any variable, other than the IV, which may affect the DV and therefore affect validity of the findings. Extraneous variables need to be controlled in an experiment wherever possible.
Field experiment	A controlled experiment conducted outside a laboratory. The IV is manipulated by the experimenter, but participants are usually unaware that they are being studied.
Fraction, percentage, decimal, ratio	Methods of expressing parts of a whole.
Generalisation	Applying the findings of a study to the population, or to situations beyond the research context.
Heuristic	A mental rule or short-cut allowing for more efficient decision making, but often leading to cognitive biases.
Histogram	A graph showing the frequency distribution of continuous data.
Hypothesis	A precise and testable statement about the predicted relationship between the variables. Should be operationalised.
Independent groups design	Participants are allocated to different groups, representing different conditions of the IV, preferably by random allocation.
Independent variable (IV)	The condition that is directly manipulated by an experimenter in order to test its effect on the DV.
Inter-observer reliability	The extent to which there is agreement between two or more observers involved in observations of a behaviour.
Intervening variables	Variables that come in between two other variables and can explain their association.
Dependent variable	The variable that is being measured in an experiment.
Inferential statistics	Statistical tests to find out the likelihood that a result could have occurred simply by chance in a sample.
Informed consent	Participants must be given comprehensive information concerning the nature and purpose of the research and their role in it, in order that they can make an informed decision about whether to participate.
Internal validity	The degree to which an observed effect was due to the experimental manipulation rather than other factors such as confounding or extraneous variables.
Interview	A research method that involves a face-to-face, real-time interaction with another individual in order to collect data.
Interviewer bias	The effect of an interviewer's expectations, communicated unconsciously, on a respondent's behaviour.
Investigator effect	Anything that an investigator does that affects a participants' performance in a study, directly (through interaction with the participant) or indirectly (through bias in the study design).
Laboratory experiment	An experiment carried out in a controlled setting.
Linear correlation	A systematic relationship between co-variables that fits a straight line.
Level of significance	The level of error we are prepared to accept, for example $p<0.05$ means there is less than 5% chance that the difference or association occurred by chance in a sample.
Matched pairs design	Pairs of participants are matched on key variables. One member of each pair is randomly allocated to each experimental condition.
Mean	The arithmetic average of a data set.
Measure of central tendency	A descriptive statistic that provides information about a 'typical' value in a data set.
Measure of dispersion	A descriptive statistic that provides information about how spread out the data are in a data set.
Median	The middle value of a data set when the items are placed in rank order.
Meta-analysis	A research method in which a researcher statistically analyses the findings of a number of different studies to investigate the overall effect.
Mode	The most frequently occurring value or category in a data set.
Mundane realism	The degree to which experiences encountered in the research environment mirror those in the real world.
Natural experiment	A research method in which the experimenter has not manipulated the IV directly for ethical or practical reasons.

Naturalistic observation	An observation carried out in an everyday setting, in which the investigator does not interfere in any way but merely observes the behaviour(s) in question.
Negatively skewed distribution	Most of the scores are bunched to the right. The mean is affected by extreme scores in the long tail to the left, so the mean is to the left of the mode.
Non-directional hypothesis	Predicts that there is a difference between two conditions without stating the direction of the difference.
Non-participant observation	The observer is separate from the people being observed.
Normal distribution	A symmetrical bell-shaped frequency distribution curve. The mean, median and mode are at the mid-point.
Observer bias	Observers' expectations affect what they see or hear. This reduces the validity of the observations.
One-tailed test	Form of test used with a directional hypothesis.
Open questions	Questions that invite respondents to provide their own answers. Tends to produce qualitative data.
Operationalise	Ensuring that variables are in a form that can be easily tested.
Opportunity sample	A sample of participants produced by selecting people who are most easily available at the time of the study.
Order effect	In a repeated measures design, an extraneous variable arising from the order in which conditions are presented, e.g. a practice effect or fatigue effect.
Order of magnitude	A means of comparing numbers by focussing on the overall size (magnitude). This may be done by expressing the number in standard form (powers of 10).
Overt observation	Observational studies where participants are aware that their behaviour is being studied.
Participant observation	Observations made by someone who is also participating in the activity being observed, which may affect their objectivity.
Peer review	The practice of using independent experts to assess the quality and validity of scientific research and academic reports.
Presumptive consent	Dealing with lack of informed consent or deception, by asking people who are similar to the participants whether they would agree to take part in the study. If they consent, it is presumed that the real participants would also agree.
Pilot study	A small scale trial run of a study to test any aspects of the procedure, with a view to making improvements.
Population	The group of people that the researcher is interested in studying, from whom a sample is drawn, and about whom generalisations can be made.
Positively skewed distribution	Most of the scores are bunched to the left. The mean is to the right of the mode because it is affected by the long tail on the right.
Primary data	Information observed or collected directly from first-hand experience.
Privacy	A person's right to control the flow of information about themselves.
Probability (p)	A measure of the likelihood or chance that certain events will occur.
Protection from harm	During a research study, participants should not experience negative physical or psychological effects, such as physical injury, lowered self-esteem or embarrassment.
Qualitative data	Non-numerical data.
Quantitative data	Data measured in numbers.
Quasi-experiment	A research method in which the independent variable is a characteristic of the individual, and cannot be manipulated by the experimenter.
Questionnaire	Data are collected through the use of written questions.
Random allocation	Allocating participants to experimental conditions or groups using random techniques.
Random sample	A sample of participants produced by using a random technique so that every member of the target population has an equal chance of being selected.
Range	The difference between the highest and lowest item in a data set. Usually 1 is added as a correction.
Reciprocity	A sense of fairness, a social rule that people should repay acts of kindness.
Repeated measures design	Each participants takes part in every condition of the experiment, i.e. every level of the IV.
Review	A consideration of many of studies that have investigated the same topic in order to reach a general conclusion.

Right to withdraw	Participants can stop participating in a study if they are uncomfortable in any way. This is especially important in cases where it was not possible to give fully informed consent. Participants should also have the right to refuse permission for the researcher to use any data they produced.
Sampling	The method used to select participants for a study. Sampling also refers to the method of recording behaviours in an observation such as event or time sampling.
Scattergram	A graphical representation of the association (i.e. the correlation) between two co-variables.
Secondary data	Information used in a research study that was collected by someone else or for a purpose other than the current one, such as published data or data collected in the past.
Sign test	An inferential statistical test to determine the significance of a difference in scores in a sample of related items.
Significance	A statistical term indicating that the association between variables is sufficiently strong for us to accept the research hypothesis under test.
Significant figures	The number of single digits (other than zero) used to represent a number. The zeros exist as place holders, to maintain the correct order of magnitude.
Skewed distribution	A frequency distribution in which the scores are not evenly distributed either side of the median.
Social desirability bias	A distortion in the way people answer questions – they tend to answer questions in such a way that presents themselves in a better light.
Standard deviation	The spread of data around the mean.
Standard form (or scientific notation)	A way of expressing any number in two parts, in the form $A \times 10^n$. A is a number between 1 and 10, and n can be positive (for very large numbers) or negative (for very small numbers).
Standardised procedures	A set of procedures that are the same for all participants in order to be able to repeat the study.
Stratified sample	A sample of participants produced by identifying subgroups and selecting participants randomly from these subgroups, in the same proportion as their occurrence in the population.
Structured interview	Any interview in which the questions are decided in advance.
Structured observation	The use of systems such as behavioural categories and sampling procedures to organise an observation.
Systematic sample	A sample obtained by selecting every nth person (where n is a number).
Table of critical values	A table of numbers used to judge significance. The calculated value of the test statistic is compared to the relevant number in the table (the critical value) to see if the calculated value is significant.
Test statistic	The number calculated in statistical testing. For the sign test, the test statistic is known as S.
Time sampling	An observational technique in which the observer records behaviours at regular intervals, e.g. every 20 seconds.
Two-tailed test	Form of test used with a non-directional hypothesis.
Unstructured interview	The interview starts out with some general aims and initial questions, then lets the interviewee's answers guide subsequent questions.
Validity	Whether an observed effect is a genuine one.
Volunteer bias	A form of sampling bias arising because volunteers have special characteristics such as higher than average motivation.
Volunteer sample	A sample of participants that relies on self-selected volunteers.

Topic 1 The experimental method

A researcher investigated the differing levels of certain hormones at times of stress. To do this he measured the levels of certain hormones in the blood – the day before and exam and just before the start of the exam. The results for one person are shown in the table.

	Measurement on the day before an exam	Measurement just before the start of the exam
Adrenaline	2	9
Cortisol	4	1

Research Methods questions are based on a question stem, like this one in the box. They will then have a number of short questions relating to this information. Make sure you keep re-reading the stem as you answer each part of the question.

(a) How has the researcher operationalised the independent and dependent variables in this investigation? *(2 + 2 marks)*

The independent variable is when the hormones are measured. The dependent variable is the levels of adrenaline and cortisol in the blood.

Both variables are correct but the IV is not fully operationalised – it should state the two conditions. 3 marks.

(b) Write a directional hypothesis for this investigation *(3 marks)*

The levels of adrenaline and cortisol will both be higher just before the exam than the day before.

Fully operationalised and directional. 3 marks.

(c) What might the researcher conclude from the results in the table? *(4 marks)*

The adrenaline was higher just before the exam than the day before, but the cortisol level was lower just before the exam than the day before. This shows that cortisol is associated with chronic stress and adrenaline is raised in acute stress, like just before the exam.

The first sentence simply describes the results, but the second links the findings about adrenaline to an interpretation of them, which is a conclusion. Not so clearly done for cortisol. 3 marks.

(d) Explain **one** ethical issue that might arise in this study. *(4 marks)*

An ethical issue is protection from harm, as participants might become stressed by having blood tests just before an exam, and also they might find it stressful to realise that they have different hormone changes going on because of stress. This extra stress might affect their performance in the exam, which could be harmful.

Good suggestion of an issue, and well elaborated and contextualised. 4 marks.

(e) Aside from ethical issues, identify **one** limitation of this study, and explain how you would correct it. *(4 marks)*

The researchers might assume that the exam is the only source of stress in these students' lives, but there may be other stressful experiences that they are having as well, such as relationship issues, or they may just be a more anxious individual. The researchers could deal with this by measuring anxiety levels a week after the exams have finished as well, so they can find out how stressed the students are when they are not having exams.

The student has suggested two limitations, but only given a way of dealing with one (the individual differences point) so this is the one that is marked. Not very clearly linked to the suggested solution, though. 3 marks.

Topic 2 Control of variables

When psychologists try to assess the effectiveness of different psychological therapies they often compare recovery rates after the use of different therapies. One study looked at 10,000 patient histories and found that 80% of patients receiving psychoanalysis had recovered, whereas only 65% of those undergoing other psychological therapies had recovered.

(a) Outline **one** conclusion you could draw from this study. *(2 marks)*

Psychoanalysis is better than other psychological therapies, as a higher percentage of people got better with psychoanalysis.

A clear conclusion linked to findings. 2 marks.

(b) (i)   Explain what is meant by 'validity'. *(4 marks)*

Validity means whether something measures what it is trying to measure. It can be internal validity or external validity. External validity means whether the findings apply to contexts or groups of people outside of the study, e.g. ecological validity or population validity.

> The first sentence describes internal validity, but this is not clear. The description of external validity is better. 3 marks.

(ii)   Outline **one** factor that might affect the validity of this study. *(3 marks)*

The different outcomes might be influenced by the type of disorder being treated as well as the severity of the disorder. For example, psychoanalysis may be used to treat less severe disorders, so people would be more likely to recover anyway, and the difference is not due to the therapy.

> A good suggestion, well elaborated for 3 marks.

Topic 3 Return to hypotheses and other things

Examiner's comments

A psychology class decides to compare the effectiveness of two methods of memory improvement, referred to as method 1 and method 2, to help them remember the content of a lesson. They expect method 1 to be more effective.

(a) (i)   Write a suitable hypothesis for this study. *(3 marks)*

Students who use method 1 will recall more of the content of the lesson than students who use method 2

> This is clear and fully operationalised. 3 marks.

(ii)   Is your hypotheses directional or non-directional? *(1 mark)*

Directional

> A single word is all that's needed. 1 mark.

(iii)   Explain why you chose this type of hypothesis. *(2 marks)*

Because the students believe that method 1 will work better.

> This is not a good reason. It should be based on evidence from previous research. 0 marks.

(b) (i)   Explain why it might be better to use an independent groups design rather than repeated measures in this study. *(2 marks)*

Because you get order effects with repeated measures, as each person does the learning twice, so they will already have learnt it using the other method.

> The student has answered the question the wrong way round – the answer must say why it is better to use independent groups, not why repeated measures is a problem. 0 marks.

(ii)   identify a suitable method to use in selecting participants and outline how you would do this. *(3 marks)*

They could use a random sample. They could use a random name generator on the computer, with all the class's names in it.

(iii)   Explain why this method is best for this study. *(2 marks)*

Because everyone gets an equal chance of being chosen for each group, it's not biased.

> Random sampling is appropriate, and the target population is identified, and a method of choosing randomly has been given. 3 marks.

> Correct and clearly explained. 2 marks.

(c) The students conduct their experiment in the classroom under carefully controlled conditions.

(i)   Identify **one** extraneous variable that they would need to control, and explain why this would be important. *(3 marks)*

The amount of distractions should be controlled. This is important because if one method was being used before lunchtime then students would be more distracted and not concentrate as well as a lesson in the middle of the morning.

> A good suggestion, and sufficient explanation for full marks. 3 marks.

(ii)   Explain why this study would be considered to be a laboratory experiment. *(3 marks)*

Because it is carried out in a controlled environment so variables can be controlled fairly well.

> This identifies the main reason it is a lab experiment, but for full marks it could mention control of extraneous variables (in contrast to a field experiment) or manipulation of the IV (in contrast to a natural experiment or quasi-experiment). 2 marks.

Topic 4 Experimental design

One way to study the duration of short-term memory is to show participants a consonant syllable such as TXR or GJP and then ask them to count backwards until a buzzer sounds. At this time they are asked to recall the consonant syllable. In one study the buzzer sounded either after 6 seconds or 15 seconds. Each participant was tested twice, once after 6 seconds and once after 15 seconds.

(a) Describe the operationalised independent and dependent variables in this experiment. *(4 marks)*

The IV is time after being shown the consonant syllable before they had to recall it. The DV is how many they remembered.

> The IV is correctly operationalised, but the DV is not quite correct. 3 marks.

(b) What experimental design was used? *(1 mark)*

This is repeated measures because the same participants are being used for both conditions of the experiment.

> 1 mark – as only one mark is available, the explanation is not necessary.

(c) Give one strength and one limitation of using this experimental design. *(4 marks)*

A strength is that any individual differences don't become confounding variables, e.g. memory ability. A limitation is that there could be order effects, like fatigue or boredom which would make performance worse in the second condition.

> Detailed and clear response. 4 marks.

(d) How should participants be chosen for the two conditions? *(1 mark)*

By random allocation.

> Correct terminology

(e) Explain how counterbalancing could be used in this experiment, and why this would improve the design. *(3 marks)*

If half the participants did the 6 second condition first then the 15 second condition, and the other half did them the other way round. That is AB or BA. Alternatively they could do ABBA where they all do each condition twice.

> The student has given two ways of organising the counterbalancing, when one would have been fine, but neglected to say why it would improve the design. 2 marks.

(f) The reason participants were asked to count backwards was to prevent rehearsal of the consonant syllable. Why was this necessary? *(3 marks)*

This prevented them from rehearsing the consonant syllable. Therefore they couldn't use maintenance rehearsal, which would keep it in their STM indefinitely.

> The first sentence repeats information in the stem so gets no credit. The next sentence gives an explanation but doesn't quite say that rehearsal would make it impossible to measure the duration of STM. 2 marks.

Topic 5 Laboratory and field experiments

A group of psychology students were studying the experiment by Loftus and Palmer, in which participants were asked questions containing different verbs, and asked to estimate the speed of a car on a video.

(a) What was the aim of this experiment? *(1 mark)*

To investigate the effect of misleading information on eyewitness testimony.

> Remember the aim is not a hypothesis, it is the area of interest of a study. 1 mark.

(b) Identify the independent variable in this experiment. *(2 marks)*

The verb used in the question about the speed of the car when they crashed, hit or bumped.

> The verb gets one mark, some operationalisation by describing or giving examples gets the second mark. 2 marks.

(c) (i) Explain what is meant by 'operationalisation'. *(2 marks)*

Stating the variables clearly in a way that they can be measured.

> 2 marks – being measurable is the key.

(ii) Write a suitable, fully operationalised hypothesis for this study. *(3 marks)*

The verb used to describe the car crash (hit, smashed etc) affects the eyewitnesses' estimates of the speed the cars were driving at.

> This is clear and fully operationalised. 3 marks.

(d) Identify one possible extraneous variable in this study and suggest how it could be controlled. *(3 marks)*

The driving experience of the participants would make a difference, as experienced drivers might be better at estimating speeds of cars. This could be controlled by asking participants how long they had been driving and matching pairs with similar experience between the two conditions.

> This is a relevant extraneous variable, and a sensible suggestion of how it could be controlled. 3 marks.

(e) Laboratory experiments such as this can be criticized for having poor ecological validity. Explain what this means. *(2 marks)*

Lab experiments are done in artificial conditions, so this one involved watching a video, which would not be as shocking as experiencing a car crash in real life.

The criticism is explained and contextualised in relation to this study, with excellent elaboration. 2 marks.

(f) The students would like to carry out a field experiment to explore the same aim, in order to improve the ecological validity. Suggest **one or more** ethical issues that they might encounter in planning this field experiment. *(4 marks)*

A field experiment would have to involve real crashes, maybe mock-ups using stunt drivers, but even so there would be a real risk of harm to participants. This could be physical harm from flying debris or psychological harm from witnessing a crash. They would have to be debriefed but some people might see the crash who were just passersby and could not be debriefed, so this is unethical.

The risk of harm is identified in the context of a suggestion of how a field experiment might operate using mock-ups, so this is a good suggestion. Issues with debriefing are also relevant and this gives a second issue that is well explained too. 4 marks.

Topic 6 Natural and quasi-experiments

The cognitive interview is a technique used by only some police forces. Other police forces continue to use the standard interview which is the traditional method used in questioning suspects or eyewitnesses. A researcher is employed to compare the two interview techniques. To do this the researcher compares two police forces. One force uses the cognitive interview and the other uses the standard interview technique. The researcher shows a set of films to 10 'eyewitnesses' and then the eyewitnesses are interviewed by both police forces. The information gathered is scored for accuracy. The results are shown in the table below.

Examiner's comments

When a large amount of information is provided in the stem, take time to read it and highlight key words.

	Mean accuracy score out of a maximum score of 100
Police Force A (uses cognitive interview)	76
Police Force B (uses standard interview)	69

(a) Identify the participants in this study. *(1 mark)*

The police officers in the two forces.

This needs to be clear before you can understand the study. Note that the eyewitnesses are not the participants in this study. 1 mark.

(b) Explain in what way this study is a natural experiment. *(3 marks)*

Because the officers were either in one force or the other, they were not randomly allocated to the two forces by the researcher.

A concise answer with three important ideas in it; the naturally occurring IV, the fact that this cannot be controlled by the researcher, and that participants can't be randomly allocated to conditions. 3 marks.

(c) Explain **two** limitations of a natural experiment in this study. *(5 marks)*

As the IV can't be manipulated, the researcher can't be sure whether the two police forces had different approaches to interviewing in other ways, different training, more intelligent police officers etc, which would be confounding variables. Also they may be in unique situations, like one in a big city and one more rural, so the social culture may be unique and the results could not be generalised.

The first limitation is well contextualised but not elaborated to explain how this would affect the conclusions, which is that changes in the DV may not be due to the IV, so we can't conclude the different interview is the cause of the different accuracy scores. The second limitation is fully elaborated. 4 marks.

(d) What do the results in Table 1 show? *(2 marks)*

Police force A, using the cognitive interview, got a higher mean accuracy score than police force B, using the standard interview. This shows that the cognitive interview may be better at getting more accurate details out of eyewitnesses.

The findings are linked to a conclusion. The 'may be better' is appropriate after the discussion of limitations, and also ∞ the difference is not great and may not be statistically significant with such a small sample. 2 marks.

(e) Explain why the mean was used to calculate the average score for accuracy. *(2 marks)*

Because it means you can compare the two forces' scores.

The researcher was also asked to compare the accuracy scores for male and female police officers. This part of the study is a quasi-experiment.

(f) Why is this a quasi-experiment? *(2 marks)*

Because gender is a characteristic of the individuals and they can't be allocated to different genders.

This does not explain fully why the mean was used, rather than just looking at all of the scores. The answer should say something about summarising all the scores. 1 mark.

Correct and concise answer. 2 marks.

Topic 7 More problems with experiments

Examiner's comments

Many years ago people did not believe that separation between parents and their children would have serious emotional consequences. One hospital decided to conduct research to see if parental contact would improve the recovery rates of children in their hospital. Each child who arrived at the hospital for treatment was assigned to one of two wards – Ward A and Ward B. In Ward A parents were encouraged to visit often. In Ward B visiting time was restricted to two hours per day. When each child was due to go home, a psychologist interviewed the child and assessed their behaviour, producing a contentment score. The results are shown in the table.

	Average contentment score	
	Hospital stay 1–3 days	Hospital stay 4+ days
Ward A	48	4
Ward B	34	2

a) Describe how the independent and dependent variables were operationalised in this study. *(4 marks)*

IV – visiting time in the two wards. DV – children's contentment at the end of their stay.

> IV correctly operationalised, DV should be contentment scores. 3 marks.

b) Display these findings using an appropriate graph or chart. *(4 marks)*

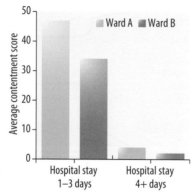

> A bar chart as the data is category data. Correct with labelled axes and key. 4 marks

c) What do the findings show about the effects of disruption of attachment? *(4 marks)*

Children in ward A were more contented than ward B, particularly in shorter stays.

> This is only one conclusion but is worth 3 marks. You can compare several ways in a two-way table. This answer compares rows, but you can also compare columns, comparing shorter and longer stays for all children.

d) Explain how investigator effects may have reduced the validity of the findings. *(3 marks)*

If the researcher knows which ward the child had been in, they might influence the way they ask questions and the way they interpret the interview and give the contentment scores. For example, if they know the child was in ward B they might expect the child to be more negative and this makes them biased in the scoring of answers.

> This gives appropriate ideas of how investigator effects might operate in this study, and how this would reduce validity.

e) This study was a field experiment. Give **one** strength and **one** limitation of using this method to investigate the effects of disruption of attachment. *(3 marks + 3 marks)*

Because the experiment is carried out in a hospital rather than a lab it has higher ecological validity. A limitation is that the researchers can't control other variables that might affect the children's contentment scores, so they might draw the wrong conclusions about what has actually caused the difference. e.g. the nurses may be nicer on Ward A.

> Ecological validity is not elaborated. The limitation is well explained, for full 3 marks. 4 marks total.

Topic 8 Sampling

Discuss methods of selecting a sample of participants for psychological research, giving examples of research studies which have made use of these sampling methods. *(10 marks)*

Most research probably uses an opportunity sample, which is convenient as it just uses people who happen to be available. For example, research done in universities often uses groups of Psychology students who are easily available so cheap and easy to recruit.

However, the problem with this is that it is a biased sample and may not represent other people in the population. Psychology students may have particular characteristics so the findings may not have population validity. For example, some of Loftus's eyewitness testimony research was carried out on groups of students.

A volunteer sample is also very easy to obtain, as you can just put an advert on the internet or a newspaper. Milgram did this for his obedience research. This is biased too, as the volunteers will all be keen to take part, so they may be more susceptible to demand characteristics, and they may have volunteered because they are short of money or have a lot of spare time, so again they may not represent the population as a whole and shouldn't be generalised.

A better type of sample would be a random sample. The whole target population would be given a number, then a random number generator on a computer would choose numbers. This is totally unbiased, but the problem comes when some of the chosen people don't actually want to take part, so then the sample becomes biased like the volunteer sample, with only willing and motivated people actually taking part.

There are also stratified and systematic samples that can be good but have limitations.

Level 4 answer (9–10 marks)

Examiner's comments: This essay discusses three sampling methods, and each is described and evaluated in its own paragraph, a sensible way of organising the content in this essay.

Overall, a well organised and clear answer, just lacking an example for random sampling.

Topic 9 Ethical issues

Research on the effectiveness of any drug treatment is often conducted by giving one group of participants the drug while a second group receive a placebo – they think they are receiving an active drug but it doesn't actually contain anything. After a period of time the two groups are compared to see whether there is a difference in their recovery. In one such study, recovery was assessed in terms of the improvement in a patient's score on a mental health questionnaire (maximum score of 50). The table shows the results.

	Drug group	Placebo group
Mean score before treatment	23	26
Mean score after treatment	37	34

a) Calculate the percentage mean improvement scores of each group, as a percentage of their score before treatment. Show your working. *(4 marks)*

Drug group: improvement = 37-23 = 14

Percentage improvement = 14÷23 x 100 = 60.9% to 3 sf.

Placebo group: improvement = 34-26 = 8

Percentage improvement = 30.8% to 3 sf.

b) What do these findings show about the effectiveness of the drug treatment? *(4 marks)*

The drug treatment group showed a much greater improvement than the placebo group. This shows that the drug treatment is effective. Although both groups did improve, so patients' mental health also improves when they just take a placebo. But neither group achieved perfect scores so the drug doesn't work that well.

c) How do you explain the findings in relation to the placebo group? *(3 marks)*

The placebo group had a higher starting score, so maybe they weren't quite as bad to start with. Also they believed they were taking an actual drug, so this is a kind of demand characteristics where they thought they were getting better, so they scored higher on the questionnaire. Maybe the attention of the doctor made them feel better too.

d) Describe **one** ethical issue with this kind of research. *(3 marks)*

The issue is that some patients are being deceived, and given a fake drug rather than the actual drug which could really benefit them. This could be seen as causing harm, when they could have been given the real drug but they weren't.

Examiner's comments

An effective first paragraph with strengths and limitations well elaborated and an appropriate example of research. This could have been further elaborated to explain how students may not represent other drivers (because of their age and lack of driving experience).

The paragraph on volunteer samples is also clear with a good example, and the discussion points are well elaborated.

This is an excellent explanation of random sampling, but there is no example from research. There is a high level evaluation point explaining how random sampling may not end up as unbiased as we would like it to be.

This final paragraph doesn't add anything as the other two sampling types are named but not explained or evaluated.

Examiner's comments

Remember that 10% of your marks come from maths-related questions. This doesn't necessarily mean calculations, as it includes knowing about sampling, data analysis etc. However, you should be prepared to calculate percentages in various different ways. These are easy marks if you have practised, read the question carefully, show all your working and take care not to make mistakes.

Correct answers, rounded to an appropriate level of accuracy. 2sf would also have been fine, as the scores are given to 2sf. 4 marks.

This answer actually gives three conclusions, so more than enough for 4 marks. Don't forget the obvious points – that both groups improved, and that neither group showed full recovery.

Three valid points are made here. The first one is not very well explained, but the other two are good. 3 marks.

This is indeed an ethical issue, in fact two have been identified (deception and harm) but they are linked and the consequences are explained so 3 marks.

Topic 10 Dealing with ethical issues

Discuss how psychologists deal with ethical issues in psychological research.
Refer to examples of research studies in your answer. *(12 marks)*

Examiner's comments

Ethical issues involve a conflict between the aims of the researcher and the interests of the participants. For example, the researcher may want to deceive them so that there aren't demand characteristics, but participants generally don't like being deceived and this can cause harm. Most of the social psychology research involved deception, like Milgram's obedience studies, Asch's conformity experiment and Moscovici's minority influence research.

> Remember that 'discuss' means 'outline and evaluate'.

> A good introductory paragraph explaining what issues are. This will not gain any credit by itself, but it sets the context in this essay for the discussion about deception and harm. The key studies are also introduced here.

Part of the problem with deception is that participants cannot give properly informed consent before the study, as they weren't told what was going to happen. This can be dealt with by debriefing them thoroughly beforehand, telling them what the study was really about and giving them the choice to withdraw their data if they want to. However, this doesn't always solve the problem. For example, Milgram said he had debriefed everyone but some critics claim that he didn't actually debrief people properly, and some participants were left feeling bad about how they'd given people electric shocks.

> Deception is now linked to informed consent, and a way of dealing with this is introduced and evaluated, with excellent linking to the Milgram study.

Nowadays the whole research study has to be approved by an ethics committee before it can go ahead. They will carry out a cost-benefit analysis, where they decide if any deception is justified in terms of the useful things that could be learnt from the study, that could benefit society as a whole. This is a good process and safeguards participants to some extent, but is it really possible to judge how much harm people will experience in a study? Even a simple one involving lines and colours like Asch or Moscovici might make people embarrassed and lose confidence about themselves. And even if people are given the chance to withdraw their data, it's too late to reverse any harm they have experienced.

> The role of the ethics committee and cost-benefit analysis are clearly explained here, with some excellent evaluation, linked to research studies. It is not really explained why people might feel embarrassed; this could be elaborated a little more.

Researchers are meant to stop the study if any participants appear to be distressed, but how distressed would they have to be? Sometimes researchers get so involved in the study that they don't want to stop it, like Zimbardo with his Stanford Prison study.

> Another dilemma is outlined here, and linked to a fourth study; although this is so briefly introduced. This should be a bit more explicit.

Level 4 answer (11–12 marks)

Examiner's comments: Overall, an excellent essay with clear line of argument, a range of evaluation points and good choice of examples.

Topic 11 Observational techniques

Examiner's comments

A psychologist studied the attachment relationship between infants and their parents to see which parent the infant was most strongly attached to. The psychologist was particularly interested to see if infants were most strongly attached to their mother or their father, or simply to the person who was the main carer (i.e. generally fed and washed the infant). Each infant was observed in the psychologist's lab by a team of two observers while playing with its mother, and in a different session playing with its father. The results are shown in the table.

	Percentage of infants most strongly attached
Mother main carer	37%
Father main carer	31%
Mother not main carer	22%
Father not main carer	10%

a) This study has two hypotheses. State possible hypotheses for this study. *(2 marks + 2 marks)*

An infant is more likely to be attached to its mother than its father.

Does the fact that a parent feeds and washes an infant make it more likely that they will become most attached to that person?

Examiner's comments

The first hypothesis is correct. The second statement is a research question, not a hypothesis. 2 marks altogether.

b) Explain why the psychologist chose to observe the parents with their infants in a lab environment. *(2 marks)*

It means the psychologist can do a controlled observation, where they control extraneous variables like noise and the objects in the surroundings. Also they can use one-way mirrors and cameras more easily.

Excellent answer. 2 marks

c) Explain **one** strength of using observational techniques to study infant behaviour. *(3 marks)*

Infants aren't generally aware that they are being observed for a study, so they will behave naturally. Also you can't ask them which parent they prefer, you have to just observe them.

Valid points. 3 marks.

d) Is the psychologist using covert or overt observation in this study? Explain your answer. *(2 marks)*

This is overt observation because the parents know they are being observed.

2 marks. Covert observation could also be an answer, as the infant doesn't realise they are being observed. The answer needs justification to get any marks.

e) How might the psychologist assess the reliability of the observations recorded by the team of two observers? *(3 marks)*

The inter-observer reliability should be calculated–the extent that the observers agreed with each other. An inter-observer reliability of over 80% would count as high.

This doesn't explain enough about *how* the reliability is assessed. 2 marks.

f) How could demand characteristics affect the validity of the findings in this study? *(4 marks)*

Demand characteristics are when the person being studied alters their behaviour to fit what they think the researcher wants. If the parents know they are being observed they may be especially attentive to the infant, so they come across as a 'good parent', which is social desirability bias. This would affect the validity because they would not be acting naturally, so conclusions will not be valid.

The first sentence is unnecessary, as the question does not ask for an explanation of what demand characteristics are. However the rest of the answer is on track and gains 4 marks.

g) A sample of 40 infants was used in this study. How many infants were most strongly attached to their father, even though he was not the main carer? *(1 mark)*

10% of 40 = 4 infants.

Correct. 1 mark. This question does not require working to be shown as there is only one mark available, but it is always a good idea to show it anyway.

Topic 12 Observational design

Examiner's comments

Ainsworth developed a technique called the Strange Situation to observe types of attachment. This technique consists of a number of different episodes involving a mother, an infant and a stranger.

a) What research method is used in this study? Explain your answer. *(4 marks)*

Full answer, 4 marks.

This a controlled observation. The researcher controls the environment by doing it in a lab, and also controls some of the events, the different episodes in the Strange Situation. They then observe the infant's responses.

These are not observable behaviours. 0 marks. They would need to be categories such as willingness to explore and crying.

b) The infant's behaviour was recorded using behavioural categories. Suggest **two** behavioural categories that could be used in this study. *(2 marks)*

Separation anxiety and stranger anxiety.

c) What sampling procedure could the observers use? Explain how this would be carried out *(3 marks)*

They could use time sampling, where they watch the video and tally the behaviour in different behavioural categories every 10 seconds.

Time sampling is OK, and a clear explanation. 3 marks. Event sampling could also be used, where the number of times the infant cries in 10 minutes is counted.

d) A team of three observers recorded the behaviour of each infant. Explain why this would increase the reliability of the observations. *(2 marks)*

It is more likely with three observers that one might categorise behaviour differently, than if they only had two. This means that if they all agree there must be good reliability.

This is a difficult question to answer, as it focuses on how having three observers would increase reliability. This answer does explain this. 2 marks.

Topic 13 Self-report techniques

Some psychology students decided to investigate the topic of memory by interviewing people of different ages about their memories. They wanted to find out early childhood memories and what kinds of things people typically remembered.

a) i) Give an example of a question that would produce qualitative data. *(2 marks)*

What do you remember about your first day at school?

ii) Explain why this question would produce qualitative data rather than quantitative data. *(2 marks)*

This would produce qualitative rather than quantitative data as it is an open question so the interviewee can express things in their own words rather than just choosing from a list.

b) Give one strength of conducting an interview rather than a questionnaire in this study. *(3 marks)*

The interviewer can probe a bit deeper and explain questions if the interviewee doesn't understand them, so they are more likely to get in-depth answers whereas with a questionnaire people might not be bothered to answer all the questions.

c) Explain why it might have been preferable to use a questionnaire instead of an interview. *(3 marks)*

A questionnaire is quick and cheap to produce and doesn't need lots of expensive interviewer's time, so it is easy to get a much larger sample of people.

d) Describe how the students might have conducted a pilot study. *(3 marks)*

A pilot study is a small scale study carried out before the main study so researchers can try out the procedure to see if it works, and make changes if needed. The students could check their questions work by trying them on a few of people before the main study.

e) Explain why it might have been a good idea to conduct a pilot study. *(3 marks)*

Because they can check that participants understand the questions and change them if necessary before doing the main study, so as not to waste time in the real interviews having to explain the questions all the time.

f) The students were concerned that some of them may have asked the questions differently when they were interviewing participants. How could the students improve the reliability of their interviews? *(3 marks)*

They could have training to make sure they all do the interviews in the same way, and they could practise asking the questions in the pilot study, video themselves, and check the interviewees all have a similar experience and the findings are more reliable.

g) Explain why reliability is important when conducting interviews.

Because if two interviewers ask questions differently or code responses differently this will bias the results and make the conclusions meaningless.

Examiner's comments

This example is fine. 2 marks

This student has wasted time writing out the question, but the rest of it is good. 2 marks.

'In this study' means that the answer must be contextualised for full marks. This one is not, so only gets 2 marks.

3 marks.

Unfortunately the first sentence describes what a pilot study is, which doesn't answer the question. The next sentence is not in enough detail. 2 marks.

This gives a good reason and explains how it would help. 3 marks.

A bit unclear as it is all written in one sentence, but it has some good ideas for improving reliability. The last section is more about why rather than how. 2 marks.

A difficult question, and this is a good answer. 2 marks.

Topic 14 Self-report design

Psychology students in a university decide to investigate cultural variations in attachment because the students at the university come from diverse cultural backgrounds. They plan to develop a questionnaire to find out about different child-rearing practices and expectations about mother-infant attachment.

a) Explain **one** strength of using a questionnaire to find out about cultural variations in attachment. *(3 marks)*

The advantage is that people may be more willing to answer sensitive questions in a questionnaire than they would face-to-face with an interviewer. This is especially true if the researcher might come from a different cultural background and the participant might feel judged in an interview, but a questionnaire is more anonymous.

Examiner's comments

A good way of addressing this is to compare questionnaires with interviews, in order to identify a strength of using a questionnaire. This student has done this well. 3 marks.

Examiner's comments

b) Write **one** question that would produce quantitative data and **one** question that would produce qualitative data. *(2 marks + 2 marks)*

Quantitative: Does your child get distressed when left with a babysitter? Yes/no

Qualitative: What do you think of mothers who ignore their child when they are distressed?

> Both good answers. Keep it as simple as possible when designing questions, and make sure you are clear which is which. 4 marks.

c) Why is useful to include open and closed questions in a questionnaire? *(3 marks)*

Because open questions allow people to express their own thoughts and beliefs in their own words, and get rich detailed descriptive data, whereas closed questions produce quantitative data which is much easier to analyse using statistics.

> This is another way of asking what are the strengths, of open and closed questions. This is a good answer, with both points well elaborated. 3 marks.

d) Give **one** limitation of open questions, and **one** limitation of closed questions in a questionnaire. *(2 marks + 2 marks)*

Closed questions have limited answers available, and they might not match participants' true opinions, so they are forced to pick an answer or leave it blank, reducing validity.

Open questions take time and effort to answer properly, so some participants might not write much and also it is difficult to analyse the responses as people can write anything.

> Closed questions – a good point, clearly elaborated. Open questions – the student has given two points, when they were only asked for one. However, both have been elaborated so the examiner, chooses one and gives 2 marks. 4 marks altogether.

e) How might social desirability bias affect the validity of their questionnaire? Suggest how this could be dealt with. *(3 marks)*

People might answer in the way that makes them look good, so they might say that in their culture mothers are attentive and they have really good attachment. Especially if they guess what the survey is trying to find out. The researchers could include filler questions that are nothing to do with attachment or culture, to put participants off the scent.

> Good answer, well contextualised, with a sensible suggestion for dealing with the issue. This demonstrates knowledge of questionnaire design. 3 marks.

f) i) Identify a suitable method that could be used to select participants, and explain how it would be done. *(3 marks)*

A stratified sample would be useful. They could find out the cultural backgrounds of everyone in the university and select people from each background in proportion.

> Stratified sampling might be useful, but this answer doesn't explain how the people would be selected from each background (using a random selection technique preferably). 2 marks

ii) Give **one** limitation of this sampling method. *(2 marks)*

There may not be enough people from some cultural backgrounds to get sensible sized samples.

> A good point, and sufficient for 2 marks.

Topic 15 Correlations

Examiner's comments

A researcher investigated the accuracy of the recall of real-life eyewitnesses. Each eyewitness answered a questionnaire about their experiences which included questions about how scared they were and what details they remembered. The graph shows the relationship between fear (score from 1 to 10, where 10 is very scared) and amount of detail recalled. A correlation coefficient of +.55 was calculated.

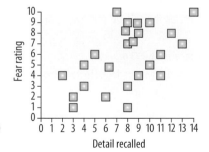

a) What does the graph show about the relationship between fear and amount of detail recalled? *(3 marks)*

The graph shows that high levels of fear lead to better recall, low levels lead to worse recall.

> This is **not** correct! This answer implies a causal relationship, and correlational research only shows a link between the two variables, not a cause-and-effect relationship. The graph actually shows a moderate positive correlation between the level of fear and the amount of detail recalled, showing the higher the fear, the more detail is recalled.

b) Outline **one** strength and **one** limitation of using correlational analysis to investigate eyewitness testimony. *(3 marks + 3 marks)*

A strength is that it enables investigators to study relationships where it might be unethical or impractical to manipulate variables. So in this study it would be unethical to create fear in order to study its effect on recall. A limitation is that it doesn't demonstrate a causal relationship between the variables.

> A full and contextualised explanation of the strength, but the limitation is not contextualised – what does that mean in this study? 3 + 2 marks

c) Describe **one** possible factor that might lower the validity of this study. *(3 marks)*

People may not remember accurately how afraid they were, or might not be honest about it because of social desirability, meaning they wouldn't report as much fear as they felt.

> Good answer, which explains why people might not report fear accurately, and what the consequence of this is on the findings. 3 marks

d) How could the reliability of the questionnaire be assessed in this study? *(3 marks)*

With the test-retest method. Participants answer the same questionnaire again a month later, and if their answers are pretty similar then the questionnaire has good reliability.

> All the key points included – test-retest; what that means; how it is used to assess reliability. 3 marks.

Topic 16   Other research methods

A newspaper article reported the case of a young man injured in a car accident. He suffered damage to part of his brain and as a result he appears to be unable to form new long-term memories. This means that he can only remember things for about 90 seconds, the limit of short-term memory.

a) A psychologist was interested in the case and contacted the injured man to test his abilities. He hoped to find support for the multi-store model of memory. Outline the aims of the case study. *(2 marks)*

To see if his short-term memory is still intact, despite long-term memory loss.

> This shows understanding of what an aim is, and expresses it clearly in relation to the multi-store model and the case study. 2 marks.

b) How might this case study support the multi-store model of memory? *(3 marks)*

If he has damage to his LTM but no damage to his STM, this supports the idea that there are separate stores which are based in different locations in the brain.

> The important aspect here is the separate stores, and this is elaborated by mentioning the different locations, which is highly relevant to this case. 3 marks.

c) Outline **one** strength and **one** limitation of using a case study to research memory. *(3 marks + 3 marks)*

A strength is that researchers can look at rare or unique cases where there aren't enough people with the same condition to be able to make a sample for an experiment. A limitation is that, because they are unique, we can't generalise from them. For example, this young man's injury will not be exactly the same as anyone else's, and we don't know what his abilities were before the accident so we can't draw any general conclusions from it.

> The strength is clearly explained but is not in the context of memory research, so this answer only gets 2 marks. The limitation is well explained and also contextualised – 3 marks.

d) Identify **one** ethical issue that might arise in this case study and explain how it could be dealt with. *(3 marks)*

An issue is informed consent, as the man would not remember giving consent. This could be dealt with by getting consent from his parents or carers.

> An appropriate issue, elaborated and with a simple suggestion for dealing with it. 3 marks.

e) The data used in a case study may be qualitative or quantitative.

   i) Explain the difference between qualitative and quantitative data. *(3 marks)*

Qualitative is rich, detailed descriptive data that can't be summed up in numbers, whereas quantitative data tries to quantify people's opinions and feelings by giving people closed questions and Likert scales to choose from.

> A question asking for a difference requires you to compare directly between two things, rather than just describing one and then the other. So you have to choose a feature that you can directly contrast, which this answer does. 3 marks.

   ii) Explain **one** strength and **one** limitation of qualitative data. *(2 marks + 2 marks)*

A strength is that qualitative data is much richer and more detailed and so is more likely to represent a person's actual thoughts and feelings. A limitation is that it is much more difficult to analyse or compare with other people's answers, as it can't be put into graphs or descriptive statistics like quantitative data can.

> Both good answers. 2 + 2 marks.

   iii) How might quantitative data have been used in this case study? *(3 marks)*

The man might be asked to do some cognitive tests like the digit span test (to test the capacity of his STM) or the trigram retention test (to test its duration).

> Good suggestions, and explanations of their relevance to the aims of this case study. 3 marks.

Topic 17   Mathematical skills

A psychologist plans to investigate whether certain types of people are more conformist than others. The table displays some of the results.

Participant type	Didn't conform	Did conform	Percentage conforming
Young (under 10)	5	7	
Older (over 40)	6	11	
Females	23	13	
Males	25	11	
Total	48	24	

a) Describe a method the psychologist could use to assess how conformist each participant is. *(3 marks)*

She could set a task like the Asch conformity task and observe to see if the participants give the wrong answer when the confederates do.

> It is perfectly creditworthy to describe Asch's study as an answer to this question, but this answer does not give enough detail. *2 marks*.

Examiner's comments

b) Give **one** criticism with the method you described in a) *(3 marks)*

There is the possibility of demand characteristics, which might have more effect on some participants than others. For example, adults might be more likely to guess the purpose of the experiment and answer as they think they are meant to.

> The effect of demand characteristics on the findings is clearly explained. *3 marks.*

c) Calculate the percentage of each type of participant which conformed. Fill in the percentages in the right hand column of the table, giving your answers to 2 significant figures. *(3 marks)*

Young: 7÷(7+5)×100 = 58%

Older: 11÷(11+6)×100 = 65%   Female: 13÷(13+23)×100 = 36% Male:

Total: 24÷72×100 = 33%   11÷(11+25)×100 = 31%

> Note that these answers needed to be written in the table, but you should still show some working in the place provided.
> Make sure you understand how to calculate percentages, as they are a really useful way of comparing findings from different sized subgroups of participants. *3 marks.*

d) What fraction of the total sample of participants conformed? *(1 mark)*

33% = $\frac{1}{3}$

e) i)   What age group did most participants fall into? *(2 marks)*

Between 10 and 40 years

> Correct, *1 mark.*

   ii)   How many participants in this age group conformed? *(1 mark)*

24 – (7+11) = 6

f) What conclusions can you draw from this study about conformity? *(4 marks)*

Only 6 of 43 people aged 10–40 conformed (14%) so people in this age group conform the least. Young children and people aged over 40 conform more, maybe because children are less certain what is required so follow the behaviour of others. Females conform more than males, although this is a small difference and may not be significant.

> Correct. (There were 12 people under 10, and 17 over 40, with 72 participants altogether. So 72 – (12 + 17) = 43 between 10 and 40.) 2 marks for a bit of adding and subtracting.
> ii) correct. *1 mark.*

> Effective linking of findings to conclusions, and a suggestion about what might have caused this difference in conformity in children. There is no suggestion relating to older people or females, although the comment about significance is creditworthy. 4 marks.

Topic 18 Measures of central tendency and dispersion

A study was conducted to see how children aged between two and four years reacted to their mother's voice, compared with the voice of a stranger. The children listened to the voices through a headset. Some children heard their mother's voice first, reading a short passage, then the stranger's voice, reading the same passage. Other children heard the voices in reverse order. The children's responses were assessed through observation and a 'happiness' score was calculated. The results are shown in the table.

Examiner's comments

Child	Happiness score listening to mother's voice	Happiness score listening to stranger's voice
1	6	4
2	5	4
3	8	3
4	1	0
5	7	3
6	9	7
7	5	5
8	5	6
9	6	4
10	4	4

a) Explain which experimental design was used in this study. *(2 marks)*

Repeated measures

> This question has two marks, so needed more than just the name of the design. 1 mark.

b) Explain why the researcher played the voices in different orders to some of the children. *(3 marks)*

To counterbalance, to avoid order effects.

> This answer is much too brief. It could have explained more about what order effects are. However, it does use correct terminology, so 2 marks.

c) Calculate a suitable measure of central tendency for each set of scores, and explain why you chose this measure. *(5 marks)*

Mother's voice: mean = 5.6

Stranger's voice: mean = 4

I chose the mean because it takes into account all the data, so it is a sensitive measure.

> The mean is correctly calculated, and can be used with this sort of data. However, the median would also be accepted. 4 marks.

d) Calculate the range for each set of happiness scores. *(4 marks)*

Mother's voice: range = 9–1+1 = 9   Stranger's voice: range = 7–0+1 = 8

> The ranges are correctly calculated. Remember that the convention in psychology is to add 1 to the difference between the highest and lowest scores. 4 marks.

e) Why might the standard deviation be a better measure of dispersion than the range for this data? *(3 marks)*

The standard deviation takes all the values into account without being distorted by extreme values – here, there are extreme values which make the range very high even though most of the scores are bunched up in the middle, especially for the Stranger condition.

> This is well explained and linked to the actual data. 3 marks.

Topic 19 Display of quantitative data and data distributions

A psychologist investigated which methods of treatment were most effective. Thirty depressed patients were given one of three treatments for 6 weeks after which their improvement was assessed on a scale of 1 to 30 where 0 = no improvement and 30 = no depressed symptoms. They were assessed again after 1 year to see if the improvements had continued. Improvement rates are shown in the table below.

	Mean improvement score after six weeks	Mean improvement score after one year
CBT	17	23
Drug therapy	20	10
Psychoanalysis	12	21

a) Display these findings graphically. *(5 marks)*

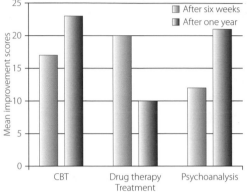

a) The bar chart is the correct graph to display this data, and it has everything it needs: gaps between the bars; axes labelled; a key for the two groups (you can't use colours in your exam, but you can use shading or just label all the bars). 5 marks.

b) Explain what these results show about the effectiveness of different therapies. *(4 marks)*

Drug therapy is the most effective straight away, with the best improvement scores after six weeks, but CBT is the best after a year. Psychoanalysis is least effective after six weeks but gets more effective after a year. Depressed patients should take drug treatment for an immediate benefit and a psychological therapy for longer term improvements.

b) The first two sentences describe what the findings show about the effectiveness of the treatments, but the last sentence moves on to recommendations, which is not what the question is asking for. 2 marks.

The drug therapy was also tested on 800 patients, and their improvement scores after 1 year were plotted as a frequency histogram, shown on the right.

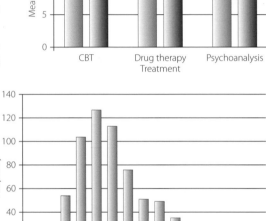

c) Describe the distribution of this data. *(1 mark)* Right-skewed

d) Give the modal improvement score. *(1 mark)* 10

e) Would the mean improvement score in this sample be to the left or the right of the mode? Tick **one** box. *(1 mark)*

Left ☐   Right ✓

c) Right skewed or positively skewed. 1 mark.

d) The mode is the highest point, so 10 is correct. 1 mark.

e) The mean is affected by the extreme high scores in a positively skewed distribution, so right is correct. 1 mark.

f) What does this distribution suggest about the effectiveness of the drug treatment? *(4 marks)*

A few patients responded particularly well to this treatment and improved enormously, giving some very high improvement scores.

f) This is a partial answer. 2 marks.

Topic 20 Types of data

Research on the effects of institutional care has looked at the behaviour of ex-institutional children later in their life. One study used in-depth interviews with a group of adults who had experienced institutional care for more than one year early in their lives.

a) Write one question to be used in the interview to produce quantitative data. *(2 marks)*

How many years did you spend in institutional care?

The question you write must be one that would produce an answer that could be counted (i.e. quantitative). 2 marks.

b) Explain one strength of using quantitative data rather than qualitative data. *(2 marks)*

Quantitative data is easier to analyse because you can show the data in a graph and calculate the mean etc. You can't summarise and analyse qualitative data in the same way.

Just saying 'Quantitative data is easier to analyse' would not be sufficient for 2 marks. The second part of the sentence adds enough for the full 2 marks.

c) Explain why it might be preferable to use a questionnaire rather than an interview to collect data in this study. *(2 marks)*

Some people can be more honest when answering a questionnaire because in an interview someone is listening and this might make you feel more embarrassed or ashamed.

Another study used records from care homes and criminal records to analyse patterns of behaviour in children and adolescents, and explore the association with adult criminal behaviour.

d) Discuss the use of primary or secondary data in research into the effects of institutional care. *(8 marks)*

Primary data is data which is collected by the researchers themselves, like the interviews. This means they can get exactly the data they want, as they are in control of the interview questions, but it takes a lot of time and therefore money to interview all those people, and then analyse all the data. Secondary data comes from other sources, like the care home records and criminal records. This means someone else has taken the time to collect it, so it is easy to access and therefore the process takes less time and money. But the limitation is that it might not quite answer the questions that the researchers wanted to know about. Also it might contain the bias of whoever recorded it, for example if the care home workers disliked a particular child and picked on them it would make their behaviour seem worse than it really was.

Examiner's comments

Again it is important to explain your answer. Therefore this answer would get 2 marks.

The answer needs to be contextualised, using the examples given in the two stem studies to show how primary and secondary data can be used. This student has done this with primary data, mentioning interviews, but it is better achieved in the secondary data paragraph. Here they have explained a limitation in the context of the secondary data from care homes too.

The evaluation is quite brief. Strengths and limitations for each type of data, could be elaborated with examples, causes or consequences. What is the consequence of it taking. 5 marks.

Topic 21 Introduction to statistical testing

The data from the study described on page 251 can also be tested for significance using the sign test.

Here is a reminder of the procedure:

A study was conducted to see how children aged between two and four years reacted to their mother's voice, compared with the voice of a stranger. The children listened to the voices through a headset. Some children heard their mother's voice first, reading a short passage, then the stranger's voice, reading the same passage. Other children heard the voices in reverse order. The children's responses were assessed through observation and a 'happiness' score was calculated.

Child	Happiness score listening to mother's voice	Happiness score listening to stranger's voice	Sign
1	6	4	−
2	5	4	−
3	8	3	−
4	1	0	−
5	7	3	−
6	9	7	−
7	5	5	0
8	5	6	+
9	6	4	−
10	4	4	0

a) State a directional hypothesis for this experiment. *(2 marks)*

The children will be less happy when listening to a stranger's voice than their mother's.

b) Complete the third column in the table above, then use the sign test to test the significance of the findings. The table of critical values of S is given below. *(5 marks)*

There are 7 minuses and 1 plus so the calculated value of S = 1

N = 10−2 = 8

The hypothesis is directional so we can use a one-tailed test.

The critical value from the table is 1 at a significance level of 0.05

The calculated value of S is equal to the critical value, so the result is significant.

The direction of the difference is as predicted.

c) What conclusion can be drawn from this data? *(2 marks)*

As the result is significant, the hypothesis is proved. Children are happier listening to their mother's voice than a stranger.

▼ **Table of critical values of S.**

Level of significance for a one-tailed test	0.05	0.01
Level of significance for a two-tailed test	**0.10**	**0.02**
N		
5	0	
6	0	0
7	0	0
8	1	0
9	1	1
10	1	1
11	2	1
12	2	2
13	3	2
14	3	2
15	3	3
16	4	3
17	4	4
18	5	4
19	5	4
20	5	5
25	7	7
30	10	9
35	12	11

Calculated value of *S* must be EQUAL TO or LESS THAN the critical value in this table for significance to be shown.

a) This is not fully operationalised. The DV is happiness scores, not just happiness. 1 mark.
b) The signs have been filled in correctly in the table. The calculation is correct, and all the stages of working are shown, so 5 marks.
c) Never use that word!! You can't *prove* a hypothesis. You should say 'the hypothesis is supported by the data' and go on to restate the hypothesis as your conclusion. This student has restated their hypothesis, which was not fully operationalised, but we won't penalise them again. 1 mark.

Topic 22 The scientific process and peer review

Discuss the purpose of peer review. *(16 marks)*

Examiner's comments

Peer review makes sure that research articles are checked by experts in the field before they are published. The researcher submits the article to a journal, and it gets sent off to other people who are researching the same area of psychology. They then scrutinize it, looking for any problems in the methodology and the statistical analysis, and to see if the conclusions are justified. They also decide if it is novel and interesting and make sure it is not plagiarising previous published articles. This makes sure that published research is reliable and valid so poor quality work doesn't get published.

> You should discuss the purpose of peer review and its strengths and/or limitations. Answers that merely outline the purpose of the peer review process can receive a maximum of 6 marks.

This is important for several reasons. First, other researchers will base their research or theories on it, so it must be reliable. Second, the public need to be able to trust that published scientific work is good quality. Third, this protects the reputation of the journal, the university where the research was done, and psychology as a whole. Also, funding for research is based on good previous research, so universities need to get research published but it must be good quality.

> This essay explains the purpose of peer review very clearly in the first two paragraphs, using correct terminology and explaining the importance of the process. This is written a bit like a list, but it has been organised in a logical way and makes a clear, readable line of argument because of linking statements like 'This is important for several reasons'.

There are some problems with this process, however. First, it may be difficult to find an expert in the field, especially if it is a new area of research, so there may not be anyone who understands the new research. This means the reviewers might just reject it as they don't understand it. Therefore it can be difficult to get really new ideas published.

> The evaluation is introduced with 'There are some problems…' which flags up the type of issues that are going to be discussed.

Second there may be bias towards famous researchers' work or important universities, which are more likely to get their work published. Again this leads to publication bias as new researchers will find it harder to get their articles published.

Third the reviewers may not want their rivals to publish work, as they might be doing something similar so they can slow the whole process down to make sure they can finish their article first and beat the competition. This means they are not objective in their decisions, and this also creates publication bias against new researchers.

> Each issue is dealt with in a separate short paragraph, which makes it easy to read. The ideas are all linked back to how they affect the achievement of the purpose of peer review. This is then summarised in the final sentence to round off the argument: 'This means the peer review process does not always achieve what it sets out to do'. It might be even clearer if this sentence had been used at the beginning of the evaluation section instead, to show that all the limitations are focused towards how they affect the ability of the peer review process to achieve its purpose. Starting off like this would also help to focus the writer's mind.

Fourth, journals themselves seem to be biased against replication studies or negative results as they prefer something exciting and new. This is also a publication bias and means that review articles or meta-analyses are not a valid representation of all the research that has taken place on a topic, as some of it didn't get published. This is called the file drawer phenomenon, where it is stuck in the researcher's drawer because they can't find a journal to publish it.

Finally, if research does get published that turns out later to be fraudulent (like Cecil Burt's twin studies), it still remains in the public domain and people might not realise it has been discredited. This means the peer review process does not always achieve what it sets out to do, but no one has come up with a better idea yet.

Level 4 answer (13–16 marks)

Examiner's comments: There is a good balance of outlining and evaluating here, with five clear, well developed evaluation points.

In a long and theoretical answer like this, keep looking back at the question to make sure you haven't strayed off track. This essay doesn't gain much credit for the first two sentences that are about the process, but they do set the context and explain that peer reviewers are experts in the field.

This is clearly a level 4 answer, and may even achieve full marks.

Topic 23 Psychology and the economy

Discuss the implications of psychological research for the economy. *(12 marks)*

Examiner's comments

Many areas of psychological research have benefits for society, which then have economic implications too. For example, the memory research of Loftus led to a new understanding of how leading questions and anxiety can affect the accuracy of eyewitness testimony.

She found that people can develop false memories if they are asked leading questions, such is her car crash research. In one study she asked participants how fast a car was going when it collided with another vehicle, but she replaced 'collided' with different verbs, such as 'hit', 'smashed', etc. She found that people made different estimates of the speed of the car depending on the word used in the question.

> This memory research is relevant, but the second paragraph goes into far too much detail of the procedure of a particular experiment, which does not gain any credit.

This research has then led on to the development of the cognitive interview, which aims to let participants tell the story in their own way without interruption. Also, interviewers are more careful to not ask leading questions. Due to this, the police get better evidence and hopefully the right people get punished for crimes, which means we are not wasting police and court time or imprisoning the wrong people and then having to pay compensation.

> Here we have the relevant part – linking to police evidence-gathering processes and the implications are clearly explained.

Another area of benefit is mental health. Researchers collect evidence about the effectiveness of different treatments, so the NHS can spend its money on the treatments that are most cost effective. That is why the government has been investing in CBT to try and get depressed people back to work so they aren't taking up time and resources from the health service, and they aren't claiming benefits for being off sick with depression. Instead they are able to go back to work and pay taxes which helps the economy.

> Mental health research is a good discussion point too. This could have been evaluated further, as 'cost effective' does not mean the same as 'effective'. However, this point is clear and has been well linked back to the economy.

The government's nudge unit tries to make direct economic improvements using psychological techniques. For example, they made the letters requesting car tax payments simpler and more personalised, and more people paid their taxes.

> The nudge unit is briefly mentioned here, and could have provided material for a whole essay if the student had known more about it.

There was a study in which researchers put a picture of some eyes above an honesty box and more people paid for their coffee and tea. This shows that we are affected by social influence without realising it, and could be used to benefit the economy.

> This last paragraph doesn't add much, as it shows limited knowledge of the study and only makes a very weak connection with benefits to the economy.

Level 4 answer (13–16 marks)

Examiner's comments: There are many possibilities of research or theories that could be included in an answer to this question. This particular version gives you complete freedom to choose any topic in psychology and show how it could have economic implications.

Overall, some good material but some irrelevant and some not sufficiently developed.

Section A Social influence

Answer all questions.

1 Which **two** of the following are factors affecting conformity investigated by Asch? *(2 marks)*

A agentic state C task difficulty

B locus of control D unanimity

C and D

2 Read the item below and answer the question that follows.

> When David started university he believed that the UK should have nuclear weapons. However, nearly all of the new friends he made were against this idea. David felt under pressure to conform so would say that he was also against nuclear weapons. By the time David graduated three years later, he strongly believed that the country should disarm and would even organise protests against nuclear weapons.

Referring to the above item, explain the difference between compliance and internalisation. *(6 marks)*

Compliance is when an individual accepts influence because they hope to achieve a favourable reaction from those around them. When David started university he was not really anti nuclear weapons but pretended to be – probably because he wanted to fit in with his new crowd and be accepted by them. Internalisation is different from compliance because now individuals' public and private beliefs match. It seems like David was influenced by his friends over time so that he came to change his beliefs about nuclear weapons. This means that he goes on protests with them not because he has to but because he actually wants to.

3 **(a)** Outline **one** of Milgram's findings from his research into obedience. *(2 marks)*

Milgram found that location affected obedience levels. When participants were expected to shock another apparent participant, they were more likely to do this when the experiment took place in a university building rather than a run down office.

(b) Briefly explain **one** limitation of this finding. *(2 marks)*

One limitation is that Milgram only studied males in when carrying out his experiment in both locations. This means his findings may be gender biased as the levels of obedience that he found may not generalise to women who may obey more or less than men.

Examiner's comments

1 This simple recognition task should be straightforward but there are still ways in which mistakes can be made. The question asks for two factors so more or less than this will obviously affect the marks. Although all of the terms will be familiar, you need to focus on those that affect conformity.

This answer would get both available marks.

2 This kind of question requires you to apply your knowledge and understanding to a novel situation (in the item). You will have learned about what compliance and internalisation are, and hopefully how they are different. You then need to think about this in the context of the David and use information from the item to help you to illustrate your point.

This answer includes two clear statements that tell us what compliance and internalisation are. More importantly, the statement about internalisation draws out a comparison between the two concepts which addresses the part of the question that says 'explain the difference'. The example of David is also used to emphasise this difference where it talks about a change in his beliefs. Overall, the item is used effectively with the candidate going beyond the information to suggest why conformity may happen in this context. All six marks would be awarded.

3 **(a)** When asked for one set of findings it best to think about them in terms of separate studies. If a study finds out a number of things, then it may be possible to separate these things out. As the question only asks about findings there is no need to go into detail about the procedure. Although this sometimes helps to make sense of the findings, you can assume that the examiner knows about the procedure already – especially Milgram's research is referred to on the specification. This answer looks at the findings from one study. There is no need to explain in detail why one participant is shocking another (as it really relates to procedure). What is important is that a relevant factor affecting obedience (location) is identified and then explained, with accuracy, how it did in the context of Milgram's research. Both marks would be awarded – one for a relevant factor and one for the explanation.

3 **(b)** This part of the question continues to focus on findings so it is important that the answer does too. It is acceptable to consider limitations of how the research was carried out but then you would have to think about how this impacts on the findings thereafter. Also note that only one limitation is required so choose carefully. For example, ethical issues may be difficult to relate to the findings. This answer focuses on a relevant limitation. The problem starts with the sample but then the candidate goes on to explain how this has a bearing on the findings. The point has been expanded on well with good use of terms such as 'gender bias' and 'generalise'.

4 Describe and evaluate **one** dispositional explanation of obedience. *(12 marks)*

Dispositional explanations of obedience look inside of the individual to understand obedience rather than assuming that people obey because of the situation.

One type of personality associated with obedience is the authoritarian personality. Adorno et al. used the F scale to measure the different components that made up the authoritarian personality. This questionnaire contained statements such as 'Obedience and respect for authority are the most important virtues children should learn' and 'Rules are there for people to follow, not change'. Authoritarian personalities were more likely to agree with these kinds of statements. The theory is that individuals with an authoritarian personality are rigid thinkers, who obey authority, see the world as black and white, and expect rules and hierarchies to be strictly followed.

Adorno et al. also proposed that people who have an authoritarian personality had a particular type of upbringing. They are raised by strict parents who often use harsh punishments when rules are not obeyed. As a consequence, children learn to accept authority unquestioningly, and expect people they see as subordinate to obey them.

Elms and Milgram selected 20 'obedient' participants from Milgram's original electric shock experiments and another 20 'defiant' participants (those who had refused to continue at some point in the experiment). Each participant did the F scale to measure their levels of authoritarianism. Participants were also asked a series of open-ended questions, including questions about their relationship with their parents during childhood. Findings showed 'obedient' participants had higher levels of authoritarianism compared to 'defiant' participants. Obedient participants saw the experimenter in Milgram's original study as clearly more admirable, and their fellow participant (who they were shocking) as much less so. They also found that 'obedient' participants reported being less close to their fathers during childhood, and were more likely to describe them using negative terms compared to 'defiant' participants. It is difficult to know how reliable retrospective data it especially when it comes through self-report. The qualitative nature of the interview data also means it is open to interpretation.

Research by Middendorp et al has suggested that education is more significant in determining the authoritarian personality than parenting styles. They found that less educated people are consistently more authoritarian than well educated people.

Altemeyer refined the concept of the authoritarian personality by identifying a cluster of three of the original personality variables that he referred to as 'right-wing authoritarianism' (RWA). They are: conventionalism; submission to legitimate authority; aggressive feelings toward people who break norms. Altemeyer tested the relationship between RWA and obedience in an experiment where participants were ordered to give themselves increasing levels of shock when they made mistakes on a learning task. There was a significant correlation between RWA scores and the level of shocks that participants were willing to give themselves. Of course, a correlation can be interpreted in a number of ways. Obedient behaviour may dictate people's judgement of their personality rather than it being the other way around.

A key feature of the authoritarian personality is their support of right wing politics. On this basis, we would expect left wing people to demonstrate lower levels of obedience. This has strong support from a study conducted by Begue et al. They replicated Milgram's study as part of a mock game show, where contestants had to deliver fake electric shocks to other contestants. Interviews showed that the more participants defined themselves as left wing, the lower the intensity of shocks they agreed to give to the other contestant.

Of course, dispositional explanations ignore the effects of situation. If we look at the vast numbers of participants whom obeyed in Milgram's experiments, it seems unlikely that so many of them shared the same personality or indeed had similarly harsh upbringings. It seems more likely to have been a consequence of the situation that Milgram set up that in turn influenced a range of personalities to obey.

An obvious compromise is to consider that obedience is a result of both dispositional factors and situational factors. It could be that certain people are raised in a way that makes them more prone to following orders and this will then happen if they are put in a situation where they feel compelled to obey.

Examiner's comments

4 This essay question asks for just one explanation of obedience so offering any more causes problems for the examiner. They would normally try to credit the first one offered – which may not be the best one! More importantly, it is a waste of your time to describe others. However, it is appropriate to use other explanations in an evaluative way by drawing comparisons and using them to generate criticisms.

This essay wants you to discuss a dispositional explanation of obedience. This is likely to be the theory of authoritarian personality as it's the one on the specification. Describing it earns AO1 marks and there are six of these on offer. The remaining six are AO3 marks. This can be earned through use of evidence, criticising your chosen explanation and considering alternative explanations, for example.

This answer gives a detailed and accurate description of the theory behind the authoritarian personality. It outlines the personality type as well as the reasons for its development. Including relevant research is a good way of bolstering the AO1 content and when this evidence is used (to draw a conclusion, to support an idea) it begins to earn AO3 marks as well. Note how this candidate evaluates some of the evidence but when they do, they link it back to the theory which is important to ensure they get credit for it. Other AO3 marks come from criticising some of the assumptions of the theory as well as considering situational factors as an alternative. The essay is well balanced between the two skills and it is impressive that they are integrated throughout the answer giving it a sophisticated structure. The essay has substance and depth, making it easy to award a top band mark. This answer would score 12/12.

Section B Memory

5 Which of the following types of memory is being used in each of the examples below? Choose one type of memory that matches each example and write A, B or C in the box next to it.

Use each letter once only. *(2 marks)*

A Episodic memory

B Procedural memory

C Semantic memory

• Daniel remembers how to mow the lawn without consciously thinking about it. [B]

• Danielle remembers how upsetting it was when she once destroyed a flower bed when mowing the lawn. [A]

6 Name **two** components of the working memory model. *(2 marks)*

Central executive and visuo-spatial sketchpad.

7 Read the item below and then answer the questions that follow.

A psychologist investigated whether it was easier to recognise faces when in their normal configuration than when the faces' features were scrambled. Participants had to identify ten faces they had been shown before from a set of 30 faces. Some participants chose from scrambled faces while others chose from normal faces. The psychologist recorded how many they correctly identified, and the results are shown in **Table 1**.

Table 1 The number of faces correctly identified (out of 10) for scrambled faces and normal faces.

Condition 1 (Scrambled faces)	5 7 3 3 4 1 0 5
Condition 2 (Normal faces)	6 0 7 8 9 8 7 8

(a) Calculate the median for Condition 1. Show your workings. *(2 marks)*

0 1 3 3 4 5 5 7

(3 + 4) /2 = 3.5

Median is 3.5 faces.

Examiner's comments

5 This question has three feasible answers to choose from so it's important that you can distinguish between your different types of long term memories. It is especially easy to confuse episodic and semantic because most events are also fact!

B is the right answer because the first statement refers to mowing the lawn which is a procedure and there is also a reference to it being unconscious which is specific to procedural memory.

A is the right answer because the second statement refers to an event (or episode) and there is also a reference to time (once) and place (when mowing the lawn).

6 With this question, it is important to distinguish between the features of the model (a phrase used in the specification) and the components. Features of general ideas are important in the model or theory (e.g. the idea of parallel processing) whereas components are distinct parts that make up the model. Try to get the names of these exactly right. Sometimes the components get named differently in other sources (e.g. visuo-spatial scratchpad) but it's best to stick with the terms in the specification.

Both the components would be creditworthy with the other two obvious ones being the phonological loop and the episodic buffer. There is no need for full sentences with a question like this and definitely no need to go into any detail.

7 (a) This is one of the questions that also tests your mathematical skills albeit in the context of Psychology. Read questions like this carefully to make sure you are carrying out calculations on the right set of data – the data from Condition 1 in this case. There will be one mark for a correct answer but also one mark for workings. So even if it's obvious to you what the answer is – show your workings. Also if your workings are right but you make a mistake at the end, you can still get one of the two marks.

Here the workings – putting the scores in order, finding the middle two, and working out their average – would get one mark. The median itself is also correct, so that's the other mark.

(b) Explain why the median is a better of measure of central tendency compared to the mean in this study. *(2 marks)*

The median is not affected by anomalous scores unlike the mean which can be skewed by this. If a mean had been used in Condition 2 then the score of zero would have seriously affected the average but the median essentially ignores it as it focuses on what is happening in the middle of the data set not at the extremes.

8 Outline **one** strength and **one** weakness of the cognitive interview as a technique for improving the accuracy of eye witness testimonies. *(4 marks)*

One strength of the cognitive interview is that it is based on empirical evidence which has investigated how the human mind works. Therefore it has been designed to enhance memory for an event rather than disrupt the recall process as the standard police interview used to.

One weakness of the cognitive interview is that any benefits may not be due to the technique itself. Because the cognitive interview lasts longer than a standard interview and allows the witness to talk more, the improved recall may simply be a result of people getting more attention which motivates them to remember better.

9 Briefly evaluate retrieval failure as an explanation of forgetting. *(4 marks)*

A strength of retrieval failure as an explanation is that supported by a wide range of evidence from laboratory experiments through to anecdotal evidence. Many people will actively use cues in real-life to help them recall something – for example, retracing footsteps to locate where a lost item was left. Critics of the explanation say that encoding specificity principle (which is part of the explanation) relies on a circular argument i.e. if a cue leads to the retrieval of an event or fact then it must have been encoded in memory but if it doesn't then it can't have been encoded. This makes this part of the explanation impossible to disprove which means it lacks scientific rigour. One obvious issue with the explanation is that it assumes all information is available if it not retrievable. This ignores the fact that information may be unavailable, For example, it may have decayed through disuse.

10 Describe the multi-store model of memory. *(8 marks)*

The multi-store model is a model that focuses on the effects of time and space on memory. The basic idea is that memory comprises a number of separate and distinct stores that differ in terms of duration and capacity, and where data is in the systems determines whether it is remembered or forgotten.

The model states that memory needs an input which comes directly from the environment via the senses. Once this data is encoded, it enters a store known as the sensory register. Although the capacity of this store is very large (as it has to hold all available data in the immediate environment) its duration is very short – a matter of seconds. If data is not paid attention to in this time, then it will not go any further and decay. This means if someone has just spoken to you, and you have not attended to what they said, then it will disappear from sensory register. However, if you 'catch' what they said within two seconds or so, then there is a chance of sending the information on.

The next stop for data is the short-term memory. As its name suggests, its duration is quite limited – data will decay in about 15 seconds. However, if it is rehearsed, the data can last longer. The short-term memory also has a limited capacity, coping with seven chunks of data (on average) at any one time. If this short-term memory is overloaded then some of the data will be lost through displacement. Like the sensory register, the short-term memory mainly uses modality specific coding where data is stored in the same mode as it entered but some visual data (words, letters, numbers) are coded acoustically.

The final store in the model is the long-term memory where only some data ends up. To get there, data needs to go through more elaborative rehearsal. Once in long-term memory, most data is stored using a semantic code as it is an abstract form. The capacity and duration of this store is said to be unlimited.

Examiner's comments

7 (b) This is a typical research methods question. You have to demonstrate your knowledge of an idea or process from research methods and then apply it to the study described in the item. Note how you are supposed to know the pros and cons of different measures of central tendency as well as knowing what they are and how to calculate them.

This answer correctly identifies a strength of the median over the mean and then makes a good job of using data from the item to illustrate the point. Easily worth the two marks available.

8 When a question asks for one strength and one weakness make sure that is all you give. It also helps to label which is the strength and which is the weakness so that the examiner can credit you accordingly. Writing about strengths can actually be quite challenging as if they are not done properly they can just read like a description of whatever is being evaluated. Be clear on why something is a strength to avoid this.

This answer clearly deals with both a strength and a weakness, and both are elaborated on. Note how the strength has been explained so that it sounds like more than just a feature of the cognitive interview. The weakness is more straightforward as it is obviously highlighting something that is wrong with the technique. The candidate would be credited all four marks.

9 This question requires you to get straight on with evaluating an explanation; there is no expectation that you describe the explanation although you may possibly highlight features you want to evaluate. Marks can be earned by covering a number of points but it is safer to focus on a few and explain them well to give depth.

This answer has a good balance of positive and negative commentary, although this is not necessary. Many candidates find it easier to just criticise a theory or explanation which is fine. The thing to note is that the points are well developed demonstrating this candidate's understanding.

10 This high tariff question only requires description but this means it needs to be a good level of description offering both breadth and depth. The structure and the quality of communication are important too, and this includes using specialist terminology. Responses like this benefit from planning. Think about all the details you want to include and think about a logical order to present them in.

This answer has a very clear structure. It starts with an overview of the model and then takes the reader through the proposed memory system in a very logical order. Each paragraph is dedicated to a different store in the model, and here the candidate outlines the key features of that store. Because they focus on the capacity, duration and coding throughout, it is also easy to see the differences between the stores. A strong response worth all eight marks.

Examiner's comments

Section C Attachment

11 Name two of the countries studied by van Ijzendoorn in his research into cultural variations in attachment. *(2 marks)*

Japan and Germany.

11 It is possible to get very fact based questions like this. However, they can only be asked about studies that are listed in the specification not any study. There are certain details you should be expected to know about a study and since this one is famed for its cross cultural research, it makes sense that you should know some of the key countries analysed.

The answer would get both marks. Germany is identified as 'West Germany' in the actual study but the candidate would not be penalised for missing this.

12 Outline **two** limitations of Ainsworth's research into the 'Strange Situation'. *(4 marks)*

One limitation of this research is that it relies on observing behaviours that are open to interpretation. Because Ainsworth started with the idea of there being different attachments types, she and her fellow researchers may have been biased in how they viewed quite subjective behaviours such as willingness to explore and level of anxiety.

Another limitation was the infants and carers were only from middle class families. There is evidence that there is a cultural element to attachment behaviours and this would apply to different classes of people within a culture. Because of potential differences in things such how educated parents are or how much time they have available to play with infants, the results may not be representative of lower classes.

12 This question asks for two limitations so do make sure that they are clearly separated from each other in your answer. Also think through all of the limitations you could use, and choose two where there is no overlap (e.g. don't do two about sample bias if you can avoid it) as this will increase your chance of getting full marks for each limitations. Here you would assume that each limitation is worth two marks.

This answer offers two distinct limitations – one that focuses on the research method used and one the focuses on the sample of participants. The first limitation uses a generic limitation of doing an observation but then earns the second mark by cleverly applying it to the Ainsworth study. The second limitation starts by identifying the issue (the bias in sampling) and then earns the second mark by explaining why this bias is an issue. All four marks would be awarded in total.

13 Read the item below and answer the questions that follow.

> A psychologist compared two groups of adolescent participants who either had secure or insecure attachments as infants. He used a questionnaire to identify their attachment type but also to rate the quality of their friendships. The higher the rating, the more positive the friendships were for the participant. The results of the study are shown in **Table 2**.
>
> **Table 2** The median rating for quality of friendships for participants with secure attachments in infancy and those with insecure attachments.
>
> | | Secure | Insecure |
> |---|---|---|
> | Median rating for quality of friendship | 12.1 | 10.3 |

(a) Explain why this study is an example of a quasi experiment. *(2 marks)*

A quasi-experiment has an independent variable like every experiment but it is not directly manipulated by the experimenter. The IV here is whether infant attachments are secure or insecure. The researcher obviously has no control of this as attachments have happened already in participants' childhoods.

(b) Outline one limitation of using a questionnaire to collect the data in this study. *(2 marks)*

One limitation of using a questionnaire is that self-report relies on respondents having certain qualities like honesty, insight and (in this case) good memories. The findings may not be valid if the teenagers have not accurately remembered their infant years, or they may be tempted to give socially desirable responses to answers because they don't want the researchers to know their friendships are not very positive.

13 (a) The question is essentially in two parts. First it is assessing whether you know what a quasi-experiment is with the emphasis on the 'quasi' part. Then, you have to apply this knowledge to the item by extracting the relevant information.

The answer correctly defines a quasi-experiment and then finds the independent variable in this study to show that it is not open to manipulation. Both marks would be awarded for this answer.

13 (b) This question relies on you knowing a limitation of a questionnaire and then applying it to the study in the item. This is where the two separate marks come from. You may know a number of limitations of using questionnaires so choose one which fits best with the study that has been described – look carefully at what is measured in the questionnaire.

This answer looks like it deals with a number of limitations but the candidate has been clever in terms of introducing the limitation as 'relies on respondents having certain qualities'. Although quite a weak statement in itself it is broad enough to include a number of issues which the candidate then goes on to explore (rather successfully) in the context of the study. Both marks would easily be earned here.

(c) Sketch a bar graph to show the median ratings for quality of friendships in **Table 2**. *(4 marks)*

A bar graph to show the median rating for quality of friendship depending on the type of infant attachment.

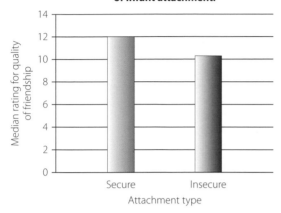

A bar graph to show the median rating for quality of friendship depending on the type of infant attachment.

14 Explain how reciprocity and interactional synchrony are involved in caregiver–infant interactions. *(4 marks)*

Reciprocity describes the situation where caregivers and infants move in rhythm with each other by coordinating their actions so that they almost take it in turns to coordinate their actions. The regularity of an infant's actions allows the caregiver to anticipate the infant's behaviour and respond appropriately. It is this sensitivity to the infant's behaviour which lays the foundations for later attachment.

Interactional synchrony is closely related to the above and happens when infants (even very young ones) imitate the facial expressions and other gestures made by the caregiver. This is seen as the start of the infant beginning to experience as others do which becomes crucial in later life for developing empathy – an important part of any healthy attachment to another.

Examiner's comments

13 (c) The number of marks awarded for a graphical display varies depending on the demand of the question. It is affected by factors such as how much data has to be plotted and how difficult scales are, and so on. This question gives a 'head start' by telling you which graph to use whereas another similar question may not. Always assume there is a mark for a title and for labelling the axes, as well as at least one for sketching the graph itself with some accuracy. Get everything as right as you can with no errors and then you should earn all of the marks!

This answer has a clear title which includes both variables being measured so this would get one mark. The y-axis uses a scale and so this is judged too, to make sure it is appropriate. The scale is spread enough to show the differences between the bars – a scale with the numbers to close together may not show this. The scale also allows the candidate to display scores to one decimal place easily. In short, the scale would get a second mark. The two axes have clear and accurate labels which would get a third mark. Finally, the bars are drawn accurately (they are separate and reach the right place on the scale) so this would get the fourth mark.

14 The question refers to two separate (but related) concepts. However, it is like having two questions really as there is no requirement to consider them alongside each other e.g. by looking for a difference. It makes sense to assume you'll get two marks for what you know about one, and then the other. To secure two marks for each, you would need to be clear about how they are involved in caregiver-infant interactions.

The answer deals with both concepts separately, and more importantly, equally. This balanced answer does the same with both concepts – describes what they refer to and then goes on to explain their role in developing attachments. Therefore, this answer would earn four marks in total.

15 Briefly discuss one of Harlow's animal studies on attachment. *(6 marks)*

Harlow did an experiment on eight infant monkeys who had been separated from their mothers. Instead, they had the choice of two wire 'mothers'. One had a head and was also wrapped in a soft cloth, the other just had a head. The infant monkeys were also able to be fed by the mothers as they had a milk bottle attached to them. For four of the monkeys the milk bottle was on the cloth-covered mother and for the other four it was on the other mother. The monkeys were observed for 165 days. Findings showed that all eight monkeys spent most of their time with the cloth-covered mother whether or not this mother had the milk bottle. Those monkeys who fed from the wire mother would only spend a short amount of time getting milk and then returned to the cloth-covered mother. When they were scared, all of the monkeys clung to the cloth covered mother and when playing with new objects the monkeys often kept one foot on the cloth-covered mother apparently for safety. These findings suggest that infants do not develop an attachment to whoever feeds them but to the whoever is offering comfort. Harlow continued to study these monkeys as they grew up and saw many consequences of their early attachment experiences. He found that these orphaned monkeys, even those who did have contact comfort, developed abnormally. They were socially abnormal e.g. they froze or fled when approached by other monkeys. They were also sexually abnormal – they mating behaviour was unusual and they did not cradle their own offspring when they had them.

Although Harlow did his research on monkeys, he generalised his findings to humans suggesting we attach more to people who comfort us than those who feed us. He also suggested that adults with problem behaviours may have experienced deprivation like the monkeys. However, critics would say that humans are more complex than monkeys and therefore the findings are unrepresentative of human attachments. Although Harlow used monkeys to get around the ethics of studying deprivation, others still argue that what he did was unethical because it still caused distress for the monkeys, including long-lasting negative effects. There was also a problem with the way the experiment was set up. The two wire monkeys had different types of head which can be seen as a confounding variable. Did the infant monkeys prefer the comfort offered by the cloth covered mother or is it possible that they simply preferred her head?

Example Paper 2

Section A Approaches in Psychology

Answer all questions.

1 Which **one** of the following divisions of the nervous system is made up of the brain and spinal cord? *(1 mark)*

A Autonomic nervous system   C Peripheral nervous system

B Central nervous system   D Somatic nervous system

B

2 Name the type of neuron that forms synapses with muscles. *(1 mark)*
Motor neuron

3 Read the item below and then answer the question that follows.

> Jasmine is a girl who has inherited a disorder that will potentially affect her verbal ability in the future. However, her parents have worked hard to stimulate her development in this area and psychologists are amazed with the progress she is making.

Distinguish between the concepts of genotype and phenotype. Make reference to the case of Jasmine as part of your answer. *(4 marks)*

Genotype refers to the genetic code that is written into someone's DNA whereas phenotype refers to how the genotype expresses itself in outward behaviour and other characteristics. This is partly dependent on how genes interact with the environment. We can see this in the case of Jasmine. Her genotype has determined that she has inherited a disorder affecting her verbal ability but the input from her parents means it may not express itself so severely. The extent of her disorder when it comes to speech and communication is the phenotype.

Examiner's comments

15 A question that asks you to discuss a study will have a number of AO1 marks reserved for you to first describe the study. The remaining AO3 marks are for evaluation. The fact the command is 'briefly discuss' tells you that not much evaluation is required so you would assume the six marks are divided into four AO1 marks and just two AO3 marks. When describing a study – and note only one is asked for – make sure that you cover both procedure and findings. There is a tendency for some candidates to miss out the findings – the crucial part!

This answer has a good balance of description and evaluation although three evaluation points is probably unnecessary for just two AO3 marks – especially since the points are quite well developed. The description of the study is appropriately detailed with the main features accurately covered – it is very clear what Harlow did and what he found out. This answer would definitely earn all six marks.

1 All of the options are feasible answers in the sense that they are all genuine nervous systems (and all named on the specification) so you do need to know how they differ – in this case, in terms of their component parts.

B is the right answer as the others a part of the same but separate nervous system.

2 This question shows that you need to know the names of different types of neurons as well as their function. Structure is important too but not relevant to this question.

Motor neuron is the right answer with the clue being a reference to muscles which are obviously involved in movement.

3 There is quite a lot to get right with a question like this. First, you need to know what genotype and phenotype are, and then also make some kind of distinction between them. When this is done, there are further marks to applying this understanding through use of the item.

This answer earns all of the marks available. The candidate states what genotype and phenotype are whilst making a distinction between them at the same time. This would earn the first two marks. Then the case of Jasmine is used effectively to show how genotype and environment can interact (worth one mark) and how this impacts on phenotype (which is worth another mark).

4 Read the following item and then answer the question that follows.

> Rory looks up to his older sister Rosie, and tries to copy many things he sees her doing. Rory is particularly keen to be as sporty as her as he sees that their parents give her lots of praise and attention for this. Rosie is also aware that Rory pays a lot of attention to what she does so she is always careful to play fair when she knows that he is watching.

With reference to social learning theory, explain Rory's sporty behaviour. *(6 marks)*

Rory clearly identifies with his sister Rosie, and social learning theory would label her his role model. This is why he tries to imitate certain behaviours that he observes his sister modelling. Rory is particularly motivated to imitate Rosie because of the process of vicarious reinforcement. This is when we observe someone being rewarded and we imitate them in the hope of being rewarded to. In this case, Rory is also seeking praise and attention from his parents suggesting that it is lacking at the moment. Rosie seems to be aware that she is role model for Rory which is why she consciously plays fair – however, sometimes modelling is a more unconscious process. In time, we might expect Rory to become a sporty individual too, if he has the capacity. At some point the behaviours will become internalised so that he is not seeking rewards all of the time.

5 Describe and evaluate the cognitive approach in psychology. *(12 marks)*

The cognitive approach focuses on information process as in the ways that humans input, store and output data and how this guides our behaviour. Information is transformed and transferred through processes such as attention, decision making and retrieval. These processes cannot be directly observed which is an issue for this cognitive approach – especially when it tries to do so in a scientific way through controlled experiments. Critics claim that mental processes are too subjective to be investigating using objective means.

Schemas are a key part of the cognitive approach where a schema is a mental framework for organising and interpreting data. There are schemas for specific events or specific roles – and these amount to a set of expectations based on past experiences. For example, a person will use a schema when meeting their new GP for the first time as they will have certain expectations of how a doctor should . Schemas allow us to filter out unnecessary data and focus our attention on what we need to know. Of course, there is sometimes a danger that schemas dictate what we perceive or recall – rather than what we actually sense. On this basis, the cognitive approach has made useful contributions to the field of eye witness testimony and to research into prejudice. The assumption is that key details can be missed or forgotten if they do not fit in with a schema. However, others argue that these kinds of details are more easily processed because they challenge a person's schema.

Computer models are commonly used within the cognitive approach. For example, they are used to test parts of the mind to do with memory or language development. The development of computer hardware and software has allowed this approach to test out its theoretical models on computers. If a computer behaves as a human does, e.g. forgets like a human – then the model is valid. However critics have argued there is no value in comparing humans and computers, as humans are more unique and much more complex. Humans also operate in an emotional and social context that is not relevant to computers.

A general criticism of the cognitive approach centres on its attempts to apply scientific principles to the human mind. Laboratory experiments are often used yet may lack ecological validity as the human mind may function differently under artificial conditions e.g. no distractions. Or if people are aware of being investigated (as they often are in experiments) this may affect the very thing that is being studied – their conscious thoughts. The scientific approach is also seen as too reductionist – as in reducing human thought and experience down to a series of machine like processes. It is also seen as too deterministic in the sense that the structure and functions of the mind are preset meaning the role of free will is not always recognised.

Section B Psychopathology

6 Identify one behavioural characteristic of;

(a) depression

(b) obsessive-compulsive disorder

(c) phobias *(3 marks)*

(a) changes in sleep patterns

(b) repetitive actions

(c) avoiding the feared object/situation

7 Read the item below and then answer the question that follows.

> Ewan was diagnosed with depression having felt overrun with despair for the last twelve weeks. His doctor suggested that the cause of this was the fact that Ewan's long-term partner walked out on him three months ago. After this happened, Ewan convinced himself that he would never find himself another boyfriend.

Using Ellis' ABC model, explain why Ewan is suffering from depression. *(6 marks)*

Ellis ABC model suggests that there are three stages to developing depression with a clear focus on cognition. It starts with an activating event (A) which has the potential to lead to depression. In Ewan's case this would be his partner walking out on him. The event is not enough in itself – it then depends on how a person thinks about what has happened – their belief (B). In Ewan's case, the belief is quite an irrational one as he believes he will never find another boyfriend which seems unlikely. However, it is this belief that dictates the consequences (C) – in other words, what happens next. Because Ewan has dealt with his loss in an irrational way, the consequence is unhealthy emotions which is why he's been diagnosed with depression.

8 Describe **one** research study that supports the behavioural approach to explaining phobias. *(4 marks)*

The most famous study in this area is the one conducted on Little Albert, an 11 month old baby. Albert had previously been tested on a series of objects to see what he feared and did not fear. During this test, he happily played with a white rat. In the actual experiment, a white rat was used to condition a fear response. Every time Albert went to play with the rat, two steel bars were banged together behind making a very loud noise that made Albert cry. This loud noise (an unconditioned stimulus) and the rat (a neutral stimulus) became associated so that after seven trials the rat alone was enough to cause a fear response. In other words, the rat had become a conditioned stimulus and Albert had learned to be afraid of white rats, and in fact other white furry objects.

9 Read the item below and answer the questions that follow.

> A psychologist tested the effectiveness of drug therapy in treating the symptoms of obsessive-compulsive disorder by comparing drugs with a placebo (a fake drug). To do this, she used a matched pairs design.

(a) Identify the independent variable in this study. *(1 mark)*

Whether a drug or a placebo is used.

Examiner's comments

6 As well as testing your knowledge about the separate disorders listed on the specification, this question is also checking that you can distinguish between the different categories of symptoms i.e. behavioural, emotional and cognitive. Remember that behaviour is to do with how people act, emotions are to do with how people feel and cognition is to do with what people think. It is possible that there may be some overlap in characteristics (e.g. anxiety is an emotion common to all three disorders) but it is still best if you can try to come up with distinct symptoms.

This answer has three characteristics which all clearly link to behaviours even if some (sleeping) are more specific than others (repetitive actions). Each one matches the disorders listed (and in the right order!) so three marks would be awarded.

7 On the surface, this looks like quite an easy question to answer. You remember what ABC stands for – write this down and link it to a statement from the item. However, the command word 'explain' is used which suggests a bit more than this is required. Indeed, that is why they are six marks attached to this question. It makes sense to assume that half the marks are for knowing about the ABC model (which conveniently has three parts to it) and then the other half are for applying it to the case of Ewan.

This answer demonstrates good understanding of the model and does more than just name the three stages. There is an outline of each and more importantly clear links are made between them. As the candidate takes the reader through these stages, they extract the relevant information from the item to illustrate the model's ideas. On this basis, the answer would earn six marks.

8 Make sure you take the time to break down questions like this. It sometimes helps to work backwards! So this question is asking about phobias. Then the focus is on explaining (rather than treating phobias). Then it is on behavioural explanations of phobias (as you should expect with this part of the specification) and also it is on a study (rather than the theory itself). Finally the command word is describe – and describing a study means you need to write about what was done and what was found out.

This answer is a sound response – both technical and detailed. The key features of the study are described with accuracy, and information is presented in a logical order so that it is easy to follow. Both procedure and findings are covered given a good overview of the study. This answer would easily earn the four marks on offer.

9 (a) Asking for the independent variable is quite a common question. You are looking for the variable that is being manipulated but remember that in some studies (quasi experiments) it is not directly controlled so look for the two conditions or the thing that is supposed to be having an effect on something else.

This is the correct answer and it is good that the candidate has clearly stated both 'sides' of the IV rather than just saying treatment or even drug/no drug. A mark would be awarded.

(b) Outline **one** advantage of using a matched pairs design in this study. *(2 marks)*

One advantage is that participant variables are reduced compared to an independent groups design. This means that if there is a difference between the symptoms of the two groups of participants it is unlikely to be due to individual characteristics if they've been matched on key factors such as sex, age, type of OCD, severity of OCD, etc.

10 Outline and briefly discuss **two** definitions of abnormality. *(8 marks)*

One definition of abnormality is statistical infrequency. As the name suggests, this adopts a mathematical approach to defining abnormality. Normality is defined by what the majority of people do – there does not have to be an exact number put on this – but it needs to apply to most. This means that what is rare – something that only a small number of people think or do – is abnormal. For example, schizophrenia is abnormal because it only affects about 1% of the population.

One of the problems with this definition is that there is not an exact number that defines the majority or conversely the minority. For example if 95% of a population believe something this more normal than if 55% do – but both are majorities. Another issue is that abnormality is often seen as undesirable but something might be desirable exactly because it is statistically rare – like a photographic memory, or a very high IQ.

Another definition of abnormality is one labelled deviation from social norms. Social norms are expected standards of behaviour which, over time, have been agreed by a society or group. An example in the UK might be queuing. So if someone pushes to the front of a queue this deviates (or breaks from) the social norm and may be seen as abnormal. Conversing with yourself in public is another deviation from social norms which is another reason why schizophrenia may be seen as abnormal. Of course, this definition closely ties with the other one as social norms are often dictated by what the majority do. However, this is not always the case. For example, homosexuality may not be seen as deviating from social norms in certain societies but it may still be a behaviour that only applies to a statistical minority.

Unlike deviation from statistical frequency, social norms does allow desirable behaviour to be classified as normal (because it won't be challenging any of society's rules even if it is rare). However, deviation from social norms relies on more qualitative decisions about behaviours so is open to interpretation. Some might even say that it is open to abuse when it comes to deciding whether someone has a disorder or not because who really decides what is acceptable and what is not?

Section C   Research Methods

Read the item and then answer the questions that follow.

A psychologist investigated the relationship between children's diet and how well they behaved in school. He used a sample of 30 children aged from 5 to 11 years. Participants were randomly selected from children where both the parents and the child's school had agreed to taking part. The psychologist measured diet by asking parents to complete a questionnaire which gave a score for how healthy the child's diet was. The higher the score, the more healthy the diet. He measured behaviour by doing an overt observation of each child, for one hour, in their normal classroom. Using a series of behavioural categories, he counted how many times a child displayed a certain behaviour. The categories were all examples of poor behaviour, so the higher the total score, the worse the classroom behaviour was.

Examiner's comments

9 (b) The trick with this question is to first to identify an advantage of the design (which will get the first mark) and then to see how this applies to the particular study that is being outlined (for the second mark).

It is useful that the candidate has included the design that he is comparing matched pairs to as it helps to qualify the advantage. For example, another advantage is no order effects but this would be in comparison to repeated measures. The candidate has probably chosen the better of these two advantages as it's easier to apply it to the study given the limited information on offer. Two marks would be awarded.

10 This question can almost be treating as two separate ones worth four marks each. Then there would be two marks for outlining a definition and a further two marks for offering some critique of this definition. However, a more sophisticated answer may try to draw the two definitions together in some way even if this is not strictly necessary.

This answer using two definitions taken directly from the specification which is a sensible starting point. Both definitions are outlined with clarity and detail, and the use of examples helps to demonstrate understanding. It is good to see the most of these examples of an obvious psychological context too. There is some comparison of the definitions in the third paragraph (and example of drawing them together) and this kind of analysis should gain AO3 credit. Other AO3 marks come from the more straightforward criticisms which are raised in the second and fourth paragraph. In the last paragraph there is further comparison of the two definitions which helps to give the whole answer more coherency. A strong response worth all eight marks.

Examiner's comments

11 Write a suitable directional hypothesis for this study. *(3 marks)*

There will be a significant negative correlation between children's score for a healthy diet and their scores for poor classroom behaviour.

11 This is a common question which normally carries three marks. You should get a mark for knowing what the hypothesis is generally predicting. However, if you get that completely wrong (in this case, assuming a difference is being predicted) then you automatically lose all marks. This question doesn't just ask for a hypothesis but is more restrictive – asking for a directional hypothesis so this will be part of the assessment. You also need to include the variables in the hypothesis and to secure full marks these need to be fully operationalised. In other words, you can't predict a relationship between diet and behaviour – you need to be specific about how these two variables will be measured. Remember it is also good practice to write hypotheses in the future tense and to include the work 'significant' for statistical purposes.

One mark for predicting a correlation. One mark for making the hypothesis directional through the use of the word 'negative'. One mark for the fully operationalised variables.

12 Outline **one** advantage and **one** disadvantage of using a random sample in this study. *(4 marks)*

One advantage is that random sampling is unbiased so the psychologist cannot be accused of just choosing children who would support his hypothesis.

One disadvantage is that freak samples may be selected by chance so the psychologist may end up with children who do not really represent the population in terms of their diet and/or behaviour.

12 This is a typical question for this topic in the sense that you are asked to evaluate methodology in some way but then also consider this in the context of the study. You need to recall the advantages and disadvantages of this particular sampling technique and then think about how can you apply it to the study in the item.

Two marks for the advantage. A mark would be awarded for the strength in general and then it is just about applied to the study through the reference to children.

Two marks for the disadvantage. A mark would be awarded for the weakness in general and this is applied to the study through reference to the two co-variables being measured.

13 Five of the children in the study were from Year 1. What fraction of children in the sample were from Year 1? Show your workings. *(2 marks)*

5/30

30 divides by 5 (= 6) so same as 1/6

13 You should expect some questions like this where you are essentially being tested on your mathematical skills, albeit in the context of psychology. Read the question carefully. It might be more common to use decimals or percentages in everyday life, but this question is asking for a fraction. Remember your good practice from Maths GCSE – don't just put down your answer, show the examiner how you got to it!

One mark for the correct answer: 1/6.

One mark for the workings. There are 30 children in the sample (see the item) and 5/30 = 1/6.

14 Explain why the psychologist needed the parents to agree to the study taking place. *(2 marks)*

The parents need to consent for ethical reasons. Because primary school children are all under the age of 16 and too young to be able to agree to take part in a study for themselves.

14 This question is not really about this study but is a question testing general knowledge of ethics. Although the word 'ethics' is not in the question hopefully you would recognise that this is what the question is about. However, make sure you focus on a specific ethical issue as it is often too general to state that a study is ethical or unethical.

One mark for recognising that this is an issue of consent, and one further mark for explaining why parental consent is needed.

15 The psychologist used closed questions in his questionnaire. Give **one** strength and **one** limitation of using closed questions. *(2 marks)*

One strength is that it's easy to quantify answers from closed questions and look for patterns. One limitation is that they do not offer much depth in terms of data.

16 Give **one** example of a behavioural category which could have been used in the observation. *(1 mark)*

One category could be 'talking when the teacher is giving instructions'.

17 (a) Briefly explain **one** limitation of using an the observational method in this study. *(2 marks)*

One limitation is observer bias. The psychologists may interpret an action as poor behaviour when someone else may not think it is severe enough to be categorised e.g. shouting out – how do we decide a child is being loud enough to count it as shouting?

(b) Briefly outline how this limitation could have been addressed. *(2 marks)*

One way of addressing observer bias is to use more than one researcher. They would have to agree on what they have observed before deciding on a final score. This makes the score more objective.

The results of the study are shown in the scattergram below.

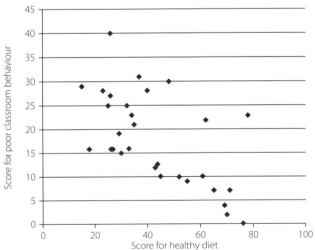

A scattergram to show the relationship between the score for a healthy diet and the score for poor classroom behaviour in a group of primary aged children.

Examiner's comments

15 Like question 12, this is also asking you to evaluate an aspect of the methodology. However, the question is only worth two marks as it does not need to be in the context of the study. Here you can just rely on your general knowledge about the pros and cons of closed questions. Remember to make it clear which is the strength and which is the weakness by heading them up for the examiner.

Both marks would be awarded here as the stated strength and weakness are clear and relevant.

16 This question is testing your knowledge of behavioural categories but through example. It is doing this by putting you in the position of the researcher. You need to make sure you are clear about what is being observed before deciding on a category. Think also about how it would be phrased in a real study.

This answer would earn one mark. It is obviously a relevant category for someone counting incidents of poor behaviour and is phrased in an appropriate way.

17 (a) Watch out, as this is one part of a divided question. Always check the other part(s) before answering. This is particularly relevant here because the second part of the answer relates to the first part. You are going to have to 'solve' whatever issue you come up with me – so try to make sure you choose a limitation where you can suggest a solution.

One mark for the general limitation of observer bias and then a second mark for applying this effectively to the study.

17 (b) This kind of question does put you 'on the spot' and it is not a response you can really prepare in advance. This is one reason why it is useful to do some of your own research as part of your learning so that you feel better equipped to deal with a design question like this.

This is a good answer as not only does it offer a solution which is then put in context but it also goes on to state what the benefit is. This answer would easily earn two marks.

Examiner's comments

18 Describe what the scattergram shows. What would the psychologist conclude from this data? *(3 marks)*

This scattergram shows that there is a strong negative correlation. This means that the children with healthier diets display less poor behaviour.

18 Pay attention to the command word 'describe' here. This shows that you need to give enough detail to earn two marks. With a scattergram that would normally mean writing something about the direction of a correlation and its strength. The second part of the question is specific to the study so there needs to be some reference to the variables being measured.

The first part of the answer would be awarded two marks – one for recognising it is a negative correlation and one for recognise it is strong (as the points a cluster around a relatively straight line). The third mark would also be awarded because it applies the negative correlation to the variables. Importantly, the candidate does not suggest causation in their final statement so would secure full marks.

19 What is the range of the data taking from the observations of poor classroom behaviour? Show your workings. *(2 marks)*

Range = highest score minus lowest score plus 1
= (40 – 0) + 1 = 41

19 Here is another maths question where it is important to show your workings, even if you are able to work out the range 'in your head'. Remember, the range is the difference between the highest and lowest score in a data set. It is also convention to add one so that both scores at the extremes are included in the calculation.

One mark for the right answer, and one mark for showing how it has been reached.

20 Give **one** limitation of using a correlation to investigate diet and behaviour. *(1 mark)*

One limitation is that a researcher cannot establish cause and effect between the two variables they are investigating.

20 The command word is 'give' and only one mark is on offer, so the answer does not have to be that elaborate. Although there is a reference to the variables in the study, the limitation of using correlation will be the same regardless.

This answer would get the mark as it offers the 'classic' limitation of a correlation. Although there isn't an explicit comparison with the experimental method, this is acceptable for just one mark.

Introduction

AO1: descriptive skills (page 9)

How many marks? Alice's answer contains many details (e.g. use of physical punishment; demand strict adherence to social rules) and is all relevant. However, not all elements have been sufficiently detailed, so 5 out of 6 marks. Tom's answer wastes too much time describing the F test and offering unnecessary evaluation so very little relevant description means just 2 out of 6 marks.

AO2: Application of knowledge (page 11)

Amalia's answer: Wastes a lot of time describing 'report everything' but sufficient remaining material for 3 out of 4 marks.

Melissa's answer: Excellent context (reference to stem). The answer does more than use the name 'Chloe' – the steps of the cognitive interview have been shaped to this particular incident (e.g. They could ask 'If you were standing on the other side of the road what would you have seen?'), 4 out of 4 marks.

Pedro's answer: There is an attempt to engage with the stem, but this is rather cursory, and the answer revolves around a general description of two of the techniques, 2 out of 4 marks.

Roy's answer: The reference to the stem is minimal and the answer is not all relevant (final two sentences on schemas), 1 out of 4 marks.

Chapter 1

Topic 1 Types of conformity and explanations for conformity

Choose the right answer: 2E and 5A

Spot the mistakes: [mistakes are in bold; correct material in brackets] Compliance is a form of conformity in which we go along with the group's view and **accept what we are told** (but do not accept what we are told). Our underlying attitude therefore **changes** (does not change). An example of compliance would be if we were pressured by our friends into stealing from a shop, but we didn't want to do that. Internalisation is when we go along with the group's view and accept what we are being told. In internalisation, our underlying attitude also changes. An example of internalisation would be agreeing to go to a party **when we didn't really want to** (and believing that we really wanted to).

Match them up: 1B, 2E, 3C, 4D, 5A

Applying your knowledge: (a) Normative social influence is conforming in order to gain approval or avoid disapproval. Even though he doesn't want to throw a stone, Dave doesn't want to be excluded from his group of friends. By throwing a stone, he will avoid their disapproval (and/or gain their approval), and so he conforms to the majority behaviour.

(b) Pete doesn't know which tube train to get on, and so is guided by the behaviour of others, because he thinks they are right. In informational social influence, we go along with a group because we accept that their perceptions and beliefs are accurate. Presumably, Pete believes the others are going to the match and follows them because he accepts that they must know how to get to Wembley.

Topic 2 Variables affecting conformity

Choose the right answetr: B, E

Drawing conclusions: There are several conclusions that can be drawn from the bar chart. These include:

- There are two factors that affect conformity, namely the size of the majority and the difficulty of the task
- A large majority is most influential with a very difficult task, but still exerts pressure when the task is very easy.
- A small majority has less of an effect than a large majority, although there is slightly more conformity when the task is very difficult compared with when it is very easy.

In order to obtain full marks on a question like this, you will need to draw at least three clear conclusions which make reference to what the chart (or table) shows.

Research issues: One ethical issue that arises in this study is that of **deception**. A second ethical issue is that of **informed consent**. Deception can be dealt with by **debriefing** participants when the study is over, that is, telling them that were deceived during the experiment and explaining to them why the deception was necessary.

Note: On this question the requirement was to 'identify' two ethical issues rather than 'describe' them. Therefore, there is no need to go beyond simply naming the ethical issues. However, if you are asked to 'describe' ethical issues, then you will need to explain what the ethical issue is. For example, informed consent 'is when participants are given comprehensive information concerning the nature and purpose of a study and their role in it. This is necessary in order that they can make an informed decision about whether to participate.' Deception 'occurs when a participant is not told the true aims of a study.'

Key words: Variable 2 Task difficulty. Key word/phrase 1 More difficult task. Key word/phrase 2 Informational social influence. Variable 3 Group size. Key word/phrase 1 Increased group size. Key word/phrase 2 Three.

Suggested answer: One variable that affects conformity is **unanimity**. Research shows that if one person in the group shows **dissent**, then conformity is **decreased**. A second variable that affects conformity is **task difficulty**. If the task becomes more **difficult**, conformity is increased, probably due to **informational social influence**. A third variable is **increased group size**. Asch found that with **three** confederates, conformity occurred 33% of the time, but that further increases in group size did not lead to more conformity.

Applying your knowledge: In part (a), Mark is being affected by the group's unanimity. When one of the team suggests 'Kathmandu', the other team members agree, and the group is unanimous that this is the correct answer. Research shows that people conform more when the group is unanimous. Mark is probably being affected by this, and perhaps does not want to give a different answer for fear of disapproval from the unanimous group members.

In part (b), the group's unanimity is broken by the appearance of a team member who suggests **the same** (correct) answer as Marks'. This **increases Mark's confidence** that he is correct and **breaks the unanimity of the group. There is now less pressure for him to conform.**

Topic 3 Conformity to social roles

Choose the right answer: A, D

Match them up: 1A, 2D, 3C, 4B

Spot the mistakes: [mistakes are in bold; correct material in brackets] Zimbardo's study is important because conformity to social roles can also be seen in the real-world. At Abu Ghraib, the guards were abusive towards the prisoners even though **the guards were accountable for their behaviour** (the guards were not accountable to higher authority) However, Zimbardo's study raises important ethical issues. One of these **is deception, because the prisoners did not know what the study was about**. (Deception was not an issue in this study, because participants were told the explicit purpose of the study). Another criticism of Zimbardo's study is demand characteristics. A study has shown that when given details about the procedure, students who were unfamiliar with the study were able to correctly predict how the prisoners and guards would behave. However, one strength of Zimbardo's study is that it has been replicated by Haslam and Reicher in a simulated prison setting in Britain. (Haslam and Reicher did not replicate Zimbardo's findings in their study, and so this could be argued to be a weakness of Zimbardo's study).

Applying your knowledge: Mike has been given a position of authority. His social role as a steward is associated with patterns of expected behaviour which he has adopted. He has a visible sign of that authority in the form of a bright yellow high-visibility jacket. In a way, this is similar to the uniform worn by the guards in Zimbardo's study. Mike's 'Aviator' sunglasses make eye contact with him impossible which, again, is similar to the dark shades worn by the guards in Zimbardo's study. Although Mike's job is to ensure that people are safe, he seems to have forgotten that, and has started to behave in an abusive and 'tyrannical' way towards a young boy. The young boy is like one of the prisoners in Zimbardo's study and, because of Mike's behaviour towards him, he has taken on the role as a member of the crowd. He has become depressed and passive, and he feels helpless. His crying is similar to the extreme reactions seen amongst the prisoners in Zimbardo's study. Although the boy wants to leave, Mike will not allow him to do that, even though the boy is perfectly within his rights to leave the football ground whenever he wants to. During the second half of the game, as a result of Mike's 'increasingly cruel and sadistic' behaviour during the first half, the boy has become 'increasingly passive' and 'accepting of his plight', just as the prisoners in Zimbardo's study did.

Topic 4   Situational variables affecting obedience

Choose the right answer: 1E, 2C, 3D

Drawing conclusions: The chart indicates that in Variation 3 (proximity) there was 40% obedience. In Variation 7 (institutional context) there was about 45% obedience. In Variation 10 (an ordinary man gives orders) there was about 20% obedience.

Spot the mistakes: [mistakes are in bold; correct material in brackets] Research has shown that uniforms can have a powerful impact on how obedient people are. In one study, Bushman found that **people obeyed more when they were told to do something by a person dressed as a business executive compared with when they were dressed in a police-style uniform** (people obeyed more when they were asked to do something by a person dressed in a police-style uniform compared with when they were asked to do something by a person dressed as a business executive). Milgram found that people were more obedient when the experimenter wore a laboratory coat compared with when he was dressed as an ordinary man. Milgram found that compared with his laboratory study, **people hardly obeyed at all** (people obeyed slightly less obediently) when the experiment was conducted in a privately-rented office. However, when Milgram conducted his study in a **police station he found that nearly everyone obeyed the experimenter.** (Milgram didn't conduct any of his studies in a police station!!)

Research issues Four examples of deception are: (1) the participants being told that the study was about the effects of punishment on learning, (2) the drawing of lots being 'rigged' so that one of the participants was always the 'teacher', (3) participants were told that they would be giving electric shocks to the 'learner', and (4) the 'learner' was not genuine, but an actor hired by Milgram to play that role. One other issue that is evident in the passage is informed consent. Because the participants were deceived about the true purpose of the study, they could not possibly have given their 'informed' consent to take part in it.

Applying your knowledge: Mike's bright yellow high-visibility jacket acts as a symbol of legitimate authority given the situation's context. It

functions like the laboratory coat in Milgram's study. When Mike removes his jacket, the crowd do not see his authority as legitimate. This is equivalent to the variation in Milgram's study in which the experimenter did not wear his laboratory coat. Milgram found that obedience was significantly reduced when the experimenter became 'an ordinary man giving orders'. The same thing possibly happens when Mike removes his jacket.

Topic 5   Agentic state and legitimacy of authority

Choose the right answer: B, E

Match them up: 1C, 2B, 3D, 4A

Applying your knowledge (1): The crowd's behaviour can be explained in terms of the legitimacy of authority. In the situation described, the doctor has legitimate authority and this is recognised by the crowd who make way for him in order to allow him to treat the man's ankle. Someone who knows about first aid has more legitimacy than someone who doesn't, so it's unlikely that the crowd would have parted for someone who shouted "Let me through I'm a bank manager". However, someone who is a trained doctor clearly has more legitimate authority than someone who 'knows first aid' but has not been trained as a doctor.

(2) Milgram's agency theory says that when we undergo agentic shift, we move from an autonomous state (in which we see ourselves as being responsible for our behaviour) to an agentic state (in which we see ourselves as an agent for carrying out another person's wishes). Susan does not see herself as responsible for the instruction to wear uniform. Instead, she sees the head teacher as being responsible. As a result, she is in the agentic state, and simply the 'messenger' who is responsible for another person's wishes, hence she says 'don't blame me'.

Topic 6   The authoritarian personality

Choose the right answer: 1E, 2A, 3B

Drawing conclusions: (a) The scattergram shows a positive correlation. (b) A high score on the California F scale is associated with a high score on the obedience measure, or as scores on the F scale increase, they tend to increase on the obedience measure. (c) The main limitation is that causality cannot be inferred on the basis of a correlation alone. Just because a high score on the F scale is associated with a high score on the obedience measure, it does not necessarily mean that changes in one variable are causing changes in the other variable. (d) Counterbalancing prevents order effects. Hopefully, any effect there is of doing the F scale questionnaire followed by the obedience measure questionnaire will be 'counterbalanced' by any effect there is of doing the obedience measure questionnaire followed by the F scale questionnaire.

Spot the mistakes: [mistakes are in bold; correct material in brackets] Adorno proposed that obedience could be explained in dispositional factors. Adorno says that it is a person's personality **and the situation they find themselves in** (Adorno does not talk about situational factors) that causes them to be obedient to authority figures. To measure the Authoritarian Personality, Adorno devised the **California AP-scale.** (California F scale) Authoritarian people are **flexible thinkers** (inflexible thinkers) who see the world in black-and-white terms. They also believe that respect for authority is an important virtue that children should learn. However, authoritarian personalities believe that social rules are **there to be broken** (there to be followed). There is a correlation between scores on Adorno's measure of authoritarianism and how likely it is that people will behave obediently.

Match them up: 1B, 2C, 3A

Applying your knowledge: One way of explaining their differences of opinion is in terms of the authoritarian personality. Authoritarian personalities agree with California F scale statements such as 'Rules are there for people to follow not change'. It is possible that Guy is an authoritarian personality and sees things in 'black and white', whereas Tony may be better educated or to the political left, hence their difference of opinion about the officer on trial.

Topic 7 Resistance to social influence

Choose the right answer: C, D

Drawing conclusions: One finding is that internals (89%) are more likely than externals (14%) to question the caretaker when no reason is given for his instructions. This shows that internals are more likely to resist social influence when told to behave in a certain way. Another finding is that when a reason is given, internals (15%) are just as likely as externals (14%) to follow instructions. This shows that personality does not influence our resistance to social influence provided that a reason is given for us to follow an instruction.

Match them up: 1D, 2A, 3E, 4B, 5F, 6C

Applying your knowledge: (a) Javed has an internal locus of control. (b) Steve has an external locus of control. (c) Steve is **least** likely to resist pressures to conform. Steve has an external locus of **control**. Research shows that people with an external locus of control believe that what happens to them is determined by external factors. Consequently, they take less personal responsibility for their actions and are less likely to display independent behaviour and more likely to accept the influence of others.

Topic 8 Minority influence

Choose the right answer: B, E

Research issues: A control condition provides us with a 'baseline' against which we can compare experimental conditions. In Moscovici et al's study, the researchers needed to know how many of the blue slides were judged to be green when *no* form of social influence was applied. Moscovici et al found that in the control condition no participant referred to the slides as green whereas in the consistent condition 8% of people were influenced to say the slide was green and only 1% in the inconsistent condition.

Spot the mistakes: [mistakes are in bold; correct material in brackets] Moscovici studied minority influence in his slides experiment. A group of six participants were used, but **one of these was a confederate** (two of these were confederates) who was told to always say **blue** (green) even though all the slides were clearly **green** (blue). Moscovici found that the minority influenced the majority about 8% of the time. In another condition, the confederates were told to sometimes call the blue slides green. Conformity decreased to about 1%. Moscovici says that minorities are more influential if they are consistent and that it is important because it suggests to the **minority** (majority) that there must be a reason for holding a view if the **majority** (minority) maintain it all the time. Flexibility is the willingness to be flexible and to compromise when expressing a position.

The exam technique mistake occurs in the last sentence. The question asked for an explanation of one of the factors that affects minority influence. The definition of flexibility is not necessary, and would not receive credit anyway because it is not an explanation!

Applying your knowledge (1):

Finding from **minority influence research**	**Advice** to Estefan
Consistency	Estefan should try to be consistent in his expressed position over time. If he takes this approach, the majority are more likely to consider his position more carefully.
Commitment	Estefan should show that he is committed to his position, because it will suggest certainty, confidence, and courage in the face of a hostile majority. This may then persuade others to take him more seriously, or even convert to his position.
Flexibility	Estefan needs to be willing to compromise when he expresses his position. He must be prepared to negotiate with the majority rather than enforce his position.

Applying your knowledge (2): Sylvia is trying to convert the majority (who do not eat sushi) to her own minority position (of eating sushi every day). Research shows that Sylvia will be more likely to be influential if she behaves consistently and demonstrates commitment in her behaviour. Unfortunately, Sylvia's friends have seen her eating a super deluxe beef burger. If Sylvia behaved consistently, and showed commitment, her friends might have considered her position more carefully. Unfortunately, she didn't, and as a result her friends are unlikely to be persuaded by her.

Topic 9 Social influence processes in social change

Choose the right answer: C, D

Drawing conclusions: One finding is that from 1960 onwards, non-violent minorities have been more successful than violent minorities in bringing about social change. This shows that minorities who adopt non-violent ways of getting their message across are more successful in changing the views of the majority and bringing about social change. A second finding is that the largest difference in percentage success rates for violent and non-violent minorities in bringing about social change is most pronounced in recent years, with 67% of non-violent minorities being successful in the years 2000-2006, whereas in the same period, only 11% of violent minorities were successful in bringing about social change. This shows that as well as factors such as consistency and augmentation being important in whether majorities change the views of the majority, it appears the way in which they do it is also important, with non-violence being more successful than violence.

Match them up: 1C, 2D, 3A, 4E, 5B

Applying your knowledge: (a) One approach Mike could use is a social norms intervention. There seems to be a misperception between how many supporters actually do put their litter in a bin, and how many supporters are *believed* to put their litter in a bin. Mike needs to correct this misperception. Perhaps one thing he could do is put up a sign with a statement such as 'Most supporters don't throw their litter on the ground' or 'Most supporters put their litter in bins'. Research shows that when peoples' misperceptions about the frequency of a behaviour are corrected, their behaviour tends to change. Hopefully, when the supporters had their misperceptions corrected their behaviour would change, making Mike's life a lot easier.

(b) The boomerang effect is an unwelcome problem with social norms interventions. Although such interventions are aimed at people whose behaviour is *less* desirable than the norm, they can also affect those whose behaviour is *more* desirable than the norm. In other words, they can also lead to people who are behaving desirably behaving undesirably. If Paul is correct about the boomerang effect, then the social norms intervention Mike introduced might have the effect of leading to those supporters who already put their litter in the bin throwing it on the ground! Such an effect would, of course, make Mike's job even harder!

Chapter 2

Topic 1 Short- and long-term memory

Choose the right answer:

Definition	Concept
The length of time a memory lasts before it is no longer available.	C
The quantity of information that can be held in memory.	B
The way in which information is changed so that it can be stored.	A

Choose the right answer:

	Short-term memory	Long-term memory
Encoding	Acoustic	**C**
Capacity	7 ± 2	**A**
Duration	**B**	Lifetime

Spot the mistakes: [mistakes are in bold; correct material in brackets] According to Peterson and Peterson (1959) the **capacity** (duration) of short-term memory is approximately 18 seconds, whereas according to Bahrick et al. (1975) long-term memory has a 70% accuracy after **34 years** (48 years). Furthermore, Miller (1956) suggests that the capacity of short-term memory is between 5-9 'chunks' of information, whereas long-term memory is supposedly **limited** (unlimited).

Applying your knowledge: Yasmin has difficulty in remembering her new mobile phone number as the capacity of STM is between 5-9 items. Her mobile number is 11 digits long so exceeds the capacity of STM. She can remember her holiday to Disneyland, however, as the duration of LTM is up to a lifetime.

Topic 2 The multi-store model of memory

Choose the right answer: A, B

Complete the diagram: 1. Sensory register; 2. Maintenance rehearsal; 3. Transfer; 4. Long-term memory; 5. Retrieval.

A marking exercise: AO1: The description of the MSM is quite basic and there are some mistakes, therefore this answer is likely to achieve mark band two. To improve the answer, information in relation to the capacity, coding and duration of the sensory register, short- and long-term memory should be provided. Furthermore, the processes of attention, rehearsal and retrieval should also be included to ensure that maximum marks are gained.

Topic 3 The working memory model

Choose the right answer: E

Spot the mistakes: [mistakes are in bold; correct material in brackets] The working memory model was proposed by **Atkinson and Shiffrin** (Baddeley and Hitch) to resolve some of the issues found with the multi-store model. It consists of separate stores for acoustic and visual information, which are controlled by the **episodic buffer** (central executive).

The central executive directs the brain's resources to one of three the slave systems, which include the phonological loop and the visuo-spatial sketchpad. The phonological loop contains the **articulatory store** (articulatory process) and phonological store. The visuo-spatial sketchpad

contains the visual cache and inner scribe. The purpose of the **inner scribe** (visual cache) is to store visual information.

Applying your knowledge (1):

Identify the psychology	Link to the WMM
Condition 1 (one visual and one auditory task) … the brain's resources are divided between the visuo-spatial sketchpad and phonological loop.	This means that… participants in condition 1 will perform significantly better as the visual task will be directed to the visual spatial sketchpad and the auditory task will be dealt with the phonological loop.
Condition 2 (two visual tasks) … the brain's resources are all being allocated to the visuo-spatial sketchpad.	This means that … the participants in condition 2 will perform less well, as their resources are all being allocated to the visuo-spatial sketchpad and therefore they will struggled to process all of the information at once.

Applying your knowledge (2): Mr Robinson is able to select pictures and listen to music at the time same, because these tasks are occupying different components of his working memory. Listening to music is using his phonological loop, whereas selecting pictures is using his visuo-spatial sketchpad. However, he finds it difficult to type information and talk with his friend, because both tasks require the uses of his phonological loop.

Topic 4 Types of long-term memory

Choose the right answer:

Definition	Concept
A detailed memory of a family holiday to Spain.	A
A memory of how to play the piano.	C
An understanding of different theoretical models of memory, including the multi-store model and working memory model.	B

Fill in the boxes:

Episodic memory is…concerned with personal experience	An example of episodic memory is…a memory of a family holiday.
Semantic memory is… knowledge about the world, which is shared by everyone.	An example of semantic memory is…language and mathematics (abstract concepts).
Procedural memory is… remembering how to do something.	An example of procedural memory is…riding a bike.

A marking exercise: AO1: The answer could be improved by adding the following information: firstly, it could mention that procedural memories are are concerned with skills and typically learned through repetition and practice and secondly, it could mention that these types of memory are automatic and therefore we are less aware of them.

Applying your knowledge: Clive is still able to play the piano and sing; therefore it would appear that he has retained his procedural knowledge, however he is unable to remember a holiday to Australia and therefore it would appear that his episodic memory is no longer intact.

Topic 5 Explanations of forgetting: interference

Choose the right answer:

Definition	Concept
When a person's past learning interferes with their current attempts to learn something new.	B
An explanation for forgetting in terms of one memory disrupting the ability to recall another. This is most likely to occur when the two memories have some similarity.	A
When a person's current attempts to learn something, interfere with their recall of previously learnt information.	C

Research methods:

1. Group A = 5+6+8+7+4+5+6+10+4+5=60. 60/10 = 6.

Group B = 11+15+12+13+19+11+12+15+16+16=140. 140/10= 14.

2. The standard deviation suggests that there is a greater dispersion (variability) of scores for Group B, in comparison to Group A. The larger the standard deviation the more spread a set of scores is about the mean, and therefore it is less representative than a set of scores with a smaller standard deviation. As a result, this may be less useful for the experimenter.

Drawing a conclusion: 1 mark for stating that this is due to retroactive interference. Plus 1 mark for either of the following explanation / elaboration points: 1) because the material is similar in both conditions; 2) new / recently learnt / acquired information has disrupted / interfered with / affected the recall of old / previously learnt / acquired information.

A marking exercise: The answer includes a detailed method section and results. However, the answer is missing a conclusion to achieve 5/6 out of 6. For example, '*These results show that the intervening task produced retroactive interference, because the later task interfered with the previously learned material.*'

Topic 6 Explanations for forgetting: Retrieval failure

Choose the right answer: D

Match them up:

Tulving and Thomson (1973)	Encoding specificity principle
Retrieval cues	Environmental context and/or a person's emotional state
Godden and Baddeley (1975)	Context-dependent learning
Goodwin et al. (1969)	State-dependent learning
Retrieval failure	The inability to access information which is stored in long-term memory.

Research issues: One ethical issue Gooden and Baddeley should have considered is protection from harm. The researchers should ensure that the testing conditions (both underwater and on land) are safe for their participants and do not place any participant at risk of physical or psychological harm. Therefore, they should have checked the underwater locations carefully to ensure that no other divers or boats would be present at the time of testing.

Applying your knowledge: The results of Godden and Baddeley suggest that information is best recalled when it is learned in the same context, or environment, as where it is later recalled. Therefore, the teacher's advice is likely to improve Emmanuel's memory, as learning the information in the room where he is going to be tested, will provide Emmanuel with environmental cues that are likely to help him remember the information.

Topic 7 Accuracy of eyewitness testimony: Misleading information

Choose the right answer: A, D

Drawing conclusions: For example, Finding 1: More participants in the control condition said 'no' there was no broken glass compared with the smashed and hit group. Conclusion 1: This suggests that the leading question about the speed did affect participants' memory of the accident.

Finding 2: The 'smashed' group were most likely to answer 'yes' to the question about broken glass. Conclusion 2: This suggests that the misleading question (suggesting that car was travelling fast) lead them to remember it was a serious accident where there may have been broken glass.

Applying your knowledge: The memory of the event may have been altered as a result of post-event discussion. Research by Gabbert et al. (2003) found that participants who discussed an event went on to mistakenly recall information that they had not witnessed, in a video of a theft. These results suggests that the people who witnessed the Space Shuttle Challenger explode, may have incorporate information from other people who had witnessed the disaster. Consequently, their eyewitness accounts may have been distorted and become inaccurate as a result of post-event discussion.

Topic 8 Accuracy of eyewitness testimony: Anxiety

Match them up:

Johnson and Scott (1976)	Anxiety decreases accuracy of EWT.
Christianson and Hubinette (1993)	Anxiety increases accuracy of EWT.
Pickel (1998)	Surprise decreases accuracy of EWT, not anxiety.
Halford and Milne (2005)	Violent crimes increase accuracy of EWT.

A marking exercise: It got this mark because the information provided about procedure (how) is basic and there is a prediction given rather than an accurate reference to findings.

Examples of further information that could be included would be more procedural detail (e.g. interviews were 4–15 months later, those who were threatened were the bank tellers) and include information about the findings (e.g. all victims had better than 75% recall, bank tellers had the best recall).

Fill in the boxes:

Anxiety reduces the accuracy of EWT One piece of evidence for this is … Johnson and Scott (1976). This suggests that … seeing a weapon increases anxiety and reduces the accuracy of EWT.

Anxiety enhances the accuracy of EWT One piece of evidence for this is … Christianson and Hubinette (1993) This suggests that … victims of a real life bank robbery who were most anxious demonstrated the best recall, suggesting that anxiety improves the accuracy of EWT.

Anxiety may sometimes reduce and sometimes enhance the accuracy of EWT

One piece of evidence for this contradiction is … Bothwell *et al.* (1989)

This suggests that … individual difference may play an important role in accuracy of EWT.

Spot the mistakes: [mistakes are in bold; correct material in brackets] Johnson and Scott (1976) investigated the effect of anxiety on eyewitness testimony. Participants were asked to sit in a waiting room where they heard an argument in an adjoining room and then saw a man run through the room carrying either a pen covered in **blood** (grease) (low anxiety condition) or a knife covered in blood (**low** (high) anxiety, 'weapon focus' condition). Participants were later asked to identify the man from a set of photographs. They found that the man accuracy was **59%** (49%) in the pen condition, compared to 33% in the knife condition. The results suggest that anxiety reduces the accuracy of eyewitness testimony, as the participants who saw the knife (**high** (low) anxiety condition) were less accurate in their identifications.

Topic 9 Improving the accuracy of eyewitness testimony: The cognitive interview

Choose the right answer: B, C

Drawing conclusions: The results suggest that the cognitive interview is more effective in increasing the amount of correct information generated, in comparison to the standard interview (45% in comparison to 32%). However, the results also suggest that the cognitive interview is no different to the standard interview in increasing/decreasing the amount of incorrect information generated (8% in both conditions).

Applying your knowledge: Any two techniques are appropriate. However, the key to this question is that you apply the answer to the extract, for example:

Changed perspective – try to recall the incident from the perspective of the teacher. What do you think she would have seen? Mental reinstatement of the original context – I would like you to think back to the day the man burst into the psychology room. What topic were you studying? What time of day was the lesson? Who were you sitting next to? Etc.

Chapter 3

Topic 1 Caregiver-infant interactions

Choose the right answer: A, D.

Research issues:

- Parental consent – as the researchers are investigating infants they would need to obtain informed consent from the parents, in order to conduct the observation.
- Confidentality – the video recording and data from the observation should be coded and kept confidential and there should be no way of identifying the infants who took part in the research.

Applying your knowledge:

Identify the psychology	Link to Darren and baby Rebecca
interactional synchrony reciprocity	perfectly in time with each other 'Darren smiled, Rebecca smiled back'

Topic 2 The development of attachment

Choose the right answer: B

Drawing conclusions:

Possible answers: 1) The strength of the infants' specific attachment increases steadily/quickly from age 21 to 36 weeks. After week 36 the infants' specific attachment continues to increase, but at a slower rate. 2) The same applies for stranger anxiety, however at a slightly slower rate (in the first 36 weeks).

Match them up:

Indiscriminate attachments	Infants start to show a preference for social stimuli, in comparison to inanimate objects.
The beginnings of attachment	Infants can now distinguish between familiar and unfamiliar people.
Discriminate attachment	Infants form one special attachment and start to show stranger anxiety.
Multiple attachments	After forming one main attachment the infant develops a wider circle of attachments.

A marking exercise:

1) Frodi et al. (1978) found that there are no differences between males and females in terms of attachment.

2) The answer has made two (correct) critical point.

3) The answer could be improved by adding numerous other points: 1) Heermann et al. (1994) found that men are less sensitive to infant cues; 2) However, there are cases when men form secure attachments with their children, which is often found in single (male) parent families; 3) Fathers have an important role as secondary attachment figures and have a more playful and physically active relationships with their children.

Topic 3 Animal studies of attachment

Choose the right answer: A

Spot the mistakes: [mistakes are in bold; correct material in brackets] Lorenz investigated imprinting in **adult** (baby) **geese** and divided his goslings into **three** (two) groups. One group was left with their natural mother, one group was placed in an incubator ~~and one group acted as a control.~~

The group which hatched in the incubator imprinted onto the first moving object they saw which was Lorenz and started following him around. Lorenz then marked the two groups and placed them together again. **All of the goslings started following their natural mother** (One group of goslings followed Lorenz and one group followed their natural mother). This suggests that goslings imprint onto the first moving object they see.

A marking exercise:

1) There are no mistakes in this answer.

2) The student has not outlined the entire procedure, findings or conclusion.

3) The answer could also include the following information: Lorenz marked the two groups (to distinguish them) and placed them together again. Lorenz and their natural mother were present and the goslings quickly divided themselves up, one group following Lorenz and one group following their natural mother. The results suggest that baby geese imprint onto the first moving object they see, which takes place during a critical period.

Topic 4 Explanations of attachment: Learning theory

Choose the right answer: A, C.

Complete the diagram:

1. Food (UCS)
2. Pleasure (UCR)
3. Mother (NS)
4. No response
5. NS and UCS paired
6. NS is now CS
7. Pleasure (CR)

Spot the mistakes: [mistakes are in bold; correct material in brackets] According to learning theory, attachments are formed through classical or operant conditioning. Food is a **neutral stimulus (NS)** (unconditioned stimulus (UCS)) which produces an **unconditioned response (UCR)** of pleasure. During the first few weeks an infant learns to associate the person who feeds them, usually the **father** (mother), with the pleasure from feeding. Through regular association, the mother becomes a **conditioned response (CR)** (conditioned stimulus (CS)), producing a **conditioned stimulus (CS)** (conditioned response (CR)). Learning theorists refer to this newly formed stimulus-response as 'mother love' and suggest that attachments occur through feeding.

Applying your knowledge: According to learning theory, Nathan may become attached to his father Jon, if Jon is providing food. Food is an unconditioned stimulus that procedures and unconditioned response of pleasure. If Jon, who is the neutral stimulus, continually feeds his son Nathan, then Nathan will form an association between his father and the pleasure from being fed. Eventually Jon will become a conditioned stimulus which produces a conditioned response, feelings of pleasure in Nathan, which results in the formation of an attachment.

Topic 5 Explanations of attachment: Bowlby's theory

Choose the right answer: A, B.

Match them up:

Continuity hypothesis	The idea that emotionally secure infants go on to be emotionally secure, trusting and socially confident adults.
Critical period	A biologically determined period of time, during which certain characteristics can develop. Outside of this time window such development will not be possible.
Internal working model	A mental model of the world which enables individuals to predict and control their environment. In the case of attachment the model relates to a person's expectations about relationships.
Monotropy	The idea that the one relationship that the infant has with his/her primary attachment figure is of special significance in emotional development.
Social releasers	A social behaviour or characteristic that elicits caregiving and leads to attachment.

Applying your knowledge:

Identify the psychology		Link to Bowlby's theory
'Big blue eyes and cute round face'	→	This means that … Liza is showing physical social releasers, as looking 'cute' elicits caring behaviours from her mother.
'Crying for my attention'	→	This means that … Liza is showing behavioural social releasers, as crying will also elicit caring behaviours and alert her mother, therefore leading to attention and possibly affection.

Topic 6 Ainsworth's Strange Situation: Types of attachment

Choose the right answer: A, D.

Research issues

The main ethical issues include: privacy and confidentiality, although other considerations such as right to withdraw are also creditworthy.

The researcher would need to ensure that the participants' information was kept confidential. This means that the responses can not be matched to the individual participants. To do this the research could assign each participant a unique number which only the psychologist is aware of. The questionnaires and results would then be analysed in relation to this unique number and not the participants real name.

Activities: suggested answers

Complete the table:

	Secure attachment (Type B)	Insecure-avoidant (Type A)	Insecure-resistant (Type C)
Willingness to explore	High	High	Low
Strange anxiety	Moderate	Low	High
Separation anxiety	Easy to soothe	Indifferent	Distressed
Behaviour on reunion with caregiver	Enthusiastic	Avoids contact	Seeks and rejects

Applying your knowledge:

Ashley is likely to be classified as insecure-avoidant. She is willing to explore the environment, however she is indifferent to separation and avoids contact upon reunion with her caregiver.

Alex on the other hand is likely to be classified as insecure-resistant. She shows low levels of exploration and is distressed when separated from her caregiver. Finally, she angrily resists being picked up upon reunion with her caregiver.

Topic 7 Cultural variations in attachment

Choose the right answer: D.

Drawing a conclusion:

The table shows that secure (type B) attachment is the most common type of attachment in all three countries. Furthermore, the results also reveal that insecure-avoidant attachment is the second most common attachment type and insecure-resistant is the least common attachment type.

Spot the mistakes: [mistakes are in bold; correct material in brackets] One problem with cultural variations in attachment is that many of the results are based on **cultures** (countries) and not individual **countries** (cultures). VanIJzendoorn and Sagi (2001) found a **different** (similar) distribution of attachment in Tokyo to Western countries. Furthermore, they also found that more rural regions had an increase in insecure-resistant individuals, in comparison to less rural regions. This suggests that cultural variations may not be comparing cultures but are in fact comparing different countries.

Applying your knowledge:

Yuna is either likely to be classified and securely attachment or insecure-resistant. Yuna is likely to become distressed when left alone, which may be the result of the traditional Japanese childrearing practices, where the children are rarely separated from their mothers.

Topic 8 Bowlby's theory of maternal deprivation

Choose the right answer: B, C.

Research issues: One issue with the use of interviews is interviewer bias which is a form of investigator effect (1 mark). Interviewer bias may be unconscious, with expectations communicated non-verbally through tone of voice, length of pause etc (1 mark). To avoid interviewer bias, interviewers must be trained to ask the questions in a neutral and consistent way (1 mark).

Applying your knowledge:

Abdul has suffered from emotional deprivation as he lost his parents when he was six months old, which is during his critical period. Abdul was then placed into care where he was unable to form a continuous relationship with a mother substitute. Although he was adopted at the age of 5, this is outside the critical period for attachment and therefore accordingly Bowlby, he would not be able to form an attachment at this stage.

The results of Bowlby (1944) can explain Abdul's aggressive behaviour, as the children who experienced frequent early separation from their mothers were later diagnoses as affectionless psychopaths and experienced no shame or guilt for their delinquent behaviour. Abdul has also experienced early separation and as he was unable to form an attachment with a mother substitute this could have caused his aggressive behaviour.

Topic 9 Romanian orphan studies: Effects of institutionalisation

Choose the right answer: B, C.

Match them up:

Physical underdevelopment	Children in institutional care are usually physically small caused by a lack of emotional care and poor nourishment.
Intellectual underfunctioning	Children who suffer from emotional deprivation often experience poor cognitive development.
Disinhibited attachment	Children do not discriminate between people they choose as attachment figures. Such children will treat near-strangers with inappropriate familiarity (overfriendliness) and may be attention seeking.
Poor parenting	Research has found (Quinton et al., 1984) that women raised in institutions experience difficulties acting as parents in later life, in comparison to women raised at home.

Apply your knowledge:

Identify the research	Link to Alin
Rutter and Sonuga-Barke	*This shows that…children adopted before the age of six months old develop 'normally' by the age of four. As Alin was adopted by 18 months old, he is likely to develop in-line with his peers, by the age of four.*
Le Mare and Audet	This shows that… the effects of institutionalization may disappear over time and any physical underdevelopment found in institutionalized children had improved by the age of 11. Therefore, by the time Alin reaches 11 years old, he is likely to have overcome any physical underdevelopment.

276

Research issues:

One strength of using case studies is that they provide rich and interesting information on a particular topic, which is difficult to examine using other methods. Therefore the researchers would generate lots of information about the effects of institutionalisation on Alin, which have high levels of ecological validity.

However, one limitation of using case studies is that they are difficult, if not impossible to replicate. As Alin is a unique example, it would be difficult to find another 'case' which is exactly the same as Alin and therefore psychologists are unable to replicate the findings to see if the same effects appear in other children.

Topic 10 The influence of early attachment

Choose the right answer: A, D.

Research issues:

One strength of using a questionnaire is that large quantities of data can be collected more easily than other methods, for example interviews. This allows the researchers to examine a larger population of people, in a more cost effective way.

However, one weakness of using a questionnaire is that the participants may answer in a socially desirable way. Participants may be inclined to lie about their early childhood experiences which can affect the validity of the findings.

Fill in the boxes:

Childhood friendships… Securely attached children in infancy score higher in terms of social competence.	**Elaboration…** This was shown in the Minnestoa child-parent study which demonstrates the importance of attachment on childhood friendships.
Poor parenting… Poor attachments can lead to later difficulties with parenting.	This was shown in Harlow's research with monkeys and Quinton et al. who found that the lack of an internal working model means that individuals lack a reference point to subsequently form relationships with their own children.
Romantic relationships Secure attachments can lead to healthy adult romantic relationships, whereas insecure attachments can lead to unstable romantic relationships.	This was shown by **Hazan and Shaver who found a link between early attachment type and later relationships.**
OPTIONAL: Mental health… The lack of attachment during the critical period can result in the lack of an internal working model and 'attachment disorder'.	Attachment disorder is now a condition included in the DSM.

A marking exercise: The student could also explore the link between the internal working model and future parenting relationships. This suggests that negative experiences during childhood influence later parent–child relationships.

Chapter 4

Topic 1 Definitions of abnormality

Choose the right answer: A, D

Spot the mistakes: [mistakes are in bold; correct material in brackets] One **strength** (weakness) of the statistical infrequency definition of abnormality is that it is culture-bound. This means that a behaviour which is statistically frequent in one culture may not be statistically infrequent in another. The diagnostic manuals for mental disorders, such as the DSM, are based on **non-Western** (Western) cultures. However, there are cultural differences in what is normal and abnormal. This means that there **are universal norms** (are not universal norms) for labelling people as abnormal.

Match them up: 1B, 2C, 3D, 4A

Applying your knowledge: (a) One way of defining abnormality is in terms of statistical infrequency. (b) Buckland's eating and drinking behaviour might be considered abnormal because most people do not eat and drink what he did. Because his eating and drinking behaviours are statistically infrequent, he would be defined as abnormal according to the definition given in (a). (c) One limitation of the statistical infrequency definition is that it does not take into account the desirability of a behaviour. Being a 'genius' and having an IQ of 'over 200' are desirable behaviours. However, because they are also statistically infrequent behaviours, they would be defined as abnormal.

Topic 2 Defining abnormality (continued)

Choose the right answer: B and E

Choose the right answer: D and E

Keywords:

Failure to function adequately: Key word/phrase 1 Cope with everyday life. Key word/phrase 2 Personal distress. Key word/phrase 3 Distressing to others. Deviation from ideal mental health: Key word/phrase 1 Jahoda's criteria. Key word/phrase 2 Self-actualisation. Key word/phrase 3 Coping with stress.

Suggested answer: The failure to function adequately definition says that a person is abnormal if they cannot **cope with everyday life**. A person whose behaviour causes them **personal distress** is failing to function adequately. You are also failing to function adequately if your behaviour is **distressing to others**. The deviation from ideal mental health definition uses **Jahoda's criteria** of mental health to define abnormality. One characteristic of ideal mental health is **self-actualisation**. Jahoda says that healthy people achieve this. Another characteristic is **coping with stress**. Jahoda says that mentally healthy people are able to cope with stress.

Applying your knowledge: (a) Sandra was using the failure to function adequately definition of abnormality. (b) One example of a behaviour that might cause people distress or suffering is being unable to get to work, although there are many other examples, of course. (c) One limitation of the failure to function adequately definition is that some apparently dysfunctional behaviour can actually be adaptive and functional for a person, since it brings increased attention for the person (e.g. depression). Again, there are other limitations that could also be used to answer this part of the question.

Topic 3 Mental disorders

Choose the right answer: B and D

Drawing conclusions: (a) Country C, (b) Country A, (c) Country A, (d) Depression (2.1)

Spot the mistakes: [mistakes are in bold; correct material in brackets] The main emotional characteristic of a phobias is a marked and persistent fear of some object or situation. People have **rational** (irrational) thoughts about things and are resistant to rational arguments. Phobics avoid the thing they fear and this interferes with their normal routine **but not** (and) their social activities.

Applying your knowledge: A cognitive characteristic shown by Hughes was his belief that because everybody carries germs the only way he could live longer was by avoiding germs. A behavioural characteristic shown by Hughes was dictating the same phrases over and over again. An emotional characteristic was the distress he felt about being contaminated by germs.

Topic 4 The behavioural approach to explaining phobias

Choose the right answer: A, C

Spot the mistakes: [mistakes are in bold; correct material in brackets] Watson and Rayner (Mowrer) proposed the two-process model to explain the development of phobias. Classical conditioning explains how phobias are acquired. If an initially neutral stimulus such as a white rat is paired with unconditioned **response,** (stimulus) such as a loud noise, then fear occurs. Because the neutral stimulus now produces fear, it has become the conditioned stimulus, and leads to the **unconditioned** (conditioned) response of fear whenever it is presented.

Match them up: 1A, 2B, 4A, 5B. 3 is left over.

Drawing conclusions: (a) Fear of snakes. (b) 6.5 (30.8 − 24.3). (c) 10.5 (34.8 − 24.3). (d) Nominal (data are in separate categories).

Applying your knowledge: (a) Mowrer would say that Stuart has acquired a phobia through classical conditioning. Pain is an unconditioned stimulus that produces an unconditioned response of fear. When the dog was associated with pain (it bit Stuart) it became a conditioned stimulus, and the fear became a conditioned response. Mowrer would explain avoidance behaviour in terms of operant conditioning. By avoiding dog, Stuart's fear is reduced, and is therefore reinforced. This is an example of negative reinforcement.

(b) Watson and Rayner found that Little Albert generalised his fear of the white rat to other objects that were similar to it, such as a fur coat and even Watson wearing a Santa Claus mask. Even though Dave was bitten by a Dalmatian, he is generalising his fear to at least one other breed of dog (Dave's Great Dane).

Topic 5 The behavioural approach to treating phobias

Choose the right answer: A, E

Match them up: 1E, 2C, 3D, 4B, 5A

Drawing conclusions: (a) The results suggest that flooding (76%) is nearly twice as effective as systematic desensitisation (41%) in the treatment of aviophobia. (b) Since flooding does not use a hierarchy whereas systematic desensitisation does, and given that flooding is much more effective, this suggests that it is not necessary for a hierarchy to be used. (c) Because flooding involves exposure to an extreme form of the threatening situation, it can be a highly traumatic procedure. People are told of this before the therapy begins, and the findings in the table suggest that more people are put off by the procedures involved in flooding than those involved in systematic desensitisation.

Applying your knowledge (1): The therapist might begin by either teaching Andrea how to relax using a technique that would allow deep muscle relaxation, or by sending her to somebody else trained in these techniques. Then, the therapist and Andrea would work together to construct an anxiety hierarchy, starting with the least feared situation, such as being in a seminar room on her own, working up to the most feared situation, such as having to speak in front of a room full of students

in the seminar room. The therapist would start by either asking Andrea to imagine the least feared situation or by showing her pictures of an empty seminar room, and helping her to remain relaxed. When that situation no longer produced any anxiety, Andrea would address the next situation in her hierarchy. When Andrea was able to imagine the most feared situation, or she could be in the most feared situation without experiencing any anxiety, then she would no longer be phobic. Note that in an examination you must engage explicitly with the situation described, and talk about how systematic desensitisation would be used with *Andrea and her phobia*. A maximum of 2 marks would be awarded for a reasonable description of systematic desensitisation without any engagement.

Applying your knowledge (2): The therapist could begin by teaching Celine how to relax her muscles completely. Celine could be taken to a building similar in height to the Eiffel Tower in order to confront her fear. Over a session of several hours, Celine's adrenalin levels would initially rise but at some point they would decrease. This would allow a new stimulus-response link to be learned, which would be between the feared stimulus and relaxation. When Celine reported no anxiety at the top of the building, she would no longer be phobic and would be free to enjoy her weekend. Hopefully, Celine would not experience so much anxiety that she was prevented from confronting her fear, but this is an issue with flooding. As with the previous question, a maximum of 2 marks would be awarded for a reasonable description of flooding without any engagement.

Topic 6 The cognitive approach to explaining depression

Choose the right answer: A, D

Spot the mistakes: [mistakes are in bold; correct material in brackets] **Ellis'** cognitive triad (ABC model) says that when an activating event (A) leads to a **rational** (irrational) belief (B), the consequences of this (C) may be depression. Musturbatory thinking is the **result** (cause) of irrational beliefs. For example, one of these beliefs is that we must do well otherwise we are worthless. People who hold these kinds of beliefs **always** (may) become depressed. For mental healthiness, these 'musts' therefore need to be challenged.

Match them up: 1C, 2B, 3A, 4D

Applying your knowledge (1): The activating event (A) in the passage is Becky telling Boris she can't go to the concert with him. The belief (B), which in this case is probably irrational, is that Becky must really hate Boris. The consequence (C) of the irrational belief is Boris being too upset to go to concert himself.

Applying your knowledge: Beck would say that Simon's father's criticism of him has led to the development of a negative schema. When Simon was asked to play in goal by his teacher, this schema was activated. The negative schema has led to a cognitive bias in Simon's thinking – he now thinks that any team he plays in goal for will lose on the basis of what his father said about his abilities. In terms of Beck's negative triad, Simon might have developed a pessimistic and irrational view about himself (I am useless), the world (I'll be useless whatever I do), and the future (I'll always be useless). Such a belief system might lead to Simon becoming depressed.

Topic 7 The cognitive approach to treating depression

Choose the right answer: A, D

Research issues: (a) One advantage of gaining qualitative data is that it offers the researcher the chance to gain in-depth information that would not be possible with a simple rating scale. For example, the patients receiving CBT could give information about the specific areas in which they felt the greatest improvement.

(b) *Factor 1*: The different therapies would have been delivered by different therapists. Research has shown that the qualities of the individual therapist are every bit as important as the qualities of the therapies in the study. Therefore these would have a strong effect on any potential outcomes for the patient. *Factor 2*: Patients may well have been referred to the different types of therapies based on the severity of their symptoms or other factors that would make one type of therapy more suitable than the others. This would also influence the speed at which they would improve, or even the amount of improvement that might be reasonably expected.

(c) One finding is that the level of self-reported improvement of patients with depression who received REBT was greater than for the other two therapies. This suggests that REBT is a more effective treatment for depression than either psychoanalysis or counseling. A second finding is that the level of self-reported improvement of patients with anxiety who received REBT was approximately the same as that reported for the other two therapies. This suggests that all three therapies are moderately and equally effective in the treatment of anxiety.

Match them up: 1D, 2B, 3A, 4C

Spot the mistakes: [mistakes are in bold; correct material in brackets] Ellis' rational emotive behaviour therapy (REBT) aims to turn irrational thoughts into rational thoughts, and resolve emotional and **biological** (behavioural) problems. The therapy challenges or disputes irrational thoughts, aiming to replace them with rational beliefs which produce new feelings. Clients complete homework assignments between therapy sessions. Homework enables irrational beliefs to be tested against **theory** (reality) and putting new rational beliefs into practice. **Conditional** (unconditional) regard is given to the client by a therapist, as an important part of REBT is convincing clients of their value as humans. Another feature is for the client to become more **passive** (active), since this leads to rewards that are an antidote to depression.

Applying your knowledge: Irrational belief 1. Sophie believes that she needs to prove her competence all the time. This could be disputed by telling Sophie that she will be happier if she achieves at a realistic level rather than strives for perfection. Irrational belief; 2. Sophie believes that it is a disaster if things don't go the way she wants them to. This could be disputed by telling Sophie that although it is unfortunate when things don't go the way she wants them to it is certainly not catastrophic, and that she can make plans for her life to be as enjoyable as possible. Irrational belief; 3. Sophie believes that she has to be approved by everyone all the time. This could be disputed by telling Sophie that whilst we would all like to be approved by others we do not *need* such approval.

Topic 8 The biological approach to explaining OCD

Choose the right answer: C and E

Match them up: 1D, 2B, 3C, 4A

Spot the mistakes: [mistakes are in bold; correct material in brackets] One biological explanation for OCD is that it is caused by genetic factors. The SERT gene creates **higher** (lower) levels of serotonin and this may be what causes OCD. Another gene which researchers think is involved in causing OCD is the COMT gene. One variation of this gene is more common in people with OCD. This gene regulates the production of dopamine and produces **lower** (higher) levels of this neurotransmitter. Ozaki et al found that a mutation of the **COMT** (SERT) gene was present in two unrelated families where six out of seven of them had OCD.

Applying your knowledge: Although people with a first-degree relative with OCD are more likely to develop the disorder than people who do not have a family history of the condition, Leon seems to have forgotten about the role of environmental influences. As well as sharing genes, families also share environments, and it could be that it is the shared family environment which is responsible for other family members developing OCD. Likewise, Andy also seems to have forgotten that as well as sharing their genes, identical twins also typically share environments as well. A further point Allegra could make concerns the concordance rate, which Andy says is 'really high'. It may be, but the concordance rate is not 100%, which means that environmental factors *must* be playing some role in the cause of OCD.

Topic 9 The biological approach to treating OCD

Choose the right answer: C, D

Drawing conclusions: One finding is that there was a greater reduction in the severity of symptoms for participants who took tricyclic drugs compared with those who took SSRI drugs. One conclusion that could be drawn from this finding is that tricyclic drugs are more effective than SSRIs in the treatment of OCD. A second finding is that the reduction in symptoms for participants who took SSRIs was less than for those who were given the placebo. A conclusion that could be drawn from this finding is that any improvement over the three months for those who took SSRIs could be solely due to a placebo effect rather than any effect due to the drug.

Research issues: One ethical issue that might have arisen is *deception*, since participants were not told which condition they were in. A second issue might have been *informed consent*. Because information about which group they were in was withheld from participants, they were denied the opportunity to give fully informed consent. It is possible that people diagnosed with OCD would not have given their consent to receive a placebo instead of a drug. A third ethical issue could be the more specific concerns associated with this type of investigation. This could include the fact that, because investigators have a *duty of care* to their participants, withholding treatment (in the placebo condition) from those who need it would be to ignore this duty of care.

Match them up: 1B, 2D, 3C, 4A

Applying your knowledge: (a) First, Paul might have told Linda that research shows that drugs are effective in reducing the symptoms of OCD compared with placebos, at least in the short-term. Second, he might have told her that drug therapy requires little effort and time on her part compared with psychological therapies, where she might have to attend regular meetings and put considerable thought into dealing with her problem. Third, Paul could have pointed out the economic benefits of drugs compared with psychological therapies. If Linda was prescribed her drugs, the cost would be much less than if she was referred for psychological therapy. (b) Caroline might have pointed out to Linda that whilst Paul was right about the short-term benefits of drug therapy, there is little evidence about the long-term benefits of drug therapy. She could also point out that all therapeutic drugs have side effects associated with them, and that these might be sufficiently unpleasant to cause Linda to stop taking the drugs. Finally, she might make the point that Linda may become physically dependent on the drugs (or addicted to them) and that even if she didn't, the drugs were only masking her condition and not actually curing it.

Chapter 5

Topic 1 The origins of psychology

Choose the right answer: A, D
Match then up:

Empiricism	The belief that all knowledge is derived from sensory experience.
Introspection	The process by which a person gains knowledge about his or her own mental and emotional states.
Scientific method	Refers to the use of investigative methods that are objective, systematic and replicable.

A marking exercise:
This answer is likely to achieve 3 out of 6 marks. The answer could also include information in relation to empiricism – the belief that knowledge comes from observation and experience and that Wundt applied empirical methods to the study of human beings, which contributed to the development of Psychology. Furthermore, the answer could also define the scientific method which refers to the use of investigative methods which are objective, systematic and reliable.

Topic 2 The behaviourist approach

Match them up:

Classical conditioning	The process by which a neutral stimulus is paired with an unconditioned stimulus, to eventually produce a conditioned response.
Operant conditioning	The process of learning through reinforcement or punishment. If a behaviour is followed by a desirable consequence then that behaviour is more likely to occur again in the future.
Punishment	Where a behaviour is less likely to occur again in the future, because it is followed by an unpleasant consequence.
Reinforcement	Anything that strengthens a response and increases the likelihood that it will occur again in the future.

Complete the diagram:

1. Food (UCS)
2. Salivation (UCR)
3. Bell (NS)
4. No response
5. NS and UCS paired
6. NS is now CS
7. Salivation (CR)

Applying your knowledge:

Identify the psychology	Link to pigeon
When the pigeon pecked the red sign saying 'exit' he was positively reinforced	This means that … the pigeon was rewarded for his/her behavior which meant that he/she is more likely to repeat this behavior in the future.
When the pigeon pecked the green sign saying 'Do NOT press' he was punished.	This means that … the pigeon is unlikely to repeat the behavior in the future, to avoid the punishing (harmful) effect of the electric shock.

Research methods: The mean is an appropriate measure of central tendency because it takes into account all of the data, while avoiding extreme scores. In this case there are no extreme scores as the researcher would expect the time to decrease with each trial.

Mean = 27
Range = 48 seconds

Topic 3 Social learning theory

Choose the right answer: A – Attitude OR behaviour.
Applying your knowledge (1):

Identify the psychology	Link to Mrs Watkins (Hint: Don't forget the question states 'vicarious').
Positive reinforcement…by praising those children who raise their hands, in front of everyone else.	This means that …the other children may learn vicariously and also want to receive praise and start acting appropriately, by also raising their hands.
Punishment… by giving the children who call out a detention, in front of everyone else.	This means that … the other children may learn vicariously and want to avoid the punishment of a detention and therefore stop calling out answers.

Applying your knowledge (2):

- Mediational processes occur between the observation (Joseph watching) and response (Joseph copying the shot).
- Joseph is motivated (keen to play well)
- Joseph pays attention (watches carefully)
- Joseph thinks about the positives of the outcome (hitting a fantastic shot)

Topic 4 The cognitive approach

Choose the right answer: D – Cognitive neuroscience shows an association (correlation) between cognitive activities and different brain regions.

Match them up:

Computer model	Refers to the process of using computer analogies as a representation of human cognition.
Inference/Inferring	Means reaching a logical conclusion on the basis of evidence and reasoning.
Schema	A cognitive framework that helps to organise and interpret information in the brain.
Theoretical models	Refers to the process of using a simplified pictorial representation of a particular mental process.

Research issues: One strength of carrying out this study in a laboratory is that the conditions are highly controlled and therefore it makes the research easier to replicate. However, one weakness is that the task is not reflective of everyday memory and therefore the study lacks ecological validity, as the findings are not applicable to everyday human memory.

Drawing conclusions: 1) 11 and 6. 2) Useful to show the distribution (spread of the score). Indicates the participants in condition 1 are more variable than the participants in condition 2.

Topic 5 The biological approach

Choose the right answer: A, B

Match them up:

Evolution	Refers to the change over successive generations of the genetic make-up of a particular population.
Gene	A part of the chromosome of an organism that carries information in the form of DNA.
Genotype	The genetic make-up of an individual. The genotype is a collection of inherited genetic material that is passed from generation to generation.
Neurochemistry	The study of chemical and neural processes associated with the nervous system.
Phenotype	The observable characteristics of an individual. This is a consequence of the interaction of the genotype with the environment.

Spot the mistakes: [mistakes are in bold; correct material in brackets] Genes are inherited from one generation to the next and carry instructions for a particular characteristic (such as intelligence). There is an important distinction between genotype and phenotype. The **phenotype** (genotype) refers to the genetic code in the **neurotransmitters** (DNA) and the **genotype** (phenotype) is the physical appearance that results from inherited information.

Applying your knowledge: Samuel and Daniel have an identical genotype as they are MZ twins. Although, they have the predisposition to develop the same personalities as each other, environment factors will result in the differences found. Their phenotypes are different, possibly because Samuel has engaged with sociable and lively people.

Topic 6 The psychodynamic approach

Match them up: 1B 2A 3F 4E 5C 6D

Choose the right answer: C

Drawing conclusions: *Finding 1*: The graph shows that there was less improvement in terms of symptom reduction for patients undergoing psychoanalysis for the first six months compared to CBT, but at one year psychoanalysis was superior. *Conclusion 1*: This suggests that psychoanalysis is more effective in the long term as a treatment for depression, whereas CBT is more effective in the short term. *Finding 2*: Both psychoanalysis and CBT show more improvement at all three points compared to a placebo group. *Conclusion 2*: This shows that there is a real therapeutic benefit to both therapies, as both have been shown to reduce depressive symptoms more effectively than a placebo condition.

Applying your knowledge: Identify the psychology: childhood trauma, repression, unconscious affecting current emotion and behaviour. Link to Sadie: her memory of trauma, not conscious, might help her to understand herself more (insight) and not blame herself.

Topic 7 Humanistic psychology

Match them up: 1D 2C 3B 4A 5F 6E

Spot the mistakes: [mistakes are in bold; correct material in brackets] Counsellors try to give their clients **conditional** (unconditional) positive regard, so that they feel accepted. They do this by listening without judgment and offering **directive** (non-directive) counselling. This results in the client **developing more** (letting go of their) conditions of worth, so that they can be more authentic and true to self. Humanistic counselling is based on the idea that people can solve their own problems with support, and may just need help understanding themselves better so they can move towards the ultimate goal of **self-esteem** (self-actualisation).

Choose the right answer: C

Applying your knowledge: For example: Identify the psychology: conditions of worth, unconditional positive regard, acceptance. Link to Jasmine's counselling: facilitate her in solving her own problems, moving upwards in Maslow's hierarchy, provide empathy and unconditional positive regard to help her to overcome the conditions of worth from parents/ broken relationship.

Topic 8 Comparison of approaches

Choose the right answer: D

A marking exercise: 3 marks. Good direct comparisons, but more elaboration needed of 'learnt by direct experience' and 'learn by watching other people'. Vicarious reinforcement not explained. The determinism difference is not fully explained either; how does SLT allow for choices when behaviourism does not? Overall, on the right lines but not enough detail.

Applying your knowledge: for example:

Approach	Explanation of Alex's preference
Behaviourist	Alex has learnt by operant conditioning and been reinforced previously for carrying out experiments successfully, so he wants to repeat this.
Social Learning	Alex has observed someone else carrying out successful experiments and being rewarded for this, vicarious reinforcement has occurred and he want to imitate this.
Cognitive	Alex has a fixed belief that experiments are better than other research methods, this makes him emotionally committed to the idea.
Biological	Alex has a particular biological disposition to carrying out experimental research as it fits his neural pathways which have been built up by extensive experience in his other studies. Maybe he studies Science subjects.
Psychodynamic	Alex has experienced some trauma and his unconscious mind is protecting him from anxiety by ensuring that he does not explore any areas of psychology which might bring up emotional memories or conflicts.
Humanistic	Alex has conditions of worth from his parents who he feels approve him based on their view of masculine scientific behaviour, and he needs to prove to them that psychology is a proper science subject by researching experimentally.

Chapter 6

Topic 1 The nervous system

Match them up: 1C 2F 3D 4B 5A 6E

Spot the mistakes: [mistakes are in bold; correct material in brackets] The autonomic nervous system allows you to carry out **conscious** (unconscious) activities. It includes two divisions, the sympathetic and **non**-sympathetic (parasympathetic) branches. The sympathetic nervous system tends to stimulate organs like the heart, sweat glands and **digestive** (respiratory) system. The neurotransmitter **acetylcholine** (noradrenaline) is mainly involved in this branch, and it is concerned with response to emergency situations. The para-sympathetic branch helps to restore a normal physiological state after the emergency has passed, and is known as the rest and **refresh** (digest) system.

Applying your knowledge: For example, Sophie becomes very tense when she sees the spider because her brain has identified a threat and sends signals via her sympathetic nervous system (SNS) to her muscles, tensing them up ready for a fight or flight response. Her SNS also stimulates her heart to beat faster and her breathing rate to increase, so she can get more oxygen to her muscles ready for this emergency response. She feels sick because her blood is diverted away from her digestive system. When Charlotte has removed the spider Sophie calms down because her parasympathetic nervous system is activated and restores her to a normal physiological state (rest and digest).

Topic 2 Neurons and synaptic transmission

Complete the diagram: Dendrite A, Myelin sheath B, Axon C, Cell body D

Choose the right answer: C

Drawing conclusions: For example, *One finding:* Students who failed maths GCSE used a lot more oxygen in condition 2 than condition 1. *This suggests that:* They were anxious in condition 2 and therefore their sympathetic nervous system was activated by a stress response, so they used more oxygen. *Second finding:* Students taking maths A level also used more oxygen in condition 2 than condition 1, but not as much more as the students who failed maths. *This suggests that* the extra mental effort of performing calculations used more oxygen anyway.

Applying your knowledge: for example, if the researchers stimulated several neurons which all caused an EPSP in the post-synaptic neuron, then spatial or temporal summation mean that an action potential is produced. On the other hand, if they stimulated a combination of neurons some of which caused IPSPs, then the post-synaptic neuron would not fire.

Topic 3 The endocrine system

Match them up: 1F 2A 3D 4B 5C 6E

Fill in the boxes: For example, Endocrine glands are glands which produce and secrete hormones into the bloodstream. Endocrine glands are regulated by negative feedback, which is called homeostasis. An example of an endocrine gland is the pituitary gland, which releases many hormones such as ACTH, LH and FSH and oxytocin. The pituitary is controlled by the hypothalamus in the brain. Hormones are chemical messengers which travel in the blood and bind to receptor molecules on the surface of target cells. Hormones can affect the brain and behaviour by their involvement in stress responses, attachment and sexual behaviour. An example of a hormone is ACTH. This hormone affects the adrenal cortex, stimulating it to release cortisol which is involved in the stress response.

Spot the mistakes: [mistakes are in bold; correct material in brackets] The pituitary gland **stimulates** (is stimulated by) the hypothalamus to produce hormones. The pituitary gland produces ACTH which targets the **adrenal medulla**, (adrenal cortex) as part of the stress response. It also sends messages to the ovaries to make them release **follicle stimulating hormone**, (FSH is produced by the pituitary not the ovaries) oestrogen and progesterone. In males, **it secretes testosterone** (stimulates the testes to produce testosterone) which acts on the testes to make them produce sperm.

Applying your knowledge: For example, Sandra's pituitary tumour may be producing excess ACTH. This stimulates production of cortisol in the adrenal cortex, a stress hormone which may increase her blood pressure and make her feel fatigued and anxious when it is present in her blood stream over a long period. This will also slow down healing processes, making her cuts take longer to heal, as it affects the immune system.

Topic 4 The fight-or-flight response

Match them up: 1F 2C 3E 4B 5A 6D

Complete the diagram:
Chronic stress: Hypothalamus (CRH) → pituitary (ACTH) → Adrenal cortex (cortisol)
Acute stress: hypothalamus → SNS → Adrenal medulla (adrenaline)

Choose the right answer: C and D

Applying your knowledge: For example, Karl seems to have a male aggressive response, which may be due to the SRY gene on his Y chromosome. This causes him to release a lot of adrenaline in response to stress, and he faces up to the group of teenagers. In contrast, Karla freezes, which is a common initial response to a threat. She still has an acute stress response to the threatening group, and the adrenaline in her blood stream cause her to become pale (as blood moves away from her skin) and shake (as her muscles tense up ready to run away).

Topic 5 Localisation of function

Choose the right answer: i) A ii) D iii) C

Research issues: for example, the patient may not be able to give fully informed consent due to the stroke, which may have affected other cognitive functions as well as speech. The researcher should try to obtain consent as far as possible from the patient, but also from his family and should keep all details anonymous.

Applying your knowledge: For example, The patient may have damage to Broca's area which is where speech production is localised. This means that the stroke has affected the posterior part of the left frontal lobe. His Wernicke's area seems to be unaffected, as he is still able to understand speech.

Topic 6 Lateralisation and split-brain research

Applying your knowledge: For example, B.L. sees the cat with her left visual field, and the information from here is processed in the right visual cortex. This information is then restricted to the right hemisphere, so can't be processed into speech as the speech production areas (Broca's area) are in the left hemisphere. However, B.L. can still pick the correct card with her left hand as this is controlled by her right hemisphere. As her right visual field sees the lion, this is processed by her left visual cortex and can be transferred to her speech areas, so she says she's seen a lion.

A marking exercise: (a) 1 mark. This does not explain that different images are presented to different halves of the visual field, although the means of testing (they have to say what they've seen) is OK.

(b) 2 marks. This answer does not focus on the usefulness of split-brain research in investigating lateralisation, although both points are valid limitations. To obtain more marks the criticisms should be linked to how this weakens their support for lateralisation in normal individuals.

Drawing conclusions: 60%

Choose the right answer: D

Topic 7 Plasticity and functional recovery of the brain

Drawing conclusions (1): Strong positive correlation. This suggests that when people spend longer working as taxi drivers this part of their brain develops more. This supports plasticity in response to experience.

Spot the mistakes: [mistakes are in bold; correct material in brackets] The brain is able to change by developing new synaptic connections and pathways. This is called plasticity. For example, playing video games **kills brain cells** (increases synaptic connections in brain areas involved with spatial recognition, strategic planning and motor performance). Even if some parts of the brain are destroyed by trauma, they can **re-grow** (other parts can take over their function). This is called functional recovery.

Drawing conclusions (2): 27.8%. Bar chart. Patients with TBI who had more years of education were more likely to achieve DFR.

Topic 8 Ways of studying the brain

Match them up: 1C 2D 3A 4B

Research issues: For example, H.M. may not have been able to give fully informed consent to this, as he kept forgetting that he was involved in research. This was dealt with by asking interested parties and family members to give consent, and he did seem to be very enthusiastic about helping people by participating in experiments throughout his lifetime.

Applying your knowledge: *Identify the psychology* EEG is useful for recognising the abnormal brain waves during an epileptic seizure. *Link to Flora* EEG would be appropriate for Flora because she has been experiencing seizures, which may be caused by epilepsy, and EEG is very useful for recognising the abnormal brain waves during an epileptic seizure. However, EEG does not pinpoint the exact source of the abnormality, as the electrodes pick up signals from a fairly wide area.

Topic 9 Circadian rhythms

Match them up: 1D 2C 3A 4E 5B

Choose the right answer: B, D

Applying your knowledge (1): For example, Katie seems to be a 'morning person' whereas Jack is an 'evening person'. These individual differences may be innate or learnt, and they could try to adjust their sleep patterns by making sure they get out in the light together during the day so their sleep-wake cycles are affected by the light in the same way. They could also try keeping their bedroom cool as temperature also affects the body clock.

Applying your knowledge (2): A line graph. The findings show that the body temperature is lowest at 4am and highest at 6pm. There is more variation in temperatures (shown by the higher standard deviation) at 8am and around 8pm, which could be caused by different activity levels of participants at those times.

Topic 10 Ultradian and infradian rhythms

Choose the right answer: B

Spot the mistakes: [mistakes are in bold; correct material in brackets] Biological rhythms that are longer than 24 hours are known as **ultradian** (infradian). For example, the female menstrual cycle is **exactly** (around) 28 days and is controlled by **the orbit of the moon** (pituitary hormones). Ovulation occurs about half way through the cycle when **progesterone** (oestrogen) levels peak.

In addition, human health follows annual rhythms. Some people become severely depressed in the winter, and most deaths occur in **December** (January).

Sleep consists of **four** (five) stages which make up an ultradian rhythm, including **NREM** (REM) sleep which is when most dreaming occurs. This cycle repeats every **hour** (90–100 minutes) through the night.

Applying your knowledge: Mr Walker could make sure that the timetable allows students to take a break every 90 minutes, to fit in with their 90-minute ultradian cycle of alertness and fatigue. He could also consider shorter college days in the winter as many people are affected by the seasons in annual rhythms.

Topic 11 Endogenous pacemakers and exogenous zeitgebers

Choose the right answer: B, C

Research issues: The children's sleep may be affected by different light levels, which could cause harm. The researcher should ensure that parents know that if their children are being adversely affected by lack of sleep, they can withdraw them from the study and replace their normal curtains.

Applying your knowledge: *Identify the psychology:* Endogenous pacemakers need to synchronise with exogenous zeitgebers. *Advice to James:* He should make use of the exogenous zeitgebers of light and social cues to reset his biological clock. He could do this before he flies east from Chicago by making sure he is exposed to bright light during the day to shift his sleep-wake cycle a bit. When he gets back home he should go outside early in the day, to be exposed to warm daylight so that his retinal melanopsin-containing cells send signals to the supra-chiasmatic nucleus that it is now daytime. He should also socialise during the day and not at night time, so that the social cues help to reset his endogenous pacemakers.

The study is an independent groups design, so the findings will be affected by individual differences; some children may naturally be better sleepers than others, or be used to thin curtains. To improve the study, a repeated measures design could be used, where both groups of children have a week with each type of curtain, half in one order and half in the other (counterbalanced for order effects).

A marking exercise: 4 marks. An accurate answer, explaining some of the issues Claire experiences during night shifts, but with no explanation of why she finds it difficult to sleep in the day. The information about the pineal gland could be further elaborated with mention of the SCN and how it is affected by the light-detecting cells in the retina.

Chapter 7

Topic 1 The experimental method

Choose the right answer: A, D

A marking exercise: *Kerry's answer:* 1 + 1 mark (neither variable is operationalised).
Megan's answer: 1 + 0 marks (second answer is not a variable).
Rohan's answer: 2 + 2 marks (both variables are operationalised)

Applying your knowledge: For example, (a) The aim is to see whether rewards affect performance. (b) IV = receiving £1 or not for doing the test, DV = score on the test. (c) Children who are offered £1 achieve higher scores on the test than those who receive nothing. (d) Directional hypothesis. (e) The children who got the reward might be smarter anyway. Therefore they would do better on the test, not because they got the reward but because they were smarter and this would confound the results. (f) One demand characteristic would be that the offer of a reward might make the children in the no reward group realise what the experiment was about and they would try very hard. (g) One strength is the experimenter could repeat this study if he had controlled all the variables carefully such as using the same test and the same reward to see if the results were reliable. One limitation is that the situation was contrived so the children might have behaved differently to how they would behave when tested at school – they probably wouldn't be offered money so it isn't very realistic.

Topic 2 Control of variables

Match them up: 1D 2C 3A 4B

Applying your knowledge (1): For example: (i) Children who used strategy B remembered more words correctly on average than those who used strategy A, so this was more effective. However, the difference was not very large. And the standard deviation was much greater for strategy B, so this strategy worked much better for some children than others, whereas strategy A had a more consistent effect as the standard deviation is smaller, so the result were less spread out from the mean. (ii) A bar chart of the mean scores. (iii) The experiment was only carried out on children, so the findings cannot be generalised to adult learners – this would be a problem of population validity. The children may already learn French, or some may be native French speakers, so their learning of French words may relate to other skills and strategies that they already possess, there is no guarantee that they were actually using strategy A and B – this is a problem of internal validity.

Applying your knowledge (2): For example: The setting is artificial, which affects the ecological validity, as the caregiver and child might behave differently in their own home. Also the caregiver may not be behaving normally, as they also know they are being watched. These demand characteristics affect the internal validity. And Mary Ainsworth only tested children from the US – other researchers have replicated the

procedure in different cultures and found different results, so there is a problem of population validity.

Topic 3 Return to hypotheses and other things

Match them up: 1C 2B 3A 4E 5D 6F

A marking exercise: A 0 marks – this is not a pilot study as the researchers have used all the participants. B 1 mark – correct but not applied to this investigation. C 2 marks – good suggestion of a reason for carrying out a pilot study in this investigation.

Choose the right answer: D

Topic 4 Experimental design

Match them up: 1E 2A 3B 4F 5D 6C

Choose the right answer: ADE

Applying your knowledge 1: For example: The repeated measures design removes participant effects, which would be a problem with an independent groups design, and could be caused by different individuals having different tolerances for caffeine. It means that each participant's results are compared before and after drinking coffee, so they act as their own control in the experiment, rather than being compared with different participants.

Applying your knowledge (2): For example: a) There are different people in each condition of the experiment, (e.g., left-handed in one condition and right-handed in the other condition) so each participant carries out the creativity test once. b) Because people are either right-handed or left-handed; they can't be in both groups. Right-handed and left-handed people are being compared: this is the IV. c) A strength is that there are no order effects, so participants do not get bored and perform worse in the creativity test, or improve through practice. A weakness is that participant effects act as a confounding variable, so there may happen to be people in one group who are more experienced in these type of creativity test and will perform better for that reason rather than because of their right- or left-handedness. This makes it difficult to draw valid conclusions about the effect of the IV on the DV. d) There will be a difference in the performance of right-handed and left-handed people in a creativity test.

Topic 5 Laboratory and field experiments

Choose the right answer: C

Research issues: For example: passers-by were not briefed so they did not give informed consent. The researcher should debrief them afterwards, explaining the purpose of the study and giving them an opportunity to withdraw their data. He should not continue with the study if people seem distressed when they are debriefed.

Fill in the boxes: For example:

	What study was it?	IV	DV	Uncontrolled variables	Task	Setting	Were participants aware?
Lab experiment 1	Loftus and Palmer car crash	5 different verbs	Estimate of speed of car	Individual differences	contrived	Lab	yes
Lab experiment 2	Jacobs digit span	Number of digits	Longest span of digits recalled correctly	Strategies used?	Artificial memory task	Lab (classroom)	Yes
Field experiment 1	Bushman the power of uniform	Confederate's clothing	Obedience rate	Distractions in the surroundings	realistic	Street	no

Topic 6 Natural and quasi-experiments

Match them up: 1D 2C 3A 4B

Choose the right answer: D

Applying your knowledge: (a) IV – watch tv more than five hours a day or not. DV – aggression ratings. (b) natural experiment. (c) People have chosen whether to watch a lot of tv or not, they have not been put into groups, so the IV was not manipulated by the researcher. It was a study of their behaviour in a natural environment. (d) It is likely to have low validity as the groups were self-selecting, so people who watch more tv may already be more aggressive; or people who watch a lot of tv don't have time to be aggressive. This means other variables are confounding the findings.

Topic 7 More problems with experiments

Match them up: 1F 2D 3A 4C 5B 6E

Choose the right answer: C

Drawing conclusions (a):

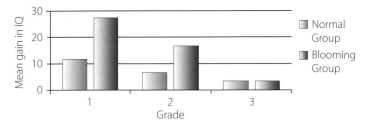

(b) The teachers' expectations made a huge difference to children's progress in grade 1, as they made more than twice as much gains in IQ when teachers believed they had high scores for intellectual blooming. In grade 2 the 'high score' group also did much better than normal children. However, by grade 3 the teachers' expectations didn't make any difference. Overall, children made most progress when they were younger anyway.

Applying your knowledge: For example, the individuals who were asked to take part in an experiment thought there must be some scientific purpose to the request, so they were willing to cooperate without knowing more – maybe they knew that researchers can't always tell you the purpose before the experiment takes place. People who were just asked to perform press-ups without being told it was for an experiment, but just for a favour, didn't see the purpose and were amazed. This shows how demand characteristics might arise in an experimental setting, as people are generally willing to cooperate with the project of Science.

Topic 8 Sampling

Match them up: Opportunity sample: C D

Volunteer sample: B E

Random sample: A F

A marking exercise: *Dylan's answer* = 3 out of 3 marks (Dylan has provided one strength and one criticism, each with some elaboration). *Carrie's answer* = 2 out of 3 marks (first sentence not really an evaluation, second sentence is a criticism with some elaboration). *Charlotte's answer* = 1 out of 3 marks (mention of 'bias' gains one mark, the rest is not relevant).

Spot the mistakes: [mistakes are in bold; correct material in brackets] Psychologists need to select participants for their research studies. One way to do this is by using a **voluntary** (volunteer) sample. This means you ask people if they want to take part. Such a sample is likely to be **unbiased** (biased). Another technique that can be used is the random sample. To do this you identify your **main** (target) population and then

put all the names in a machine like they use for the lottery and randomly select the number you require. A third method is the opportunity sample. The people who are chosen are the ones most **willing** (available).

Applying your knowledge: For example, (a) Could be any of the 3 methods plus an explanation of how, e.g. one method would be an opportunity sample. You could just go up to people in the street and ask them how many calls they make per day and also rate their friendliness. (b) Strength as appropriate to part (a) but should include some context related to the stem as the question says '… in this study', e.g. this is the easiest method you could do because you can straight away go get your 30 people in the street rather than waiting for volunteers or contacting a random sample. (c) Independent groups. (d) Mobile phone use (1 mark), number of calls per day (1 mark for operationalisation). (e) It is a natural experiment because the IV has not been controlled by the experimenter. People are put in categories according to their existing behaviour.

Topic 9 Ethical issues

Match them up: 1B 2C 3E 4D 5A

Choose the right answer: B

Applying your knowledge: for example, participants could have had more accurate briefing so they knew what to expect; to avoid harm, an objective observer could have stopped the study or given the participants the option of withdrawing when they appeared distressed; closed circuit tv could have been used to monitor the participants; they could have been given a means of recording their feelings so that their level of distress could be assessed on a daily basis.

Topic 10 Dealing with ethical issues

Choose the right answer: A, B, D

A marking exercise: Ahmed's answer gets the full 1+ 3 marks as he has stated the point (don't identify) and then said two further pieces of information (don't use photos/names, or change them). Christian's answer only receives 1+ 1 out of 3 marks. Only the third sentence is creditworthy. The final sentence is too vague.

Applying your knowledge: For example, (a) It is a laboratory experiment because the IV is age and this has not been manipulated by the researcher .(b) If you used repeated measures you would have to use the same participants as children and adults and have to wait a long time. (c) One issue is deception and another issue is informed consent. She could deal with deception by debriefing participants at which time she would tell them the real aims and might offer that they could withhold their data. She would discuss any concerns they had. A second issue is informed consent. She would deal with this by seeking some outline consent before the study began, especially to gain consent from the children's parents. She would give an outline of what will be involved (e.g. tell them they would be watching a film of a robbery and answering a questionnaire). (Other options: confidentiality, or psychological harm) (d) Children may be impatient and not pay attention very closely to the task, either when watching the video or when identifying the photographs. This means their results would lack internal validity. (e) The purpose is to advise psychologists about what is not permissible ethically, and also about how they should deal with any situations where ethical issues arise. (f) The mean is a measure of central tendency where all the values of the data are taken into account in the final calculation. (g) Younger children performed less well than adults. This suggests that they wouldn't be as good as eyewitnesses. The spread of the data (standard deviation) is bigger for the adults. This suggests the children were more consistent in terms of accuracy. The adults varied more in their accuracy than the children, and some may have even been less accurate than the children.

Topic 11 Observational techniques

Match them up: 1A 2F 3E 4B 5D 6C

Research issues: For example: privacy is an issue, as the young people would not expect someone to be listening in and recording their conversation. He could debrief them afterwards, asking their permission to use the data (anonymously) and destroying it if they are not willing.

Fill in the boxes:

	Covert	Overt
Participant observation	High internal unless affected by observer bias High ecological	Low internal – high demand characteristics
Non-participant observation	Low demand characteristics	Low ecological Low internal

Applying your knowledge: Study A (a) controlled (b) overt (c) non-participant (d) yes, because parents gave consent and the study was stopped if children became unduly distressed. Study B (a) naturalistic (b) overt (c) non-participant (d) yes, as participants gave consent and were in normal everyday situation. Study C (a) naturalistic (b) covert (c) non-participant (d) Yes, as long as consent was obtained from parents, as children were in their normal situation. Study D (a) naturalistic (b) covert (c) non-participant (d) maybe not, as privacy was being invaded and he could not get any retrospective consent for using data. Study E (a) naturalistic (b) covert (c) participant (d) yes, as long as they gained consent retrospectively to use the data. Or no, as they were deliberately deceiving psychiatrists and other staff.

Topic 12 Observational design

Applying your knowledge (1): For example, (a) Avoiding a stranger (stranger anxiety), closeness to mother on her return (reunion behaviour). (b) The observations may not be reliable because the observer may misinterpret a behaviour and think a child was avoiding someone when they might have been playing a game. (c) It means you can arrange the setting to be able to test what you are interested in, such as arranging for the stranger to come and go.

Applying your knowledge (2): For example, (a) Playing with other children. (b) The list of behavioural categories would be used to record the behaviour of individual children by watching each child for a period of time (e.g. an hour) and ticking the behaviours observed in a behaviour checklist. This could be used to calculate a score for social development. (c) (P) One limitation is that the behavioural categories might not include every behaviour that the children do. (E) Therefore the record would not accurately reflect what they were actually doing. (E) This means that the results would lack validity. (L) It might be better to do a pilot study at the beginning to get the behavioural categories right.

Choose the right answer: D

Drawing conclusions: (a) smile, laugh, give (b) time sampling (c) to assess inter-rater reliability (d) The two observers scores were exactly the same for observations of boys. For girls, there were some differences in interpretations of behaviours, for example observer 2 only saw a total of 5 smiles whereas observer 1 saw 10. (e) Girls showed a much greater variety of prosocial behaviours when playing, such as smiling, laughing, giving and receiving, which the boys didn't display during that time period. The boys, however, spent more time looking at each other and facing each other.

Topic 13 Self-report techniques

Choose the right answer: B

Research issues: For example, one issue would be confidentiality. People who answered would not want their identities to be recognizable because then other people might link what they said to their families, and criticize their parents for poor attachment. A second issue is informed consent. People should be given information before they agree to take part, so they know what kind of data will be collected about their family relationships, and how it will be used, so they can decide whether or not to take part.

Drawing conclusions: For example, *Finding:* The largest number of respondents identified just one primary attachment figure. *Conclusion:* Bowlby's idea of monotropy continues into adolescence.

Applying your knowledge: For example, (a) The psychologist might want to check whether the questions for the children were easy to understand and could also check the standardised instructions are clear. (b) The psychologist can give the questionnaire out to a lot of children so you get a lot of replies to analyse. If you were conducting interviews each would take a lot more time than questionnaires which would reduce the number of participants that could be involved. (c) It might be better to use an interview so you could encourage the children to elaborate and explain their answers about their experiences of day care. Children also might find it difficult to write their answers down so an interview would be better.

Topic 14 Self-report design

Match them up: 1C 2A 3B 4E 5D 6F

Choose the right answer: D

Drawing conclusions:
(a) $(6 + 3 + 5 + 6 + 7 + 5 + 2 + 3 + 6 + 6) \div 10 = 4.9$. (b) Jess has a lower score than the mean for the group, so she is less excitement seeking.

Applying your knowledge: (a) For example: For how many years have you smoked? – 0 1 2 3 4 5 6 more than 6. (closed question). What do you dislike about smoking? (open question). (b) (P)The interviewer should be careful to be neutral, (E) not showing any response which might increase social desirability effects, (E) such as seeming to disapprove of smoking. They must be careful with their tone of voice and facial expression, (L) so that their behaviour does not affect the responses that the interviewee gives. (c) 'Do you think smoking is really disgusting?'

Topic 15 Correlations

Match them up: 1A 2E 3D 4B 5F 6C

Drawing conclusions: (a) 18. (b) Scattergram.

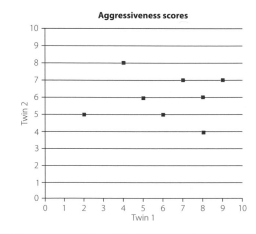

This is a zero correlation. (c) This suggests that there is not a genetic basis for aggression.

Applying your knowledge: For example, (a) Ask teachers to rate each child on a scale of 1 to 10 where 10 is very aggressive. (b) There is a correlation between hours spent in day care per week and aggressiveness rating. (c) A correlational analysis only demonstrates a relationship, it cannot tell us whether one variable caused the change in the other. In this case whether day care caused aggressiveness.

Research issues: For example, it would be appropriate to use a pilot study to check that key aspects of the design worked. For example, to check the standardised instructions are clear enough for the participants (the parents or teachers who are rating the children's aggressiveness) to understand what they are required to do. Also to check the method of assessing how many hours a week children were in nursery to see if the method was reliable.

Topic 16 Other research methods

Match them up: 1E 2C 3I 4A 5F 6B 7K 8D 9G 10J 11H

Applying your knowledge (1): For example, (a) They might use psychological tests to assess the emotional development of some of the children who had been there. (b) They might use a volunteer sample where they advertise for an institution who would be willing to take part.

Research issues: For example, the psychologist would not reveal the adopted woman's name nor the names of any other people involved. Any information that is stored should be protected so it cannot be accessed by other people. The psychologist should also ensure that any details that would identify the adopted woman, such as where she lives or works, are not included in the study.

Applying your knowledge (2): For example, (a) One technique would be interviewing. The psychologists would interview people arrested for rioting and also people who had been affected. (b) One limitation would be that people don't tell the truth, especially the people who had committed crimes, who would try to put themselves in a good light (social desirability bias). The people affected might also not tell the truth, they might exaggerate the effect the riots had had. Another limitation would be that it is retrospective recall and people don't always remember past events accurately. (c) One strength is the rich detail that could be collected, which might give new insights into rioting behaviour and change our views about the causes and effects of rioting.

Topic 17 Mathematical skills

Match them up: 1/10 = 0.1 = 10%, 1/25 = 0.04 = 4%, 3/16 = 0.1875 = 18.75%, 1/8 = 0.125 = 12.5%, ½ = 0.5 = 50%, 83/150 = 0.55 (to 2sf) = 55% (to 2sf).

Applying your knowledge (1): (a) $(12 \div 40) \times 100 = 30\%$. (b) $(6 + 4) \div 40 = \frac{1}{4}$ (c) 30 second intervals.

Applying your knowledge (2): (a) 37.5% = 38% to 2sf. (b) There are fewer girls than boys. (c) 2/100 = 1/50. (d) For example: $4200 \div 42 = 100$. (e) 9. (f) $0.25 \times (72 + 72) = 36$. (g) $0.1 \times (96 \times 3) = 28.8 = 29$ to 2 sf.

Topic 18 Measures of central tendency and dispersion

Match them up: 1C 2G 3H 4B 5D 6F 7I 8E 9A

Drawing conclusions: For example, *One finding:* Group A were slower on visual task 1 than Group B. *This suggests that* doing a second visual task at the same time interferes with the first visual task. *Second finding:* Group A were slower on visual task 1 than visual task 2. *This suggests that* interference doesn't affect both tasks equally.

Applying your knowledge:
(a) $(72 + 67 + 61 + 55 + 56 + 34 + 39 + 43) \div 8 = 53.4\%$ to 3sf. (b) For example, standard deviation as it takes into account all of the data but is not affected by extreme values.

(c) A line graph.

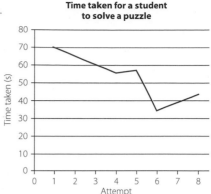

Time taken for a student to solve a puzzle

Horizontal axis = attempt, vertical axis = time taken. (d) The student got faster up to the 6th attempt, which was probably due to learning, as the puzzles are similar. The student then got slower for the last two attempts, which may have been due to tiredness or boredom.

Topic 19 Display of quantitative data and data distributions

Match them up: 1G 2E 3C 4A 5H 6F 7D 8B

Choose the right answer: A

Drawing conclusions: For example, *One finding:* In general the day care children had higher social development scores than the home care children. *This suggests that* day care had a positive effect on social development. *Second finding:* There was a a big difference in social development score at age six between the day care and home care children. *This suggests that* the effect was most marked when children started school and perhaps were better able to cope with peers having been in day care.

Applying your knowledge: (a) bar chart (b) histogram or frequency polygon (c) scattergram (d) bar chart (e) frequency polygon or grouped bar chart.

Topic 20 Types of data

Choose the right answer: B, C

Applying your knowledge: (a) Describe behaviour, use photos or video clips to demonstrate different examples of aggressive behaviour, for example pushing, aggressive facial expressions. (b) Make a tally chart of behavioural categories, for example hitting, pushing, use time sampling to tally each behaviour. (c) Qualitative data gives a rich description of behaviours, and allows for the recording of unexpected behaviours, but it does not give a representation of how frequent they were. Quantitative data is useful for comparing frequencies of different behaviours in individual children but does not indicate how important they were, what led up to them, or how other children responded. Also any unexpected behaviours which do not fit into an existing category will be missed out of the analysis. Quantitative data is more suitable to address the hypothesis about boys playing more aggressively, as 'more' suggests a quantitative comparison. (It would also be valid to argue for qualitative data, with a suitable reason.)

Topic 21 Introduction to statistical testing

Match them up: 1D 2B 3F 4A 5C 6E

Choose the right answer: C

Applying your knowledge (1): 1. Hypothesis: People will lose weight in three months on this slimming programme. Directional. 2. - - + - - 0 - + - - 3. $S=2$ 4. $N=9$, critical value of $S = 1$. 5. This is not significant. The hypothesis cannot be accepted.

Applying your knowledge (2): (a) The mean weight loss and the standard deviation (or median weight loss and range). (b) Mean weight loss = $(6 + 23 - 1 + 21 + 14 + 0 + 8 - 1 + 22 + 28) \div 10 = 12kg$. (c) The programme was very effective as the mean weight loss was 12kg in 3 months. (d) Two people's weights increased so the sign test was not significant, but they actually only increased by a kilogram, whereas seven people lost large amounts of weight. (e) Yes, as it seems to be very effective for weight loss and even the people who gained weight only gained a tiny amount.

Topic 22 The scientific process and the peer review

Choose the right answer: D

Research issues: For example: Why the paper was rejected: 1. Poor methodology; 2. controversial findings; 3. a replication study. How this affects the meta-analysis: 1. Improves its validity; 2. Reduces its validity; 3. May not affect its conclusions but weaker statistical analysis as sample size is smaller than it would be.

Applying your knowledge: For example: Issues: 1. Case studies should not be used as the basis of theory as they are the experiences of individuals and should not be generalised; 2. Interpretation is highly subjective. Problem: 1. Poor reliability; 2. Poor validity. Suggestions: 1. Try to gather broader data using other research methods such as questionnaires, interviews, longitudinal studies of samples not just individuals; 2. Offer theory more tentatively until there is substantial evidence.

Topic 23 Psychology and the economy

Choose the right answer: B

Research issues: For example: citizens are not aware that they are being influenced by the Nudge Unit, so this could be said to be an invasion of privacy or autonomy of individuals, with a lack of consent. They are unelected and people may not like the idea that they are being influenced without their knowledge by psychologists and economists. On the other hand, people are constantly influenced by advertisers without realising, and the Nudge Unit was appointed by an elected government in order to improve society as a whole. There is substantial evidence of positive outcomes which benefit individuals via improving the economy. There should be safeguards in place, and the Nudge Unit should be accountable to a disinterested Ethics Committee for their actions.

Drawing conclusions:

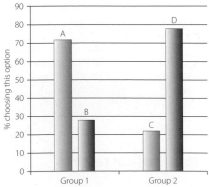

Conclusion: The way that the statements were framed (positive or negative) affected people's choice of treatments, so positive framing persuaded people to choose treatment A rather than B, and negative framing caused them to choose D rather than C, even though the outcomes were exactly the same.